The South African War
1899–1902

Bill Nasson

Professor of History,
University of Cape Town, South Africa

ARNOLD

A member of the Hodder He
LONDON • SYDNEY • AL
Co-published in the United Stat
by Oxford University Press Inc

First published in Great Britain in 1999 by
Arnold, a member of the Hodder Headline Group
338 Euston Road, London NW1 3BH

http://www.arnoldpublishers.com

Co-published in the United States of America by
Oxford University Press Inc.,
198 Madison Avenue, New York, NY 10016

British Library Cataloguing in Publication Data
A catalogue record for this book is available from the British Library

Library of Congress Cataloging-in-Publication Data
A catalog record for this book is available from the Library of Congress

ISBN 0 340 61427 7 (pb)

1 2 3 4 5 6 7 8 9 10

Production Editor: Wendy Rooke
Production Controller: Iain McWilliams

Typeset by J&L Composition Ltd, Filey, North Yorkshire

What do you think about this book? Or any other Arnold title?
Please send your comments to feedback.arnold@hodder.co.uk

One of the most unhappy, and to those concerned in it, disastrous wars since the fall of Napoleon is, in South Africa, now working itself to a close apparently still remote, and in every way unsatisfactory. There is reason to think that the conflict was unnecessary in its inception; that by timely and judicious action it might long since have been brought to a close; and that it now continues simply because the parties to it cannot be brought together to discuss and arrive at a sensible basis of adjustment... Nevertheless, as the cable despatches daily show, the contest drags wearily along, to the probable destruction of one of the combatants, to the great loss of the other, and in utter disregard of the best interests of both.

Charles Francis Adams, *Lee at Appomattox and other Papers* (New York, 1902)

The war in South Africa has exceeded the limits of barbarism. I have fought against many barbarous Kaffir tribes in the course of my life; but they are not so barbarous as the English, who have burnt our farms and driven our children into destitution, without food or shelter.

The Memoirs of Paul Kruger, vol. 2 (London, 1902)

As to any sign of their ablutions, you will very seldom see a Boer with a clean face. One of them has written to a Cape Town relative that his people will not wash until they have driven the hated British into the sea. That sounds most impressive, but will hardly entail much hardship upon his people.

Clarion, 1 September 1900

The pro-Boers were wrong about the Boers; they were right about the war. The great underlying issue at stake was not whether the Boers stood for a moral cause, but whether the British Empire stood for one.

A. J. P. Taylor, 'The Boer War', Manchester Guardian, 11 October 1949

Freedom Front Leader, General Constand Viljoen, has advised Parliament that he had been assured by the Minister of Arts and Culture, Lionel Mtshali, that the 1899–1902 Anglo-Boer War would not be renamed the South African War.

Cape Times, 14 February 1998

Contents

List of Maps

General Editor's Preface

One of the principal theorists of war in the twentieth century, Major-General J. F. C. Fuller, who fought in the South African War as a young infantry subaltern, called it 'the last of the gentlemen's wars'. The description has stuck, part of an overdrawn and misleading picture – that of a tactically backward, ponderously flat-footed, and still (at least metaphorically) red-coated army forced to confront modernity by a non-army. The Boers, by contrast, compensated for their numerical inferiority and civilian status with operational astuteness, combining fire and movement to devastating effect.

The war's position on the road to modernity is confirmed by its chronological position. It began as the last war of Queen Victoria's reign and finished as the first of the twentieth century.

But these easy images confront a paradox. Over the previous half century, the British army had conquered and held an empire by responding to scientific and technological innovation and by exploiting the advantages of industrialization. It was wearing a form of khaki in the Indian Mutiny. It had learnt the value of long-range and disciplined firepower on the North-West Frontier of India and in the Sudan. Medicine had enabled it to penetrate areas where diseases hitherto fatal to white men were endemic. Survey and cartography had rendered its knowledge of the territories it had acquired comparable with, or even superior to, that of the indigenous populations.

The defeats of 1899 were therefore surprising precisely because they were inflicted on an army that had long appreciated the danger of underestimating either its opponents or the variety of local conditions it would encounter. These were principles driven home by its Commander-in-Chief in 1899, Garnet Wolseley. His victories had been predicated on methodical preparation and excellent logistic support; indeed, his excessive attention to both had been largely responsible for his one major setback, the campaign to relieve Gordon at Khartoum. Wolseley advocated the creation of a strong expeditionary capability within Britain ready for rapid despatch overseas. His hand is to be seen in the speed with which the small force in South Africa at the war's outbreak was reinforced from Britain. None the less, part of his defence for the events of 1899 rested on the argument that he had not got all that he had asked for – or at least, not a force sufficiently big to overcome the evils of taking on a commitment more extensive than previous colonial wars in a policy driven by the ambitions of the government rather than by military practicalities.

Britain's weakness at the war's outset handed the Boers an initial strategic advantage, as Bill Nasson makes clear. But it was not long-lived. Moreover, it certainly does not explain the army's operational or tactical inferiority. A more important but still not fully satisfactory explanation for the latter was evident in Wolseley's public criticism of Lord Lansdowne, the Secretary of State for War, and was reproduced at many levels and in many guises throughout the army. This was a war about whose purposes many British soldiers felt uneasy. The Boers were devout and self-sufficient farmers, the embodiment of exactly those religious and moral ideas to which the army itself wished to subscribe. In fighting them, the British army seemed to be being asked to service a type of modernism different from the technology which underpinned its tactical predominance in colonial warfare – the interests of big business, high finance, and urbanization. One of Wolseley's 'ring', Sir William Butler, the Commander-in-Chief at the Cape before the war, clashed with the High Commissioner, Sir Alfred Milner, on precisely this count. During the war, as Keith Surridge has recently shown, British soldiers were the advocates of a compromise peace. Politically and socially conservative, many were unhappy about destroying a way of life to which temperamentally they themselves were drawn. Nor were they alone in their reservations. At home 'pro-Boers' were vociferous in their criticism of government policy. However, these opponents of the war drew on British radicalism's nonconformist and pacifist roots, and could not easily strike a deal with the army.

The 'gentlemanly' aspects of the conduct of the Boer war owe much to this ambivalence about its political necessity. Both sides took prisoners and saw their opponents in the field as fellow human beings:

in an African context it was not the 'last' of the gentlemen's wars, but possibly the first. Hitherto neither Boers nor British had been sparing in the deliberate use of terror as an instrument of conquest. However loath it may have been to take the war to the women and children of the Boer republics, therefore, the British army knew well enough from recent experience in the Sudan and elsewhere what was required. One legacy of such methods was the deep distaste for war which charac-terized the reactions of many veterans of South Africa when they heard of the outbreak of war in Europe in 1914.

The fact that this was a war about big ideas – religion, political self-determination, the credibility of the British Empire – gave it many of the trappings of 'totality'. Ultimately, however big and however long it became for Britain, it remained for London a limited war – geo-graphically self-contained, and more aggressive than defensive. But the British used the instruments of 'totality' for the achievement of victory, not least because for the Boers it was a war for existence. Determined not to compromise, the Boer 'bittereinders' were answered by concentration camps, the destruction of their farms, and even the danger of social revolution; and so the war threatened to eliminate the very way of life it had been designed to defend.

The 'bittereinders' could never accept that the outcome of the war was anything other than a humiliation. In 1914 they rebelled rather than side with Britain in the First World War. But ironically, as Bill Nasson points out, it was a younger, more liberal generation – Botha and Smuts pre-eminent among them – who reinvigorated the Boers' military effort in 1900. From that sustained effort they gained suffi-cient leverage to strike the deal in 1902 which allowed Afrikanerdom to survive. Bill Nasson picks up on his own earlier work to show how involved in the war many of the black population became. But the victory did not topple white supremacy, and as the Union of South Africa evolved the defeat of Boer values became less evident. The cal-culations of Paul Kruger looked less self-defeating in the medium-term perspective of the 1960s than they did in 1902. The success of the Boers in the field, as well as the trials and tribulations of their families, restoked an Afrikaner identity which became a key element in the policy of apartheid. One definition of modernism might embrace the assumption and presumption of liberalism. The fact that South Africa is only now, a hundred years later, confronting mod-ernism in this sense is itself an indication of how pervasive and long-lived the legacy of the South African War has been.

The Boers therefore did not lose everything: they conceded polit-ical independence to retain social and cultural identity. The British army gained in ways that demand a more prosaic vocabulary. What it learnt about fieldcraft and firepower made it the best army, man for man, in the execution of minor tactics in 1914. In many respects (and herein was one of the causes of defeat in 1899) South Africa was atypical: the air was clearer, the ranges longer, the fields of fire less cluttered than would ever be the case in Europe. But the tactical lessons which these differences imposed were progressive in their impact. Moreover, the subsequent reform in the army's higher administration did much to end the polarity in civil–military relations characteristic of the nineteenth century, and set a path towards the greater integration of political and military objectives which proved so vital in two world wars. When the British set about the reform of their military institutions after the South African War, they did not think they were preparing for a war in Europe; they were simply making sure that they dealt with the next war of empire more efficiently. But they certainly benefited by the fact that some at least of the skills were transferable.

Hew Strachan
University of Glasgow

Preface

The South African War 1899–1902, or Anglo-Boer War, or Boer War, or even Anglo-South African War (invariably, you will still take your pick) was a war which finally completed the British imperial conquest of Southern Africa. It was the biggest ever 'small war' of late-Victorian 'New Imperialism', and has a recognized significance in world history. This is a book which tries to provide an account of how that war came to pass – how the political contest between Boer republicanism and British imperialism developed into a violent struggle; how the warring sides conducted their operations; how adversaries saw each other; how the conflict affected belligerent societies and some beyond; how the combatants finally turned to peace; and, finally, how the war has come to be remembered in the country across which it was fought and how it might be seen now.

The South African conflict has long been part of modern historical memory, and if you rummage for its contemporary traces you could as well go wide as deep. In Britain's Merseyside, hardened Liverpool football fans still bunch into a stand known as the 'Kop', after the January 1900 Battle of Spion Kop. The Netherlands has clusters of Transvaal neighbourhoods or *Transvaalbuurten*, with streets named after celebrated Boer generals like Louis Botha or Christiaan de Wet. Popular Parisian folk art of the early twentieth century includes robust images of anti-British, French–Boer republican fraternity. Russian soldiers in the First World War sang a folk song, *Transvaal*, as a surrogate expression of their sense of national suffering. Peasants never sang so gloriously as when in adversity. For years, radical

Quebecois nationalists have defaced Montreal Anglo-Boer memorials to the empire patriotism of Canadian troops who died in South Africa. More than one British and Antipodean town has its Pretoria Road or Mafeking Avenue, to say nothing of memorials to imperial sacrifice. In South Africa, as commemoration has grown more universal through changing political conditions, so gestures have increased for public recognition of a still unknown tally of black casualties. Meanwhile, the graves of thousands of British and Boer combatants in military cemeteries and in more scattered farm locations, as well as those of Boer civilians, are maintained as sites of remembrance, but not without difficulty. A harsh African climate and nibbling land-hunger continues to sweep away crosses; the slabs of concentration camp victims or soldiers' headstones would always stand their ground more easily in Western Europe than in the Orange Free State.

There are also many deposits of the war's more picaresque colonial legacy. South African fruit stalls sometimes sell a brand of orange-pink mango called 'Tommy Atkins'. The sports press has for years greeted British Lions rugby tour sides with warnings that the (overwhelmingly Afrikaner) Springbok team is bristling to resume and pay back the Boer War. And the anti-English term 'redneck' or *rooinek* for soldiering British Tommies has long formed one of the more disparaging elements of Afrikaner masculine tradition, not least when the Anglo-Boer War has been replayed as some bruising school rugby match, near to war, but not quite war. In this vein, the writer Robert Greig has recalled that white liberal students in the 1970s were dubbed foreigners or *Uitlanders* by their hostile Afrikaans peers, who rubbed in 'old injuries', like the myth of British army concentration-camp commanders lacing food for interned Boer women and children with 'ground glass'.[1] Had Britain lost in 1902, perhaps twentieth-century Afrikaner society would have come off badly for some war immorality of its own creation.

The relevance of the South African War to the run of South African history does not wholly explain the much wider fascination which the Anglo-Boer conflict continues to exercise. Some part of that historical interest is undoubtedly made up of lingering popular nostalgia for an imagined Victorian colonial war. Through this rosy filter glows an episode in which hardy British regiments fought clean and courageous engagements with decent Boer combatants, or in which those gripping symbols of empire besieged, Mafeking, Kimberley, and Ladysmith, came to be lodged forever in the imperial psyche. Another part is a growing stock of specialized historical reference, some of it quite outlandish. Anyone curious about the merits of the Boer republicans' Krag-Jorgensen rifle now has a handbook with an impressive technical sweep. Equally, the pivotal role of Rudge, Raleigh, or BSA in scouting and dispatch cycling has received its fair due. The unique use of dolomite and sandstone in British fort and blockhouse construction has also not gone unnoticed in the historical record, nor has the technical modification of Royal Navy guns for use as land artillery.[2]

We probably still do not know how many ways there are of skinning a cat: very probably the same number of ways there are of trying to write a history of the South African War. The present volume is undertaken partly because no new general narrative treatment in English has appeared since the end of the 1970s, when Thomas Pakenham produced his capacious military depiction, *The Boer War*. Since then we have had only one or two photograph-driven texts, such as Emanoel Lee's *To The Bitter End*. The present work could perhaps also be read as a response to the memorable plea from the novelist Kathy Lette's Australian anti-heroine, Maddy Wolfe, 'go on, rewrite history then! . . . it's a time-honoured English tradition. The Boer War, Gallipoli, the Fall of Singapore.'[3]

This then, is, a book which seeks to inform, but which aims also to appeal to the general reader. Now a century on since 1899, a return to some consideration of that harsh imperialist–republican fight is timely. It was hatched as a war to demonstrate, in the words of Britain's prime minister, that in South Africa 'we, not the Dutch, are boss'.[4] It commenced as a war of misjudgement, or 'miscalculation', in the view of the Acting Transvaal President, Schalk Burger, in which the Boers hoped to wrap things up before major British forces arrived, and many on the imperial side expected the colonial enemy to yield without too much of a struggle. But it turned into a bitter war of waste, civilian suffering, and grief, while still embodying a keen awareness of cause, reason, or motivation. And like other more modern colonial wars, it had an annoying tendency to last somewhat longer than virtually everyone initially anticipated. As Saki wrote of its perambulation in 1902:

> Dwindle, dwindle, little war,
> How I wonder more and more,
> As about the veldt you hop,
> When you really mean to stop.[5]

Its outcome was mutual disappointment. The Boers lost their grim battle to hold on to republican independence from Britain. While the

British won, it was not without hand-wringing over the costs of victory, military efficiency, and national fitness to continue the imperial task.

As a large small war of modern empire, the South African War tested the ability of invading British forces to adapt to tricky and demanding local circumstances, put pressure on Britain's military and financial resources, handed the Boers fatal strategic choices, dragged republican society close to the edge of social and political disintegration through something close to total war, and ultimately changed the face of South Africa. An agrarian conflict with industrial corrugations, in its conditioning and conduct the South African War was perfectly transitional, a traditional war of movement, with cavalry and mounted infantry carrying the fight over enormous spaces, yet connected to modern firearms, railways, electric power, a grid of censorship, the early use of field telephone communication, and the refinement of tough imperial policies of destruction, resettlement, and exile to break the enemy and win the war.

Although the following account recapitulates much of the staple history of the war, it naturally does not attempt to reproduce every well-known detail about campaigns, sieges, personalities, regiments, and units. This is partly because such technically descriptive detail can be found elsewhere, and also because my main purpose here is to provide a fairly compact interpretation, rather than an exhaustive treatment of what has at times also been called the Transvaal War, the Great Boer War, or even The Grate Bore War.

In conceiving of this work, I had in mind the idea that readers would fall into roughly two groups. One consists of those interested in a digestible general portrayal of the war, with minimal prior knowledge of the conflict, or perhaps even no basic comprehension of the episode at all. To this end, I have limited the bibliography to a modest sample of books, essays, and articles as helpful signposts to further reading on particular topics or themes. Any South African War study of a reasonable length is an attempt to squeeze quarts into pint pots, and I am only too aware of aspects which have had either to be left out or given cursory treatment. The second category of readers comprises those who may have an outline grasp of the conflict, or even a grasp of some central detail. In the ensuing perspective they may find something over which to ponder, or about which to quibble. Greater understanding of the war can only benefit from the critical judgement of readers, as well as the continuing dialogue of historians.

Lastly, there are debts to express. I gratefully acknowledge the financial assistance of the Centre for Science Development (Human

Sciences Research Council, South Africa) towards this research. Naturally, opinion and argument are those of the author, and are not necessarily to be attributed to the CSD. Bits of this study were thought about and tinkered with during visiting fellowship sojourns at Cambridge University and the Australian National University. For the opportunity of a congenial berth in Cambridge I must thank the managers of the Smuts Memorial Fund for Commonwealth Studies, the president and fellows of Clare Hall and, most especially, John Lonsdale. In Canberra the History Programme of the ANU Research School of Social Sciences provided stimulating collegiality, and here I would particularly like to acknowledge and thank Ken Inglis. Australian hospitality far beyond the boundary of the Manuka Oval was generously supplied by Donald Denoon and Mary Mortimer, and Ken and Amirah Inglis. For another home in just about every sense during a stint as an Oppenheimer Fund visitor at Oxford University, I am grateful to Stanley and Barbara Trapido.

As always, there are other writing debts. Over the past several years various individuals have offered encouragement, ideas, comment, references, and chance suggestions which have left their mark. For such influence, frequently unwitting, I am grateful to Stanley Trapido, Ian Phimister, Albert Grundlingh, Greg Cuthbertson, Lance van Sittert, Kate Angier, Vivian Bickford-Smith, Helen Bradford, Stephen Watson, Yvette Abrahams, Nigel Penn, Anne Mager, Johan Loock, Kees Greshoff, and the mass Expeditionary Force of fellow participants in the August 1998 'Rethinking the South African War' conference at the University of South Africa in Pretoria. Obviously, for what follows the usual disclaimers apply. I am similarly indebted to several colleagues of the Historial de la Grande Guerre in Peronne, France, whose searching historical thinking on the Great War, and occasional curiosity about the Boer War, has been suggestive in thinking about how best to capture the essence of the South African War. General acknowledgement is also due to fellow members of the War Graves Committee and Jean Beater and Leonie Marais of the War Graves Division of the South African National Monuments Council. Through conscientious public custodianship, they seek to preserve the sombre memory of the ways of war in South Africa.

I should also like to express particular thanks to Hew Strachan for encouraging me to revisit the South African War for this series, providing an opportunity to turn from an older specialized focus to a broader canvas. At Arnold, gratitude is due to Christopher Wheeler, Elena Seymenliyska and Wendy Rooke for having the patience of an oyster. Thijs Verloren, publisher of the Dutch version of this work, also needs special mention for his helpful interest. At the University of Cape Town, Nick Lindenberger helped with the preparation of maps, and I would also like to thank Phil Ford for crafting them. Finally, as ever, I am wholly indebted to Ann and Leah for the usual combination of moral encouragement and artful distraction, and for displaying not the slightest interest in whether it was those pints of champagne or the Natal humidity which rather clouded General Buller's grasp of offensive tactics at Colenso. Still, they share the view that there is probably nothing quite like war to remind one that history, if anything, is the story of human folly. Indeed, perhaps one of the reasons why academic South African historians still give military history a wide berth is that the continuing sound of gunfire on so many of the country's streets brings home the realities of close combat better than any writing. As South Africa approaches the end of the twentieth century, Clausewitz should be here.

Bill Nasson
University of Cape Town

Preface Notes

1. *Sunday Independent,* 20 Apr. 1997.
2. Ron Bester, *Boer Rifles and Carbines of the Anglo-Boer War* (Bloemfontein, 1995); D. R. Marce, *Bicycles during the Boer War* (Johannesburg, 1977); South African National Monuments Council submission, 9/2/097/0011, May 1998; Tony Bridgeland, *Field Gun Jack versus The Boers: The Royal Navy in South Africa 1899–1900* (London, 1998).
3. Thomas Pakenham, *The Boer War* (London, 1979): this has since been reissued in a substantially abridged and pictorial format, *The Boer War: Illustrated Edition* (Johannesburg and London, 1993); Emanoel Lee, *To the Bitter End: A Photographic History of the Boer War 1899–1902* (Harmondsworth, 1985); Kathy Lette, *Foetal Attraction* (London, 1993), p. 96.
4. Quoted in Selborne to Milner, 27 July 1899, in *The Crisis of British Power: The Imperial and Naval Papers of the Second Earl of Selborne, 1895–1910* (London, 1990), p. 92.
5. Saki (Hector Munro), *The Westminster Alice* (London, 1902), p. 46. I am grateful to Andrew Thompson for this reference.

Introduction

By the end of the nineteenth century, the colonized African region that had become known as South Africa had been moulded by over three centuries of European imperial influence. To begin with, the Dutch mercantile seaborne empire moved beyond seeing the tip of South Africa as a handy port between Amsterdam and Djarkarta, to expansion and settlement throughout the later seventeenth and eighteenth centuries. Unlike those of Australia, the Southern African coastline and hinterland looked worth breaking into, while holding the Cape of Good Hope and Table Bay gave the Dutch, not the English, sure command of the sea route to India. Conquest and capitalist agricultural and commercial growth, ruinous for independent indigenous societies like the Khoikhoi and the San, produced a gradual melding and blending of settler cultures and classes into a new social outgrowth. A distinctive Dutch African or 'Boer' ('farmer') order came into being as a dominant European colonial society. By the end of the eighteenth century the settler men and women of emergent Boer society had no doubt that they belonged to a quite new commercial and trading order with a developed race and status consciousness, although they were as yet in no sense a unified or ideologically coherent Boer or Afrikaner nation. A free patriarchal society of town and countryside, the intensely Protestant *burgher* (citizen) bourgeoisie was in possession of a good many chunks of the Cape colony that were obviously worth possessing, and even a few that were not.

As the nineteenth century drew near, itchy frontier colonists were

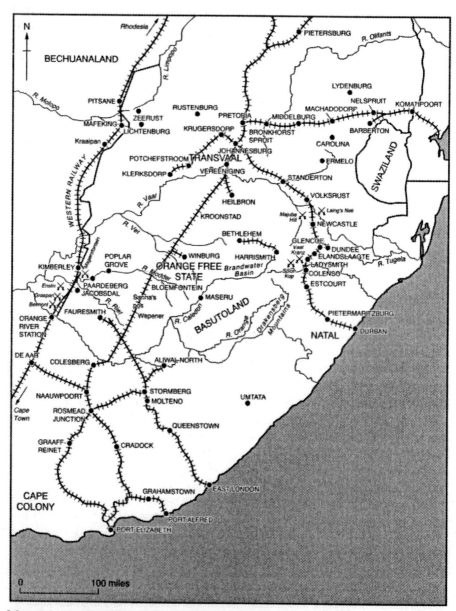

Map 1.1 *South Africa at the Outbreak of War*

finding that expansion into lands beyond was still being checked by the density and defensive resilience of their African peasant inhabitants. Dutch interests were pushy, but something stronger was needed if further European conquest was to get its way. That fire came from Britain. Up to the end of the eighteenth century, its port option on the key trade route between Western Europe and India and the Orient had been the island canteen of St Helena in the south Atlantic, or disagreeable dependence on the Dutch harbour of the Cape. The only British nibble at Southern Africa had been in 1785, when a parliamentary committee had suggested Das Voltas Bay between Portuguese Angola and the Dutch Cape as a bracing spot to which to exile British convicts. In the event things were settled by Botany Bay, and South Africa lost the opportunity to become Australia. But Britain was soon back, and with more ambitious intentions. By the 1790s growing imperial rivalry and jostling for spheres of influence and strategic sites in the Indian Ocean was poisoning relations between Britain, France, and the Netherlands. Some of these issues on the periphery were resolved by the Napoleonic wars, in which Britain exploited its decisive naval supremacy to hit the imperial posts of its continental adversaries. Driven by the demands of war and the strategic imperatives imposed by trading interests, British forces invaded the Dutch-controlled Cape. The defences of a rapidly weakening Dutch East India Company crumbled to pieces at a touch, and by 1815 the permanence of Britain's colonial control of the Cape was finally sealed by treaty recognition.

The impact of the new nineteenth-century empire was large. To its Cape colonial heartland it brought British culture, the ideological predominance of free-trade capitalism, and an immigration impetus which gave rise to a new English-speaking settler community which was resolutely British in its circumstances and outlook. A segment of the wealthier urban-rural Dutch élite was happy to get into bed with British administrators in a marriage of class convenience, but such Anglicizing accommodation did not go far. In general there was no British assimilation with a continuously fertile and preponderant rural Boer population. But there was much more to growing British intervention than the implanting of an imperial civilization. South Africa's incorporation into an industrializing British empire enlarged the colonial capitalist economic system, and greatly increased its dynamism. In the Cape the accumulative imperatives of efficiency and improvement cleared the way for free wage labour to supplant the bondage of the earlier Dutch slave-holding period. An inflow of mercantile capital provided reservoirs of credit for agricultural development and speculation, driving up land prices and closing doors to poorer Boer pastoralists. And increasing imperial-backed military expansionism delivered African land and labour to sweeten the inventories of the settler élite.

But many ordinary Boers groaned under the burden of a predatory Britishness, the loss of traditional tied labour through slave emancipation, drought, and a bruising struggle for landownership and security. In a movement towards the end of the 1830s, thousands of pioneer migrants or *Voortrekkers* left the Cape colony with their Coloured and African servants, in an exodus into the interior in what would become known as the Great Trek. This represented a rebellious escape from the arrogance of British rule and economic ascendancy to find some new emigrant tenure north of existing colonial frontiers. These land-hungry trekkers had a hard time in search of easier livings. An initial enclave in the eastern coastal settlement of Natal was uprooted in the 1840s when the British annexed it as a colony, locking up its valuable acres for speculative land and commercial exploitation. Having failed in Natal, many Boer trekkers rolled on to find better pickings in the interior. After much floundering and political squabbling amongst themselves, and with creeping imperial authority, precarious truces and tributary relations with some African chiefdoms, and warfare with others over land, the Boers founded two independent white republican states. The independence of these republics, the Orange Free State or *Oranjevrijstaat*, and the Transvaal or South African Republic or *Zuid Afrikaansche Republiek*, was formally recognized by Britain in the 1850s. For imperial interest, nothing very much hung on them.

In large territories in the interior highveld, the republican Boer populations were fractious and their administration tottery; in this impoverished hinterland, sparsely settled trekker communities, greatly outnumbered by indigenous inhabitants, battled to assert effective control over the expropriated African land and labour to which they laid sweeping claim. The early agricultural Boer states established a solid ethnic and cultural identity, but in other respects struggled to assert their nominal independence from British trading and other influence through established colonial market towns. The Boer diaspora was just the unproductive edge of an expanding colonial market, and was recognized as such by many Cape and Natal Boers, for whom equal rights with British settlers and a stable colonial environment did quite nicely; accepting the legitimacy and citizenship of an imperial order, they were disinclined to pack up for the uncertainties of a rickety republicanism.

It is a commonplace for modern histories to argue that nineteenth-century Boer expansion represents a tributary of the great world flood of European migration, colonial conquest, and settlement, tugged along by long-distance hunters and traders, and powered by

the bullock wagon, the horse, and the musket. It is equally customary
for scholars to emphasize that the Boer migration was one strand in
a web of Southern African population upheavals and movements
which created new African states and societies in the first half of the
nineteenth century. In this, the demographic disruptions throughout
the interior highveld plateau as a result of conflict centred around the
Zulu kingdom in the Natal lowveld turned out to be favourable to the
wants of Boer independence, delivering land for appropriation by
trekker republicanism while weakening the capacity of some African
inhabitants to repel invaders. While all this helped the Boers to hold
their ground and assert their sovereignty, in most respects it was a
tenuous business until well into the later nineteenth century.[1]

If British power in South Africa waxed and waned during the
course of the nineteenth century, there was never any lack of exertion
to defend and rub in its perceived economic, political, and strategic
interests. On the secure outer rim colonial ports controlled external
trade interests, while the navy had command of the coast and the sea.
Inland, the creeping conquest of independent African people for the
extraction of tax and labour required fighting, and there was a good
deal of that to be done by imperial troops. Through the increasingly
violent closing decades of the nineteenth century, British armies
and settler colonial armed forces, sometimes in warrior alliances
with shrewd African collaborators, inexorably rolled up African
chiefdoms.

Behind the increasing momentum and coordination of British conquest and intervention lay the emergence of diamond and then gold
mining as the interior flywheel of the Southern African economy,
unleashing massive demands for capital, transport, and industrial
infrastructure, and labour for diggings, plantations, and commercial
farms. With the sub-continent suddenly a vital economic and strategic interest, Britain's subjugating requirements became more intrusive, and any remaining polities sufficiently independent and powerful
to hinder imperial economic and political paramountcy were an
impediment to this. So, when the upstart Zulu declined to supply
labour and taxes, their peasant kingdom was destroyed and dismembered in the 1870s Anglo-Zulu War. That left one remaining obstacle,
the Transvaal Boers, now marked up by their gold holdings.

The South African Republic asked only to be left alone but, from
the 1870s onwards, Britain had little time for such opinion and began
to paw at the Boer state. Its immense gold deposits were turning it
into the economic hub of the entire Southern African region, putting
into the centre of affairs a now viable settler state which not only

showed no allegiance to British imperialism, but which was ominously strengthening its republican nationalism in response to rising external pressure. Without prevailing influence and control over the Transvaal, Britain's grand dominion over South Africa looked anything but assured. Even without anyone at first necessarily wanting war, Anglo-Boer relations were getting into a mess over issues which increasingly looked worth fighting over. Amidst deepening tensions by the 1890s, there was one imprudent military attempt to try to deal with the Transvaal without the price of war. This was the 1895 plotting by well-connected British settler interests of a small armed invasion and insurrection to topple the republican state. The ignominious failure of this hare-brained coup, which became known as the Jameson Raid, meant that four years later Britain's Colonial Secretary, Joseph Chamberlain, and its South African High Commissioner, Alfred Milner, were confronted with the higher price of a real war to get their way.

The story of this conflict has certainly been told more than once in past decades, and among scholars there is probably no longer much serious debate over some of its more defining features. It is well understood, for instance, that for Britain the war proved to be a far larger and more costly undertaking than had been initially envisaged. In one grisly calculation, by 1901 it was costing the Treasury £140 to knock out a single Boer combatant; put another way, that was the price of a ton of bullets required by the average British infantryman to topple a republican commando.[2] Similarly, it is known that shattering defeats in the early months of the war induced a sense of crisis for imperial power, and called into question national fighting efficiency and British 'racial' vitality, initiative, and competence. On the other end of the scale, there is agreement that the Boers generally fought and resisted with agility, guile, and tenacity in what in many ways came to resemble a people's war, with numerous rural women involved in the republican war effort or otherwise sucked into hostilities.

Myths about the character of the war have also had their lengthy run. There is the idiosyncratic notion that this conflict came at the end of some imaginary set of chivalrous male encounters, making it 'the last of the gentlemen's wars'.[3] Given the rigour of modern British tactics to strangle the enemy in South Africa, this has long been an antiquated hangover from the Hundred Years War. There is no dispute that imperial methods of warfare, especially in the closing guerrilla stages of the contest, increasingly shredded the agrarian basis of settler society in the Boer states, threatening its very future. Just as diplomacy failed to prevent war in 1899, so imperial politicians were short on sops to provide for a bargained peace; Britain would not relent until the republics caved in.

Equally, some Boer men and women die-hard bitter-enders, or *bittereinders*, were all for fighting to the end, rather than swallow unconditional surrender. In that sense the war ran away with some elements on both sides. Yet in making peace thereafter, Britain moved smartly from destroying the Boers to negotiating with them. However implacable in forcing surrender, calculated magnanimity in victory ensured that while the Boers may have lost the war, their more reconciliationist leadership none the less won a sizeable slice of the peace. Finally, after more recent scholarship there is broad recognition that older perceptions of the struggle as a 'white man's war' are quite illusory. Black inhabitants were not always off-stage as passive spectators, as many earlier historians of the war have accepted or implied; their reactions to the conflict and engagement with its flow were a significant ingredient in the making of a South African War. While the essential meaning of the war lies in its Anglo-Boer, European character, the weight of evidence on ancillary black involvement in military operations on both sides, on the ways in which blacks intervened on the margins on their own account, and on the bleak experience of African refugees in British concentration camps, means that we can eliminate once and for all the myth of a war conducted on the basis of black exclusion or neutrality.[4]

That said, the war's claim to continuing historical study remains unassailable. For its importance is marked, and not merely for the history of South Africa. The Anglo-Boer encounter represented a sharp test of arms and will between European adversaries overseas, in a protracted contest marked by strategic and tactical difficulties and moral anxieties over war conduct. On the issue of the survival of national independence against imperial gain, it can be seen as the most important colonial war of the early twentieth century, as an example of advanced African colonial warfare ranking, perhaps, alongside the Italian wars of conquest for Ethiopia.

Moreover, in its range and complexity the South African War also went beyond being a limited Victorian backyard war. As a European war fought out in Africa it also had a notable international impact. In early twentieth-century Britain issues of popular patriotism, relative imperial decline, and the efficiency of structures and institutions were brought sharply into scrutiny by its disquieting impact. For Australia, New Zealand, and Canada, empire military involvement watered the ground for those Dominion myths of masculine war sacrifice and national identity which were to ripen in the Great War. For sardonic Indian nationalists in Delhi and Calcutta, Britain's political aversion to deploying Indian combat troops to put down what they enjoyed calling the 'Boer Mutiny' or the 'Dutch Peril' provided another insult to the rightful stature of loyal Indians. And for ordinary Dutch, Belgian, French, German, Russian, and other European peoples, as well as many Americans, the distant war brought home the saga of a tiny white Christian nation's heroic challenge to bullying British imperial power. Around the world, the war became some mighty if symbolic anti-British cause, encouraging the foolish to make all sorts of flatulent gestures. One, Tsar Nicholas II, considered withdrawing his fortune from the Bank of England, and dreamed of chancing a Russian invasion of British India while London was distracted by Pretoria. Only in Tokyo was there popular support for the British interest.

There are other factors, too, which imbued the South African War with the overall sense of a modern war. Some part of this lay in its scale, levels of technology, logistical organization, armaments, and robust ideological ardour. At another level, it was also a conflict which fell squarely within one of the most belligerent phases of capitalist imperialism, and within an epoch of rapidly modernizing industrialization. While the most aggressive eruptions of the 'scramble for Africa' were over, the offensive impetus remained strong; a resort to war was always justifiable for the safeguarding of perceived interests, one of the instinctive assumptions of 'an age of victors and vanquished nations'.[5]

Then, too, there was the war's imaginative scope, or the powerful codes through which its harsh realities were expressed. The shadows cast by dead British soldiers in the trenches of Spion Kop, by rebel Boer executions under martial law, by blackened farms and razed fields, and by dead Boer infants in British camps, nudge the mind forward to the imagery of furrowed corpses, suffering, and destruction associated with industrial war in the twentieth century. If this was not yet a truly total war, like the American Civil War, it was, perhaps, a conflict waged well up that evolutionary scale.[6] It was also a war waged on the very edge of modern memory, inspiring a contemporary imaginative literature on the justice, pity, or 'truths' of 1899–1902, not only in Dutch/Afrikaans and English, but also in European languages. In these cultural terms, new Afrikaans war fiction a century on is finally beginning to break with ingrained myths of British bestiality and Boer purity, to explore a more universal imagining of the horrendousness of the conflict and the rawness left in its wake.[7]

Above all, for its white colonial protagonists this encounter was a chastening experience of the ugly side of a European culture of warfare, in which they confronted a stiffness of purpose which in South Africa had usually been reserved for black adversaries. Previously, both British and Boers had been blooded in fierce combat with Africans, save for the tiny and fleeting first Anglo-Boer War of the early 1880s. When these enemies now clashed wholesale, European affinities counted for something, such as not finishing off the wounded after battle (common enough for warring sides in such episodes as the Anglo-Zulu conflict), but not for too much. Boer republicans found the British virtually as committed to grinding them into submission as had Xhosa or Zulu chiefdoms, decades earlier. Equally, as it buckled under the pressure of British offensive and containment techniques, Boer society caught a whiff of what its own warriors had dished out in expeditions to obliterate frontier San communities in the later eighteenth century. Here was a situation not without some tragic irony, even though hardly any republican contemporary seems to have been the least aware of it. As Victor Kiernan has nicely observed, the 'habit of treating troublesome natives as "vermin" was bound to brutalize white men's treatment of one another when they fell out'.[8] And, it might well be added, some men's treatment of some women.

Lastly, while the direct experience of formally waging war involved only about one-fifth of the population of the region, a combined British and Boer total of just under one million, the 1899–1902 conflict was a powerful historical hinge. While it would be trite to call it history in which everyone took part, some knew instinctively the importance of its outcome to the future not just of dominant English and Afrikaner colonial societies, but of the colonized black majority as well. In this light, quite apart from what the war would teach the Edwardian War Office about the levels of British military performance, or its impact upon South African port trade and labour, it also helped to create modern South African history, its 1902 peace bringing to an end more than a century of smaller wars of colonial conquest. It is, then, impossible to miss the crucial role of this war in anchoring modern South Africa, laying the keel for a reconstructed and unified capitalist society as the basis of a twentieth-century white segregationist state. In that, there is certainly something to Iain Smith's suggestion that 'it was as important in the making of modern South Africa as the American Civil War was in the history of the United States'.[9]

There are one or two overarching concerns which have informed treatment of the war in the pages to follow. One is an attempt to relate the primary business of what happened, how the contest was prepared for and fought, and how the war was lost or won, through a straightforward narrative of the military course of events. Another is a characterization of the war as an episode struck in the image of the imperial and colonial societies which waged it. In that respect this study is more an interpretation of how the conflict was waged, and how it was seen, rather than being part of the perennial academic historical controversy of why it came about.

Any historian who has a stab at giving an account of this war cannot but be aware of the hard flesh of widely held popular understandings, a staple of some general imperial histories and many general histories of South Africa. In this view, novice Boer successes in the field provided evidence of high military talents despite meagre means; stumbling British arms were at first overawed, and then later foiled and exasperated by gifted and gritty republican campaigning abilities. Britain prevailed over sparsely equipped, rough farmers, but only through merciless sacking, burning, and herding of civilians. There is an element to this of the farmer and novice weekend soldier as a kind of David, holding out against the lumbering regimental Goliath of the British imperial army.

Yet, at least at the outset, the Boers were not entirely short of means. And while most of them were indeed farmers, they were not simply shy colonial cousins of Welsh sheep drovers, Highland crofters, or Hertfordshire stud farmers, as some of the more romantic British pro-Boers fondly imagined them. In masculine socialization and a political culture which linked citizenship to a universal obligation to perform armed service, the Boers were a long way from the shires, and were quite a different kettle of fish. African societies like the Ndebele and the Venda, who had earlier faced the guns and horses of a predatory and militarist Transvaal, knew well just how formidable an adversary republican settlers could constitute, fortified as they were by the moral guardianship of settler women.

The obvious challenge for the British was in coming to terms with the demands and difficulties of a campaign fought at a great distance, in an imposingly large country (bigger than France, Germany, Italy, and the Low Countries combined), against a well-gunned, highly mobile, and increasingly dispersed native enemy traversing a terrain which it knew intimately. A feature of the war was the British achievement in gradually making good their initial blunders, in improving the professional running and direction of South African operations, and in eventually fighting a flexible and ruthlessly effective big-countryside war to break the enemy off the battlefield.

In this respect, the stiffest stage for Britain was not the short period between October 1899 and June 1900, when its forces confronted the assembled armies of the Boer republics. Then, after several expensive defeats, the British inevitably recovered, and skewered the republicans through pressure and organized thrusts. What was more difficult was the ensuing longer and fluid guerrilla phase. This was the real nut to be cracked, in which the key to final victory lay in adapting to a long-range, irregular campaign, and in maintaining an edge in fighting conditions in which success depended on grinding down the enemy, and in which the most embittered foe was not just what was left of the Boer armies, but also their civilian front of women and families.

Ultimately South Africa provided an instance of a stretched imperialist power comprehensively winning a modern war against proficient and sinewy colonial opponents. There are not too many instances of that during this century. At the same time, the Boer struggle *was* different. The republicans lacked the revolutionary zeal, sense of sustained common purpose, and crucial integration of military discipline and popular political unity which, in actual anti-imperialist revolutionary armies, has made up for more conventional deficiencies. In this sense, the classic single command eluded the largely indisciplined Boers, and they could not avoid going the way of their nineteenth-century African counterparts in military confrontations with superior imperial forces.

Against that there is the question of how the Boers measured up to the real opening possibility of winning, or at least forcing an early, bargained peace. For this, they had their advantages of mobility, speed, surprise, and a temporary superiority in resources to bring decisive victory in the field. Certainly, they and their adversaries were 'ill-matched',[10] but not necessarily from the word go. However, despite a frisky advance, the Boers lacked the strategic vision and early flexibility to keep things tilted their way; and afterwards they faced, in the great distances of the South African interior, a remorseless war to defeat them step by step. Shrinking numbers and a crumbling economy of provision produced what at best ended up as a war of running evasion. As time ran out, this became a glum guerrilla strategy of staving off defeat, while counting a fearful and rising social and political cost; it was never a realistic basis for winning against a powerful and committed industrial enemy.

The impetus of a white war in Africa meant that something else also got going. For, once war broke, the contested legacy of their own recent African conquests became the republicans' albatross. The problem for Pretoria and Bloemfontein was that there was always something more than London to contend with. Not only had the empire to be beaten back; the lines of authority and control had to be held against black people hostile to the Boer position and its claims. And when republican strategy required the invasion of British territory, the practice of hammering in occupation authority was bound to turn many of these inhabitants against the Boers. For Britain, on the other hand, fighting the war did not entail open confrontation with black communities. If it involved inflicting hardship upon some, this was tempered by a judicious currying of favour with others. It worked. One need not necessarily accept the assertion of some leading African historians that Boer defeat 'was in large measure due to their inability to garner any significant African support', or that the real Boer predicament lay in political isolation, a failure to draw Africans into an 'anti-imperial alliance'.[11] This could never have been an option: republican authority was riveted to meaningful occupation and control of conquered African land and labour. They could not but hang on to their colonial order, while some Africans perceived the possibility of their being dislodged by the war. While the Boers desperately needed black neutrality as British flying columns, blockhouses, barbed wire, and farm incendiarism choked their cause, what they eventually got amounted almost to another aggressive front, and was a factor in forcing their surrender.

If one point about this episode is that of British achievement in coming to grips with the demands of a land war of immense dispersion and punishing endurance, it might even be suggested that London came to manage its South African campaign reasonably effectively, even though almost all observers at the time, to say nothing of the morticians of its Royal Commissions, seemed to see little else but an appalling mess. Indeed, it goes almost without saying that a significant feature of the war was that it provoked a bitter conflict of opinion in Britain, and no little moral disapproval of the ways in which it came to be waged. 'The Boer War,' as Samuel Hynes has suggested, 'began jingoistically in one reign and ended without glory in another ... for the first time in a century an English war had been fought in the face of serious and outspoken opposition at home.'[12] At the most general level, colonial wars rarely seem to offer much by way of honour or moral credit. Readers can form their own judgement of whether British farm burnings and internment of women and children 'was a sad but very necessary part'[13] of its South African operations. Perhaps what can be said is that while imperial military policy was not famous for restraint, in their own, smaller, way the Boers were not saints either. Still, in one respect there is no doubt that this war differed from some earlier colonial wars in Southern Africa: warring sides took prisoners, and did what they could to keep them alive.

Like many such encounters, it was a war which was expected to be brief. As in August 1914, popular opinion in October 1899 was that hostilities 'would be all over by Christmas', with few observers having any realistic comprehension of what was to come. For the British, even though South African experience had recently administered the bitter pill of imperial military humiliation at Isandlwana (at the hands of the Zulu, 1879) and Majuba (at the hands of the Boers, 1881), too many still assumed that this would be Afghanistan, or Egypt, or the Sudan. Used to moving mostly effortlessly against primitively equipped tribesmen, most officers and men had yet to run into a European enemy. Their guesses as to what to expect tended to be dangerously uninspired.

As for the republicans, with a comfortingly Liberal Gladstone no longer in Downing Street, but with an abundance of gold now on the Witwatersrand, this was not to be a re-run of the 1880–81 Transvaal War of Independence. Then, Pretoria's Pathans had seen off an outnumbered British expeditionary force in a fight which lasted only three months, and which produced a negotiated outcome fairly pleasing to the separatist aspirations of Boer society on the highveld. The war which now broke would be fought for all of 32 months, and would leave a considerably more expensive balance sheet. For, following the American Civil War and the Franco-Prussian War, it would become the third major military conflict of the industrial age. But before we turn to that telling and tragic confrontation, we need first to consider why and how the British and the Boers were carried to war.

Introduction Notes

1. Donald Denoon, *Settler Capitalism: The Dynamics of Dependent Development in the Southern Hemisphere* (Oxford, 1983), p. 38; Timothy Keegan, *Colonial South Africa and the Origins of the Racial Order* (Leicester, 1996), p. 196.
2. Clive Trebilcock, 'War and the failure of industrial mobilisation: 1899 and 1914', in *War and Economic Development*, ed. J. M. Winter (Cambridge, 1975), p. 141.
3. J. F. C. Fuller, *The Last of the Gentlemen's Wars* (London, 1937).
4. Peter Warwick, *Black People and the South African War, 1899–1902* (Cambridge, 1983); Bill Nasson, *Abraham Esau's War: A Black South African War in the Cape, 1899–1902* (Cambridge, 1991).
5. Daniel Pick, *War Machine: The Rationalisation of Slaughter in the Modern Age* (New Haven and London, 1993), p. 86.
6. See John Horne, 'Introduction: mobilizing for "total war", 1914–1918', in *State,*

Society and Mobilization in Europe during the First World War (Cambridge, 1997), p. 3.

7. Christoffel Coetzee, *Op Soek na Generaal Mannetjies Mentz* (Johannesburg, 1998).

8. V. G. Kiernan, *The Lords of Human Kind* (Harmondsworth, 1972), p. 235.

9. Iain R. Smith, *The Origins of the South African War 1899–1902* (London, 1996), p. 10.

10. Brian Bond, *The Pursuit of Victory: From Napoleon to Saddam Hussein* (Oxford, 1998), pp. 97, 99.

11. Bill Freund, *The Making of Contemporary Africa: The Development of African Society since 1800* (Bloomington, Ind., 1984), p. 106; Basil Davidson, *The People's Cause: A History of Guerrillas in Africa* (London, 1981), p. 31.

12. Samuel Hynes, *The Edwardian Turn of Mind* (Princeton, 1968), p. 17.

13. Frank Myatt, *The British Infantry, 1660–1945* (Poole, 1983), p. 157.

I

The Anglo-Boer Crisis and the Coming of War

'The Boer War ... brought first the culmination and then the end of an arrogant, boastful epoch, in which British public opinion seemed to have abandoned principles for power – the political equivalent of that *fin-de-siècle* spirit in art and literature which produced decadence and Oscar Wilde.' So wrote A. J. P. Taylor in the *Manchester Guardian* on the fiftieth anniversary of the outbreak of the Anglo-Boer War. For Taylor, an appalling litany of miscalculation, blunder, and sheer folly had forced the pace of events in South Africa. On the face of things, the long-term salvation of a British South Africa lay in policies of gradual persuasion, moderation, and conciliation, cosseted by 'wise economic planning' and improved living standards for the black majority: yet all the impetus ran the other way. With the ground cleared for impatient men with a liking for impetuous action, the 1896 Jameson Raid not only failed to net Britain the Transvaal; it destroyed the position of compromising Boer moderates, blackened the Colonial Secretary, Joseph Chamberlain, and ensured that Britain's South African High Commissioner, Alfred Milner, a man of 'German dogmatism', would be pitted against a crop of Boer leaders 'as violent and as obstinate as himself'.

While war had assuredly been made inevitable by the Raid, its personal motivation was obvious: Britain's Prime Minister, 'Salisbury, was dragged into war by Chamberlain; and Chamberlain was dragged into war by Milner'. Perpetually in search for the expedient of the moment, it was Milner who wanted to rush in at the end of the 1890s, unwilling to wait for the incremental establishment of a British dominion through 'the passage of time'.[1] Would that this were the only ink spilt on the cause of the South African War, or that the explanations down the decades of 'Milner's War' or a 'Capitalists' War', and sometimes even 'Chamberlain's War' had resolved the knotty question of why war came in 1899. Instead, the debate over its origins still shows no sign of drying up. Historians still ponder a basic question: why did Britain resort to a war which its Colonial Secretary had earlier predicted could be 'a long war, a bitter war, and a costly war'?[2]

Perhaps the first point to emerge from those who have laboured on the subject is that the war was not made by hustling imperial figures. Responsibility cannot simply be ascribed to the individual motivations or peevish personalities of Salisbury's Colonial Secretary or his South African High Commissioner, however influential their position in the spectrum of British policy instincts and policy-making. While the urgings of Chamberlain and Milner were inextricably part of the immediate slide into war, they are not 'guilty men' upon whom the war can be blamed. This risks substituting effects for causes, by failing to grasp that a big man like Milner 'may have helped to stir the pot, but he did not supply the ingredients'.[3] A whiff of those clearly requires another starting-point.

Here, one factor on which all historians are generally agreed is that the South African War serves as a textbook illustration of Geoffrey Blainey's argument that it is hard to find any war which could be termed 'accidental or unintentional'.[4] This was a war deliberately initiated in the conviction that the objectives of victory or staving off of defeat could not be pursued effectively other than through fighting. Another given is that, in its origins, this was emphatically a British rather than a Boer war.

Naturally, both during the war itself and in its immediate aftermath imperialist commentators claimed that the Boer republican leadership and their Transvaal oligarchy bore responsibility for the war. An obdurate President Paul Kruger lacked the moderate good sense to yield to the essential internal reform of his state necessary to ensure harmony and security in the Southern African region. Hard-faced in its diplomatic dealings, it was the belligerence of the South African Republic which forced the pace, by getting the Orange Free State into line behind a blunt Boer war ultimatum of 9 October 1899.

The fact that it was the Boers who issued that ultimatum rather than the British (who had already drafted one under wraps in September in case the Boers dawdled) made the republicans the aggressor. They were outfoxed diplomatically and, perhaps equally importantly, initially surrendered some moral ground to their adversaries and critics. For an appreciative Salisbury, this relieved his government of the need to explain 'to the people of England why we are at war'.[5] By then, influential imperial pressure groups and much of the metropolitan press required little further explanation. For some time they had already been working up the notion of a combined South African Republic and Orange Free State conspiracy to dismantle British supremacy in the region, in order to impose a unified Boer or Afrikaner republican dominion over the rest of South Africa.

Perceptions of a wilful and hard-nosed Transvaal also coloured settler reaction in British South Africa. Even for leading conciliatory and pacific Cape liberals such as John X. Merriman and James Rose Innes, the 'hostility' and 'impracticable attitude' of the Transvaal leadership, and of Paul Kruger in particular, were making it impossible for a reasonable Anglo-Boer settlement to be given a chance. The Boer President's bloody-minded exercise in warnings and ultimatums, and failure to grasp the need for progressive reforms 'as necessary for his own future as for that of the whole of South Africa', meant that he risked 'forfeiting all claim to sympathy and consideration'. As the war crisis deepened, some prominent members of the Cape Afrikaner Bond party who had little stomach for war were similarly alarmed by the Transvaal. J. M. Hoffman (who would go on to work in a Boer ambulance unit during hostilities) was one, whose view of the 'attitude' of 'Krugerism' turned to 'contempt'.[6]

In fact, within the Transvaal political establishment itself there were voices which sounded not so very different. Kruger's Progressive Party political opponents, including generals like Piet Joubert, insisted that war was by no means inevitable, and that what was preventing a peaceful accommodation was the Boer President's 'blind obstinacy', a trait which played straight into enemy hands. For the prominent attorney Ludwig Krause, Kruger was playing an exceptionally dangerous card: fearful that any reform of the Transvaal would mean 'the weakening of the Kruger Party', he concentrated on demonizing Progressive critics as 'traitors' and Anglophile fanatics or *Engels-gezind*, indulged in calculating brinkmanship, and 'played the fool all over the country with a matter of life and death'. Krause was adamant that the war was 'engineered' as an ill-judged trial of armed strength 'in order that the Kruger party might remain in power'. In this despairing judgement, an autocratic Kruger regime was risking war so as to escape domestic reform. In chancing a dubious hand against Britain, the Boer President was not lacking the courage of 'a sincere patriot'; he simply lacked statesmanship.[7]

Such rumblings suggest that the Transvaal did not move to war as a 'united people', nor did its leading social classes necessarily endorse some pre-war national compact. In any case, did Kruger actually want war, rather than merely being resigned to it? Of course, the Boer leadership was convinced, with good reason, that a hard line in any crisis of survival would reinforce its position and raise its legitimacy. Yet this was not the same as wanting to plunge the Transvaal into a major war. On the Boer side, the war which came was entirely defensive, and it was on this basis that Kruger and President Marthinus Steyn of the Orange Free State had little difficulty in convincing their populations that the taking up of arms was to defend the certainties of an independent existence. On the basic score of republican survival and security, not even bilious anti-Kruger Progressives like Ludwig Krause had any doubts about turning out for war.

The Transvaal President was certainly convinced that if they did not go to war at that moment their position would deteriorate and Boer power and control would pass into British hands. His famous mid-1899 charge against Milner, 'It's our country that you want', remains a crisp expression of what was ultimately at stake. While military calculations were to play their part in the crucial decision-making a few months later, a declaration of war against Britain had become a desperate gamble by a cornered opponent, and one which simply had to be taken. Milner's relentless gunning for Boer capitulation, and his willingness to resort to force to achieve this, had ruled out any practicable policy of further stalling or appeasement. Eventually, it became time to act. Why wait for Britain to pick the moment for battle?

A further, equally more contemporary view of things saw the origins of the war not as an 'accidental' conflict with mainly short-term and contingent causes, but as the sheer inevitability of an evolutionary human struggle through which progressive civilizations shoulder aside conservative, stagnant, and outmoded societies. Interpreted in this way, the war was a progressive colonial landmark 'in the perennial evolution of human society towards a higher state, one of many similar struggles in that unstoppable process of development'.[8] Grounded in those later Victorian biological and evolutionary arguments which accepted war as indispensable to progress, the South African War was both natural and necessary. For individuals ranging from Alfred Milner in South Africa to metropolitan figures like the eugenicist Karl Pearson and Fabians like *English* Sidney Webb, to the editorials of the *Economist,* the Boers were *Supremacy* seventeenth-century frontiersmen, a medieval racial oligarchy, primi- tive stock-breeders, or sluggish nomads whose parasitic lifestyle was a drag on rates of economic expansion. Their maintenance of feudal barriers to progress was wilfully blocking progressive development associated with a Great Power imperial civilization, sanctioned 'by God's will'.[9] In some more threatening anti-English associations, the Boers were also the Picts and the Irish. The underlying issue was not whether the war had a particular cause, or whether that cause was moral or just: it was its acceptance as a conflict between antique and modern centuries, made inescapable by the imperatives of a Darwinist militarism.[10]

Marxist-influenced interpretations of the conflict took more than one form in Britain. For some writers in *Clarion* and *Justice* the war was a structural or functional necessity of capitalist advance. It became in some sense a 'bourgeois revolution', an enforced stage in completing South Africa's transition from a traditional non-capitalist civilization to a fully modern society. Through the handmaiden of war, a restive industrial and financial capitalist class sought to secure a political and economic system that would further its interests, burst- ing through the stifling incubus of protectionist landed proprietors. The South African War became a version of the English Civil War played out in a colonial context.[11]

Other radical opinion focused on the perceived relationship between the war and imperialism: here was ample illustration that militarism had become an essential cog of newly expansionist capitalism. The deployment of armaments, and the 'egging on' of *Economic* conflict in South Africa, revealed the manner in which war had *Hobson* become a weapon in the competitive struggle between capitalist nations for imperial areas as vital markets for surplus production and as investment opportunities for surplus capital. Accordingly, the increasingly frenzied drive of European imperialism by the last two decades of the nineteenth century made the Boer War inevitable.[12]

While the rampant character of capitalism and the accepted relationship between capitalism and imperialism was part of such contemporary explanation, other more precise factors were also identified. For some Labour critics as well as Radical Liberals, war *individual* was being fomented by shady special or 'sectional' interests intent on provoking a situation which would lead to colonial annexation. Such meddling by meretricious colonial capitalists had already been detected in places like Egypt and China; now it seemed to be South

Africa's turn. Thus, Fabian dissenters like Ramsay Macdonald and Bertrand Russell blamed 'the imperialism of capitalism' for manipulating 'vainglorious nationalism' as a cover for greedy individual capitalists to grab all they wanted. The Radical Liberal intellectual J. A. Hobson, in various articles and in his 1900 book, *The War in South Africa*, charged that sordid interests in the shape of Transvaal mining magnates had pulled the levers of war and conquest as a contemptible alternative to the 'natural' growth of commerce. Such British criticism was directed towards 'militaristic' and 'speculative' means, not at expansionist ends; it was anti-war, not anti-imperialist.[13] Within the Transvaal, too, leaders such as the State Attorney, Jan Smuts, and the State Secretary, F. W. Reitz, along with papers like *The Standard* and *Diggers News*, proclaimed that behind the intensifying war crisis lurked intriguing mine-owners and capitalist speculators.

Smuts concluded confidently that the war was not being unleashed as a fight for British 'national' interests. 'As the Boers read the situation,' he declared, 'the one issue was whether the mine-owners had to govern the Transvaal in their own interest; the British flag was a minor phase of that fundamental issue.'[14] In this he was much of the same mind as Hobson, who in his 1901 *The Psychology of Jingoism* lambasted the manipulation of patriotism as a 'screen' by suspiciously cosmopolitan capitalist forces. In the case of the British cause in South Africa, when 'businessmen...require a screen, they find it in the interests of the country, patriotism. Behind this screen they work, seeking private gain.'[15]

For radical British interpretations of the war the issue was invariably capitalist imperial aggression and not empire itself, for by the late nineteenth century the dominant feeling was that Britain needed continuing worldwide expansion to stay alive, just as a fish required water. Thus, for Macdonald, while the war was a blatant instance of naked capitalist greed, the desired evolutionary outcome in South Africa was British supremacy. Similarly, the Liberal David Lloyd George assumed 'that the peace and prosperity of South Africa depend upon British rule being supreme in that part of the world', something which would have been attained naturally and legitimately 'by pacific methods'. There was thus no need to work up an expensive war on the basis of bogus motives in order to extend British control, especially one which would consume funds urgently needed for domestic social reform.[16]

Whatever their various understandings, these contemporary perceptions engage with the question which has preoccupied historians up to the present. The coming of war should not be taken as the outcome of a single event, and clarifying its cause still boils down to explaining why Britain harried the South African Republic to a point where the Boers opted to attack in order to try to preserve their independence. Moreover, while the weight of argument has also shifted from the view up to the 1960s of seeing the war mostly as the product of individual stimulus, towards locating it as the outcome of more complex structural forces, debate continues. At one level it is about the balance of causality: how far was the 1899 clash of arms determined by more gravitational or underlying forces, and how crucial was the immediate stirring of politicians and officials?

To make basic sense of how the war crisis developed, a short narrative context is necessary, if simplified for present purposes. By the second half of the nineteenth century the patchwork region that had become known as South Africa was held together not by any remotely common culture or political coherence, but by an encrusted British imperial presence which either enjoyed acceptance or commanded pragmatic accommodation. Roughly one million white inhabitants populated four settler states, consisting of the Cape Colony, Natal, and the distinctly backwoods interior Boer states of the Orange Free State and South African Republic. While these cast a jaundiced eye upon the intrusive influence of the British and their largest colonial berth, the Cape, whatever 'the ambitions of their creators, the Afrikaner states were inexorably part of the informal British Empire.'[17] Under the 1852 Sand River Convention and 1854 Bloemfontein Convention, that cost-conscious 'reluctant empire' was content to leave emigrant Boers alone to manage the ramshackle establishments which represented the frontier of the colonial market.

British interests puttered along through the 1850s and 1860s in an imperial situation which had no very obvious points of urgency. There was no rival European challenge to Britain's domination of external South African trade, and its strategic position appeared impregnable. Transvaal attempts to establish an outlet to the sea through Delagoa Bay on the Portuguese territory of Mozambique had failed, sealing Boer commercial dependence on the British ports of Natal and the Cape. And Simon's Town naval base, the symbol of Britain's control of the sea route via the Cape of Good Hope, was more than safe. At some stage Britain could usefully try to cajole all the settler states into some collaborative white federation under imperial auspices, not least to stitch together a common policy towards governing conquered Africans and organizing the supply of their labour. While this looked potentially awkward given independent Boer republican instincts, it was equally a fairly distant policy interest.

Affairs remained like this until the beginning of the 1870s, when the rapid development of the Kimberley diamond fields began to galvanize and transform what had previously been a mercantile agricultural economy. South Africa suddenly became more valuable as a field for large-scale capital investment in mine-based industry and in railways, driving the British stake deeper. For those with an eye on future share prospectuses there were also reports of possible gold deposits in the eastern Transvaal. The unresolved issue of extending imperial control now moved sharply up the agenda. Speculative capitalists were keen on seeing growing investment and trade backed by the British flag, settler federation appeared a more urgent and also more affordable enterprise, and for strategic interests concerned with the security of the Cape sea route to the east it was now preferable to have South Africa's hinterland and its mineral deposits under Britain's thumb. To these considerations were added disputes involving competing Boer and black claims to diamond diggings, chronic armed skirmishing between Boers and Africans driven by the rising market for land and labour assets, and friction over Transvaal meddling in the flow of African migrant labour to the Cape and Natal. It was apparent that 'informal British hegemony' could no longer suffice.[18]

Following British annexation of the Griqualand West diamond fields in 1871 the Colonial Secretary, Lord Carnarvon, initiated a confederation policy for the South African territories to craft a cohesive and stable general union within the orbit of British supremacy. Carnarvon's 1870s push for a sturdy centralized state put a premium on economic imperatives. By phasing out rickety and inefficient non-British states an integrated governing entity would be able not only to service mounting industrial demand for transport provision and labour supplies, but more than anything, it would provide the teeth to close remaining pockets of African landed independence, incorporating its inhabitants as the mass labour force of a humming imperial dominion. For Whitehall, national settler responsibility would also be likely to reduce future demand on imperial military expenditure and other colonial financial aid.

Yet, instead of opening the sluices, federation won few converts. Absorption did not excite the self-governing Cape, and the northern Boers were less than lukewarm about negotiating away their independent identities. But Carnarvon was the dog with the bone. With the Transvaal bankrupt and menaced by powerful Zulu armies, he bounced the republic into the British empire, annexing it in 1877 in the quaint belief that this would achieve all his aims. Instead, it scuppered the federation initiative completely. Annexation inflamed anti-imperial feeling within Boer communities throughout South Africa, and was also condemned as a blunder by moderate English Natal opinion. Undeterred, Sir Garnet Wolseley, Britain's Transvaal overlord, announced that 'so long as the sun shines, the Transvaal will be British territory'.[19] It did not shine long. By the end of 1880, the republican Boers had had enough, and rose in armed rebellion. Flagged on by militant women, commandos with customary logistical support from African combat auxiliaries overwhelmed the slim and poorly prepared British garrisons, and in February the following year heavily defeated their redcoat enemy at Majuba Hill, a loss which included the life of the British general George Colley.

Although not quite Khartoum on the scale of late-Victorian imperial trauma, a leaden Majuba came to symbolize the blemishing of national honour, provoking mockery everywhere, even in the Caribbean, where it became parodied in a popular calypso melody. Like the preceding 1879 Isandlwana defeat by the Zulu, the disaster rankled especially because it represented humiliating loss to a congenitally inferior colonial adversary. In the political culture of Tory imperial patriotism, this bruising loss of face was not something to be easily brushed over. There was lost glory to be restored. For the republican Boers, meanwhile, Majuba signalled not merely an ignominious British retreat, but the potential to push their power into the Southern African region more generally, probing the empire's soft spots and making other kinds of trouble.[20]

With Irish troubles already on its plate, Gladstone's Liberal government opted for a negotiated peace rather than renewed battle, something which greatly irritated the crusty Queen Victoria, who grumbled, 'I do not like peace before we have retrieved our honour.'[21] Under the 1881 Pretoria Convention, the Transvaal reverted to full internal independence, while Britain retained a token 'suzerainty' in respect of its relations with foreign powers, frontier zones, and the distinctly petty issue of African rights. Through a diplomatic Resident in Pretoria, British interests were to be upheld, if in a some-what antechamber style. While a forward federation policy had been derailed by the War of Independence and its settlement, Boer or Afrikaner nationalism did not yet present any immediate threat to Britain, even though a good many Conservatives and Liberal Imperialists warned that it did. So did some English opinion in Natal, which worried that the wider nationalist stirrings sparked by the war of 1880–1 presented 'a threat to British supremacy and the future of Natal as a British colony'.[22] In reality, with its earlier annexations of Basutoland in 1868 and Griqualand West in 1871, the margin of security for Britain's essential interests continued to be substantial, even massive.

That margin of trade and influence was also watched both in the west and to the east. The imperial gaze grew especially vigilant in 1883, as strategic power rivalry reared its head with Germany taking possession of Angra Pequena Bay on the west coast, north of the Cape Colony border. Two years later, Britain annexed the Tswana territories of Bechuanaland to block oozing Transvaal growth which looked as if it might eventually lap up against the recently declared German protectorate of South West Africa, even if Germany's acquisition was in itself 'relatively worthless or utterly insignificant'.[23] Eastwards, the remaining free parts of coastal Zululand between Natal and Mozambique were annexed between 1884 and 1887 to block off Transvaal access to the sea which might have freed it from commercial dependence on colonial British ports. Then, at the end of the 1880s, the perpetually hungry mining baron, Cecil Rhodes, pushed through an occupation of Matabeleland and Mashonaland to the north. This British-imperial company enterprise not only provided a base for expansion beyond the Zambezi, up Rhodes's favoured 'Suez Canal to the interior.'[24] It also completed the handy triangular cordoning of the South African Republic.

In all this, Britain was still careful not to tread too heavily upon Transvaal corns, by observing a loose contract of balanced needs and rights. Thus, one annexation was accompanied by a relinquishing of residual controls over republican 'native policy'; similarly, in return for Boer restraint upon westward movement, Britain dropped the term 'suzerainty' from the provisions of the 1884 Anglo-Boer London Convention. This intriguing period of empire and republican interplay, based on a kind of nervous stability, served to establish Transvaal independence or 'sovereignty' as something continuously debatable, its meaning and limits inherently renegotiable or redefinable. While a restored post-Majuba Republic was keen to assert its control over its own affairs, and not yield to such impudent British claims as the right to move imperial troops through Boer territory at will, treaty or convention-based dealings prevented another 1877 breakdown.

Equally, while it merely slumbered within an imperial Southern African economy, the South African Republic could only dream of real independence. Its new post-1883 President, Paul Kruger (a flinty figure who had risen to power during the detested British occupation), continued to seek that elusive railways artery to Delagoa Bay, a direct line to Kimberley, and a customs union with the Cape to beef up its revenue. By the mid-1880s these initiatives were either barely making headway, or were more or less dead. Given some new forward movement, it seemed that London might yet be able to nudge along a settler state association, a bloodless sub-Limpopo version of the 1867 Dominion of Canada. With federation a reliable tenant of British ascendancy there would also be no need for the War Office to fret over the potential political difficulties of having to turn the Cape peninsula anchorage into 'a Gibraltar' to police the Indian sea route.[25]

But seemingly fluid conditions were not destined to solidify in quite the way anticipated by Britain. In 1886 the discovery of Transvaal gold dramatically transformed the position and prospects not just of the Republic but of South Africa as a whole. The emergence of a mineral revolution in a marginal state long saddled with virtual insolvency rapidly renovated Kruger's republic. More than this, it turned the Transvaal's Witwatersrand into the economic hub of the entire sub-continent, the power of its industrial revolution producing 'a pronounced northward shift in the balance of economic power in southern Africa'.[26] Gold rapidly overtook diamonds in export importance, and in not much over a decade the fabled Rand mines had become the world's largest single source of gold, their rising production accounting for more than a quarter of total international output. Everything that had gone before, whether Cape wool and diamonds or Natal coal and sugar, was eclipsed by a gold industry which began to squeeze the economic and political structures of South Africa into the grid of an industrial civilization. The tremendous impact of this mineral-based industrial revolution forms one of the most powerful themes in the historiography of modern South Africa, and has generated a body of writing longer even than Paul Kruger's imposing beard.[27]

As Transvaal gold set the pace in sustaining the complex late-nineteenth-century international monetary, financial, and trading system presided over by the Gold Standard and centred on London, capital investment flooded in. Overwhelmingly from *rentiers* abroad, including French and German capitalists, the lion's share of mining investment was British; most estimates suggest that this comprised three-quarters or more of the £75m foreign investment on the Rand at the outbreak of war. While countries such as Australia, Canada, and Argentina were also key markets for British investment and trade in this period, they were certainly not collared as an investment enterprise with anything like the fervour of the South African mineral boom. One significant outcome was that South African ore reserves became an increasingly crucial commodity for the protection of Britain's commercial advantage in the world economy and its supply and servicing position in the international trading system. It was due to the Rand, for example, that the Bank of England was able to double its volume of gold reserves in the first half of the 1890s.

For an impoverished agrarian Boer state, the swarming mineral revolution had its own decisive outcomes. First, in becoming the wealthiest region in southern Africa, revenue mushroomed: by the mid-1890s income had already multiplied more than 25 times over the immediate pre-1886 years. Previously 'the Dutch in South Africa had had the numbers but not the money; now they had the money too'.[28] Second, the effects of gold radically reshaped the social framework of the Transvaal. Production demands required a new mass inflow of cheap, unskilled African migrant labour from elsewhere in the region, including the British South African colonies. Within Boer society itself, inflated land prices due to vaulting agricultural opportunity, and speculative enclosure for prospecting, intensified pressures on available land. This accelerated growing class stratification, worsening the malaise of landless, labouring tenants or *bywoners* yoked to the farms of wealthier Boers, and increasing the difficulties of many other displaced 'poor whites'.

Within this white underclass, cultivated populist resentment perceived foreign capitalists and prosperous black peasants as a principal threat to prosperity. At the same time, a patriarchal ruling class of Boer notables on the make, including such leading Calvinist squires as Paul Kruger, Louis Botha, and Piet Joubert, freely exploited major or minor government office and backstairs influence to amass land for large commercial farming.[29] The seismic pressures exerted by growing industrial and agricultural mobilization naturally affected both republics, making settler society increasingly restive. To some extent, centrifugal social forces could be knitted together by populist perceptions of 'alien' domestic or foreign perils which endangered a traditionalist male burgher order of 'the people' or *het volk*, threaded with large families and buttressed by a robust tradition of women's involvement in social and civic spheres and in rural homestead life.

A no less interesting side of this picture is the singular failure of Boer capitalist enterprise to break into the mining industry itself. No indigenous mine magnates or Randlords homed in, and skilled white mine-work was not for uneducated and inexperienced Boer workers.

Accordingly, with no defining social shift into the new industrial sector, the political structure and sense of identity of Transvaal settler society remained pinned to an essentially conservative agrarian order. At the same time, that population occupied a country which had now become home to fragmented and divergent white societies. Into a Calvinist religious state traditionally riven by localized rivalries and factionalism, yet stitched together by kinship, communal social solidarities, and an independent identity hardened by recent anti-imperial conflict, came an enormous influx of overseas immigrants or *Uitlanders*. Mostly European, and overwhelmingly British, a mosaic of skilled industrial workers, professionals, merchants, managers, and fortune-hunters became concentrated in the mining mecca of Johannesburg.

This mostly parvenu imported society of over 100,000 people, some 75,000 of them British, and over two-thirds consisting of single men, entrenched itself as an alien, English-speaking frontier vanguard. Held in low regard by many republican burghers as transient shysters of dubious morals, and tolerated by the Kruger government as economic mercenaries who had no legitimate claim to citizenship or a political stake in the republican order, the intrusive Uitlander presence could not be anything other than a growing predicament for the Boer authorities. And this was not solely because of the British habit of using Transvaal Sundays for pigeon-racing rather than prayer.

By the later 1890s, republican male burghers may already have been outnumbered by Uitlander men; while this fanned anger over continuing disenfranchisement of a white Johannesburg community 'which provided the Republic with a very sizeable proportion of its public wealth', it also stiffened the resolve of the ruling Boer oligarchy to resist any democratizing encroachments upon its closed governing system. Stern from the start, the Boer constitution barred Jews, Catholics, and any other male non-Protestants from parliamentary or *Volksraad* membership, and from holding any civil or military office.[30] A flood of foreigners could not be assimilated into republican politics, for conceding meaningful rights would fatally undermine the Boer monopoly of power. Enfranchised immigrants could tilt the balance of power towards mining interests, deliver political control of the state to English profiteers, and finally square the circle by easing the republic back into British hands. Of course, for opposition Boer Progressives, the outcome of a more liberal white supremacist constitution looked nothing like as apocalyptic. A nicely balanced clientele alignment of reformist Boers and moderate

English Uitlanders would not necessarily mortgage Transvaal national interests. Instead, it would increase legislative pressure from the People's Council (Volksraad) upon the Kruger regime over government corruption, largesse, and the cosy fixing of profitable economic arrangements to enrich the state's cronies.

Within the ruling establishment and its small political community, there was no question of transforming the political character of the state, and a series of stringent laws were enacted to make the acquisition of citizenship hard going. Through the later 1880s and 1890s, this was a leadership which conceived of itself as both rightfully predominant and increasingly threatened. Security lay in absolute mastery of the political apparatus, fiscal levies upon the gold mines, and manipulation of the economic arena through tariffs and preferential monopolies or concessions over dynamite, railways, and alcohol. These costs yielded increased state revenue and fattened German, Dutch, and other capitalists who buttoned Paul Kruger's ear, but they also burdened the mining industry.

General anti-Boer Uitlander antagonisms (over everything from education to policing) and sectional mine grievances (over the industry costs imposed by state policies) mounted through the post-1886 decade, culminating in the emergence of a patchy and ineptly led political reform movement on the Rand. This pressed for liberalization of a state 'in which those who felt that they contributed most to the wealth and revenue of the country were effectively discriminated against and excluded from citizenship and political power'.[31] In Britain, the imperialist press and other forces swung noisily behind an ill-treated Uitlander interest; enfranchisement, it was claimed, would turn a corrupt Boer fiefdom into a modern and purposeful industrial state, efficiently serving the needs of its wealth creators rather than those of an arrogant, obstructive, and anti-modern rural dynasty. For Whitehall's High Commissioner, Sir Henry Loch, a potential revolt over Uitlander rights seemed to clear the ground for renewed imperial intervention. With a nod from influential mining interests, in 1894 he began to tinker with the game of staging an imperial annexation in support of rebelling immigrants, in order to make the Transvaal a British colony. But the Colonial Office would not wink at this, fearful of condoning a deluded insurrection which could well spark off another Anglo-Boer war.

Meanwhile, by no means all Uitlanders were anti-republic malcontents. To be sure, there were influential business and professional coteries quite intent on putting down permanent roots, and psychologically incapable of playing second fiddle to the Boers, whom they considered not to be up to the job of managing a modern urban industrial civilization. But outside this boardroom of pro-imperial interest, attitudes were more mixed. Content to make their pile as temporary migrants, many Uitlanders had no interest in the franchise; others had no relish for the more onerous obligations of republican citizenship, such as compulsory commando service; artisan radicals wavered between an anti-Johannesburg capitalist rap-prochement with the government, and visions of a cosmopolitan smallholder republic, with as little love for British imperialism as for the existing Boer system. Lastly, German, Scandinavian, and other continental Europeans, to say nothing of nationalist Irishmen, had some difficulty in identifying with an Uitlander campaign run as a unified British imperial cause.[32]

With the mining community issue simmering away, events lurched deeper into crisis around the mid-1890s. In 1894 the Transvaal completed an eastern rail link from the Portuguese Delagoa Bay to the Witwatersrand, not only giving it coastal access beyond Britain's exclusive sphere of influence, but also threatening the important goods revenue of the two British colonies. As if this were an insufficient demonstration of the Transvaal's independent new wealth and greater assertiveness, it also established diplomatic relations with Germany. While Berlin's extension of patronage did not necessarily imply an immediate challenge to British regional supremacy, it was not there simply because Paul Kruger was inordinately proud that his family lineage was east of the Elbe. German approval of Boer refusal to enter a Cape-based customs union looked to be an ominous encouragement of greater republican independence from British commercial arrangements; so did the deposit of German capital to assist the 1894 formation of a South African Republic National Bank.

For Whitehall such moves did not bode well for protection abroad. Then, in 1895, an emboldened republican government sought to rub in its improved railways position by imposing steep haulage tariffs on Cape goods trains and blocking colonial efforts to circumvent this through the use of road transport across Transvaal territory. This 'Drifts' crisis (so-called after Boer closure of transport fords or 'drifts' over the Vaal river) produced a standoff with the Salisbury government, which swung hard behind Cape insistence on rights of free commercial access under the London Convention. With a terse ultimatum which took things suddenly to the brink of war, Britain threatened forceful intervention unless the traffic blockade was lifted.

Kruger grudgingly capitulated to this sabre-rattling and re-opened the drifts, thereafter accepting a tariff agreement. Yet this appeasement could not rescue a deteriorating British situation to the south and east. With increasing trade diversion, the economic grip of the Cape (and, to a lesser extent, Natal) had been growing more slippery. Now there was a further unsettling possibility: might the Transvaal's new influence not turn to decisive leverage over the Cape Colony? Might the northern Boers not try to reel it in, in their evident aspiration to slip the leash of British supremacy?

As imperial attitudes hardened, the key men of the 1890s bustled forward. Frustrated by failure to check the Transvaal's rising wealth and power by encirclement and the raising of a countervailing Rhodesian 'Second Rand', a pathologically plotting Cecil Rhodes hatched a conspiracy in 1895 to tip the Transvaal into British hands. The ambitious Cape premier, who fancied himself as a would-be viceroy of a united white South Africa, established a secret armed enterprise to overthrow the Kruger government with the connivance of Chamberlain and his South African High Commissioner, and some mine owners who sought a more amenable business order than that currently provided by the republic. While a harnessing of capitalist interests with imperial political objectives seems to have been perfectly evident, which was the cart and which the horse has long remained the subject of historical controversy.[33]

Rhodes's rash plan was to cook up a seething Uitlander rebellion as a pretext for a protective British colonial police column led by a trusted crony, Dr Leander Starr Jameson, to stage a supporting invasion to safeguard imperilled nationals. Once the Rand had been seized, a solicitous imperial power would intervene to bring peace and mediate a safer British future for the troubled Boer state. What spoiled things was the Uitlander failure to take up arms on cue, and the madness of Jameson's hopelessly undermanned and poorly primed raiders in pressing on with their quixotic invasion regardless. Having already lost any element of surprise days before, Jameson was easily cornered by smirking Transvaal commandos early in January 1896. An utter fiasco, justly termed one of the 'great cock-ups of history',[34] the Jameson Raid inspired a flood of clashing imperialist and pro-Boer literature, animating such diverse figures as G. K. Chesterton, Rudyard Kipling, and Olive Schreiner; it also convulsed the Boer nationalist cultural community, whose writers trumpeted the preservation of sacred freedom against underhand imperial violence. As an example of chancy and bungled British imperial action the Jameson Raid is without modern parallel, with the inevitable exception of Suez.

Predictably, the results of 1896 were dismal for London. Rhodes was disgraced, Britain was condemned internationally for its implication in a mucky conspiracy to snatch an independent Christian state, and there was heightened bickering amongst British Liberal Imperialists and Radical Liberals over imperial claims upon political morality; the Raid had raised the issue of power over principled diplomacy in a most uncomfortable way. In South Africa, far from toppling Kruger, Jameson's intervention strengthened his position. Justifying suspicion of British intentions, it enabled the Transvaal to solidify further its republican alliance with the Orange Free State, boosted Kruger's previously rocky electoral popularity, and spurred the growth of anti-British, republican, and nationalist passions within Boer populations elsewhere in the region. For a breathless Jan Smuts, the Jameson Raid was the greatest stimulus to a pan-Afrikaner consciousness since the 'glorious liberation in 1880', quickening the 'national heart' of the Afrikaner.[35] While this may have been stretching things a bit, colonial Boer sympathies for their beleaguered Transvaal kin certainly increased substantially. Even the Cape African newspaper proprietor and journalist John Tengo Jabavu found British buccaneering against the Boers as distasteful and illegitimate as any predatory sortie against Africans, although few blacks would have shared this view.

For his part, Kruger was remarkably adroit. Despite a baying Volksraad, he dealt magnanimously with seditious Uitlander conspirators and sweating Jameson raiders, and became more accommodating of the grievances of Randlords who yearned for a less parasitic agrarian state, more favourable industrial legislation, and labour policies which would hasten the delivery of more African migrant workers to the Rand. While the mines remained discontented over such thorny matters as government-imposed monopolies and a regime burdened by tribal graft and inefficiency, scholars now recognize that the Boer landed oligarchy became far more solicitous of industrial needs after 1896.[36]

At the same time, Kruger's ruling clique did not neglect to apply some stick. Just as British and South African public attention focused ever more intensely on the Uitlander question, Uitlander political activities were curbed, and Transvaal leadership was stiffened against any constitutional compromise in which political control might slip out of its hands. Its defensive capability shaken by the Jameson incursion, the Transvaal also began to prepare for a war which looked as if it might well be around the corner. A new military alliance treaty was concluded with the Orange Free State in 1897, affirming mutual support against any external threat to independence. Kruger, long criticized for being too sluggish about modernization, now embarked upon just that, but to provide security rather than economic deregulation. The republic embarked upon an expensive programme of major defence works, stockpiling of supplies, and a rearmament of its forces with imported weaponry, largely from Germany.

Previously the Dutch had had only the numbers and the money. Now they had the Mauser rifle too. They also had a further token of German approval. The Kaiser despatched a congratulatory cable to Pretoria on the defeat of the Raid; even as a watered-down version of Wilhelm's personal idea of landing German marines to strut around Delagoa Bay, the gesture was bad enough. It incensed the British government and touched off a wave of imperial patriotic sentiment, providing a powerful tide for the Conservative administration to ride its South African preoccupations. Still, although some in South Africa saw in the Kruger Telegram evidence of Germany as a future patron and protector of Pretoria, it did not imply a clear-cut German challenge to British assumptions of regional paramountcy, but was more of a cavalier diplomatic manoeuvre, with repercussions which Berlin tried quickly to contain, though one which seriously deepened London's unease over developing relations between Germany and the South African Republic. In a significant way the Raid had crystallized the linkages between 'Transvaal power, the wealth and needs of the mining industry, Uitlander rights, British supremacy and the prospects of a united South Africa'.[37] Equally, while it further inflamed British–Transvaal tension, historians are divided on whether or not it made war inevitable. For one thing, in the immediate aftermath of the Raid neither side wished to press for war through risky ultimatum or threat. None the less, it certainly remains a watershed moment, for hereafter the republican regime had the internal cohesion and hardened resolve to ensure that if Britain wanted its way, it would have to be through war. Jameson's lunge confirmed for many just what the stakes were: not merely the position of Kruger's regime, but the actual fate of a free republican nation.

For two further years or so there was stalemate and restraint, although no sign of any resolution. Chamberlain's decision to turn Uitlander grievances into a high-minded infatuation with civil liberty and political freedom took off as a popular campaign for the cause of empire, mobilizing press opinion and pressure groups like the pro-British South African League in both Britain and South Africa. Determined to force the pace through steely diplomatic pressure, in

1897 the Colonial Secretary posted Alfred Milner as South African High Commissioner. Haughty, supercilious, and a self-proclaimed 'British Race Patriot', Milner was contemptuous not only of Boer republican claims. A flinty advocate of a more highly integrated imperial order, he also regarded Cape and other colonial Boers with considerable disdain and suspicion, viewing them as unassimilable disloyals, part of a rising 'Afrikanerdom' constellation which had to be smashed.[38] This was not too promising a basis for productive Anglo-Boer diplomacy.

Although Salisbury and Chamberlain disliked the idea of war, hoping that Kruger would succumb to bluff or threat before snapping, they were equally firm on forcing imperial supremacy or paramountcy on the Boers, 'whether peacefully or not'.[39] If this meant war, there was natural concern about public opinion and diplomatic repercussions on British interests elsewhere. It was essential that things looked intolerable for Britain; negotiations for a reformed Transvaal had to be genuine, and the chosen *casus belli* legitimate. For his part, Milner was increasingly dismissive of what in March 1898 he termed 'the waiting game'. Acknowledging the only conceivable outcome as 'reform in the Transvaal or war', he was more impatient than his political masters to clear the decks for a conflict he not only accepted, but craved.[40] In effect Chamberlain relinquished things to Milner, a man unlikely to go fishing or to the races when there was a crisis to worsen. Hope of acceptable reform looked lost by the end of 1898, a year of resounding electoral victory for Kruger in which the legitimacy of Transvaal nationalism was effectively reduced to the presidential incumbent.

Prodding and cajoling English press and public opinion into talk of intervention over the franchise and other Uitlander 'wrongs' and 'injustices', a beavering Milner and his subordinates and allies proceeded to do what was necessary to scupper any Anglo-Boer compromise, and to nudge along a final showdown. Early in 1899, bargaining between the republicans and the Randlords over possible franchise concessions was sabotaged, as this threatened to cool a hot political temperature. Ideas from pacifist Cape and Natal elements for regional South African policy conferences on such ticklish issues as European immigration met with indifference. Instead, a series of trumpeted Uitlander petitions to the Volksraad and the Queen, requesting reform and protection, focused things nicely for the High Commissioner, who fired a round of sulphurous despatches, enlarging old complaints against the Boer regime and dredging up further disputes. These included a famous May telegram, in which Milner depicted British subjects as 'helots' enslaved by Transvaal tyranny, a grand scandal crying out for forceful resolution.

Deaf to the conciliationist pleas of poor old Cape colonial moderates, anxious anti-war Natalians, and some Orange Free State and Transvaal 'progressives', Milner kept pushing to the limit on the franchise disagreement; he had energetically massaged British opinion on this, and believed that if the Transvaal did finally cave in, it would be delivered through its British vote. With his back to the wall, an outwardly intransigent Kruger was ultimately prepared to concede a franchise liberalization in return for some respectful imperial restraint. But such bargaining was spurned. For its part, the republic rejected demands for a joint Anglo-Boer enquiry into the Uitlander political problem, on the reasonable basis that it undermined its sovereign rights to internal autonomy.

Following the failure of a mid-year Bloemfontein Conference to achieve any compromise deal, and Kruger's memorable observation that what Milner wanted was not the franchise but his country, the Boers grasped at a last straw in August. They consented to a five-year retrospective franchise right demanded by Milner, in return for guarantees of no interference in their internal affairs, a relinquishing of the assertion of imperial 'suzerainty' or supremacy, and submission of outstanding disputes to future independent arbitration. There was by now little possibility that Britain would agree upon statutory conditions, especially not those suggested. Rejection again confirmed thinking in Pretoria and Johannesburg that the issue was not Uitlander rights, but their national autonomy. Given that balance, it is not surprising that even friendly German, Dutch, and Belgian diplomatic advice to Pretoria not to bring on war by refusing to meet British obligations failed to sway the Transvaal.

In response to the reassertion of claims and demands for further Uitlander concessions, the republic withdrew its compromise settlement offer on 2 September, and fell back on its earlier 1899 proposal of a franchise based on a seven-year residence qualification, again contesting Britain's 'suzerainty'. A week earlier Milner had declared the 'South African question' to be 'purely military', and Chamberlain had obligingly assigned troop reinforcements; Britain had also already begun to use its diplomatic leverage over Portugal to try to curb Transvaal arms imports through Delagoa Bay. Such brinkmanship increased republican determination not to yield. For Smuts, the Transvaal would sooner 'again take up arms' than submit to a 'humiliating solution'.[41] Tortuous political exchanges continued through September, as Britain bided its time. This was spent awaiting reinforcements, preparing brusque war terms, and hoping for a prior Boer ultimatum which would provide the handy just cause needed to still lingering Liberal and Labour rumblings that republican short-comings did not warrant war. At its last pre-war Cabinet meeting on 29 September, the Salisbury government was confident of national circumstances.

Meanwhile, the Orange Free State readied itself to fight alongside its neighbour. Satisfied that Transvaal independence was at stake, at the end of September President Steyn's Volksraad pledged full treaty and other assistance. On 2 October, with both states mobilizing their commando forces, Kruger advised the Transvaal legislature that war was now imminent. Convinced that a snap offensive would be to Boer advantage (and mindful of being caught napping, as in 1896), Kruger and his ally presented a joint 48-hour ultimatum to the British Agent in Pretoria on 9 October. Just pipping Britain's ultimatum timetable, republican demands left no room for any further wrangling. Britain was to agree to arbitration on all 'points of difference', and to an immediate withdrawal of all its forces, be they those menacing Boer borders, reinforcements stationed elsewhere, or troops already *en route* from any part of the empire. On the evening of the next day these terms were tersely rejected. It was already disagreeable enough for a great power to have to negotiate with a small African state managed by ruffianly Dutch farmers. This last impertinence was intolerable.

With a formal declaration of war on 11 October, and the first cross-border advance into Natal, Britain and the Boer Republics commenced hostilities. Publicly sure of a capacity quickly to overawe the enemy, Chamberlain was sanguine, even smug. A week earlier Milner had scoffed at the notion that simple farmers could hold out even for a moment against regular soldiers. Wrapped in Calvinist puritanism, an ageing Kruger was bitterly apocalyptic, assuring an American paper that the price Britain would have to pay for gaining the republics would beggar the most metaphysical imagination.[42] So much for the relentless pace of events. It is easy to see why figures as various as Smuts and Winston Churchill considered the Jameson Raid the real declaration of war, or why an apprehensive Merriman feared that its 'first shot may well be a South African Lexington', with consequences far more unpredictable and dangerous than in 1881.[43]

While the broad run of immediate events suggests why the crisis failed to be resolved diplomatically, to turn from these to the under-lying causes of war is to contemplate some historiographical Mount Everest, a consummation of years of detailed scholarly research and reassessment. It is not the present aim to add to an intricate debate, but only to touch on the main arguments. Any war casts a long shadow, and to have a reasonable view we need to clear away things which are contingent or subsidiary to a larger interpretative picture. Thus, however important their individual responsibility, the bringing on of war cannot simply be ascribed to Milner and Chamberlain or Kruger. Nor can the cause of Uitlander rights be seen as a prime motive, whatever its obvious centrality to the 1890s crisis; at bottom, this was really a functional pretext for the larger issue of who should enjoy untrammelled authority over southern Africa.[44] It is no easier to accept that war arose from republican intrigue or design to reclaim all of South Africa as a Dutch 'Africander' possession. While the spectre of an ascending 'alliance' or 'dominion' of Afrikanerdom had become increasingly influential in British thinking after 1896, there was little material basis for a republican-ruled Cape and Natal. On its own, the Orange Free State had no particular quarrel with British power, and the Transvaal and pre-war Natal maintained a cosy coexistence for good economic reasons. Crucially, too, there was also no common vocabulary of united purpose between colonial and republican Boers, whose sense of nationality and identity derived historically not just from membership of a constructed people, but also from territory and regional political cultures.[45]

Of long significance to explaining causation is the thesis, in various versions, that the war was basically a product of late-nineteenth-century economic imperialism, a push to exert control over or entrench leading access to the Transvaal gold fields and their crucial sterling supply. As already noted, the notion of a conspicuously capitalist war gripped republican leaders as well as late-Victorian British radicals; that conclusion has also been echoed by such eminent modern historians as Eric Hobsbawm, for whom, 'whatever the ideology, the motive for the Boer War was gold'.[46] But this argument has not had an easy ride from critics. In the first place, it has been pointed out that Britain did not invade the Transvaal directly to control the mining industry; its capital saw to that. Similarly, British access to bullion did not require the creation of a Crown Colony and British governance.[47]

Nor, in this assessment, is it tenable to claim that a clump of grumbling mining capitalists amounted to an impatient conspiracy, exploiting Anglo-Boer antagonisms to engineer the removal of Kruger's regime and its replacement with an administration more attuned to the special needs of the mining industry. In reality, Rand capitalists were not a united pro-war front; if anything, war looked frightening and costly for mine operations; and the most than can be said is that the anti-Kruger antagonisms of the mining interest and its local press allies helped to feed an atmosphere of crisis. Indeed, for the most part, capitalists remained willing to deal with the Boers, and would assuredly have settled for more helpful labour accords, industrial commissions, and accelerated modern state reform. As the only partisanship was that behind dividends, interest, and profits, the Transvaal might as well have been in South America. Moreover, there is no really clinching direct evidence that in resorting to war the Salisbury government was itself animated by concern over the conditions and profitability of the gold industry.

In this view, all that can be said is that the mining interest went along with force, trusting that battlefield victory would usher in a freer kind of capitalist regime. For Britain's end was not the gold supply as such, but the imposition of its political will over the Transvaal, and affirming British supremacy for the laying-down of a loyalist South Africa. The push was not economic determinism but the decisive affirmation of imperial political supremacy.[48] Equally, that Britain did not go to war *for* gold does not mean that the war was not essentially *about* its overarching effects. This takes us back to the old argument over whether or not war was necessary to modernize the Transvaal.

Its image as intrinsically torpid and anti-modern now appears much less clear-cut, and one suggestive argument is that what disturbed Britain was not just antipathy towards mine costs and other Uitlander complaints, but the use of protectionist state economic policy to foster indigenous national industrial growth. For Kruger, who personally thought gold a divine provision to end an era of hard times, greater economic autonomy through such things as the state dynamite monopoly, republican mint, national bank, and control of the railways could now realistically be pursued. Coupling political sovereignty to economic independence would increase Boer capacity to dictate the development of a wealthy and powerful state with the impetus to draw in slack British colonies, while any such protectionist trend would strike at the heart of British preference. As both imperial politicians and capitalists swung behind demands for a more accommodating Transvaal, so there was shared anxiety over its drift towards economic modernization on a tide of tariff protectionism which would inflict a serious blow to British and Cape interests.[49] The peculiar assertion in much imperial propaganda that the Transvaal's problem was that it was somehow either 'feudal' or 'medieval', and yet also South Africa's potential 'centre' or 'capital state', is a contradiction still well worth considering.

Linked to the latter perception were renewed late-1890s concerns over the Delagoa Bay connection. Britain had long wanted to block the Boers' eastern port link and to exclude any rival European power like Germany or France from commercial or political holdings in Mozambique. An 1898 Anglo-German Agreement on Britain's Transvaal paramountcy was meant to stabilize the Delagoa Bay position; but it was to prove less than perfect, as it conceded business development of the port. When that concession went to a German-backed company, Britain faced a newly awkward situation for its Southern African position and 'vital interests'. It was no idle speculation to see the consequences of an improved port facility serving the Transvaal as well as European rivals. And this deepened worries about the commercial interests of the Cape and Natal and the health of their sizeable British investments, about the future flow of gold to Berlin and Paris money markets, and about the continuing predominance of British trade with the Transvaal should Germany or France use an expanded Delagoa Bay route to penetrate a growing Boer market at British expense.

Aside from the economic stake, by the end of the 1890s there were naval fears over the strategic implications of independent Mozambican dock development. With conveniently direct access to Transvaal coal, any European maritime rival with a Delagoa base could menace the vital Cape route as well as bolting a door on inland British trade. Whether it was foreign commercial interests squeezing in on trade routes, or apprehension over rivals securing naval bases in the territory of weaker powers (as had recently already happened in China), security also moved up the imperial agenda. Disquiet was not eased by speculation in 1897 that Berlin would boost German business development of a Delagoa Bay concession to service a planned new Transvaal steamer line, entrenching advanced German marine expertise in Lourenco Marques. Against this, talk of Simon's Town being put at risk on account of the Transvaal was a sideshow.[50]

Deep down, and intersecting with British economic and strategic interests, was the critical question of who southern Africa was *for*. The answer, Britain, had always seemed obvious enough. But, by the late 1890s, this looked easier said than done. If there were no declared German ambitions in the Transvaal, German nibbling on the seaboard to its southeast still threatened to dilute that paramountcy or prestigious 'exclusive predominance' which so preoccupied Downing Street. Supremacy looked to be no less unsettled by both Germany and France entering the auction for Transvaal favour, thereby inflating its influence and independence: all this appeared as a discouraging eventuality for the Cape, and, especially, a financially rocky Natal.[51]

In imperial defensive scenarios, there were two maturing and corrosive insecurities by 1899. One was that a straining and protectionist Transvaal, aided by railways spoils and port advantages, might simply cast off. What would happen then? Shrugging off remaining dependence on British territories, it was conceivable that the republic might get a larger share of South Africa after all. But the worry was not so much that of the Transvaal sucking adjacent territory into some anti-British, republican *Mittelboer* zone as the prospect, clear to the Prime Minister's son-in-law, Selborne, and other officials, of the damage a restive, demographically expansionist and increasingly cosmopolitan republic could do to British interests if left to develop unchecked. What guarantee was there that a defensively nationalist Transvaal thick with Americans, Germans, Scandinavians, or other European 'riffraff' would not ally itself with a foreign power?

Influential 'continental' republicans were already embedded in the Transvaal state, recruited by Kruger to make good technical and managerial deficiencies in its infrastructure. For those British officials who believed that all this spelled Germany, bodies like the Pan-German League provided brooding confirmation of their worst fears, with their notions of German–Boer racial affinity and assertions that the Boers were the outriders of German expansion.[52] Even as things stood, the challenge of entrenched Boer republicanism to Britishness jeopardized the attainment of a South African federation as a segment of that 'unified white empire' which Chamberlain felt could help to rebuild Britain's competitive advantage over newer world powers like Germany and the USA.[53]

Any dribbling away of British power was considered disastrous, and not merely because of its consequences for the control of South Africa. Resolution of this problem had also become essential to maintaining confidence in Britain's ability to defend its known vital interests and to be the guarantor of imperial stability and integration. What was at stake was more than British domestic prestige, in Southern Africa or in Europe: it was the public standing of its governance throughout the empire. For the Colonial Office, the case for upholding British 'prestige' was virtually as compelling here as on the Indian frontier. Therefore, for Chamberlain, if the British position in South Africa was 'at stake', so was 'the estimate of our power and influence in our colonies and throughout the world'.[54] If the Transvaal provided a peephole into an imagined imperial abyss, the only way to lock it was a convincing demonstration that defiance of British paramountcy would not pay. That made a showdown imperative.

None of this is to discount the momentum of deadlock diplomacy and mutually misguided military conceit. Nor is it to overlook the impact of the bellicose and militarist surge of late-Victorian public opinion, across class and party lines. Having implanted an aggressive imperial campaign to jack up British prestige and secure the sovereign rights of freeborn Britons in the colonial world, it would have been difficult for any British government with a mass electorate to back away from so great and public a cause.[55] Neither, in broader terms, is it to argue that Britain made war only to protect its trade and investment, or just to make certain it retained its supremacy.

What, then, emerges by way of conclusion? It is now probably generally accepted that the precise balance between economic, strategic, and political factors remains difficult to strike. But in any equation the critical importance of gold reserves and supply to Britain's financial position in the international economy cannot be left out of any war context. At a time of growing menace from rival economic powers, London's traditional world money-market role needed the tacit assurance of uncomplicated political arrangements in the Transvaal. With a friendly regime in place, the mining industry would then finally be free to concentrate fully on improving its efficiency and performance in a more economically liberal environment, and the British government could sleep easier in the knowledge that the Bank of England would retain control over the disposal of South African gold, and remain impregnable in its leadership of the international gold standard.[56]

The other weighty consideration is the connection between confidence in Britain as the world's financial and commercial centre, and the peace and security of its empire. As the power of that empire gradually declined through the later nineteenth century, relations with economic competitors and peripheral colonial societies became more 'marked by increasing demands and diminishing tolerance'.[57] Less and less could be left to chance when secure possession of a formal empire was more essential than ever to international predominance. Chamberlain in particular made much of this, a politician who 'sought to convince the public as never before of the cardinal importance of the Empire and of the need to cultivate and consolidate it'. And that public was as much Toronto and Auckland as Glasgow and Birmingham.[58] Chamberlain stood for an authentic imperialist collectivism, fed by policies which would combine integrated imperialist development abroad with domestic economic and welfare reforms. In time this organic unity would become a largely self-generating affair, its chief benefit being a national renovation of the British imperialist race. Its commercial basis lay in the idea of a preferential imperial customs union, within which free trade would prevail, removing any protective colonial tariffs against goods from the mother country. For a Chamberlainite advocate of imperial preference and gradual, overarching imperial federation, it was only through a more efficiently organized empire that Britain would stop losing ground and be able to hold on in a tough world economy.

The highveldt had become one of the more vulnerable spots for that empire to start bleeding. Possibly as pivotal as Egypt to the British position in Africa, South Africa also appeared to be a case of nudging at back-door independence. This would not do, especially as British 'vital interests' in southern Africa were not solely strategic, a matter of safe naval stations and open ocean lanes in which the Cape of Good Hope remained vital to maritime communications with India. The broad future of capital and commodity trading markets had become no less an issue, as had the need to resolve Cape–Orange Free State and Natal–Transvaal railway disputes in order to establish a financially viable rail communications network. In the face of a potential erosion of such influence, there was something to be gained by ramming home imperial supremacy, and much to be lost by not doing so. For, in a fundamental sense, South Africa had become an exemplary case of national interest for the British governing élite. After all, for much of the nineteenth century it was axiomatic that 'the security and vitality of Britain's economy and society depended upon the retention, defence and whenever necessary, the extension of the empire'.[59] South Africa fused all these imperatives, and added the upholding of Great Power prestige. If Britain was willing to threaten war with France over its West African interests in 1898, there could be no question of its political readiness to use force for South Africa; but the irony is that the Transvaal itself was scarcely one of those great destabilizing world rivals which had become so troubling to British imperialists.

The cause of this war is fortunately not everything, although the continuing flow of literature on the topic sometimes suggests that. If some part of the South African crisis had been less about railway tariffs and more about railway timetables, A. J. P. Taylor might well have settled this question years ago. But we have another memorable Taylor observation to which we can now turn: that is, that forcing a war was not the same as determining its course, or Milner's mistake that in manoeuvring the enemy into war you needed to be sure that your generals were ready for it.[60] In this, even Chamberlain was not an entirely ignorant politician. Just a week before war, his slight worry was that 'our troops, unlike the Boers, cannot mobilize with a piece of biltong and a belt of ammunition, but require such enormous quantities of transport and impedimenta'.[61]

Still, there was nothing new in that. For some years Chamberlain had been urging the Cabinet to strengthen Britain's South African military presence, something which had usually been resisted by the Treasury and by colleagues uncertain of a popular mood for war and not wanting to overdo things. Yet, for much of this time, the Colonial Secretary himself had been thinking of armed force more as a means of keeping matters astir, as an intimidating factor in negotiation rather than for bringing on actual warfare. On the other hand, others in the Cabinet, not least Salisbury and the War Secretary, Lord Lansdowne, grasped the eventuality of the war to come more firmly, and took its requirements a bit more seriously. At the same time they also shared Chamberlain's grasp of the consequences of a binding operational commitment with a tame ending. Without a war, how could the value of any expenditure wrung from a reluctant Treasury be reasonably recovered?

From August 1899 onwards, the stage was set for Britain to handle its war preparations very gingerly, with a War Office full of misgivings about Cabinet equivocation over military measures, and with the government deliberately ambiguous over whether it would be peace or war. The classic calculation, for Lansdowne, was to avoid any step too far which could push the Boers and start a war which, just conceivably, might still be avoided. It was precisely this risk, that of a pre-emptive enemy strike, which Chamberlain continued to dismiss.[62] This sort of political balancing was all very well, but did not do much to advance the state of British military preparedness for an impending war which was likely to come sooner rather than later. If threatening words could not be backed up convincingly with military deeds, there would be a price to pay.

Chapter I Notes

1. A. J. P. Taylor, *Essays in English History* (London, 1976), pp. 184–5.
2. Quoted in Bernard Porter, *The Lion's Share: A Short History of British Imperialism 1850–1970* (London, 1975), p. 175.
3. Iain R. Smith, *The Origins of the South African War 1899–1902* (London, 1996), p. 415.
4. Geoffrey Blainey, *The Causes of War* (Melbourne, 1988), p. 141.
5. Quoted in G. H. L. Le May, *British Supremacy in South Africa 1899–1907* (Oxford, 1965), p. 28.

6. *Cape Colony Hansard (Legislative Assembly Debates)*, 18 Oct. 1898, p. 46; *Sir James Rose Innes: Selected Correspondence 1884–1902*, ed. Harrison M. Wright (Cape Town, 1972), p. 200.
7. *The War Memoirs of Commandant Ludwig Krause 1899–1900*, ed. Jerold Taitz (Cape Town, 1996), pp. 1–3.
8. Andrew Porter, 'The South African War (1899–1902): context and motive reconsidered', *Journal of African History*, 31/1 (1990), p. 43.
9. Samuel Hynes, *The Edwardian Turn of Mind* (Princeton, 1968), p. 19.
10. Bernard Semmel, *Imperialism and Social Reform: English Social-Imperial Thought 1895–1914* (New York, 1968), pp. 30, 57; Paul Crook, *Darwinism, War and History* (Cambridge, 1994), pp. 80, 89–90.
11. *Justice*, 12 July 1900; *Clarion*, 17 Nov. 1899.
12. Generally, *Marxism and the Science of War*, ed. Bernard Semmel (Oxford, 1981), pp. 13–18.
13. Bernard Porter, *Critics of Empire: British Radical Attitudes to Colonialism in Africa 1895–1914* (London, 1968), pp. 123–30; Miles Taylor, '"Imperium et Libertas": rethinking the radical critique of imperialism during the nineteenth century', *Journal of Imperial and Commonwealth History*, 19/1 (1991), p. 16.
14. *Jan Smuts: Memoirs of the Boer War*, eds S. B. Spies and Gail Nattrass (Johannesburg, 1994), p. 130.
15. Quoted in David Feldman, 'Nationality and ethnicity', in *Twentieth-Century Britain: Economic, Social and Cultural Change*, ed. Paul Johnson (London, 1994), p. 157.
16. John Grigg, 'Lloyd George and the Boer War', in *Edwardian Radicalism 1900–1914*, ed. A. J. A. Morris (London, 1974), p. 13.
17. Leonard Thompson, *A History of South Africa* (New Haven and London, 1990), p. 109.
18. Shula Marks, 'Scrambling for South Africa', *Journal of African History*, 23/1 (1982), p. 101.
19. Quoted in Brian Bond, 'The South African War 1880–1', in *Victorian Military Campaigns*, ed. Brian Bond (London, 1967), p. 204.
20. Joseph Lehmann, *The First Boer War* (London, 1972); Maria Hugo, 'Wapenstilstand', in *Die Eerste Vryheidsoorlog*, eds F. A. van Jaarsveld, A. P. J. van Rensburg, and W. A. Stals (Pretoria, 1980), p. 201.
21. Quoted in Paul Hayes, *Modern British Foreign Policy: The Twentieth Century 1880–1939* (London, 1978), p. 19.
22. Albert Grundlingh, 'Prelude to the Anglo-Boer War, 1881–1899', in *An Illustrated History of South Africa*, eds Trewella Cameron and S. B. Spies (Johannesburg, 1986), p. 184.
23. Andrew Porter, *European Imperialism 1860–1914* (London, 1994), p. 70.
24. J. D. Omer-Cooper, *History of Southern Africa* (London, 1987), p. 124.
25. D. M. Schreuder, *Gladstone and Kruger: Liberal Government and Colonial Home Rule 1880–85* (London, 1969), p. 15.
26. Peter Richardson and Jean-Jacques Van-Helten, 'The gold mining industry in the Transvaal 1886–99', in *The South African War: The Anglo-Boer War 1899–1902*, ed. Peter Warwick (London, 1980), p. 21.
27. Studies of particular distinction include *Industrialisation and Social Change in South Africa: African Class Formation, Culture and Consciousness 1870–1930*, eds Shula Marks and Richard Rathbone (London, 1982); Charles van Onselen, *Studies in the Social and Economic History of the Witwatersrand 1886–1914*, 2 vols (London, 1982).
28. Porter, *Lion's Share*, p. 98.
29. Stanley Trapido, 'Reflections on land, office and wealth in the South African

Republic 1850–1900', in *Economy and Society in Pre-industrial South Africa* (London, 1980), eds Shula Marks and Anthony Atmore (London, 1982), p. 357.

30. T. R. H. Davenport, *South Africa: A Modern History* (London, 1991), p. 85; Richard Mendelsohn, *Sammy Marks, The 'Uncrowned King' of the Transvaal* (Cape Town, 1991), p. 93.

31. Smith, *South African War*, p. 83.

32. Diana Cammack, *The Rand at War 1899–1902: The Witwatersrand and the Anglo-Boer War* (London, 1990), pp. 12–32.

33. Mendelsohn, 'Thirty years' debate on the economic origins of the raid', in *The Jameson Raid: A Centennial Perspective* (Johannesburg, 1996), pp. 55–87.

34. Neil Parsons, 'The Jameson road', *Southern African Review of Books*, 8/1 (1996), p. 7.

35. Quoted in J. A. Coetzee, *Die Politieke Groepering in die Wording van die Afrikanernatie* (Johannesburg, 1941), p. 185.

36. Patrick Harries, 'Capital, state and labour on the nineteenth-century Witwatersrand: a reassessment', *South African Historical Journal*, 18 (1986), pp. 25–45; Elaine N. Katz, 'Outcrop and deep-level mining in South Africa before the Anglo-Boer War: re-examining the Blainey thesis', *Economic History Review*, 48 (1995), p. 326.

37. Alan H. Jeeves, 'The consequences of the raid', in *Jameson Raid*, p. 172.

38. *Selections from the Correspondence of Percy Alport Molteno*, ed. Vivian Solomon (Cape Town, 1981), p. 185; Saul Dubow, 'Colonial nationalism, the Milner kindergarten and the rise of "South Africanism", 1902–10', *History Workshop Journal*, 43 (1997), p. 57.

39. Andrew Porter, 'Lord Salisbury, Mr Chamberlain and South Africa, 1895–9', *Journal of Imperial and Commonwealth History*, 1/1 (1972), p. 22.

40. Milner to Chamberlain, 23 February 1898, in *The Milner Papers*, ed. Cecil Headlam (London, 1931), p. 220.

41. Smuts to Te Water, 4 September 1899, in *Selections from the Smuts Papers*, vol. 1, eds W. K. Hancock and J. van der Poel (Cambridge, 1966), p. 309.

42. J. L. Garvin and Julian Amery, *The Life of Joseph Chamberlain*, vol. 3 (London, 1949), p. 476.

43. *Selections from the Correspondence of John X. Merriman*, vol. 3 (1899–1905), ed. Phyllis Lewsen (Cape Town, 1966), p. 95.

44. David Reynolds, *Britannia Overruled: British World Power and Decline* (London, 1991), pp. 67–8.

45. Mordechai Tamarkin, *Cecil Rhodes and the Cape Afrikaner: The Imperial Colossus and the Colonial Parish Pump* (London, 1996), p. 181.

46. Eric Hobsbawm, *The Age of Empire 1875–1914* (London, 1987), p. 66.

47. Porter, 'South African War', pp. 47–8.

48. Ronald Robinson and John Gallagher, *Africa and the Victorians: The Official Mind of Imperialism* (London, 1961), pp. 457–61; Smith, *South African War*, pp. 393–413.

49. Ian Phimister, 'Africa partitioned', *Review*, 18/2 (1995), p. 375; 'Unscrambling the scramble for Southern Africa', *South African Historical Journal*, 28 (1993), pp. 216–19; Grundlingh, 'Paul Kruger', in *Jameson Raid*, p. 232; Shula Marks and Stanley Trapido, 'Lord Milner and the South African state reconsidered', in *Imperialism, The State and the Third World*, ed. Michael Twaddle (London, 1992), p. 84.

50. Peter Henshaw, 'The "key to South Africa": Delagoa Bay and the origins of the South African War, 1890–1899', unpublished seminar paper, Department of History, University of Cape Town, 1997; 'The "key to South Africa in the 1890s": Delagoa Bay and the origins of the South African War', Rethinking the SA War Conference paper, UNISA, 1998.

51. Ritchie Ovendale, 'Profit or patriotism: Natal, the Transvaal, and the coming of the second Anglo-Boer War', *Journal of Imperial and Commonwealth History*, 8/3 (1980), pp. 225–7.
52. John Bottomley, 'The application of the theory of "economic backwardness" to South Africa's early modern period: the development initiatives of the various governments from the Zuid-Afrikaansche Republiek to the Pact Government of 1924', unpublished South African Economic History Society conference paper, University of Natal, 1992; Andrew Porter, 'The origins of the South African War', *South African Historical Journal*, 35 (1996), pp. 159–60.
53. Andrew Gamble, *Britain in Decline: Economic Policy, Political Strategy and the British State* (London, 1990), pp. 55–6.
54. Quoted in Robinson and Gallagher, *Africa and the Victorians*, p. 454.
55. Porter, 'South African War', p. 55; J. M. Mackenzie, *Propaganda and Empire: The Manipulation of British Public Opinion 1880–1960* (Manchester, 1984), p. 2.
56. Russell Ally, *Gold and Empire: The Bank of England and South Africa's Gold Producers 1886–1926* (Johannesburg, 1994), pp. 24–5, 136–7; David French, *British Economic and Strategic Planning 1905–1915* (London, 1982), p. 16.
57. P. J. Cain and A. G. Hopkins, *British Imperialism: Innovation and Expansion 1688–1914* (London, 1993), p. 360.
58. Peter Marsh, *The Discipline of Popular Government: Lord Salisbury's Domestic Statecraft, 1881–1902* (Hassocks, 1978), p. 273; *Joseph Chamberlain: Entrepreneur in Politics* (New Haven and London, 1994), p. 420.
59. K. E. Wilburn, 'The climax of railway competition in South Africa, 1886–1889', D. Phil. diss. (University of Oxford, 1982), pp. 148–9; Paul Kennedy, *The Realities behind Diplomacy: Background Influences on British External Policy 1865–1980* (London, 1981), p. 108.
60. A. J. P. Taylor, *From the Boer War to the Cold War: Essays on Twentieth-Century Europe* (Harmondsworth, 1996 edn.), p. 39.
61. Quoted in Marsh, *Joseph Chamberlain*, p. 472.
62. Ibid., p. 471.

2

Lining Up

The republican war aims were simple and straightforward: retention of the internal political independence of the Transvaal, respect for its post-1881 independent status, a repudiation of imperial 'suzerainty', and a destiny in which command of the South African Republic would remain unequivocally in Boer hands. It was by no means Paul Kruger alone who was profoundly influenced by the belief that through years of struggle and sacrifice the Boers had come to own the Transvaal. Members of its Calvinist clergy and intelligentsia, its professional classes, and its leading urban commercial and financial strata shared the Presidential view that the mineral wealth of the Witwatersrand was a final vindication of their nineteenth-century Israelite quest for the promised land, a providential reward to make up for beleaguered and impoverished migrant beginnings. Endowed by history and sanctified by Calvinist Protestantism, the republican nation state required resolute defence against predators, be they Zulu impi (warriors), anti-republican Uitlanders, or British redcoats.

Among the white rural landless and other poor there was a dusting of Old Testament prophets, millennial visionaries and archaic fundamentalists for whom a defensive war was something to be met with more than a religious sense of fatalistic acceptance. It was also an emotional opportunity to bring about a purification of the Transvaal. Successful resistance would see off both foreign invaders and the corrupting modernization represented by their mines, ideologies, and value systems; what could then be reclaimed was some lost Boer Arcadia, in which pre- or non-capitalist needs and practices could once more prevail in a gentler and more communal society. Here was a feeling that if peace could no longer be preserved, so be it. An anti-alien war could renew the republic, with victory providing the basis for a protective social order which expressed the 'true character' or 'real spirit' of its people.[1] Naturally enough, judging from the work of historians of the pre-1886 Boer republics, the good old days were somewhat less rosy for the poorer whites who lived through them than for those tramping demagogues who now nostalgically imagined them.[2]

For most ordinary Boer men and women, a war against Britain was a matter of survival. Even if the chosen method of defence would be the invasion of British colonial territory, it was widely understood to be a defensive enterprise. At the same time, the extent to which this support for war represented some universal nationalist ardour must surely remain an open question. There is no doubt that modernizing, urban-aligned and educated middle classes identified deeply with a republican state patriotism exemplified by such national figures as Jan Smuts and Marthinus Steyn, ironically the bearers of a Cambridge and London education respectively.[3] But Dutch/Afrikaans 'continental' republicanism is unlikely to have encompassed the entire Boer population, most of whom inhabited an agrarian world thick with localisms, resilient family loyalties, and devoted ties to farmsteads. Yet if this meant little or lukewarm identification with a republican statism, it did not mean lack of popular support for taking up arms. Instead, what it suggests is that the basis of support for a national war effort rested upon some quite discrete understandings of the meaning and objectives of a defensive mobilization. To put it another way, for the anti-imperialist Pretoria press this was a war to ensure the continued existence of the Boer state and the future of a free republicanism; for Transvaal and Orange Free State big rural patriarchs it may have been more an effort to defend defined territorial influence and known community; for ordinary farmers the stakes probably narrowed down to responding to a perceived threat to their homes and agricultural livelihoods; and for agitated women it amounted to a fight in defence of a traditionalist home community against unknown outsiders.[4]

While there was no uniform Boer republicanism, at the outbreak of war these impulses intersected to form a holding line based on defence of the homeland. This, as many writers on war have noted, has long been one of the most powerful motivations in the will to fight. And here there was something for burghers to defend. Part of the legitimacy of the Boer state lay in the fact that it was not completely neglectful of the welfare needs of its poorer rural burgher electorate, hard hit by severe drought in 1893 and a crippling Rinderpest cattle epidemic in 1897, to say nothing of locusts and malaria. By the late 1890s the Kruger government was spending almost one-third of its annual budget on relief to distressed whites. Imperialism was, then, a further pestilence, threatening the peace of a republic trying to protect its burgher society on sound nationalist grounds.

While the standpoint of justified defence was obviously vital to the persuasiveness of the Boer case in Europe and North America, the republicans were not wanting in pugnacity. Responding to bullying British diplomacy with a strong threat of their own, Reitz and Smuts declared it the task of all Boers to unite militarily to bring about a 'Free, United South Africa', an ambitious national Afrikaner republic stretching from the Zambezi to Table Bay.[5] This confirmed the most apprehensive imperial speculation about the Transvaal and its sub-imperial intentions. But the Reitz–Smuts grand design remained more offensive bluster than an achievable objective. The first republican columns assembling on the Natal front may have been itching to get at the enemy, but few in their ranks could seriously have believed that this would be a fight to knock the British right out of South Africa altogether. Many more, egged on through September by a pro-war republican press and a seething Volksraad war faction, simply fancied their prospects of achieving a headlong military victory and thereby swiftly repelling Britain. Newspapers on the tables of Pretoria's generals, such as *Ons Volk* and *Land en Volk*, pointed out repeatedly that Boer arms had been effective on a previous occasion. Why not again? The Transvaal wished for nothing more than another General Colley.

On the other hand, the Boers wished for nothing less than the involvement of surrounding African communities. The war aims of republican society turned upon the objective of a limited political community; its fight for independence required black compliance rather than alliance. Not only was there no basis for Africans in the Boer republics to be convinced of the necessity for war against Britain; there was every basis for assuming that discontented peasants and labourers would be more likely to favour the imperial side. For them, invasion might well be a blessing. In this sense the immediate reality of war confirmed the narrow territorial legitimacy of the republican state. It was not least for this reason that Boer war policy excluded any arming and enlistment of African groups as contractual allies. And the issue was not simply one of weighing up the risk or reliability of black collaboration. As Donald Denoon suggested years ago, 'the prime condition for Afrikaner survival', more vital even 'than independence from the Empire', was 'the constant subordination of the African communities'. For Smuts this meant that on no account could 'the coloured races' be allowed to become 'the arbiters in disputes between the whites' for fear that they would become 'in the long run the predominating political factor or "casting vote" in South Africa'. This was 'the cardinal principle in South African politics'.[6]

Because of source limitations, it remains exceptionally difficult to obtain a full picture of the range of African sentiment and responses to republican war preparation. Very broadly, what can be said is that in parts of the countryside there would have been indifference and antipathy, or some level of anticipation or even conviction that an imperial invasion of the republics could overturn Boer authority and lead to more favourable terms of existence for black workers and agricultural tenants. On the other hand, for those male servants traditionally socialized and acculturated as loyal commando after-riders or *agterryers*, here was another war in which their functions of skilled military aid and dependent solidarity would be utilized by Boer masters. If there was a recognizable black loyalty to the republican side it was here, in the individualistic and personalized form of the experienced and trusted auxiliary.

Other positions were fairly clearly defined. Some pre-war British propaganda had focused on the discriminatory treatment meted out to British Coloured citizens in the Transvaal, with a straight-faced Chamberlain even announcing that one of the causes for which Britain was going to war would be to ensure that victory over the Boers brought 'kindly and improving treatment' of 'countless indigenous races of whose destiny' a self-reproachful imperial power had been all 'too forgetful'.[7] Steeling themselves for war, the small Coloured community on the Rand looked to British success. So did many African mineworkers, fondly believing that an imperial order would in some way relieve them of an oppressively regimented labour regime.

Many more did not await the outcome of a Transvaal war. Between May and October 1899 economic slump on the Rand, and growing fears of what looked to be an unavoidable conflict, triggered a 'mass exodus' of around 100,000 African, Coloured, and Indian people, who scrambled for the Cape and Natal to escape being stranded in the republic. In flight they joined a corresponding mass of white foreigners. Nearly 100,000 miners, artisans, and other able-bodied Uitlanders 'not interested in fighting for Kruger's franchise' or fearful of 'impressment by the Boers' headed for the refugee sanctuary of coastal colonies.[8]

If republican war aims were plain, those of the British were a little less so: they hoped for a transfer of power in the Transvaal to install a pro-imperial government which would keep it unambiguously within the British orbit, and the upholding of regional paramountcy, bringing the republic into line with unification or federation objectives and ensuring that a dense web of imperial economic interests would be secured against slipping into an increasingly hegemonic, nationalist Transvaal economic bloc. As Chamberlain put it in September 1899, what had to be terminated was 'the existence of a pure Dutch Republic flouting, and flouting successfully, British control and interference'.[9]

Initially, this did not necessarily mean the practical imposition of sovereignty over the Boers; this was not conceived of as a classic war of colonial conquest to annex the Transvaal and make it a directly ruled colony. Most historians now accept that that decision was only taken after the war had started. First prize for the Colonial Office was a client regime in Pretoria which would create a pro-British state based on more modern and efficient institutional structures. The Transvaal could then be safely left to make itself. On the face of it, it is at this level that the wants of vested capitalist interests, like mining and its industrially based social groups, coincided fairly neatly with those of Whitehall.

Naturally, both sides had an eye on the international repercussions of war. Given the strains of nationalist rivalry among the Great Powers, and Britain's growing diplomatic isolation by the end of the 1890s, the Foreign Office sought to keep the Transvaal crisis confined to an Anglo-Boer domain to determine that it would not become a factor in established imperialist rivalries. In the weeks leading up to war there were certainly some recurring worries about potential German, French, or even Russian meddling, which could seriously heat up the conflict. A particular concern, already well-represented in public debate because of anxiety over economic competition, was Germany. The Transvaal was depicted as an incubus of this alien growth, with the *Pall Mall Gazette* even classifying its Boers as 'honorary Germans'.[10]

Such spleen was predictable given the mood of the later 1890s, a climate animated by periodic international crises, naval challenges, patriotic vigilance, and a shrill distrust of foreigners and their intentions. The same anxieties gripped some British colonial politicians in Natal and the Cape. Prominent amongst them was

Merriman, convinced that military entanglement would render Britain so dangerously exposed that unfriendly states could hardly be expected to remain aloof or neutral. When he termed the commencement of war a South African Lexington he had in mind France and the discomfiting eighteenth-century colonial precedent of the Franco-American alliance against George III's British empire.[11] Yet apprehension over European rivals or opponents being drawn into hostilities was misguided. Governments and the public in Germany and France may have greatly relished Britain's Transvaal difficulties, but in the imperial partition of Africa, South Africa was acknowledged to be British turf. The Transvaal would receive no pledges of official military assistance. At the same time, Britain had no need to secure allies: it had, if need be, the resources of an empire.

Just as it was in Britain's interest to keep the struggle at the level of a backyard colonial war, so it was highly desirable for the Boers to encourage European interference. W. J. Leyds, the Transvaal Foreign Secretary and Kruger's envoy in Brussels, did what he could to try to bring this about, by cultivating the more ferociously anti-British press in France, Germany, and the Low Countries, and by opening urgent lines of diplomatic communication with Britain's principal continental rivals.[12] On their part, involvement was never seriously contemplated, although in the opening phase of the war Germany, France, and Russia would briefly mull over the idea of diplomatic intervention to try to put pressure on London to come to terms with the republicans. But, as a military proposition, any move by other powers to help the Boers in countering the British was never practically feasible. Intervention would be nothing more than a lingering dream, as remote as the notion that the war in South Africa might become a world war.[13]

Nevertheless, the mirage of Cossacks to Klerksdorp or Prussians to Potchefstroom loomed over what constituted the Boer war plan. This, by all accounts solely devised and presented by Smuts, was some years in the making, and was both bold in conception and fairly detailed in its grasp of the essential requirements for a successful offensive. Evidently the only plan for war the Boers had, it was certainly the closest the republics came to formulating a strategic vision. Although ambitious and imaginative, like some other rather better known offensive plans, it was longer on the importance of timing than on sound and intelligent generalship.

Constructed as a carefully planned and intricate memorandum, tabled on 4 September for submission to the Transvaal Volksraad, Smuts's perceptions came to form the basis of a common strategic plan for both republics, for much of its effectiveness lay in close coordination between a Transvaal and Orange Free State war effort. For the young State Attorney, vigorous political and economic mobilization was as crucial as decisive military action. The first thing was sedition, or at least an attempt at encouraging it. In an assessment of enemy weak points, one assumption was that Britain had now grown vulnerable under the sheer weight of its empire. With an 'imperial structure' increasingly 'strategically over-extended', Whitehall was at the mercy of a worldwide Malthusian army of impoverished and discontented subjects, countless rebels, and innumerable plotters.[14] By encouraging Fenianist inclinations within the empire, Boer republicans could hamper any enemy war effort by helping to ignite difficulties on other fronts, and not only on the Irish Sea.

Pretoria officials foresaw the possibility of Britain's Transvaal troubles being eclipsed by ever greater difficulties elsewhere. Pressure on Britain in South Africa could open India to pressure from Russia; more widely, it could pose a temptation for the Franco-Russian Alliance to become aggressive, a recurring concern for both the War Office and the Admiralty.[15] Such Boer calculations were by no means implausible. Smuts was right about the low level of British self-confidence in Central Asia, and about rising anxieties over imperial defence capacity and costly military burdens. But he also failed to appreciate two critical considerations. One was the nature of British national interest in South Africa; its Transvaal problem, unlike India, was bound to be temporary and one which was likely to be put right. The other was the British foreign-policy imperative of working negotiations with rival powers over the protection of interests. Last, the idea of a contagious Boer republicanism corroding the worldwide imperial fabric implied a formidable propaganda campaign far beyond the slender means of the republican camp.

Local horizons were more realistic. Acutely aware that the republics could not necessarily command the total loyalty of their populations in an anti-imperial struggle, Smuts put a high priority on domestic propaganda efforts. These were directed not only towards Boer citizens of British colonies but also at neutral or irresolute republican inhabitants, such as those in the Orange Free State who had not necessarily come to view Britain as a natural foe. Trade and commercial affinities between Free Staters and the British Cape were deep, and neutrality seemed reasonable enough. Against this, northern republican appeals promoted a heightened sense of 'Afrikaner' nationhood and national patriotic duty in the event of war. Depicting a Manichean conflict between the rapacity of mercenary Rand financiers and mine magnates, and the 'Freedom', 'Independence', and 'Righteousness' of a small and plucky 'Africander people', leading republicans sought to fashion an expectant war culture rooted in moral mobilization.[16]

Smuts's own influential contribution, produced with the assistance of a no-nonsense lawyer, Jacobus de Villiers Roos, was an impassioned 1899 republican tract, *A Century of Wrong,* which denounced the enemy as 'the lion, the jackal, and the vulture', driven by 'the lust of robbery and the spirit of plunder' to fall upon a 'wounded antelope'. Concluding that what approached was 'no War' but rather an 'attempt at Infanticide', Smuts fashioned a compelling polemical vocabulary which resonated with familiar Boer religious, national, and carnivorous imagery.[17] It was also carried to Britain and published in English by the Radical W. T. Stead's *Review of Reviews.*

What connected *A Century of Wrong* to the September war memorandum was a sense of righteous Boer power, and a feeling that its time had come, provided the republicans could take the upper hand. Smuts, therefore, also envisaged an effective wartime economic policy. For a start, there was ample agricultural capacity which could be readily diverted to creating a food supply for fighting forces without squeezing domestic consumption in the countryside. In the absence of farmers mobilized for commando service, continued agricultural production could be sustained by controlled African tenant labour or commandeered work parties. In a farming community, one of the benefits of the mobile commando system was its flexibility, through which all men in the field need not be removed completely from critical stages of the agricultural cycle. Food crops would become a servant of strategy.

To enhance the production of war material, the plan called for accelerated development of new light industries, aided in urban areas by the requisitioning or commandeering of raw materials and the brisk procurement of plant by a powerful Commissariat Commission. This would ease the supply of clothing and basic nutritional requirements (such as bread, jam, and biscuits) to Boer forces. To build up stores, commissariat organization was also able to siphon off supplies held by wealthy capitalists or lean on fat individuals for patriotic donations. Some leading Transvaal industrialists, like Sammy Marks, knew a smart move and responded positively to Kruger's call. At the same time, great importance was accorded to the need quickly to set about controlling and boosting armaments production by coordinating the conversion of Rand mine foundries and machinery firms into munitions factories to hammer shrapnel and turn out shells. Provision had also to be made for import-substitutionist technical services for such things as artillery maintenance. With war under way, the British Fleet would be able to mount an arms blockade close in to Delagoa Bay, the Boers' only free provisioning point.

An irony for the Boers was the fact that the commodity which had helped to bring war upon them was also the vital means of bankrolling their own war effort. Smuts's planning assumed continuing gold production, a 20 per cent war levy on output, and the provision in return of a 'protective' regulatory environment to maintain the supply of materials and labour, and to encourage skilled mine staff, even if British, to remain on the Rand. It also envisaged increased output, if need be through the republican administration exerting direct control over the most profitable mines, or through actually taking over some operations and working them as government mines.[18]

While the Transvaal state had the ability under its 1898 Gold Law to mine gold, or confiscatory powers under martial law to scoop up raw gold supplies and coin, it would be able to pay for the war without any panic over its fiscal capacity to sustain large increases in expenditure. The solution to another Treasury concern was simple. To stop money leaving the republic as the wages of departing Cape and other African mine-workers, systematic frontier action was taken to seize all earnings. Sullen and despairing black labourers were among the first to sacrifice for the Boer war effort. Given a policy of radical government economic intervention and controls over reasonably good resources, no major war borrowing was envisaged, and nor was there any need to worry about the political consequences of heavy taxation, even if the republics had possessed the rural administrative capability to levy new cash taxes on their farm populations to fund defence.

Best characterized as an executive discussion document, Smuts's September strategy is a singular but significant indication of the ways in which the governing republican élite, or at least those elements which believed that everything had to be subordinated to the needs of war, fixed on the broad methods necessary to organize a major war effort. This was to be based on intensely ideological popular mobilization, and the first resolute steps towards the development of a command war economy. Yet to what extent the Smuts Plan came to structure the Boer war effort is not so clear. While the Kruger government and Transvaal Volksraad appear to have backed it strongly, the level of support within military command remains an unresolved question, with some Afrikaner historians even suggesting that, far from there being any binding strategic consensus, the Smuts vision had little serious impact on actual Boer strategy.[19] Indeed, at this strategic level what evolved was not necessarily a coordinated operational agenda so much as contending perspectives or understandings of the republican campaign. These were embodied in leading personalities, not all of whom were famous for tactical flexibility or for consulting with others about what to do.

There was, of course, general acceptance that the Boers had to wage an offensive war. Here again, it was Smuts who articulated a clear strategy of deep penetration. Given the military situation, everything lay in timing. Schooled in a crucial breeding-ground for master strategists, the largely student Stellenbosch militia, Smuts urged Boer generalship to prepare for a rapid offensive at the outset of hostilities. By concentrating their armed weight for a pre-emptive knockout blow before the arrival of reinforcements for the British troops, the republicans could immediately gain the advantage. Eastwards, a shaky Natal could be taken at minimal cost, while a sharp westerly thrust would cut the vital single-track rail artery connecting the Cape Colony with Rhodesia and the intermediate supply links between Cape Town, Kimberley, and Mafeking.

The scales were were finely poised. An attack could not be launched until seasonal rains had provided adequate grass to relieve mounted commandos of the lumbering encumbrance of strings of forage carts, and the need to establish and maintain a run of fodder depots. Delay, however, inevitably provided Britain with further time to ship in reinforcing contingents. Running against the clock, and gambling on good grass, the Boers had to launch a war before an expeditionary force seriously threatened.[20]

In the first instance, then, the key was to be a rapid, heavy advance on British colonies while conditions remained easy. Once they had broken through light British forces already mustered on their borders, the republicans anticipated that not much else would stand in their way. Having punched through Natal and the Cape, taking all of the former and much of the latter with the aid of Cape Boer allies, movement would be replaced by position. With northward supply lines secure, the Boer armies would plumb sturdy, first-line defensive positions deep inside occupied colonies. Holding down enemy territory would enable them to frustrate any forward movement of the main British reinforcements, due before the end of November. In this scenario, victory was considered perfectly attainable, provided war could be carried to the neighbouring colonies and kept there, even if it turned into Smuts' nightmare of a lengthy and draining struggle.

It was essential to block any move on the republics. With over 2000 miles of frontier, their borders were exposed on too many flanks, and they were far too short of soldiers for adequate defensive fortification. Their only bastions were designed to overawe the enemy within; four costly rearguard fortresses for Johannesburg and Pretoria served little purpose other than to give any uppity Uitlanders a fright.[21] A deep Natal–Cape attack would be beguilingly simple, and looked a fair gamble: if it did not bring a quick victory to weaken the British position, it could still produce a stalemate or deadlock to compel London to make a compromise peace. However, resolving things through a prompt offensive was due to more than the prevailing military doctrine that in war attack was essential, even for defence: it had also come to form a crucial ingredient of Boer military culture. African fighting, whether with Zulu, Pedi, Sotho, or Swazi had invariably been a test of movement and charging down. Recently, headlong and headstrong burghers had also overwhelmed their British enemy in short order at Laing's Nek and Majuba. The natural fighting heritage embodied in nationalist discourse was not so much staying-power as supreme will for the unstoppable offensive of 'wild' Boers.[22]

Beyond this there were more inflated hopes of what could be achieved thereby. Again, in Smuts' conception, a spearhead which tore right through to the coast could prompt otherwise hesitant European powers to intervene, particularly if the Boers had provided the necessary tokens of diplomatic goodwill (or mining rights) to continental capitals beforehand. Astonishing as it may seem, this assumption lay behind the idea and planning of a singular 'march' or 'ride' to encircle and capture Durban. Among some mobilized burghers there was excitement about a conquest of the British colonies, including a ripple of millennial relish that the republics would gain the bounty of the sea. In this view Natal was a great prize, a lost natural cornerstone of republican power which years ago had been rolled away by avaricious British 'usurpers'. Invasion was to be nothing less than a just restitution of the lost 'heritage' of a mythical Boer land, originally validated by civilizing trekker possession.[23]

Even an otherwise level-headed Deneys Reitz, the capable son of the Transvaal State Secretary, recorded that as Boer 'salvation' lay in 'rapid advance', there was 'not a man' amongst invading commandos 'who did not believe that we were heading straight for the coast'.[24] A case of chewing off more than one could swallow, like one of those memorable strategic dreams, this was lunch in Ladysmith, dinner in Durban. Once accomplished, Britain would face humiliation: its soldiers would be steaming for a hostile port, and could well find themselves on ships which commanded the sea, yet were unable to make land. If armed hostilities remained a swift affair, resolved 'perhaps within one year', Smuts envisaged the subsequent creation of his 'United South Africa', a non-imperial state in the form of an Afrikaner Republic, 'stretching from Table Bay to the Zambesi'.[25] Equally, the price of failure was seen as chilling: a war which might bleed the Boers into submission through attrition. This sober reflection would come to prove bleakly prophetic.

But, at the outset, the Boers had the initiative; all that mattered was ensuring that they retained it. For a start the republics seemed to have the means to launch a climactic assault on British positions. Their armoury was extremely well stocked, Kruger having lost no time in getting things going after partial mobilization in response to the 1896 Raid that had revealed inadequate equipment, obsolete firearms, and ammunition shortages. The amateurish legal tradition of the Boer citizen army, which prescribed that each burgher provide his own personal gun and ammunition, was superseded by government issue at a cost which exceeded £1m. Between 1896 and 1899 Transvaal annual budgets allocated over one-third to defence expenditure. Commandant-General Piet Joubert, the dapper Transvaal Commander-in-Chief and a fairly consummate operator, was able to order virtually everything he thought was necessary. Adding to around 42,000 older model British and Austrian rifles, he procured over 37,000 of the latest .276 Mausers, 'the finest infantry arm in existence',[26] the same effective Krupp weapon which had mown down many of Theodore Roosevelt's Rough Riders in the 1898 Spanish–American War. To this store Orange Free State command added around 13,000 further Mausers, making it virtually sufficient to meet Kruger's grand desire for each burgher to have a reserve rifle.

In all the Boer armies had over 102,500 good-quality rifles, a supply augmented by a large rural stockpile of personally owned arms, some in the hands of farming women.[27] Effectively overprovisioned with guns and ammunition reserves, it was envisaged that surplus material could be utilized by Boer republican rebels in the Cape Colony. As it was, commando reserve weapons transportation on that scale would require the use of sizeable numbers of mounted commando servants or agterryers as gun-bearers and in gun maintenance. An awareness of having the men and even more guns undoubtedly had an impact upon republican morale; while obviously not every mounted infantry-man was cocky, it is easy to see why many burghers felt so strong and confident about their chances.

The Boer commando's elevated relationship with the rifle, its mythic measure set by the early nineteenth-century tradition and history of the Voortrekker and his lethal *voorlaier*, was modernized.

Through natural aptitude the marksman could carry the older romantic inheritance of prowess with the trusty family musket into the handling of new, regulation-issue firepower. Not for nothing did Boer General Staff lay such store by possession of the Mauser. So did their men, with many burghers personalizing weapons by engraving their names on the butt.

Moreover, the Boers had more than just the pick of modern rifles. Their artillery corps or *Staadtsartillerie* (the republics' sole, and miniscule, standing army) had guns which were newer and considerably more modern than those of the British Army. As limited training and financial capacity would obviously never have sustained a gun-for-gun arms race with Britain after 1896, the Transvaal concentrated on acquiring the most modern available weaponry and high-quality expertise in tactics and other gunnery procedure. To this end, whopping commissions fattened Kruger's various contract agents in continental Europe, who increased in number, and in price, after the Jameson Raid. Their orders amounted to an emergency rearmament programme. One of the more ingenious post-1896 Transvaal rumours was that of a conspiracy by a couple of powerful Randlords to spirit Kruger away and replace him with a more pliable Piet Joubert. This was supposedly tumbled by European arms dealers, who alerted the President's Secret Service or *Geheime Dienst*; they had no wish to see a profitable Anglo-Boer war averted.

In addition to French Creusot heavy guns and field guns, and Krupp howitzers and field guns, Joubert plumped for a batch of advanced Maxim-Nordenfeld quick-firing field guns, British but not yet in British Army service. The Orange Free State, whose heavy arsenal was leaner than that of her wealthier republican ally, still had an established *Artillerie Korps* equipped with new Krupp field guns, as well as older Armstrong and Whitworth ordnance. Serviced by a series of new state foundries and ordnance workshops, in all the republics could deploy over a hundred highly mobile guns, some two dozen of these being quick-firers, with rates of fire far faster than anything currently in the hands of the Royal Artillery. With these went a shell stock of about 108,000 rounds laid in from Continental manufacturers. Along with ample powder and metal for some local shell assembly, this was generally considered sufficient for a short offensive war.

Marking a grand exhibition stage in Boer military history, a few of these pieces were kept warm in the later 1890s through African sideshows, bombarding recalcitrant nearby chiefdoms into submission with minimal wastage of shell. These, it has to be said, were mainly a way for old Majuba fire-eaters, like Commandant-General Joubert himself, to put on imposing new airs. In a longer war, of course, shell supply was bound to become a complication, as it was simpler for the Boers to buy stock than to invest in large-scale armaments production. This would indeed prove to be the case in the coming war. Quite apart from the effect of its naval blockade, Britain paid off several French and Belgian firms to ensure that they would not supply war material to the republics for the duration of any conflict; not much could be got after March 1899, with a £25,000 order for Creusot quick-firing guns and another for field-gun rounds failing to arrive. Inevitably, artillery replacement was also destined to be a problem; anything captured could not be replaced by foreign suppliers. In the long run the Boers would be hampered by a limited import-substitution capacity in this area.

Scholars have concluded that the Boers paid little attention to gunnery in tactical planning.[28] But this was plainly not the case after the Jameson jolt. Younger officers from leading Boer families were despatched to Germany and the Low Countries for artillery training, and the Staadtsartillerie barracks in Pretoria contracted former German gunners and engineers to provide technical training for recruits; their German drill books were rapidly translated into Dutch.The 500-man Orange Free State Artillerie Korps also engaged several German officers. Some, like Major Erich Albrechts, were veterans of the 1870–1 Franco-Prussian War, in which artillery had been of crucial importance to the Prussian side. Expansion of the Transvaal artillery corps from 100 to 400 gunners, with a well-trained and disciplined reserve of 550 men, also occurred under close German supervision. Field artillery preparation concentrated on rapid mobility in the field, the use of long-range, heavy guns using shell with time-delay fuses, accurate range-finding across large, open terrain, and the stealthy deployment of equipment. It was fitting that Boer heavy gunnery tactics, like so much of their weaponry, should be adapted in one form or another from an obliging German army.[29] In their imported Prussian hats trained personnel regarded themselves as distinctive heirs of the Prussian fighting tradition, even though they might be a bit short of siege experience against European capital cities.

Drawn from landed or other wealthier backgrounds, and far more educated and self-disciplined than the average republican burgher, Europeanized artillerymen formed a small standing-army élite, an enlisted cadre of Boer army careerists set apart from those whose routine commando obligations did not run to knowledge of trigonometry and ballistics. As with those Boer professionals and students in Holland, Germany, and England who returned home at the outbreak of hostilities to take up arms, here was a cluster of men acutely aware of the national cause, and with a consuming soldiering will; as one of them declared, if it took war to secure 'the future destiny of our nation on earth', so much the better. Obviously, a big war could also provide opportunities for national fame and personal promotion, through battle experience more challenging than the occasional bombardment of peasant enemies.[30] These men carried little trace of the entrenched civilian mentality which common burghers carried into commando service as part of the tissue of their fighting sentiment.

Confidence and optimism in the potential of artillery tactical mobility was shared by republican commanders. General Ben Viljoen, for instance, immersed himself in the study of technical conditions, penning a series of articles on the lessons of Franco-Prussian War strategy and tactics in the prominent Transvaal papers, *Land en Volk* and *Ons Volk*.[31] Indeed, Boer generals were fond of the didactic study of foreign wars, with professional knowledge of the conduct of not only the 1870–1 conflict but also the Napoleonic Wars, the American Civil War and, by no means least, the American War of Independence, because of its inspirational legacy as a war of national independence. It is thus wrong to assume that all the Boer military leadership knew of were African colonial clashes; it is equally misleading to suggest that only a single Boer soldier (General Piet Cronjé) 'ever made a serious study of modern war';[32] and it is at best whimsical for one modern writer to conclude, of this prominent 1880–1 veteran, that 'his military studies were almost certainly restricted to the campaigns of Joshua and the prophetess Deborah'.[33] The spiritual inspiration of the Old Testament may well have been deeply instilled in Boer generals, but they were not without some knowledge of Napoleon and Clausewitz. While professional military leaders were few, the Boers were able amateurs and were not unmodern in their knowledge of how to go about waging war.

One element of this was the skilled use of heliograph apparatus in commando training; mirror messages could be flashed over distances of up to 100 miles by operators specially trained by the artillery corps. Another was intelligence. Between 1896 and 1898 the Transvaal Intelligence Department spent over £286,000 on information-gathering, expanding its roll of agents and rewarding snoops lavishly. Monthly monies for men in Natal and the Cape Colony reached £1,500. On the Rand, £850 went to trusted or *vertrouwbaarde* foreigners keeping a watch on any British Uitlander intrigue, and over £900 was remitted abroad to agents in Britain. Some of these, it was reported, had been briefed to keep tabs on and to evaluate the loyalty of Irish troops or other 'alien elements' in the British army.[34] As far as can be determined, republican intelligence efforts were not so much directed at clarifying enemy intentions and strategy; Boer leadership considered these to be fairly self-evident. The greater concentration was on an intelligence picture of the state of imperial preparations and British morale, on what Britain might deploy to South Africa when mobilized, the speed with which it could be shipped there, and the strength of local British garrison forces. On the last score information was accurate enough; the British had barely 20,000 troops in South Africa, while the Boer states could quickly field at least 50,000 men. The republicans knew well that their military advantage was sufficient for the immediate move, with Smuts, for example, calculating that the enemy would require an army corps of at least 150,000 troops to match the republican forces.

British intelligence in the later 1890s stressed that mounting Boer military spending had not worked to much advantage in administrative coordination and in establishing more cohesive supply systems. Staff work remained particularly weak, and fragmentation of command over support activities made for an organizational machinery which was at best inefficient, and at worst simply incapable of focused operational planning. Entrenched discretionary powers at lower levels in the chain of command also bred corruption in the handling of stocks, with requisitions favouring those merchants most willing to nod through backhanded commissions to commissariat stores officers. It seems that only bibles for commandos were entirely exempt from requisitioning deals, probably due to God's design. Given the feeding frenzy of widespread graft under the Kruger administration, it is not surprising to find that the War Commissariat or *Krijgscommissaris* was similarly contaminated by shady practices. With inefficiency and corruption diluting the preparedness of their bureaucratic machinery, there is undoubtedly a good deal to the view that the Boer armies were 'administratively weak and not really capable of a major offensive'.[35]

Boer operational organization was certainly short on good inventory control and centralized systems of materials procurement and handling. Still, leadership generally did not conceive of the war lasting any extended length of time, and the campaign envisaged was considered sustainable by the republics' logistical capacity. Second, for the majority of Boers this was neither a war cooked up by government, nor a burdensome minor expedition imposed by their ruling élite; it was 'a war for their national independence, which concerned every single burgher'.[36] Individual motivation, ingenuity at cutting corners, and their famed independence would compensate for any systems deficiency – or that, at least, was the anticipation. Third, the conflict may well have been 'the last *laissez-faire* war'[37] for Britain, but this was less so for the Boers. The Transvaal government took over the Netherlands South African Railway Company and assumed direct control of major wagon convoys and their routes; by September 1899 it was requisitioning draught animals, carts, horses, grain, fodder, tinned food, and clothing from merchants, shopkeepers, and ordinary burghers. As *The Times History of the War in South Africa* recognized, the Boers relied very heavily 'on the power of commandeering'.[38] Fourth, and no less significant, was the degree to which the provisioning work of Transvaal and Orange Free State Commissariat commissions, councils, and committees was augmented and eased by the private supply of essential commodities. Its basis lay in a coil of social relations thickly oiled by custom, prerogative, usage, and prerequisite. Wealthier burghers entered the field not merely with their obligatory mount and initial ration reserve, but with an accumulation of carts, wagons, horses, reserve stores, and dependent or coerced African servants to attend to running and maintenance. Supplemented by commandeered horses and transport, this helped to ensure that poorer burghers who had no war goods of their own would be provisioned. At the base of the Boer war-supply system was an acceptance that defensive need might require some social distribution of surplus property. There were also strong voluntarist impulses. Newspapers and well-heeled residents funded commando supplies of tobacco and spirits. From abroad, France provided army hospital stores, while Scandinavian and Dutch sympathizers opened subscription lists to fund equipment and even weaponry.

The final logistical cog was the household, especially in helping to service nutritional and clothing requirements. While formal fighting mobilization was obviously a male affair, directed through a stoutly patriarchal Boer political system, output and distribution needs incorporated substantial numbers of women. As producers of food, as seamstresses or boot repairers, or as overseers of African servants and herdsmen, mobilized wives or sometimes mothers ran supplies of meat, biscuits, clothing, and footwear to individual burghers in commandos. The image of the hardy woman or *vrouw*, or of dutiful servants despatched by her, trekking from the farm to a commando camp with a desirable cartload of protein, fat, wool, and leather, is perhaps one of the more telling symbolic constructions of the scale and commitment of the Boer national war effort. In reality it reflected the closeness and intimacy of ties between commandos massing for the front and their fortifying domestic domain, and the significance of powerful familial exchange between Boer soldiers and their female home front of hard-working households. Here the worth of women was substantial, as was their customary responsibility, and with it came an area of corresponding authority in crisis.

If women were accustomed to getting commandos off the mark, what kind of republican citizenship soldiering did this represent? Here, a summary comment on the nature of the Boer commando army and its place in society is appropriate. A distinctive creation of eighteenth century Dutch-colonial frontier society, the armed civilian militia or *kommando* initially had no roll, but relied on the turnout of a rough assortment of Dutch East India Company soldiers, white farmers, and Khoikhoi and Coloured men who were either collaborators or forced conscripts. Service at this early stage lacked both structure and any developed notion of racial preference: there were too few Boers and many ducked call-ups, and shirking Cape farmers would frequently elbow Coloured labourers into military duties as substitutes. In the later eighteenth century settlers often comprised only a minority of men fulfilling combat obligations in commandos assembled by white frontier communities.[39]

As the classic military formation of the Boer republics, the commando system experienced continual institutional development through the latter half of the nineteenth century. In a significant recomposition it became more white under Transvaal and Orange Free State gun laws which forbade Africans from possessing firearms. It also became more centrally planned. From improvised arrangements in which dispersed male civilians were subject to service on a territorial basis, there was a transition to commando law in the Orange Free State by the 1850s, in which all white males between 16 and 60 were obliged to register for armed duty. By 1890 Free State men had to participate in annual military camps or *wapenschouwingen*. It became a statutory requirement for men in both republics to own and maintain weaponry and basic military equipment, to have equipment inspected regularly, and to participate routinely in designated field exercises and camps.

What this amounted to in the Transvaal by the later 1870s was an obligation that able-bodied men complete at least three months' full-time military service. Mobilized through a spread of some 40

Transvaal–Orange Free State electoral or magisterial districts, the timing of deployment was quick. In the event of threatening hostilities, individual commandos, each providing his own rifle with 30 rounds and horse (mostly rugged, unbending, and fleet Basuto ponies), could be ready in a week, mustered in four rising age-bands starting from 18 to 34, and ending with an under-16 reserve. For the Boer states, the advantages of commando-based defence were clear: it was an economical option for governments which lacked the fiscal base and tax-extraction capacity to maintain anything other than a negligible standing force and small police corps. A lack of any system of divisions and corps, and the practice of only appointing establishment staff for actual war, also meant large savings in services, professional officers, and administrative staff. In sum, the commando net institutionalized a cheap form of reservist conscription which trawled virtually the whole of the able-bodied male population. Peacetime in the republics meant regularly replenishing the appetite and fitness for war. In war, not only republican citizens but all official 'inhabitants' (such as Orange Free State British male residents) were liable to be commandeered for commando duty.

How many of a combined burgher force could be counted as really effective or competent soldiers seems not to have greatly worried Boer onlookers and commentators in the 1890s, nor sympathetic Dutch, German, French, and other foreign observers. If rather short on drill, dress, and systematic discipline, the 'spirit', 'dash', 'reliability', and inherited 'frontier talents' of commandos were considered more than compensating virtues.[40] No longer were Boer riflemen simply seen as capable of despatching any 'uncivilized' enemy still spoiling for a fight, like aggrieved Pedi or Swazi. Having already bloodied Britain's nose, they were judged sufficiently tough, resourceful, and tactically adept for a major offensive war. There was no shortage of romance about Africa's Boers being born to soldiering by instinct and by the blood tax of service, rather than, as with slack metropolitan Europeans, having to be made into soldiers by parade-ground generals.

These forces had a fairly well-articulated chain of command, with 'democratic' or elective structures which were completely alien to the currency of authority in regular armies. Based on commando territorialization, every district had a peppering of military commanders or *veldkornets*, who served under another elected principal military officer or *kommandant*. Higher command of militiamen and all professional forces was assigned to a Commandant-General or *Kommandant-Generaal*, also elected and invariably a Boer notable, well encumbered by worldly goods of the landed variety. A final feature was the direct insertion of the elected state president into military matters. In both republics, war declarations and martial law authorizations were not simply imposed by the State President and his consultative executive council. Each Transvaal and Orange Free State commando had a powerful elected Council of War or *Krijgsraad*, its legitimacy resting in the elected status of veldkornets, or district field officers, and commandants in statutory association with the President. This war collective voted on operational movements and battle planning after consultation, in a kind of shotgun caucus. At the end of the chain, going into battle was an elective business. Rhetorically, this participatory military democracy was underpinned by a good deal of flannel about equalizing citizenship. But muddiness was its virtue. Contentedly democratic propertied men used their office, clientage networks, political toadying, and dodgy cattle or land transactions to secure the rewards of nominations or the attachment of high political patronage. The result, in the Transvaal, was a system of popular military participation checked by the élite purchase of numbers of favoured 'Krugerite' officers, as with General F. A. Grobler, whose 'chief qualification seemed to be the power to utter silly jokes and to laugh at them himself... probably he was chosen for the purpose of keeping the burghers in a good humour. But, then, he was a staunch supporter of Kruger.'[41] In command, the persistent deference and oligarchic balance of forces within Boer political culture assuredly left their mark.

Even so, the egalitarian plumage of the commando remained an article of faith, and one which increased in standing as war approached. *Land en Volk* and *De Republikein* reminded literate Boers of their proud eighteenth-century republican inheritance, straddling the Jacobin tradition of the 'nation in arms' and the heady, manhood suffrage democracy of the American Revolution, with its citizen army fighting successfully for popular rights and independence against a degenerate and old aristocratic foe. In assessments of their army's effectiveness, the more bookish of Boer generals, like Ben Viljoen, celebrated as unique the imagined lack of social divisions within commandos, in which officers and men were indistinguishable, and where an ordinary soldier of poor social origin could be promoted on ability through the ranks to the very top of the officer corps.[42] In this fanciful notion, such camaraderie produced a fighting unit far more cohesive and dedicated than a British army hampered by the isolating rigidity of class hierarchy between officers and men.

By the late nineteenth century, to be a male citizen of the Transvaal's republican people's democracy or *volksdemokrasie*, or to be of military age in the Orange Free State (16 years), was more or less by definition to be a commando. This was the key to citizenship and the franchise, to masculine status and identity, and to any sense of both military and civic duty to defend land, freedom, and the state. Bearing arms was also pivotal to the socialization of young Boer men, with competitive traditions of individual marksmanship and horsemanship providing a distinctive 'rite of passage'.[43]

As a site of individual ability bound to a virtuous communal endeavour, the commando was a regimental expression of Boer ethnicity, the redcoats, in spirit, of frontier republicanism. This ethos was reinforced by the status of blacks on commando as auxiliary retainers, and by the mating ritual of substitution, whereby conscripted wealthier burghers could meet military obligations by stumping up for a poorer stand-in. With the fee running at up to £90, rich sleeping-partners were providing capital for lean fellow-citizens.

Around this apparent unity under arms, however, Boer society continued to carry its old troubles of fierce factionalism, regional and district animosities, and class and religious rifts. And not all ordinary citizen-soldiers were happy to make good their legal obligations to attend annual field camps and perform unpaid commando duty. The main source of discontent over militia demands was a substratum of poor whites who lacked the means to equip themselves with weaponry and equipment, and whose families faced increased privation through the loss of productive male labour to periods of military requisitioning. In the Orange Free State in the 1890s, there were growing concerns over the reliability of the bywoner class, which were centred upon its preparedness 'to take up arms in defence of republican independence'.[44] Still, by 1899 only about 10 per cent of burghers were not effectively armed.

No less interesting, if perhaps more obvious, were some other commando characteristics. Membership was by no means confined to individuals with barns. Some were banded in distinctive town commandos or *dorpskommando*, drawn from lawyers, merchants, and other sectors of the urban bourgeoisie. If they were sometimes said not to put up too easily with slumming down alongside common farmers, they were not short of an ideological sense of national obligation and were organizationally adept. Republican armies had no formal training establishment; nor did they develop any regular disciplinary regime for soldiers, leaving it to individual commanders to devise their own instruments for control. Although wearing no regular (or recognized) uniform, their soldiers' garb and bearing announced their business. Generally neatly jacketed, frequently wearing a collar and tie or even a cravat or bow-tie, commando dress peaked with a customary felt hat, the Boer answer to the French army's sacrosanct *le pantalon rouge*. For added dash, these were often worn tipped up on the right, a fashion to be later mimicked by nationalist Irish Volunteers in the 1916 Easter Rising, who would dub their slouch hats 'De Wets' after the admired republican general. The primacy of experience and seniority, as well as patriarchal authority, was marked by heavy beards, displayed by most men over 30 and the object of considerable grooming and preening.

Wholly at ease as a mounted infantry, commandos had their rifles slung across their backs and leather bandoliers strapped over their chests. As befitting a force which believed it had God on its side, men all carried a bible: even in their doctrinal Calvinist diversity, they shared a common understanding about religious devotion. They also shared a liking for military ceremonial, fashioning glorifying battle insignia, flying flags, pennants, and banners, and commemorating significant past victories by putting up stone cairns or scoring rockfaces.

Boer militia also gained by continuing to use black auxiliaries as a labour and technical-skills subsidy to keep them in the field. While Africans were excluded from the republics' gun-bearing culture, their martial law provisions or *krijgswette* made allowance for Coloured men or *kleurlingen* to be called up. Of course, what it meant to be Coloured was by no means all that obvious; in places, the colour line in white supremacist Boer society was just a trifle porous, and not all enlisted commandos would have changed complexion when scrubbed. Far more than this, though, it was the incorporation of agterryer ancillaries which counted. As able mounted servants and gun-bearers, these men serviced a range of vital needs: gun-loading and maintenance, transport of reserve ammunition, tending of horses and repair of saddle equipment, carrying of bulk rations, treatment and bearing of the wounded, dispatch riding, and scouting.

To them also fell responsibility for the finer conveniences of life on the hoof, cooking, and the brewing of morning coffee. When pressed, Boer command could swallow hard and sometimes deploy auxiliaries in direct combat roles. The leading modern historian of the commando, Fransjohan Pretorius, has ventured an average operational ratio of one agterryer per every four to five burghers, in a normal commando complement of 1200 men. At the outbreak of war, this meant that well over 10,000 auxiliaries were pulled into campaigning.[45]

Estimates of the total strength of republican forces at this juncture still vary. By October there were some 55,000 to 60,000 men available for deployment, of whom between 35,000 and 42,000 were mobilized and in the field on the southern borders of the Boer states. Depending again on differing calculations of the degree of mobilization, the effective field force represented no more than roughly 56 to 65 per cent of Boer fighting capacity.[46] The balance did not comprise idle stay-at-homes. Men had to be assigned to other sectors, such as policing and the guarding of farms against African interlopers, and to stamp Boer garrison authority on the frontiers of potential African enemy territory such as Basutoland and Swaziland. There could be no question of flinging them all at the British.

The republics could also count on some loyalist pro-Boer combat reinforcements. Internally, upwards of 2000 pro-Boer Uitlanders either joined standing commandos or formed national fighting brigades and corps, which quickly also attracted a clutch of late-adolescent adventurers (such as bull-necked American Indian fighters) from countries partial to the Boer cause. This volunteer list was long, mustering Germans, Dutch (including the military attaché to the Transvaal), Scandinavians, French, Italians, Irish, Americans, Greeks, even a Jewish Ambulance Unit, and Russians, some of whom threw in their lot with the Boer cause in the belief that it would provide handy experience for that inevitable future war with Britain.[47]

Externally, the republics banked on the armed collaboration of improvised bands of colonial Boer rebels who were expected to oppose the British wherever they chose to strike; even though prominent Cape Afrikaner Bond politicians like J. H. Hofmeyr made it clear to Kruger that a mass Cape rebellion looked rather improbable, northern leadership remained convinced that at least 5000 to 6000 dispersed rebels would be ready for war. This calculation made some sense. Indeed, in the war itself, more like 10,000 men would turn out, and prospective rebel numbers might have been far greater had invading Boer forces charged harder through the Cape and Natal.[48] But even without these colonial collaborators, the republics assembled easily the largest modern army yet seen in South Africa. Its backbone was the cream of the mounted militia. Physically tough, crack shots with advanced, clip-loading, and smokeless Mausers, formidable in the saddle, and proud of their *veldcraft*: these were good soldiers, quick to the colours, and high on confidence. Springing from a settler society attuned to warfare, their commanders knew how to manoeuvre riflemen to maximize the impact of their fire, and how to minimize exposure to anything returned by opponents.

Even if the coming war turned out to be lengthy, leading figures like Smuts envisaged that when things turned towards irregular warfare the independent Boers would shine in a guerrilla struggle sustained here, there, and everywhere. What 'everywhere' meant was probably not quite decided. At this stage most ordinary burghers were not conditioned by any pan-republican nationalism. Unlike the Boer élite, they were bounded by their borders, which confirmed them as Free Staters and Transvaalers.

This did not frighten more bellicose pro-imperial voices, either in Britain or in its South African colonies. For the *Economist* and the *Spectator* Boer fighters were no more than 'stock-breeders of the lowest type', at best 'a rough mob of good marksmen' who would be unlikely seriously to test a British army ready simply to bundle them up at negligible cost to the Treasury. 'Preposterous', concluded the *Cape Argus*, for whom Boer claims 'evoked contemptuous amusement, mingled with satisfaction at the tension being at last ended ... the ultimatum was received in military circles with the greatest enthusiasm'.[49] Such equanimity was bolstered by common press perceptions that the War Office had things well in hand. Even if there were any delay in the arrival of an expeditionary army corps, it would not hamper the British mission. The Boer army had no men of talent, its organization was too much of a muddle for any sustained campaign, and many commandos were likely to return to their farms before any action, through going without food and stores. This was the view not merely of the *Liverpool Echo* or *Huddersfield Examiner*: it was also Chamberlain's assurance to the Queen on receiving the Transvaal ultimatum. Perhaps this was the only opinion his obstinate monarch wished to hear.

As already noted, there had been some initial uncertainty over how best to handle the issue of beefing up Britain's South African position. Although the realistic possibility of a military contest had been on the cards for several years, up to the very eve of declaration the roll of the diplomatic dice had still assumed that Kruger's nerve might finally fail. The Transvaal would yield on the franchise demands, given a clear British undertaking not to challenge 'the independence of the South African Republic'. For a Cabinet insistent on dragging out the matter, it was obvious that any premature strengthening of the imperial garrison would expose Britain's aggressive calculations, increase the Orange Free State's gravitation towards the Transvaal, and risk a row with the Cape and Natal, neither of whose governments was keen to see a diplomatic confrontation turn military through impetuous warmongering.

Granted, a negotiated settlement tolerable to both sides would have stilled the Salisbury government's worries over domestic opinion and partisan parliamentary division if it came to war. Even so, the logic of any tactic of keeping up intimidatory pressure upon the enemy while continuing to negotiate with it would have justified significant mobilization well before it looked as if talking would dry up. Crucially, this did not escape the notice of the army Commander-in-Chief, Lord Wolseley, who grasped the facts of the situation: Britain's negotiating posture had to be fortified. In memoranda through June and July 1899, an apprehensive Wolseley pressed Lansdowne for authorization to amass essential stores and food reserves in South Africa, and to swiftly strengthen the British garrison establishment through the despatch of 10,000 troops to Natal and the Cape. The estimated cost of these measures was £500,000.

In sharp warnings to the Cabinet, Wolseley held that not to stiffen the military position would be a dangerously false economy, for Britain's whole situation would be thereby imperilled; the only hope of getting the Transvaal to cave in, and thus to avert war, would be to despatch a strong show of force. His recommendations were turned down twice by Lansdowne on the grounds that circumstances did not yet justify heavy reinforcements, and that it was too tricky to do anything until all negotiating options had been exhausted. All that could be risked by August was the despatch to Natal of a small contingent of 2000 men. To Lansdowne and Salisbury this may have seemed diplomatically prudent; but in military terms it was folly.

Wolseley was incensed by what he saw as misjudgement by Lansdowne and other politicians, and an alarming inability to grasp the true situation of British military strength in South Africa. His retort to Lansdowne's rejection of his proposals was that unless enough was done to put British forces into a strong position, if war broke out the initiative would be surrendered to the Boers with serious repercussions for British national prestige. For an infuriated Commander-in-Chief the problem was not British inferiority; it was a lack of political will to utilize its superiority. Baldly summarized, such ill feeling between War Office soldiers and the politicians over activity – or lack of activity – clearly made proper war preparations difficult. It was not until September, conspicuously late in the day, that the British Cabinet turned seriously to the fundamental problem that its South African garrison was far too weak to do much. It was obvious that its established force would not only have to be brought up to strength, but also increased in size through the shipping in of a strong expeditionary force. Now a worried Salisbury wanted

Chamberlain to ease up on Kruger so that Britain could first get things into place.[50]

Worries over the delay in sailing time apart, in these early days the British army did not take long to get going. A mobilization scheme operated exceptionally smoothly, and the raising and despatch of the first regular army expeditionary corps of 30,000 men to Natal ran like clockwork, prompting a satisfied Under-Secretary for War to declare the army 'more efficient than at any time since Waterloo'.[51] Indeed, so effortless was mobilization that between early October and the end of January 1900 over 112,000 regular troops were equipped and transported to South Africa. Victorian merchant enterprise, embodied in Britain's mercantile marine, worked effectively to imperial strategic order.

If the early position in Natal and the Cape was looking a little precarious, the arrival of reinforcing troops from India would be sure to extricate Britain from any difficulties. That, at any rate, was how a good few saw it at the beginning. At the same time, not everyone in London was sure that this was a war which would be quickly decided. Just as Smuts had pondered the terrible possibility of a lengthy and wasting struggle, so Chamberlain weighed up the prospect of 'one of the most serious wars that could possibly be waged', to follow his earlier, sobering Commons remark on the chances of a long, bitter, and costly engagement.[52] On the Left, a few socialists predicted that financing a major war effort would spell trouble for the Treasury and lead to possible social unrest, as a lingering colonial conflict would take an inevitable inflationary toll of workers' living standards.[53]

But most calculations were extremely sanguine; for months, war with the Boers had hardly been thought to require much serious preparation. Initially the Salisbury government estimated that the task would require no more than 75,000 troops, would incur a negligible casualty rate, would last between three and four months, and would cost perhaps £10 or £11m. This Cabinet sum, in effect the equivalent of about ten Majestic-class warships, was not the kind of figure to give the Chancellor, Sir Michael Hicks Beach, too many sleepless nights. War would get under way with no long-term approach to cost and only the most minimal short-term provision, with the Treasury estimating £5m for the mobilizing and transporting of 50,000 troops. Victory would be secured for no more than £600,000 per month.[54]

Away from South Africa, Britain's generals also believed that they had the measure of the Boer republics. Possibly the most famous illustration of this was an exchange between Lansdowne and General Sir Redvers Buller prior to the latter's departure as Commander-in-Chief to assume command of British forces in Natal. By this account, all was now set for Buller to commence his planned advance around two days before Christmas, requiring no more than a month to knock out the Orange Free State and then plunge beyond into the Transvaal, and needing only a further fortnight to reach and take Pretoria.[55] It was all as if there would be virtually nothing in his way.

Back in South Africa, however, informed military staff tended to spot one or two impediments. For this we need to go back a few months, to a moment when Milner had thought that a tough show of force would perhaps cow the Transvaal. With tension mounting in May 1899, the High Commissioner and his Military Secretary, Hanbury Williams, had had a sharp exchange with Sir William Butler, Commander-in-Chief of the British garrison in South Africa since late 1898. As ever, Milner wanted a sabre-rattling initiative. In this case, he wanted to see whether Kruger could be intimidated by a feint, the advancing of Natal British troops to the northern frontier shoulder of Laing's Nek, just inside the colony, an unhappy spot where in previous Anglo-Boer fighting Colley's infantry had been all but routed in January 1881. It seems that Butler had scoffed at the idea, insisting that a minimum of 40,000 men would be required even to begin to face down the republicans.[56] He did not share Milner's breezy belief that the Transvaal's social crises of the 1890s had so checked its economy and weakened its defences as to make it ripe for rolling over.

Butler's inclinations were to go more carefully: hence his reluctance to antagonize the republicans by also reinforcing Kimberley, and a determination to concentrate on guarding the interior approaches in expectation of a moving Boer encirclement. Acutely aware of its vulnerability, Butler was panicky about the defence of Natal, for which he claimed to have secret strategic proposals which were kept firmly under wraps. An officer with South African experience dating back to the 1870s, he was also of pronounced conciliationist instincts. In his view, rogue mercenary elements for which he cared little (Rhodes, Uitlanders, the South African League) were criminally intent on causing a terrible and needless war which would place Britain under dangerous defensive pressure.

Recognizing that he was unlikely to get an energetic offensive commitment from Butler, Milner successfully intrigued against him, carping on his Irish Catholic origins to paint him as a suspiciously lukewarm imperialist and an Irish Home Rule milksop. Too much in the rear, too prone to worry, too prejudicial towards and contemptuous of the Randlords of 'Jewburg',[57] and rather too respectful of the rural virtues of the yeomen Boers, the general had to go. Milner engineered this early in August, a tricky month for dealings with Kruger, and a time when British South African forces still consisted of only two cavalry regiments, six full-strength regular infantry battalions, and three light field batteries, their howitzers easily outranged and outmanoeuvred by Boer Krupps. Troops brought in from India raised regular-force strength for the defence of Natal and the Cape, with a further small infusion of New Zealand and Australian contingents; but British forces were still outnumbered by virtually two to one. Still, for most observers, national superiority against a 'mob' or 'tribe' of marksmen was expected to take care of any deficit.[58] The efficiency of mobilization and smooth despatch of a regular army corps to Natal seemed almost to brush away serious questions of military preparedness for a war which would require different tactics, a different administrative establishment, and different methods of command from the routine small-war expeditions of most of the nineteenth century.

For generations, commencing with the 1904 Royal Commissions on the War in South Africa, writers have addressed the question of the inability of the British government and its War Office to perceive properly and prepare for a difficult war of which there had been at least three to four years' warning. It would be tedious to catalogue in detail once again the pre-war deficiencies in preparation and infrastructural machinery, and the strains to which the military establishment would now become subject. The problem was that no one listened to the few who rang alarm bells over inadequate preparation for the task ahead. For, in its distance from the home base and the extent of its operational area, South Africa, even for a campaign of short duration, was likely to be a tough business. While comprehension of what would be needed to maintain, service, and supply a large force in a distant field would improve significantly in time, its absence at the beginning was striking. For Lansdowne and Buller, too much was seen through a glass darkly, if it was seen at all. That applied quite widely, for 'staff, troops, and service corps were scarcely better prepared than their commander to face the task ahead'.[59]

Ammunition of all kinds was in short supply, as were modern quick-firing guns, with ordnance factories poorly placed to change stride quickly. Field Artillery could deploy more guns than the Boers, but it was disadvantaged by theory and rigid drills which were dear to it. Deployment in far-forward positions and in bunched batteries may have been fine against spear-carrying warriors and for Woolwich and Salisbury Plain drills; it was not the most ideal preparation for a campaign in which exposed gun teams and horse lines would be within reach of coordinated, long-range rifle fire from entrenched positions.

The standard British infantry weapon, the .303 Lee-Metford rifle, was accurate and reliable, save for an occasional tendency for its wood to shrink in very hot weather, loosening rivets and causing the butt to slide off.[60] If infantry tactics and fire training had been sharpened up in recent years, accuracy was not their most obvious strong point. While close formations and steady volleys had thus far served against a charging peasantry on foot, this was not necessarily the best kind of instruction for coping with a more modern colonial 'small war'. Moreover, most newer infantry recruits were urban men from large industrial cities, with little experience of movement across wide open spaces, and unused to operating in the dark or in extreme weather. For these, there was little realistic prior training for South African conditions.

There were other limitations in both strength and ability. The Ordnance Department was short of hands, stores, and servicing capacity, with no planned systems for field-depot ammunition supply to the front. Warehouses lacked replacement reserves of basic equipment such as saddlery, and hospital reserve stores were non-existent. The decisive element in all of this was the severe logistical demand to be made on Britain's supply services for a South African campaign, ranging from the provision of transport and the international procurement of things like mules, to the moving of arms, stores, animals and food, and other equipment. Supply-service need was likely to be immeasurably greater than in any conflict since the Napoleonic Wars.

To these problems could be added a further difficulty. If British statesmanship had been insufficient to prevent war, the craftiness of the Colonial Section of the Intelligence Division had been sufficient to aid contingency planning, but to little effect. When war was declared ministers complained that the government had had as much anticipation of war with the Orange Free State as with Switzerland, with Buller declaring his surprise that 'the enemy who declared war against us is much more powerful than we expected'.[61] Enemy strength and armaments greatly exceeded expectations, nothing on the theatre of operations had been furnished to assist tactical training, and the pitiful inadequacy of mapping had left imperial forces in a precarious position. In fact, under Sir John Ardagh, Director of Military Intelligence, gathering of information on the enemy had been systematic and remarkably accurate, despite the most pinched resources. As he was later to point out to the Elgin Royal Commission, when the Division discovered that the Boers had been spending £340,000 on intelligence in the two years leading up to war he requested £10,000 per year for counter-activity. After argument, he was grudgingly granted £100; typically, the devising of a comprehensive military map of the theatre of war came to nothing, as it would have needed a large grant and several years of 'secret service' work by fake civilian travellers to chart topography, and document the location of roads, rail connections, bridges, rivers, and other features essential to the requirements of military cartography. Such an enterprise was considered politically impossible in the sensitive circumstances of the late 1890s.

Where Ardagh was able to do something, intelligence was impressive. In 1897 and 1899 the Division issued a series of early reports on the likelihood of war, warned that it would be costly and difficult, and accurately determined enemy intentions, military expenditure, and arms levels. Memoranda in June and August 1899 stressed the probability of full Orange Free State–Transvaal military collaboration, and a handbook on South Africa provided a fairly precise tabulation of what the enemy had. This all revealed an alarming disparity in the capabilities of opposing forces in October 1899, an intelligence tool flawed only in the sense that the problems were possibly even worse than those portrayed.[62] Ardagh's warnings did not go entirely unheeded; military personnel (including Buller) foresaw danger in moving too rapidly towards a war ultimatum while they did not have a full army corps on hand. But his warnings were not effectively absorbed by a War Office which lacked a proper General Staff for advanced contingency planning and for seeing to appropriate levels of preparedness. Communication between those who were posting key intelligence information, regular staff administration, and decisive government figures, like Lansdowne, remained laconic, incomplete, or otherwise poor.

Taking into account reservists, the size of the British army in October 1899 was about 320,000 men, drawn from a society in which military values had been spreading, so that by the end of the 1890s over 22 per cent of the male population of Britain and Ireland aged between 17 and 40 had had some kind of army or semi-military experience. As yet, 'there was little expectation that such a potential reserve of military experience would need to be tapped in any way'.[63]

The Victorian army had undergone a long period of organizational reform under Edward Cardwell in the 1860s and 1870s, and economy-based policy adaptation in the late 1880s under the Secretary of State for War, Edward Stanhope. To assist government estimates, provision allowed for the army's despatch of no more than two corps for any overseas service, after calling up its Reserve. The Stanhope policy was now about to fail its South African test.

The garrison battalions stationed in South Africa were experienced and strong, as were units despatched from India, Mauritius, and the Mediterranean. But the army, in general, was rather less so. Previous campaigns had invariably been short and limited in scale, with little need for large-scale manoeuvres and a complex communications tracery. Most generals had little experience of handling very large bodies of troops, and instead of a standard system for the transmission of information between commanders and their subordinates there was an unpredictable space. Meanwhile, at the bottom, the general calibre of ordinary soldiers was not high. Suffering from wastage of trained soldiers through short-service enlistment, 'unable to compete with urban rates of pay, and handicapped by the contraction of its traditional sources of supply – the rural population and the Irish in particular – it depended heavily upon the urban unemployed'.[64] A few months of regular food and barrack-square exercise achieved something towards becoming fit, but South Africa was a fairly tall order in endurance: weeks on packed troop-ships, hours in poorly ventilated trains, days alongside insanitary rivers and streams, and fatiguing marching and fighting across difficult terrain.

From their inception, from one angle or another, general studies of this war have stressed that all was not well with the British war effort in coping with its coming challenges. Levels of 'preparedness' or 'readiness', particularly in minor tactics and logistical planning, were to prove woefully low. While that much is obvious, it would equally not be accurate to suggest that the British army had by now somehow grown short of war experience, or had no idea of what to expect in a colonial clash. By the end of the nineteenth century, a great variety of colonial campaigns had provided it with very considerable 'small war' experience.

On the face of things, this should have aided better preparation for a war in South Africa, and eased an effective transition to the running of a more weighty and complex campaign. But instead, as the Boers now moved to cut the first thread, the British would begin by making a mess of things. Why had past war experience not served well in preparation? In terms of the war reality to be now encountered, it is perhaps that these wars of empire were not much of a guide. Small wars were highly varied in nature, and did not easily provide a standard model for operational planning; too much was unpredictable for lessons or principles, whatever the efforts of C. E. Calwell's *Small Wars, Their Principles and Practice* (1896), to provide generalized strategic assumptions. Arguably, what counted no less were the basics of Victorian small wars. In these, Britain had superior rifles and guns, better-trained, better-disciplined and better-nourished troops; under the inspired generalship of a sole commander, victories against weaker colonial adversaries came about through early decisive victories, avoiding the need for any development of prolonged campaigning, and for the absorption of new tactics to meet the modern firepower of new weapons already seen in the Franco-Prussian War and American Civil War.

Small wars with small armies were not about expansion, duration, technical adaptation, or administrative capacity: they were about running success based on personalized qualities such as courage and moral character, negligible casualties, and minimal cost. When the odd thing did go wrong, this was easier to brush aside than to absorb fully into military thought. Thus, for Wolseley and those in his 'African' army faction, much of the blame for Majuba lay with the use of an Indian army contingent, by nature indisciplined, full of drink, and ridden with venereal disease.

As this implies, the British were not without some lessons in what fleet and proficient colonial opponents could do against regular troops – but they profited curiously little from earlier South African experience. And Britain would now learn, far more resoundingly, that the Boer republics were not 'backward' in the sense of Egypt or the Sudan. Sweeping advances with machine guns which had shredded the Sudanese along the Nile would not do against a camouflaged and entrenched enemy able to make best use of broken terrain. Inadequate longer-term logistical planning would not do against a mobilized 'national patriotic' population able to keep up prolonged warfare. And professional British troops with Maxims would not rapidly be able to overcome twice their number of even untrained Boer irregulars, despite Wolseley asserting this towards the end of 1899. While it is true that the British army in 1899 was not entirely without any idea of the need for adjustment to changing tactical conditions, and the training requirements of 'a new and flexible discipline of the battlefield',[65] this was still some way short of practical application. The ruling assumptions of the next war were that that it would again be small, and that nothing fancy need be attempted.

Chapter 2 Notes

1. *Het Zuid-Oosten*, 24 Oct. 1899.
2. Timothy Keegan, *Colonial South Africa and the Origins of the Racial Order* (Leicester, 1996), pp. 279–80; Stanley Trapido, 'Aspects in the transition from slavery to serfdom: the South African Republic, 1842–1902', *Collected Seminar Papers on the Societies of Southern Africa in the 19th and 20th Centuries* (London University, 1976), pp. 26–8.
3. J. J. Oberholster and M. C. E. van Schoor, *President Steyn aan die Woord* (Bloemfontein, 1953), p. 19; Smith, 'Jan Smuts and the South African War', Rethinking the SA War Conference paper, UNISA, 1998.
4. M. A. Gronum, *Die Engelse Oorlog, 1899–1902*, vol. 1 (Cape Town, 1971), p. 46; G. J. Schutte, *De Boerenoorlog na Honderd Jaar* (Amsterdam, 1997), pp. 25–6.
5. Memorandum, Sept. 1899, in *Selections from the Smuts Papers*, vol. 1, eds W. K. Hancock and Jean van der Poel (Cambridge, 1966), p. 327.
6. Donald Denoon, 'Participation in the "Boer War": people's war, people's non-war, or non-people's war', in *War and Society in Africa*, ed. Bethwell A. Ogot (London, 1972), p. 110; Smuts to W. T. Stead, 4 Jan. 1902, in *Smuts Papers*, vol. 1, p. 484.
7. *Further Correspondence Relating to Affairs in South Africa*, Cd.547 (1901), p. 34.
8. Diana Cammack, *The Rand at War 1899–1902: The Witwatersrand and the Anglo-Boer War* (London, 1990), pp. 40–2.
9. Quoted in Iain R. Smith, *The Origins of the South African War 1899–1902* (London, 1996), p. 368.
10. *Pall Mall Gazette*, Nov. 1898, p. 19.
11. For which, see Stephen Conway, *The War of American Independence 1775–1783* (London, 1995), pp. 59–64.
12. Michel Maubrey, 'Les Francais et la "veau d'or": la question sud-africaine (1896–1902)', in *La France et Afrique Du Sud*, ed. Daniel C. Bach (Paris, 1990), pp. 55–8.
13. As suggested, improbably, by Richard B. Mulanax, *The Boer War in American Politics and Diplomacy* (New York, 1994), p. 219; G. D. Scholtz, 'Die Tweede Vryheidsoorlog in Wereldverband', *Historia*, 1/2 (1975), p. 141.
14. *Jan Smuts: Memoirs of the Boer War*, eds Gail Nattrass and S. B. Spies (Johannesburg, 1994), p. 24.
15. Sneh Mahajan, 'The Defence of India and the End of Isolation: A Study in the Foreign Policy of the Conservative Government, 1900–1905', *Journal of Imperial and Commonwealth History*, 10/2 (1982), pp. 174–6.
16. *Ons Volk*, 7 Aug. 1899; *Ons Land*, 13 Sept. 1899.
17. Smuts to Stead, 4 Jan. 1902, in *Smuts Papers*, vol. 1, pp. 464–92.
18. Smuts to Executive Council, South African Republic, 4 Sept. 1899, in *Smuts Papers*, vol. 1, pp. 322–6.
19. J. H. Breytenbach, *Die Geskiedenis van die Tweede Vryheidsoorlog in Suid Afrika, 1899–1902*, vol. 1 (Pretoria, 1969), p. 157.
20. William McElwee, *The Art of War: Waterloo to Mons* (London, 1974) p. 217.
21. Thomas Pakenham, *The Boer War* (London, 1979), p. 42.
22. Andre Niemann, *Pieter Marits: Lotgevallen van een Transvaalschen Boerenjongen* (Arnhem, 1885), pp. 82–130.
23. Loren Kruger, 'The drama of country and city: tribalization, urbanization and theatre under apartheid', *Journal of Southern African Studies*, 23/4 (1997), p. 569.
24. Deneys Reitz, *Commando: A Boer Journal of the Boer War* (London, 1931), p. 26.
25. Memorandum, Sept. 1899, in *Smuts Papers*, vol. 1, pp. 322–6.
26. Howard Bailes, 'Military aspects of the war', in *The South African War: The Anglo-Boer War 1899–1902*, ed. Peter Warwick (London, 1980), p. 70.

27. Breytenbach, *Geskiedenis*, pp. 77–90.
28. Bailes, 'Military aspects', p. 70; Michael Glover, *Warfare from Waterloo to Mons* (London, 1980), p. 209.
29. Robert Scales, 'Artillery in small wars: the evolution of British artillery doctrine, 1860–1914', Ph.D. diss. (Duke University, 1976), p. 219.
30. Jacques Malan, *Die Boere-offisiere van die Tweede Vryheidsoorlog, 1899–1902* (Pretoria, 1990).
31. J. W. Meijer, 'Die Vroeë Militêre Loopbaan van Generaal Ben Viljoen, 1896–1898', *Historia* , 39/2 (1994), pp. 50–1.
32. John Keegan and Andrew Wheatcroft, *Who's Who in Military History from 1453 to the Present Day* (London, 1996 edn), pp. 68–9.
33. William McElwee, *The Art of War: Waterloo to Mons* (London, 1974), p. 233.
34. Raymond Sibbald, *The War Correspondents: The Boer War* (London, 1993), p. 22.
35. Hew Strachan, *European Armies and the Conduct of War* (London, 1983), p. 77.
36. Sibbald, *Boer War*, p. 22.
37. Clive Trebilcock, 'War and the failure of industrial mobilisation: 1899 and 1914', in *War and Economic Development*, ed. J. M. Winter (Cambridge, 1975), p. 159
38. *The Times History of the War in South Africa*, vol. 1 (1899–1900), ed. Leo Amery (London, 1900), p. 371.
39. C. M. Bakkes, 'Die Kommandostelsel', in *Die Kultuurontploiing van die Afrikaner*, ed. P. G. Nel (Pretoria, 1949), pp. 64–8.
40. Schutte, *Boerenoorlog*, p. 40.
41. *The War Memoirs of Commandant Ludwig Krause 1899–1900*, ed. Jerold Taitz (Cape Town, 1996), p. 6.
42. Ben Viljoen, *My Reminiscences of the Anglo-Boer War* (London, 1903), p. 309.
43. Sandra Scott Swart, 'The rebels of 1914: masculinity, republicanism and the social forces that shaped the Boer rebellion', M.A. diss. (University of Natal, 1997), p. 39.
44. Keegan, *Rural Transformations in Industrializing South Africa: The Southern Highveld to 1914* (Johannesburg, 1986), p. 25.
45. Fransjohan Pretorius, *Kommandolewe tydens die Anglo-Boereoorlog, 1899–1902* (Cape Town, 1991), p. 316.
46. Peter Warwick, *Black People and the South African War, 1899–1902* (Cambridge, 1983), p. 179.
47. Apollon Davidson and Irina Filatova, *The Russians and the Anglo-Boer War 1899–1902* (Cape Town, 1998), p. 63.
48. Denis Judd, *Someone has Blundered: Casualties of the British Army in the Victorian Age* (London, 1973), p. 164.
49. *The Economist*, 15 Sept. 1899; *The Spectator*, 19 Aug. 1899; *Cape Argus*, 19 Oct. 1899.
50. Peter Marsh, *The Discipline of Popular Government: Lord Salisbury's Domestic Statecraft, 1881–1902* (Hassocks, 1978), pp. 283–5.
51. George Wyndham to his mother, 6 Oct. 1899, in *Life and Letters of George Wyndham*, eds J. W. Mackail and Guy Wyndham (London, 1926), p. 361; John Gooch, 'The armed services', in *The First World War in British History* , eds Stephen Constantine et al. (London, 1995), p. 185; Bailes, 'Technology and imperialism: a case study of the Victorian Army in Africa', *Victorian Studies*, 24/1 (1980), p. 86.
52. *Hansard*, Fourth Series, vol. XI. cols. 915–18, 8 May 1896.
53. *Justice*, 27 Sept. 1899.
54. Marc Yakutiel, 'Treasury control and the South African War, 1899–1905', D.Phil. diss. (University of Oxford, 1989), p. 23.
55. Col. C. G. Melville, *The Life of Sir Redvers Buller*, vol. 1 (London, 1923), pp. 2–4.
56. Peter Dudgin, *Military Intelligence: The British Story* (London, 1989), p. 32.

57. Keith Surridge, ' "All you soldiers are what we call pro-Boer": the military critique of the South African War, 1899–1902', *History*, 82/268 (1997), pp. 588–9.
58. Kevin Booth, *Strategy and Ethnocentrism* (London, 1979), p. 33; W. S. Hamer, *The British Army: Civil–Military Relations, 1885–1905* (Oxford, 1970), p. 175.
59. W. S. Hamer, *The British Army: Civil–Military Relations, 1885–1905*, (Oxford, 1970), p. 176.
60. Andrew Page, 'The supply services of the British Army in the South African War, 1899–1902', D.Phil. diss. (University of Oxford, 1976), p. 239.
61. Jock Haswell, *British Military Intelligence* (London, 1973), pp. 48–50; Dudgin, *Military Intelligence*, pp. 31–3.
62. Thomas G. Fergusson, 'The development of a modern intelligence organization: British military intelligence, 1870–1914', Ph.D. diss. (Duke University, 1981), p. 203.
63. Ian F. W. Beckett, *The Amateur Military Tradition, 1558–1945* (Manchester, 1991), p. 200.
64. Edward Spiers, 'The Late Victorian Army, 1868–1914', in *The Oxford Illustrated History of The British Army*, ed. David Chandler (Oxford, 1994), p. 193.
65. Bailes, 'Technology and tactics in the British Army, 1866–1900', in *Men, Machines and War*, eds Richard Haycock and Keith Nelson (Toronto, 1988), p. 42.

3

The Republican Offensive

Hostilities commenced not with any great engagement, but with a skirmish. At Kraaipan railway siding, some 30 miles south of Mafeking, a Boer patrol from forces commanded by General Piet Cronjé sabotaged a railway line on 12 October, checking the advance of a British armoured train conveying munitions and other urgent stores to the town garrison. Led by Koos de la Rey, soon to become a rising star, the 800-strong commando called up Field Artillery which briefly bombarded the stationary train from a distance of 2000 feet. This impressive onslaught produced a swift surrender, with the Boers capturing the train and taking its wounded and others prisoner, including African and white railway workers. The mechanized passage of arms and troops between Mafeking and the south had now been cut, and the Boers commanded its southern approaches, ready to open a line of advance.[1] Yet to sustain a casualty they had inserted the first wedge of the overall republican move to sweep into Natal and the Cape Colony, and to seal off the railways as a strategic avenue of British advance northwards by throttling the line at the key points of Kimberley–Vryburg–Mafeking in the Cape and the Ladysmith junction, the principal northern Natal town and railhead up from Durban.

Logically enough, the whole Boer strategic conception turned on control of the rail system, its trunk routes a key element in transport and communication over the great distances between the colonial coastal fringe and the republican heartland. Invasion routes were all aimed at denying the enemy use of lines of advance, the Boer purpose

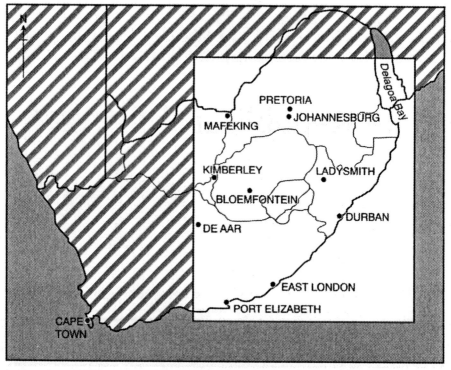

Map 3.1 *Eastern, Central, and Western Front Towns and Ports*

being to sever rail routes to the coast to prevent the British from moving reinforcements from the ports to an interior theatre of operations.
At the far head of a successful offensive lay the hemming in of
Durban and Cape Town, and the promising augury of a negotiated
peace before it all became too bloody and destructive a slog. For the
republicans' invasion lines, this meant menacing several areas at the
same time. Commandos moved westerly into Bechuanaland and
Griqualand, southerly across the Orange River to threaten the
internal territory of the Cape, and easterly into Natal.

This opening balance strongly favoured the Natal front, for
reasons involving a fine mix of military hubris and judicious political
calculation. First, Transvaal leadership was understandably partial to
the known campaigning advantages of the territory around Majuba
and Laing's Nek, the imposing but manoeuvrable ridges straddling
the main eastern corridor of advance from the Boer republic through
the Drakensberg mountain range into Natal. First Boer War veterans
like Piet Joubert, Piet Cronjé, and Christiaan de Wet had a good nose

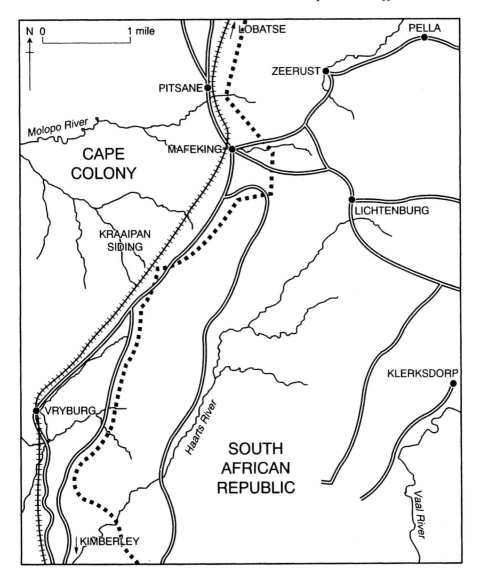

Map 3.2 *Opening of Hostilities, Western Cape Colony*

for the inspirational significance of a site where Britain's red line had previously been too thin and too short. Second, there had been a forward deployment of some British cavalry and infantry to the northern junction and colliery areas of Dundee and Glencoe. This had been ordered by Major-General Sir William Penn Symons in response to urgings from the colony's governor, Sir Walter

Hely-Hutchinson, that Natal be reinforced well inland of Ladysmith, headquarters of the main British force in South Africa. A further consideration was the political need for some show to remind Boer stock farmers in northern Natal to stay put, and also to keep surrounding Zulu communities calm. Inquisitive Africans were to remain neutral, at least until nodded into controlled collaboration on British terms.[2] With reinforcements on their way, Penn Symons in Dundee appeared confident. But Glencoe and Dundee were weak spots, and the siting of an inferior British force of 4000 troops during September and early October provided the Natal front Boers with an inviting opportunity to punch a hole right through the first enemy lines. Preparation was simplicity itself. Joubert concentrated a mass of 14,000 Transvaal commandos, reinforced by 6000 Orange Free Staters led by General Marthinus Prinsloo, along the upper northern reaches threatening the apex of Natal. The chances of failure were small.

Third, Natal was fancied because the Transvaal did not have an entirely free hand to dictate republican strategy. The Steyn administration was lukewarm about mounting a major invasion of the Cape from the Orange Free State, due in part to the honourable tenacity with which the Cape Prime Minister, W. P. Schreiner, and its Chief Justice, Sir Henry de Villiers, had pursued Anglo-Boer mediation through the last few months of the crisis. Even if virtually everyone in Bloemfontein understood that a big rush at the colony could well deliver rebel recruits to the republicans, a prevaricating Marthinus Steyn remained concerned with proper presentation of a 'just-cause' defensive alliance with Kruger. As correspondence with Joubert made clear, it was Pretoria's war, and the role of Bloemfontein was to keep up as its ally.[3]

Given that understanding, the Transvaal could not count on the Orange Free State taking the initiative to open accounts with a heavy push southwards into the northern Cape. So, again, a major Natal effort proved irresistible. Not only was it a geographically difficult region over which to establish coordinated defence; not only had the British made their position more assailable by helpfully dividing and exposing their available forces beyond the Tugela river; not only did the Boers find the route through the Drakensberg barrier fairly soft going, with no bridges blown, no passes mined, and the Transvaal–Natal railway route in nice repair to enable a moving invader to run in supplies. The further advantage was that armies could be combined with relative ease, on almost equal terms, for an easy breakthrough.

Major-General Sir George White, the dithering Commander-in-Chief of the Natal British forces when war erupted, had grudgingly agreed to urgent pleas from Penn Symons and Hely-Hutchinson for an advanced detachment to be posted far north. This dispersal, while retaining only 8000 men at Ladysmith, increasingly alarmed White because a bisecting Boer push could break communication lines between Dundee and Ladysmith, and rapidly isolate them from the rest of the colony. As expeditionary commander, an incoming Buller foresaw an even more calamitous opening outcome. In an intelligent judgement, he concluded that as the entire northern Natal salient was so vulnerable to frontal attack as to be indefensible, any position there would be overwhelmed. To make matters worse, the net could also close in another direction, through additional flanking offensives from the eastern Transvaal and western Orange Free State, across the Drakensberg. Just as Dundee and Glencoe were being lopped off, so a converging pincer movement could menace Ladysmith. Believing that there was too much dangerous ground to contest, Buller favoured pulling the British defensive line right back, if need be even well south of the Tugela.[4] He did not get his way with Penn Symons, White, or the War Office, and was in any event not in an effective command position before 9 October; and thereafter he was to have other problems on his plate, which would culminate in the rapid shredding of a good soldiering reputation.

It did not take long for Natal to become seriously disputed territory. On 19 October an advance Boer unit pushed through to Elandslaagte on the rail line just south of Dundee and Glencoe, pounced on a British supply train, and easily occupied the settlement. Under British noses, connection between Ladysmith and Dundee was swiftly cut. For triumphant commandos, the mounted photographic pose in front of a captured train was to become an early celebration of power and optimism, and one destined to be repeated. Meanwhile, in Dundee, Penn Symons did not feel that he had much to do. Writing off the taking of Elandslaagte, a headstrong and opinionated commander did not expect the republicans to have the bottle to turn to an attack on a full and capable British brigade. Although alert to the moving presence of Joubert's forces, a peculiar insouciance seemed to settle upon Penn Symons, who made no effort to entrench his troops or to devise other effective cover. He had a cynical view of the Boer armies, believing that their mounted riflemen were semi-trained levies, and no match for the superior technical preparedness and disciplined aptitude of his regulars.

But his enemy was full of fight, and was to choose its ground well.

The Boer forces were large enough to divide into two attack formations. One, under General Daniel 'Maroela' Erasmus, placed itself on the flat Impati highland overlooking the plain occupied by the small colliery settlement. The dominating Talana Hill, with heights reaching 500 feet above the depression in which Penn Symons' troops were encamped, was occupied by a force led by General Lukas Meyer. Erasmus, a figure normally known for wilfulness and for being out of touch with events, was one of those considered by the patrician Ludwig Krause as 'hardly fit to be employed, even as common soldiers'.[5]

From these crowning vantage points, the Boers sat down to unleash a thumping bombardment of Dundee below. Before fire commenced, a drifting British patrol stumbled on Meyer's assembled force of 4000 commandos in the dark, with one sergeant managing to slip off to warn his garrison commander of the strength of the republican approach. Naturally, his alarm was disregarded by Penn Symons. At dawn on 20 October, the Boers' intentions became clear. Thousands of enemy soldiers could be seen lining the hills, from which a direct artillery bombardment of the British position commenced. With customary surprise and preparation the Boers had quietly run guns up by hand in the darkness, digging small pits along hillcrests to keep muzzles at low level and to provide alternating dug-outs for the routine shifting of artillery pieces. Gunners also took particular care to water the ground heavily, or to lay the skins of freshly slaughtered cattle under their Krupp howitzers, to minimize dust being thrown up on discharge.[6]

The surprise was total for soldiers of the British Field Force, who also found that Boer weapons had been positioned beyond the range of their own garrison artillery. Penn Symons' troops managed to rally, to limber artillery into a more effective position, and to direct a screen of returning defensive fire against the Boers. This was sufficiently ferocious not merely to silence their guns, but to spread panic through their firing line; over 1000 battered and shaken commandos melted away. An emboldened Penn Symons then ordered a frontal attack on Talana, sending his cavalry between the two hills. With Erasmus' troops bedded down on Impati, this was risky, but his opponent was not one for wait-and-see or any further alarmist observation. Meyer, meanwhile, sited part of his force on Lennox Hill, adjoining Talana to the south. Luckily for the British and maddeningly for the Boers, a lethargic Erasmus was in no mood to harry enemy troops. The commando culture of a combination of independent equals always had a price, as leadership now discovered. Within republican ranks there

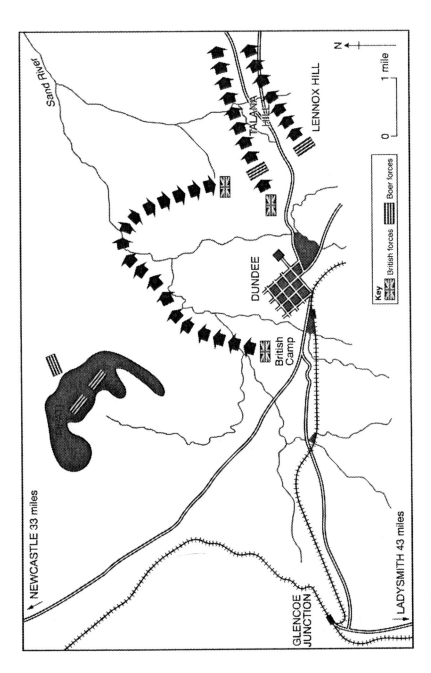

Map 3.3 *Talana Hill, October 1899*

were to be murmurs about replacing senior officers like Erasmus with men of stouter character, and even a dark belief that the republican position would have been better advanced if 'independent' commanders, who had decided 'to carry on the war' according to their 'own bright ideas', had 'been shot as early as Dundee'.[7]

In the event, it was Penn Symons who died, fatally wounded in the Talana assault and carried away by his soldiers as they held off the Boers and retreated to Ladysmith. The high ground of Talana was taken by the British, and Dundee was saved, in a fairly sombre victory. Great damage had been done to British confidence, and the cost of prevailing was quite considerable. Boer casualties were 140, while Field Force losses were 546, more than 10 per cent of the total complement deployed. Some British infantry were the victims of shrapnel fire from their own guns, as battery rounds fell short of the crucial margin between friend and enemy.

During this engagement the British decided to confront the Boers at Elandslaagte, northeast of Ladysmith, as this striking position presented a further threat to White's base. Scouting information reported that it was lightly defended, although General Johannes Kock and 1000 soldiers were in the vicinity to raise its numbers and to secure things for a move on Ladysmith. But here the initiative had already passed to the British, who on 21 October pressed forward from Ladysmith to re-establish the head link between Elandslaagte and Dundee. The men who planned the blow were two of the British army's most efficient and austere tacticians, infantryman Colonel Ian Hamilton and Lieutenant-General Sir John French, an expert cavalry force commander and 'prototypical blimp'.[8] For the occupying Boers, it was a question of being outnumbered and outmanoeuvred by a coordinated infantry and cavalry attack. Entrenched and behind earthworks threaded around the ridges and kopjes just south of Elandslaagte, they were squeezed by a pincer movement which brought continuous and thick rifle fire, while British infantry drawn up in a flanking stab closed in. Attempting to establish a defensible retreat, the Boers withdrew to a hill position from which to try to make a stand; their two commando guns could do nothing to counter the shell-fire of 18-gun British field batteries. In intense fighting, embattled Boers resolutely defended their position against repeated attack, and counter-attacked. After a final climactic British assault, Kock's defending Transvaal and Orange Free State commandos crumbled as French and Hamilton's troops stormed through.

The surviving Boer force was routed. But this collapse was to bring further slaughter. As commandos fled their trenches and took to their horses, traditionalist hard-riding cavalry swooped down with lance and sabre to cut down the cornered and presumably terrified Boers, whose famed fleetness had deserted them. The gruesome effect of men being slashed to death was terrible, with one infantryman repelled by his vision of 'a stinking knacker's yard'. For exultant cavalrymen, the outcome confirmed a mentality that even an unmistakably 'hard' enemy was to be overwhelmed solely by 'dash'. If anything, Elandslaagte, with its aged and broken General Kock himself mortally wounded, diminished that enemy, turning it into inferior prey. For Lancers, 'it was not even ... as though their army were fighting real soldiers. The enemy were a mob of farmers, dressed in black frock-coats, riding ridiculous little ponies and carrying Bibles under their arms'.[9] Their virtual annihilation of escaping Boers left the republicans with a legacy of virulent hatred of British cavalry, with commentators in Bloemfontein and Pretoria reacting with revulsion at what was considered an atrocity, akin to the earlier spearing of Christian trekkers by 'savage' or 'barbarous' Zulu or Sotho adversaries.

Despite the Boers having broken and run, for the British the outcome of the Elandslaagte affray was mixed. Even though Boer casualties amounted to half their forces, the British were not unscathed, having lost just under one-tenth of their strength. And this price had still not tipped the strategic balance in northern Natal towards the British. They lacked the power to continue holding a salient which remained vulnerable, and lacked the means to engineer a decisive battle to try to extinguish the republican offensive. So White now abandoned Dundee and Elandslaagte, and drew back to Ladysmith, leaving behind a well-provisioned camp and a dying Penn Symons.

With Boers closing in on retreating and increasingly fatigued British troops whose progress was hindered by flooding rivers and enveloping mud, White resolved on carrying the fight to his opponents before they bore down and attacked him. In a last movement before Ladysmith became encircled, he launched a concerted flanking assault with strong infantry brigade and cavalry detachments, aimed at surprising the Boer position and doing sufficient damage to reverse the entire course of their eastern offensive. In fact, his planning ambitiously addressed the need to make provision for a northwards thrust to cut off retreating Boers who were expected to make a run towards Newcastle before skulking back to Majuba and Laing's Nek, this time to lick their wounds. The weight of a century of satisfactory colonial campaigns or punitive expeditions was still keeping buoyant what John Mackenzie has neatly termed 'the "over by Xmas" mentality'.[10] But on 30 October it was all to turn out badly for the British. Poor reconnaissance, misjudgement of Boer positioning, and a blur of confusing and hesitant orders left White's dispersed forces in disarray and at great risk from the Boers, who had been anything but idling.

With his luck running out, White then deepened confusion by ordering a wholesale retreat in response to an unverified alarm that Orange Free State forces were massing to attack Ladysmith from the west. By now, the republicans had become too knowing and too strong, and were given a tenacious lead by Lukas Meyer. At Lombard's Nek they outflanked the enemy and maintained devastating fire until resistance petered out. Simultaneously, at Nicholson's Nek, the British played into Boer hands by basing themselves on the more precarious half of the pass, allowing their adversaries to occupy the more secure other half from which to mount an attack. Orange Free State commandos under de Wet overwhelmed the British. When his troops began to surrender at their own initiative, their commander, Colonel F. R. C. Carleton, resigned himself to the inevitable, declaring a ceasefire and surrendering around 1200 men, some of whom were tugged across Boer lines by African servants 'dressed in kilts', evidently stripped from the corpses of Gordons at Elandslaagte.[11] The republicans sustained some 200 casualties. These essentially diversionary battles had involved something like evenly matched forces: their outcome for the British was especially galling.

White's hand was spent. His troops, demoralized by having been shot to pieces for no gain, fell back towards Ladysmith as the encircling Boers closed in. By the end of October the largest British force in the country was trapped inside a town which some felt was the last remaining obstacle to the invaders taking Durban. In itself no great prize to be gained, Ladysmith waited to be swallowed by republicans whose communications and supply were rapidly improving. But then, instead of capitalizing on its gain, the Boer command proceeded to squander its precious advantage at a moment when time pressed as imperial troops were seaborne. As local British forces headed for Ladysmith under hastily improvised artillery cover, Joubert relieved the pressure: instead of running his mounted forces in rapid pursuit, as some of his chafing commandants and many of his veldkornets expected, he reined in his army. With the town still poorly barricaded, the chance to force through a British capitulation was lost. Then, having declined to press home its advantage before the defenders could dig themselves in, Boer leadership decided to sit out the confrontation. Joubert encircled Ladysmith and laid siege from 29 October, an investment which was to last a full four months, ending only on 28 February 1900, when British reinforcements finally relieved it. The republicans thereby effectively immobilized their Natal offensive, locking their forces into a fixed position.

Petrus Jacobus Joubert's hour was over. Before the war, the assignment of the ageing 68-year old veteran to preside over the eastern invasion had met with scepticism and even scorn from his younger and more fiery and imaginative opponents. The 'old General' or 'Kruger's dog' was judged at best irresolute and procrastinating, and at worst feeble and timid.[12] There was particular contempt for his attachment to an afternoon nap and household comforts. An evident believer in marching on his stomach, on campaigns Joubert routinely took along his spouse, Hendrina, accompanied by her servants and household cattle, partly to ensure that it would not go empty. But, as Ladysmith revealed, he was no Napoleon, with a reach which constantly threatened to exceed the grasp of his armies. Despite enjoying almost every advantage, and despite full knowledge of where and when Ladysmith defences were fairly thinly held, Joubert risked little in attempting to find a back door through which to overrun the town. One has no need to be too hard on him, as he has been well enough derided already for bull-headed tactical inflexibility and a failure of imagination. But it must be said that he was a mediocre commander who had probably got too far on political cronyism.

Smuts may have had his strategy, but clearly it could not be laid down to generals in the field. In order to report to the Transvaal government on campaign conditions, he personally visited the Natal front on a number of occasions during the opening phase of hostilities. What he saw around Ladysmith was a costly bind, at a stage when the strategic need was to leave the siege lines just near enough and strong enough to deter any major British garrison counter-attack, while investing the bulk of the commando forces in maintaining the prime offensive towards Durban. If the Boers were to settle for a war of place and position, it had to be in a commanding spot on the coast, either menacing Durban or, ideally, entering it. Then, and later, he and other younger leaders were to fume over a stubborn subversion of grand strategy by generals too old, too cautious, and too cranky to perform.

With the backing of his personal Council of War, Piet Joubert saw the siege of Ladysmith as an achievement: the Boer priority was not to capture it, but to keep it ringed in depth with commando encampments or *laagers*. Maintaining the investment was the means of impeding a British offensive against the Transvaal from Natal. It was, however, a misconceived calculation, which has rightly been termed 'one of the most serious Boer tactical errors of the war'.[13] The siege diverted thousands of troops from offensive campaigning, and mostly kept them idle. At the same time, the republicans lacked the numbers to do much during an extended investment. For their war effort, this represented a damaging confusion of strategic intentions. Moreover, the state of affairs created by Joubert played right into British hands, even if he failed properly to comprehend it. White found himself able to tie up much of the invasion force in a tactical concentration for which it was especially unsuited, and for which it was ill equipped with heavy guns. Boer military culture and disciplinary capacity did not raise commandos to conduct interminable fixed siege operations.

The siege of Ladysmith, like the other celebrated republican sieges of British towns in the opening phase of the war, was to remain a desultory business throughout. Besiegers rarely looked as if they had the will actually to take the town; despite increasingly grim conditions which were to see 10 deaths per day from disease, and dwindling reserves, white and black besieged rarely looked as if they were about to be bled into surrender by Boer attrition. Both sides seemed to conform to tit-for-tat shelling and tit-for-tat forays against each other's lines. Scarcely serious fighting, all this really did was to underline the extent to which they were not merely becalmed, but marooned. If this set-piece illustrated anything, it was the degree to which both republican and British command were becoming reliant upon the labour or other services of black workers, much of it commandeered, some of it collaborative, to maintain siege operations. The British exploited the presence of the large number of African and Asian labourers who, after fleeing the Natal coalfields, had sought refuge in Ladysmith before the siege commenced. For their part, the Boers conscripted Africans into work parties to destroy railway track and to dam up the local river, and armed a small number of chosen followers to stand relief in outposts at night.

Whatever wearing down of the British garrison was accomplished, those outside were hardly elated. Some Africans who deserted the Boer camp actually slipped into Ladysmith, in the belief that siege conditions inside might be better than being constantly ill-used.[14] More telling was the damage to the spirit, morale, and discipline of ordinary burghers, who were simply ground down by the lack of any sense of gain or purpose. Joubert's troops whiled away their days boozing on brandy, pilfering, slipping away on leave to check on

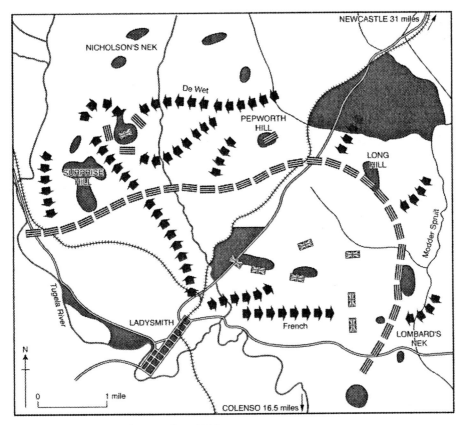

Map 3.4 *Ladysmith, October 1899*

home harvests or market conditions, and pining for beaches and bananas. Their loss of faith in Joubert in particular seems to have been all but complete. In December there was already mounting frustration with his brusque dismissal of ideas at lower-level commando ranks to commence construction of moving 'zig-zag trenches so as to get nearer and nearer the town every day' in order to 'have the enemy under rifle fire from all sides'.[15] Similarly, commandants were despondent that their general was not moving swiftly to adopt what seemed to them the obviously inviting tactic of damming up the town's Klip river in order to flood the trapped British into surrender. Such was the glum Ladysmith record: several months of mutually dispiriting endurance, and random deaths from shrapnel and typhoid.

Equally, the republicans were not in any sense contemplating a reversal of their occupation position in this eastern theatre. In December 1898 Butler had been advised that while the 'northern strip of Natal may be occupied by the Boers', it could be considered 'unlikely that any further serious advance ... would be undertaken'. At most, 'raids' involving '2000 to 3000 men' were 'to be expected' and to be adequately guarded against.[16] But this had missed something. By now, Boer gains in Natal were also causing trouble for still-vague British campaign planning. This was the 'interior strategy', in which a strong expeditionary force would roll directly through the Orange Free State and assume control of Bloemfontein. In the immediate present, Sir George White's job had been to hold off any Natal offensive until his position could be strengthened by a weighty western expedition against the republicans. In this, however, he failed. Indeed, the British inability properly to secure the colony against its predator, and the apprehension this produced, completely changed the picture. At the outset, Britain would first have to restore its battered position in Natal.

The other purpose of the Boer dual offensive was to make a hole in the Cape Colony. Here, General Piet Cronjé and a well-provisioned force of between 8000 and 9000 men which had at its disposal almost a dozen guns, including a heavy Creusot siege cannon, fixed on Mafeking as a first target. Dozing close to the western internal border of the Transvaal, Mafeking was a typically small colonial African town in the vast dry wastes between the grasslands of the veldt and the fine sand and bare scrub of the Kalahari desert. It presented an opportunity for action against a place with a name barely known to outsiders; if it was known at all, this was doubtless only for the fact that it formed the largest railway depot between Kimberley on the Orange Free State border and Bulawayo in Rhodesia. In some ways, Mafeking offered itself to the republicans. Its siting on the rail link to the north affirmed some strategic significance; as a commercial and trading enclave in the Bechuanaland Protectorate within the Cape Colony, it held useful stores and provisions; lying less than 10 miles from the Transvaal border, there was barely any need to bother about supply lines; and finally, there was a powerful emotional and patriotic reflex about the Mafeking area. It was from here that Jameson and his raiders had set out to wipe out Transvaal independence; and the man who had run them to ground then had been Pieter Arnoldus Cronjé. For all this, however, from a detached viewpoint Mafeking was not necessarily an obvious military focal point for sharp Boer campaigning.

Appointed as General for the Western Front by Joubert in September 1899, the 63-year-old Cronjé had a reputation for being dour and headstrong. A religious fundamentalist prone to prophetic visions, he occasionally expressed his ideas through symbolism and allegory rather than clearly formed Dutch sentences. In anticipating the war Cronjé was confident that Britain would not be able to crush the Boers. His assigned military adviser, the younger Jacobus Hercules ('Koos') de la Rey had nothing like the same confidence in him. But this did not mean that Cronjé did not count: a pottering siege was precisely the kind of eventuality with which his temperament could cope. Indeed, as with Joubert, holding position enabled Cronjé to retain a close connection with femininity and family. His wife, Hester, accompanied him, one of a small number of Boer women in laagers and trenches in the early stages of the war who ignored directives barring them from the field and from entering the front other than as nurses. For Hendrina Joubert and Hester Cronjé, infiltration of a masculine world of fighting was more than simply an adjustment to the dislocation of war; it was equally an active identification with the republican war effort and the adoption of a nurturing role as its camp followers. For an American press correspondent with the Boer forces, the most steely expression of that support of the campaign was the ritual oiling and loading of Cronjé's rifle by his spouse. In a limited way the Boers were simply replicating common African practice in areas like west and equatorial Africa, where the practical sustaining of military campaigns had long been something of a family business.

What ensued at Mafeking left unclear what ground that war effort had gained. It was by no means automatic that a fight should have been carried on here at all, let alone a confrontation which would last a whole seven months. The defences of the administrative capital of Bechuanaland had been roundly neglected by the Cape government for, as war approached, it was reluctant to provoke the Transvaal by carrying a military position to its very border. Far from requiring force and firepower to protect it against the possibility of republican invasion, Mafeking was considered sufficiently remote, and sufficiently small (1500 white inhabitants and 5000 blacks, mostly in the adjoining African settlement of Mafikeng), to be spared. Denied military protection by Cape authorities who shrugged off pleas and warnings, the white town fathers eventually acted for themselves and roped in Baden-Powell and his Bechuanaland Protectorate Regiment.

At first reluctant to consign any of his men to garrison Mafeking, by the latter half of September Baden-Powell was persuaded of the need to concentrate his force for the defence of the town rather than have it quartered in one or other part of the neighbouring countryside. Given the position of the Cape government, which was to keep out of the way of trouble, Baden-Powell's defensive preparations were effectively undertaken in secret, although the significance of large supplies being run into Mafeking was not lost on nearby Boers. He then moved his entire regiment in to strengthen the town and deny it to the republicans. Fully assembled, this contingent was not large. Baden-Powell had 750 trained troops and mounted police and a scratch rifle guard force of around 450 semi-trained volunteers raised from the local white citizenry. His artillery provision was also seriously inadequate, consisting of a few outmoded, slow-firing muzzle-loaders and a clutch of light guns. In all it did not look to have the makings of a strong defensive position.

Mafeking hostilities commenced with a handful of skirmishes and light sniping; as Cronjé's forces closed in, Baden-Powell launched several flanking sorties to try to break up the front of the advance while the republicans were still at a distance. Easily beating this off, the Boer general pressed him to surrender to avoid loss of life and damage to the town. Still firing to harass the invaders, Baden-Powell rejected the surrender offer, and pulled back into Mafeking. Having failed to force the issue in the field, the Boers then surrounded Mafeking and, having consolidated their lines, commenced a siege on 14 October. Peculiarly, aside from this initial belligerence, hereafter 'relatively little real fighting took place for the remainder of the siege', to quote the most informed historian of late-Victorian Mafeking.[17]

However much the siege of Mafeking (and of Ladysmith and, to a lesser extent, Kimberley) would go on to saturate the popular imagination of the British public, there was just not much to it. For here the war ground to a virtual standstill. Inside, Baden-Powell established a defensive ring of trenches linked to a cluster of small forts, looping for five miles around Mafeking and Mafikeng. Outside, the republicans threw up an encircling siege chain, its largest links being several commando laagers. Behind their cordon, the Boers also held several fortified elevated positions. Some bemused journalists pondered a military situation which at first glance looked somewhat ambiguous: was Mafeking actually being besieged, or were the republicans simply laggard in not surging forward and carrying the town's defences? For his part, Cronjé seemed content to behave as if he had plenty of time. It was only when British relief forces began to break through in May 1900, that Cronjé launched an extended attack to try to take the position.

For most of the time, the point of operations was to keep the siege alive. Reluctant to risk real losses, Boer command resorted to shelling and 'Mausering' the town from a secure distance to increase the burden of defence. Cronjé's heavy Creusot 'Long Tom', capable of engaging a target from a distance as great as 10,000 yards, looked a fearsome weapon, with the mechanical capacity to flatten and terrorize a besieged population into submission. In fact, while it powerfully combined military power and myth, it was not especially more lethal or destructive than the Krupp field guns which the commandos ranged against Mafeking to no very great effect. Ammunition was of uneven quality; fuse malfunctions were common, and shells produced relatively limited explosive power.

Mafeking was closed up by the Boers in the sense that normal communications between the town and the outside world were severed, but never in the sense that it was sealed. The relative ease with which both white and black inhabitants could on occasion weave their way through the republican sentry lines was doubtless facilitated by their thinning. While the siege started with the installation of around 6000 Boers to operate around the town, after just a few weeks this complement was whittled down to little more than 2000, as burghers decamped to do a turn on their farms, were diverted to other fronts, or were hauled away into diversionary raiding elsewhere. As the strength of the siege force was allowed to fluctuate, so the power to mount anything much more than intermittent assaults drained away. Cramped around Mafeking, some of Cronjé's more obvious problems mirrored those of Joubert at Ladysmith: maintaining the adhesion and commitment of immobilized soldiers, holding the loyalties of grumbling commandants and veldkornets, ensuring that burghers did not skulk in laagers to avoid line duties, and having to daily coordinate artillery, light sortie, and picket operations. It settled down to finding ways of sustaining momentum beyond campfires and breakfasts. Inside the town, Baden-Powell had to take special pains to organize a reasonable muster of able-bodied defenders, obviously a vital requirement for the holding of its defensive circuit. For the most part wanting nothing to do with the war, Mafeking's white citizenry resigned themselves to having to provide 300 men for the Town Guard, and even this was grudgingly given. Traders with Transvaal commercial connections had a greater interest in buying peace than in fighting for victory; they felt no pro-British attachment and considered service obligations unfair. Others resented having to turn out as substitutes for troops who, in their view, should have been despatched by either the Cape colonial or the imperial government. Even more loyal and conscientious recruits in the Town Guard and Bechuanaland Rifles became glum, their distrust and disgust rising in response to the haughty treatment and mean rewards doled out by

Baden-Powell's military authorities. As white citizen soldiers, the well-off Cape English colonists resented the rather unequal sharing of physical discomfort and material deprivation between their world, of exposed and wet trenches and airy neglect by commanders, and that of Baden-Powell and his staff officers, with its solid shelters, medals, and brandy with soda.[18]

Given that tactics again mattered more than politics, the presence of blacks around and within the sphere of Mafeking operations partly assisted the needs of both sides, and partly complicated them. Reclaiming local loyalties, Cronjé's force secured the willing cooperation of old Boer allies, the Rapulana-Barolong, whose leadership furnished scouts, messengers, and labourers; approximately 300 men were also armed and posted to trenches and fortified points, while others not dug in were deployed as cattle guards and to raid enemy livestock. But not everything could be taken for granted. Working at cross purposes with Boer designs, the wilful Rapulana seized chances thrown up by the siege to pay off personal scores with the Mafeking Tshidi-Barolong. These wilful acts of random aggression added to Boer uncertainties about the keeping of order in the surrounding region.

Similarly manoeuvring, operating, and pulling, Mafeking command was able to let loose the Tshidi, who had long experience of collaboration with the British against the Boers. Baden-Powell knew better than to leave Mafikeng exposed beyond his lines of defence, a fatal gap through which Mafeking's defensive foundations might slip. About 500 armed Barolong were stationed to defend the African *stad* and to provide cover for the southwestern cordon of the town's defence, while small armed companies were organized from other inhabitants, such as Mfengu and Coloured communities. These intermediaries, far larger in number than white defenders, both stocked defensive lines and ground away at intermittent and risky raiding of Boer lines to scoop up cattle and hit their foe, at some cost. The rudimentary labour required for fixing defensive works like shelters and dug-outs was provided by Africans, while the crafty retrieval and delivery of black scouts, spies, and runners made up the kernel of Baden-Powell's local military intelligence. At great personal risk, especially in the early months of the siege, these runners also kept wires and newspapers in the world outside in touch with the Mafeking crisis, or at least that jaunty version of its truth patted through by Baden-Powell and his vigilant military censors.

Described wryly as 'young, as men go in the Army, with a keen appreciation of the possibilities of his career',[19] by Angus Hamilton,

The Times' siege correspondent, Baden-Powell proved a dab hand at releasing outnumbered, poorly briefed, and ill-prepared forces to attack well-fortified Boer positions, at a smarting cost and to no productive gain. This did nothing to damage his rising reputation as the Mafeking siege commander, and still less were there serious questions about what had possessed him to station his Protectorate force in a spot where it would be holed up uselessly for months. Left to flourish, by the end of 1899 'The Defender of Mafeking' was projecting its siege for all the world as if it were some Troy of the Bechuanaland Protectorate. This impression was not too widely shared by white and black townspeople, who were already growing sceptical of the benefits of making imperial history under the command of a man of enormous determination and rather less humanity. Even though food for whites would never seriously be in short supply, in the early months the authorities improved the odds by denying provisions to trapped African refugees. Baden-Powell's ultimate intention was to drive those Africans who were surplus to essential defence needs out of Mafeking so as to conserve stores. For people who were liable either to be cut down or hounded by the Boers, the choice was intense privation and virtual starvation inside, or possible massacre by the republican lines. The Mafeking commander probably did more to worsen African mortality rates than to inflict damage on the Boer invaders.

The day after this dreary sideshow got under way, the republicans commenced their third large investment operation, putting Kimberley to siege on 15 October in an action which would last for four months. While not an obvious strategic cornerstone of British defence like Ladysmith, it had enough as an upcountry communications site to draw on the Boers. Unlike Mafeking, for both military and political opinion there was a sense that here was a weighty prize, the loss of which would both damage and humiliate the imperial camp. Kimberley housed the De Beers diamond industry, making it a plum deposit of capital, coal, foodstuffs and other stores, railway equipment, engineering workshops, scrap iron (potential shrapnel), and dynamite. General Christiaan Wessels, Commandant-in-Chief of the Orange Free State forces, and his War Council had little hesitation in committing resources to a move on Kimberley in the hope of spooning its captured materials onto the republican war plate. Kimberley and its diamonds were synonymous with the cavalier imperialist Rhodes, a tempting nose waiting to be bloodied. A number of republican journalists and politicians wanted Kimberley solely because it would mean the capture of Rhodes: as an exquisite political blow, it was assumed that this would raise morale in the field and inspire the Boers to ever greater efforts. Even in a phase of the war often short on sense, to make Rhodes the point of an assault on Kimberley was peculiar.

Kimberley ended up as the culmination of a very minor offensive south of Mafeking, running along the line of the rail system. Koos de la Rey and other more decisive commandants, who were determined to hurry on the war, coordinated a rapid movement through small Griqualand West villages like Taung and Kuruman, riding virtually at will, picking up republican rebel recruits, forcing white police and Coloured guards into frontal engagements where they could be outnumbered and outgunned, and scaring estranged black civilians into passivity. There was nothing to halt their advance until Kimberley, a town of 13,000 whites, 7000 Coloured people, and 30,000 Africans, 11,000 of them mine workers. Awaiting encirclement, its surrounding terrain was not particularly to the Boers' liking. Unlike Ladysmith and Mafeking, it had little by way of kopjes or other elevated ground as strong points from which to direct firepower.

Under the command of Colonel Robert Kekewich, an able and clear-thinking North Lancashire Regiment officer, Kimberley had a small but effective garrison, its professional core consisting of 400 troops of his own regiment, a Royal Artillery company, and one from the Royal Engineers; these regulars were augmented by a mixed force of trained and experienced colonial mounted infantry and police, and a town militia. With De Beers itself raising and arming about 3000 irregulars, the town rapidly mustered over 4000 men under arms. While the Cape government again dawdled over a defence commitment here, Kekewich knew very well that time was running out. In the days immediately preceding the arrival of besieging Boers he had pegged out a line of field fortifications around the town, arranged artillery around vital spots, like the water reservoir, and worked out where reserves were most likely to be needed to seal gaps sliced by any republican breakthrough. Largely due to Kekewich's initiatives, the Kimberley force did not stand around to await the arrival of the enemy. Morale was fairly high, and early on cavalry and infantry raiding parties made an intrepid effort to topple several enemy bridgeheads being planted ahead of a strike. They were efficient in creating some obstruction, but after losses they had to fall back from ground controlled by the converging republicans.

The keys to Kimberley were also what increased its defensibility; aside from levies of armed men and the capacity to draft supplies of non-combatant labour, De Beers' jutting mine dumps (up to 70 feet high) became fortified vantage points, while the mining industry provided barbed wire for fencing (hard on horses, to say nothing of their unseated riders), ample telephone connections for perimeter look-outs, engineering floorspace, machinery and skilled labour for diversion to the production of armaments and armour, searchlights to keep any creeping Boers blinking, and deep mine tunnels as shelter from bombardment for white women and children.

This was not all. 'It is hardly an exaggeration,' concluded *The Times*, 'to say that Kimberley is De Beers and De Beers Mr. Rhodes, so huge is the property and wealth of the company and so great the power exercised over it by Mr. Rhodes.'[20] Inevitably, then, the mines also supplied their omnipresent master. A man who had made his pile by making serious war on the capitalist monopoly front, he now turned his vaulting ambition to influence and command in military dealings. Here, Rhodes laid out his claim to a big say in the conduct of Kimberley's defence in a way he knew best. By provisioning and providing a large company of irregulars, supplying rifles, and extracting ammunition from mine workshops, as the embodiment of De Beers he was effectively financing siege defences from his own pocket. Contemptuous of the garrison commander, Rhodes constantly rowed with Kekewich over needs and tactics, second-guessing his orders, making independent preparations, and otherwise meddling to try to influence the running of defence operations. If garrison commanders or, for that matter, the British Cabinet could not be bought or dragooned, they could at least be shouted into listening to the Rhodes line on the Kimberley siege. For Kekewich the problems of the Boers outside were probably little worse than the travails of an interfering Rhodes inside. As one historian has suggested, 'If one of the main objectives of the Boers was the capture of Rhodes, there must have been numerous occasions during the four-month siege when the garrison commander would have been glad to hand him over to their tender mercies.'[21]

The Rhodes line emerged in the first few weeks of the Kimberley investment, and was to do the rounds for the rest of the siege: that there were 'hordes' or 'legions' or 'swarms' of Orange Free State Boers massing to storm the town, that pressure was mounting rapidly, that things were perilously close to breaking-point, and that the fall of Kimberley was imminent. On 16 October he commenced what would become a bombardment of urgent requests to highly placed contacts like Milner and Lord Rothschild, pleading for the immediate despatch of relief forces to avert 'a terrible disaster', even a 'catastrophe'. A shrill demand was that no British offensive against the republics could even be contemplated before Kimberley was saved. Clearly, its capitulation would settle the entire future of the British expedition against the Boers.

This ran counter to Kekewich's grasp of things, which was that the position was not absolutely critical. Rhodes therefore did not disclose the sending of these telegraphic alarms, and it was only when an African despatch runner brought a query from British general staff that the garrison commander discovered that he was near to surrender. Kekewich was stunned. Hereafter, relations with Rhodes became somewhat tense, and were only to worsen through the coming months. Unfortunately for imperial command, Rhodes could not be quietened. After Kimberley's southwards telegraph line was cut on 14 October, and the garrison had to resort to heliograph transmission to a watchdog station further down the line, Rhodes simply had his own heliograph equipment constructed in De Beers' workshops. He had no intention of complying with censorship provisions, of double-checking with military authorities, and least of all of having to await a turn on the official mirror. Observers began to report that the frequency of Rhodes' communications soon exceeded those of the garrison, many of them directed at an already cultivated British press which was taken with the imperial allure of Rhodes and was ready to create a heroic Victorian siege persona. Here was a bold and independent figure, once again identifying the need of empire as his need and acting with singular energy and resolve to deal with its military crisis. While recognizing the degree to which Rhodes was using his personal influence and power to ensure that Kimberley would not be lost, some of his more astringent critics hinted that the De Beers heliograph was also being used for the usual cost–benefit analysis. There was something to this. Rhodes did not sacrifice share dealing and capital commitments when Wessels arrived, and even managed to scoop up a small independent Kimberley mine during the siege.

As Rhodes maintained his personal grip, the 4800 Orange Free State commandos around Kimberley maintained their strategic grip. Steyn had judged a force of this size sufficient to overrun Kimberley, or at least to mount a siege of such concentration as to make its defensive position untenable. Further to strengthen the assault, with the support of Kruger he urged Cronjé's War Council to despatch Transvaal troops to supplement his ranks; de la Rey and his commandos were then sent southwards from the Vryburg district on 17 October to provide Wessels with additional weight. Being not far away himself, the Orange Free State president set out for Kimberley on 23 October, believing that such personal showings at the front would boost morale and raise levels of patriotism; a politician with the right patter and an imagination, Steyn needed the aid of no pollsters to know his good rating on the lines. Apart from inspecting Boer positions and meeting ordinary burghers for expressions of personal solicitude and encouragement, he attended field briefings and discussed attack preparations and other war planning with officers.

The republican President was not the kind of political leader who had little to do with war other than to authorize the mobilization of men and approve expenditure. Steyn took the Kimberley action very seriously, and assiduously outlined his understanding of what would follow its success. With the town secured, enlarged Orange Free State and Transvaal forces would maintain their combined strength in the area. One part would stand on the defensive, protecting the southern border of the Republic, while another would clip across the Orange River near Hope Town and push hard into the northern Cape Colony. Here, Steyn confidently anticipated, large numbers of republican loyalists would rise in rebellion and throw in their lot with the invaders.

The offensive might perhaps have taken this shape had republican command in Griqualand West opted for really heavy attacks to breach Kimberley defences and storm through. Instead, the siege was allowed to grind forward dismally to no very obvious territorial purpose. Early in November Wessels decided that he could destroy Kimberley without risking his troops by resorting to strong and sustained bombardment. Hesitating, he signalled his intention of delivering this fatal stroke. A general not lacking in a strong personal sense of moral decency and honour, his surrender ultimatum to Kekewich allowed a period of grace in the event of its rejection for the evacuation of all women and children before the commencement of shelling. It was 'civilized' war and a bit more: a shrewd psychological tactic to sap male nerves.

Wessels also produced an astute deal providing relief for 'any Africanders' who wished to leave Kimberley for the safety beyond Boer lines. In this political game, Kekewich and Rhodes were willing accomplices in duplicity. So as not to undermine morale, they buried Wessels' offer of general security for those traditionally most at risk under fire, and only posted the offer to receive anxious Boer families. Few of these budged: they were nervous about what could be seen as a declaration of republican allegiance, or were worried about dispossession of property in reprisal under martial law conditions or the likelihoood of hostile social isolation when they returned to resume life in Kimberley.

When heavy Creusot shell did begin to rain down there was considerable fear and panic, as brief but intense bombardments threatened not only key sites such as the mines and water reservoir works, but several other parts of the town, killing or wounding a small trickle of white and black civilians. But relatively little fell apart under concentrated bombardment or intermittent stray shelling, much of which just spent itself. Kimberley was not short of men with respectable military engineering talent or of conscriptable African labour; and fortified tunnels, sandbagged bunkers, and thick earth cushioning provided by shelters dug into mine dumps were proof against even heavy 100lb shells. While this helped to minimize white casualties, even exposed black inhabitants were largely untouched by random artillery strikes. If heavy gunfire was meant to suppress Kimberley's defences and soften things up so that it could be seized at low cost to the Boers, it was to be a conspicuous failure. As with their other misguided and drifting investments of garrison towns, what the Kimberley republicans lacked as much as anything were the banks of heavy artillery and reserve shell supply necessary to resolve stubborn sieges successfully. So the Kimberley action turned into another familiar story of stalemate, a low-intensity affair with republican forces seemingly unable to do much more than trade artillery fire with the defending garrison, give as good as they got in turning mounted sorties against enemy redoubts, and lubricate their food supply system through sporadic cattle raiding and the seizure of other agricultural produce from their surrounding supply area. As a point of assault, all Kimberley really did was to hobble a planned republican war of movement in the west.

At the same time, the corrosive impact of Boer investment was considerably diminished by the ability of garrison authority to shield the dominant political community from some of its most deleterious effects. Here, as elsewhere, there was no acceptance of any 'equality of sacrifice', or any attempt by the authorities to enforce 'fair shares' to sustain and protect whole populations. In Kimberley, supply and distributive problems were nicely resolved by displacing much of the routine deprivation and danger of siege life onto blacks. This meant, for example, that when control of De Beers' ample fresh food reserves was taken over by military command, the focus of official provisioning became white inhabitants; while scurvy was deflected here, it soon engulfed the compounds of African mine labourers, adding to the death toll from typhoid and dysentery. Of some 1500 Kimberley deaths during the course of the siege almost all were black, and a good number of these were children. The Africans were supposedly mellow about all this, their behaviour 'throughout the siege was very good; they were quiet and orderly and there was little grumbling'.[22]

Republican generalship's insistence on keeping men and materials committed to these clearly unproductive siege offensives has prompted a number of historians to account for their failure in terms of customary Boer tactical mentality or 'natural' mobile combat instincts. It is the immobility which was remarkable. Traditionalist military culture and a shallow disciplinary reach did not raise commandos to conduct fixed siege operations; on the contrary, a loss of flexible mobility in the field stifled innovation, spontaneity, and fighting conviction. Typically, therefore, Pakenham has stressed 'the first principle of Boer tactics' to have been 'mobility above all'.[23] In the main, the conduct of all of these fixed-position engagements was of a sort from which one can reasonably generalize in this way about the Boer mode of warfare, fashioned by a direct heritage of roaming pastoralism and flurried frontier or land wars.

Yet the practice of besieging the enemy until its resistance broke was hardly novel for Boer command. In the mid-nineteenth-century Transvaal, resisting Ndebele had been readily put to siege by commandos. In the 1870s some of the Mafeking Baralong had defied encircling Boer forces for a stupefying two years; the 1899 siege of Mafeking amounted to their sixth experience of being walled in by battering commandos. Indeed, in the previous year Joubert had used heavy artillery against African foes who had gone to ground, blasting away the only obstacles – those provided by nature – in order to tighten the noose. The problem for the republicans was more that the present sieges were a different story. Town garrisons with reserves, firepower, coordination, and more modern defensive technologies proved a far harder nut to crack; the Boers had artillery, but not enough to hand for continuous massive bombardment. On the other hand, any attempt to overwhelm the enemy by running at them in preponderant force involved an inevitable acceptance of casualties far in excess of those to which Boer forces were accustomed. If the attack approach of Joubert, Cronjé, and Wessels was exceptionally careful and cautious, this was probably due at least in part to a sense that they had to go carefully with their men.

While they obviously enjoyed a numerical advantage in the opening offensive, Boer reserves were not abundant, and little thought seems to have been given to the contingency that at some point the British might arrive as a relieving army. In such a case the want of numbers to repel the advancing forces would be bound to tell. Furthermore, this time, unlike colonial siege operations of the 1840s and 1850s, there was no straightforward battering-ram tactic to wrap things up. Previously, breaking the back of resisting Africans who had bunkered themselves into defensive mountain strongholds had been brutally simple. Commandos, sometimes with the assistance of African allies, would either blast in the roofs of caves, block off water supply, or touch off engulfing wood fires across cave fronts to suffocate those besieged.[24]

Still, the republicans' strategic siege problems did not mean that they were unable to advance fairly easily where British defensive lines were appreciably thin and hopelessly stretched. At the end of October, Steyn abandoned tact in respect of the quivering Cape Colony, bringing to an end the moderate and conciliatory hopes of its W. P. Schreiner administration that it might be able to duck a colonial combat involvement. On 1 November Orange Free State commandos crossed the Orange River and, confident in the knowledge that they had farms and stockpiles to draw on and local rebels to recruit, the eagerly advancing forces overran rural frontier districts, driving both eastwards and westwards. They achieved immediate success. Able to count on only a small minority of white colonial loyalists, the magistrates turned to the willing help of anxious African and Coloured citizen volunteers to try to defend their villages and tiny towns, and held their breath. Confronting superior combined invasion forces, well-armed and amply provisioned, novice local militia and scratch guards with little training and less depth could barely do anything more than exchange a few blows before giving up the unequal exchanges.

During November Steyn's army, with strong collaboration from insurrectionary Cape Boers dreaming of the juicy patronage of republicanism, took places like Aliwal North, Dordrecht, Albert, Colesberg, and Barkly East as it cut a swathe through the east; to the west, the Boers ran through Vryburg, and later Kenhardt, Prieska, and Gordonia, virtually at leisure. This wedge, driven in from the Orange Free State and with a rear reserve line, established a threatening strategic perimeter for the Boers, extending gains across a pocket of eastern and central or midlands localities. The occupation of Colesberg by the combined Transvaal and Orange Free State commandos of Schoeman and Grobler actually took them to within striking distance of the important Naauwpoort railway junction, as they assembled just 35 miles to the north; in Burghersdorp, a force under Du Plooy and Swanepoel had the potential to do something other than rest and routinely plunder local black inhabitants. Positioned only 40 miles southwest of an Aliwal North rearguard, they were set for a joint disruption of British communications by attacking the main coastal rail line to East London.

The speed of such mounted breakthroughs surprised and alarmed even usually edgy British observers. In these areas, invading Boers now had a fairly solid base, not stiff enough to give them meaningful control over the edges of their boundaries of occupation, but enough to lay further claims and to look increasingly scary. In the view of some commandants, as imperial and colonial forces in the Cape might have to be reduced or pulled out altogether to reinforce relief actions in more urgent siege theatres of operation, they could continue to take villages and other minor settlements with decreasing potential resistance from Cape Mounted Riflemen and Cape Police contingents. While Buller was compelling queasy Cape authorities to mobilize 4000 African Field Force levies to hold the borders of eastern Mfengu and Thembu districts, all this meant was that Boer forces would think twice before going to the Transkeian Territories to run off livestock, grain, and forage.[25] With control of key rail points in the central Cape midlands, and an accumulating rebel colonial reserve, commandos could form an offensive line running west from Barkly East to Gordonia, secure from any British flanking attack or counter-offensive from the rear. The route to Cape Town, Port Elizabeth, and East London then lay open: at least, that was how some more optimistic spirits in the field saw matters evolving.

Consolidating captured ground was obviously crucial to all of this. In this respect, while the Boers were not usually famous for being like-minded, like-willed, and obediently disciplined, they moved pretty sharply to coordinate their linked occupational authority into a form of rough and rolling republican conquest regime. Geopolitically, as in Natal, occupied districts were formally annexed as republican territory. Northern Boer command created a new administrative structure which rewarded southern Cape rebels for their military, political, protein, horse, and grazing subsidy of the invasion by lifting them into upstart positions of official authority as district veldkornets and *landdrosts*, or magistrates. In effect, invasion forces and their local collaborators suspended Cape Colony sovereignty in an ambitious sweep to 'republicanize' British territory through armed encroachment. If Cape Boer rebels welcomed an instant, fictional, Orange Free State territorial legitimacy, settler loyalists and black citizens bonded to a subject sense of imperial Britishness were affronted by misrule. In annexed republican districts, customary colonial domination through wage dependence, clientage, other social lubricants, or the rhetoric of common British rights gave way to fierce sanctions as occupying Boers indulged in various exhibitions of new oppressive power. As studies of wartime black experience have emphasized, new 'Boer' pass controls were rigorously enforced, labour was forcibly commandeered to service commandos and to work on friendly supplying farms, standing labour disputes were resolved through a brusque tightening of social discipline, tribute was exacted, and better-off blacks were dispossessed of rights, both propertied and petty.[26]

To be sure, the Boers did not permit themselves much discretionary choice over the conduct and terms of occupation; there were no obvious friendly gestures towards any classes of black society calculated to yield a deferential return. This left an immediate need to make the meaning of conquest tell, through tough and showy exhibitions of authority and power which simply made tenants and workers intensely resentful of the abrupt and unwanted change of masters. What might have remained sullen acquiescence or neutrality in these frontier areas became simmering hostility which would soon begin to take its own mounting toll on the republican camp. At the same time, while rising black resistance to commando incursions was the outcome of the irreconcilable conduct of the Cape campaign, it was equally also the product of the established white supremacist doctrine of Boer populism and the repeated desire to assert what commandants habitually termed Republican Native Law across the Orange River.

In other respects, even though the frontier districts invasion had failed to trigger a large-scale Boer colonial rising, the republicans had exploited the political ecology of small urban enclaves in the Cape countryside, and had created distracting problems for the British through isolation and capture of pockets of territory and a bearing down upon dispersed sectors of their communication system. For all this, there were some oddly neglectful things. Amidst the excitement at the symbolic stroke of Boer armies crossing the Orange River, no move was aimed at seizing the strategically important railway bridge on the Orange. And, more generally, while the chances of reeling in active Boer support were reasonable in the Cape while comparatively negligible in Natal, the southern campaign commitment remained fairly limited.

By the last week of November the pattern of the opening offensive was set. The degree to which imperial command had misjudged the level of reinforcements required to ward off an early republican strike, and the time it took for the British to get things going locally, ensured that Boer leadership could exploit the edge of temporary superiority without having to test the issue in major battle. In Natal, British garrison power had been knocked back and immobilized. To the west, attack against border garrisons had sealed them off, obliging them to dig in, while other cantering incursions chipped away at the British position, opening a menacing frontier gap between ground ceded and a British colonial rump which still had fairly little by way of defensive depth. But then the republican impetus started to run down. Seemingly left hanging in the air, Boer forces turned towards a defensive stance as their forward thrusts began to ebb. With a British counter-offensive already beginning to darken the picture, it seemed there would be no easy resolution: a suspicion which would indeed prove to be true, and not only for the Boers.

Whatever had been accomplished, the advance was obviously not enough to create conditions for the war to be ended speedily, and on reasonable bargaining terms. For Leyds and other Transvaal diplomats there was no crushing blow to emulate 1881, upon which the Boers could have tried to exploit their military successes politically by, say, recalling Milner to to open peace negotiations. For many republicans and their sympathizers in the Cape and abroad this could have settled the war fairly, and could also have finally cleared South Africa of future Anglo-Boer quarrels.

Interesting as they may be, these speculations are less important for historians of the war than the associated question of where the republicans went, and where they might have gone. One view is that the Boer war plan 'was achieved. With three main towns invested, the British would now have to try to relieve them.' This meant having to tackle the Boers 'where they had all the advantages, in prepared positions, held in strength but which they could abandon when they wanted and operate as guerrillas against the more stereotyped British'.[27] Unlike the Zulu, the Boers were less compelled by the economic strains of mobilization to seek out decisive early frontal battles. Or, taking another tack, despite letting opportunities slip, 'the Boers had achieved their first strategic aim: to seal off all the garrisons'. With that accomplished on 'all three fronts, it was time for the second strategic aim: to dig in and block the advance of Buller's forces. If they could hold them off, it should be possible to starve the three beleaguered towns into submission.'[28] These actions represented soft gains, for which a low price would be paid.

Against this, there is what is perhaps best termed a might-have-been argument or proposition. Here, several factors are of particular relevance. While the war crisis pushed the Boer states together, it took Steyn too long to get proper mobilization going. With both republics having to mark time to synchronize their joint operations, the mobilization timetable only came into effect in the Transvaal on 28 September, and in the Orange Free State on 2 October. Had the threat of war been accepted to mean the commencement of war for all practical puposes, the Boer time advantage would have been that much greater, and the first imperial reinforcements would not have been disembarking in Durban before the October ultimatum.

A second inference, already touched on in passing, is that by grounding so much of their campaign in 'coalescing around Mafeking, Kimberley and Ladysmith, the Boers lost their best opportunity of avoiding ultimate defeat'.[29] By immobilizing their forces, a desultory siege movement proved to be a trap for the besiegers. Poorly led and lethargically conducted, the wrong engagements sapped offensive spirit and doomed the hope of a successful short war. If anything, the grizzly, ageing generals in charge of these essentially futile operations behaved as if the republics wanted a long one.

This deepened division and acrimony within the Boer officer corps. From the outset questions had been asked about the ability and vision of high command to run the offensive. The stalled pace of that offensive did much to strengthen ongoing doubts about the competence of a supreme command consisting of elderly and dilatory men like Cronjé or Joubert. Criticism was partly generational: able, ambitious, and impatient younger commanders such as Koos de la Rey, Christiaan de Wet, or Louis Botha were contemptuous of those they considered arthritic amateurs. It was also social and political: those with the drive and faith to renew momentum lacked the authority to pull things off, because older military notables had the prerogatives of patriarchal seniority to block them from power in the field. High command rested in the hands of those who owed their position less to ability than to favouritism, factional twists, or fawning personal services for the Transvaal President and his clique. Lastly, among the small but restive urban 'educated Africander' soldiery, lawyers, teachers, ordinary state officials, beneficiaries of European travel, and the like, there was a bemoaning of the failings of a rump of 'country' or 'bush' Boer generals who were too pre-modern to ensure success. Inflexible, obstinate, and ignorant of anything other than hugging the ground and holding defensive positions, they were incapable of addressing fundamental campaign problems.[30]

One of these, leaving aside the bottleneck of delayed mobilization, was the imposing level of order demanded by the strategic plan of a two-front war. This assumed that the republics would not gain enough if they fought at full campaigning strength on a single front. Smuts was not wrong about this. But a combined two-front attack required that more time be spent on detail, precision planning of a pattern of aggressive operations, and the machinery for centralized command to ensure effective coordination between Boer generals. Those in charge were not brilliant at unity of command. By most accounts rather slow to tell one another what was going on, Cronjé and Joubert were isolated, indecisive, and unable to organize their strength in such a way as to take decisive advantage of opportunities, such as the ease with which their forces were being provisioned on the Natal southern front.[31] Thus, if Boer forces were increasingly under-extended in their Mafeking and Kimberley operations, commandos were not transferred quickly to maximize force against Natal. For that matter, given the promise of the Cape as a theatre of operations because of its republican loyalist support base, the effort here was too small-scale and sporadic to make a really deep hole. Commandos ended up staying, rather than pressing forward to positions from which it would be more difficult for them to be knocked back.

It more or less goes without saying that want of numbers was an obvious hindrance; while thousands were sent to be locked out of Mafeking and Kimberley, only about 2000 men were available on the western border of the Orange Free State for forward deployment. On this last point, Lord Carver's suggestive comment on the misdirection of republican strategy is forceful. The inevitable conclusion is that the Boers allowed themselves to become too hypnotized by sieges, by the reclamation of the spiritual lower plateau of Natal, by the harvesting of Durban, and by the triumph of an artery to the sea. Had more weight been added to the western front, the unleashing of between 30,000 and 40,000 well-prepared riflemen into the Cape Colony might conceivably 'have radically altered the course of the war'.[32] As things stood now, that course was set for a British counter-offensive. It would go to Natal.

Chapter 3 Notes

1. J. H. Breytenbach, *Die Geskiedenis van die Tweede Vryheidsoorlog in Suid Afrika, 1899–1902*, vol. 1 (Pretoria, 1969), pp. 387–90.
2. John Lambert, *Betrayed Trust: Africans and the State in Colonial Natal* (Pietermaritzburg, 1995), p. 160.

112 The South African War 1899–1902

3. *Cape Argus*, 6 Nov. 1899.

4. Gordon Blaxland, *The Middlesex Regiment* (London, 1977), p. 55.

5. *The War Memoirs of Commandant Ludwig Krause 1899–1900*, ed. Jerold Taitz (Cape Town, 1996), p. 21.

6. Robert Scales, 'Artillery in small wars: the evolution of British artillery doctrine, 1860–1914', Ph.D. diss. (Duke University, 1976), p. 219.

7. Krause, *War Memoirs*, p. 21.

8. John Keegan and Andrew Wheatcroft, *Who's Who in Military History* (London, 1996 edn), p. 106.

9. Leo Cooper, *British Regular Cavalry 1644–1914* (London, 1965), p. 193; Geoffrey Powell, *The Green Howards* (London, 1968), p. 72.

10. *Popular Imperialism and the Military 1850–1950*, ed. John Mackenzie (Manchester, 1992), p. 20.

11. John Laffin, *Scotland the Brave: The Story of the Scottish Soldier* (London, 1963), pp. 36–7.

12. Krause, *War Memoirs*, p. 31; Pretorius, 'Afrikaner nationalism and the burgher on commando', Rethinking the SA War Conference paper, UNISA, 1998.

13. Johannes Meintjies, *The Anglo-Boer War 1899–1902* (Cape Town, 1976), p. 45.

14. Peter Warwick, *Black People and the South African War, 1899–1902* (Cambridge, 1983), p. 131.

15. Krause, *War Memoirs*, p. 31.

16. Michael Langley, *The East Surrey Regiment* (London, 1976), p. 47.

17. Brian Willan, 'The Siege of Mafeking', in *The South African War: The Anglo-Boer War 1899–1902*, ed. Peter Warwick, (London, 1980), p. 141.

18. Edward Ross, *Diary of the Siege of Mafeking, October 1899 to May 1900*, ed. Willan (Cape Town, 1980), p. 50.

19. Quoted in Raymond Sibbald, *The War Correspondents: The Boer War* (London, 1993), pp. 144–5.

20. Ibid., p. 117.

21. Ibid., p. 114.

22. *South African News*, 26 Feb. 1900.

23. Thomas Pakenham, 'The Anglo-Boer War, 1899–1902', in *An Illustrated History of South Africa*, eds S. B. Spies and Trewella Cameron (Johannesburg, 1986), p. 204.

24. Isabel Hofmeyr, *We Spend our Years as a Tale that is Told: Oral Historical Narrative in a South African Chiefdom* (Johannesburg, 1993), pp. 109–11.

25. Warwick, *Black People*, p. 116.

26. Bill Nasson, *Abraham Esau's War: A Black South African War in the Cape, 1899–1902* (Cambridge, 1991), pp. 113–17.

27. Alan Barker, *Battle Honours of the British and Commonwealth Armies* (London, 1986), pp. 92–3.

28. C. J. Barnard, *Generaal Louis Botha op die Natalse Front, 1899–1900* (Kaapstad, 1970), pp. 29–30.

29. Howard Bailes, 'Military aspects of the war', in *The South African War: The Anglo-Boer War 1899–1902*, ed. Peter Warwick (London, 1980), p. 72.

30. *Jan Smuts: Memoirs of the Boer War*, eds Gail Nattrass and S. B. Spies (Johannesburg, 1994), p. 69; Johan van Loggerenberg, 'Schalk Willem Burger as Boeregeneraal', *Historia*, 37/1 (1992), p. 43.

31. Pretorius, 'Die Voorsiening van Lewensmiddele aan die Boerkommando's in die Anglo-Boereoorlog, 1899–1902', *Historia*, 35/2 (1990), p. 100.

32. Field Marshal Lord Carver, *The Seven Ages of the British Army* (London, 1984), p. 150.

4

The First British Offensive

During the first weeks of the war, correspondents to pro-imperial newspapers in Natal and the Cape gradually tempered their boasting. The republican advance implied that things were less than 'perfect' for the British position, declared a writer to the *Umtata Herald*, while another concluded that insufficient heed had been taken earlier in the 1890s of the alarming increase in the power of 'Boer militarism'. Instead of time having been wasted on who was to be given the benefit of the doubt over the Jameson Raid mess, Britain should already have moved decisively there and then to put the 'emboldened' Boers out of business. From Durban, a *Natal Witness* correspondent queried the reliability of journalists who had been scornful of republican capabilities, and were now having to report the 'dangerous' and 'injurious' gains of the Boer forces. Anti-imperial reaction is well illustrated by an awareness in *Ons Land* and *Het Zuid-Oosten* of immediate vindication of a 'just' war by the victims of calculated aggression. One reader reminded others of F. W. Reitz's rousing 1899 Manifesto to the Orange Free State burghers, calling for exertions to make 'a great day', its success affirmed by certainty that 'the God of our Fathers will be with us in our struggles'. Not all resorted to a religious vocabulary to link republican war achievement to fundamentalist Protestant doctrine. Some colonial Boers merely expressed a mild optimism that British 'difficulties' would help along a compromise peace, without victors or vanquished, on 'honourable' terms; with Britain now facing calamity in Ladysmith or Mafeking, the war was surely unlikely to be prolonged.[1]

Within British territory, this combination of loyalist settler unease and knowing republicanist satisfaction did not represent any crisis of civilian morale, in the sense that we would understand the significance of that factor (and its influence upon army morale) in a context of 'total war'. In all, it was too spasmodic and too diffuse; moreover, if General Sir George White was short of victory, colonists in Cape Town and Durban were not short of food. Here, the real effect of the republican strike was an unsettling of more confident opinion. While there was continuing anticipation of a short war and decisive British victory, it had become clear that if matters were not to be too prolonged, far more would have to be provided. The British would have to dislodge the occupying enemy from colonial territory and then carry the republics.

Given the balance at the outset, it was not altogether surprising that the war should have gone badly for the British; the Boers had the troops, the equipment, the field intelligence, the mobility, and the armaments to shake their enemy hard. Britain now moved to recover its position against the background of a still-pervasive fighting mentality whose simplicity has been sketched by many writers on this war. In essence, to quote one historian, its basis was an indefatigable sense of unreality or of illusory beliefs, 'the Boers with their memories of Majuba, the British because they refused to admit that a handful of farmers could withstand large numbers of regular troops accustomed to victory'.[2] It was no less illusory to suppose that the British had a properly planned offensive strategy. As the 1904 Royal Commission on the War would go on to note, while Britain had an agreed 'line of advance', its expeditionary force lacked the guidance of a formulated 'plan of operations' upon which to base detailed campaign organization or an envisaged sequence of battle. The lack of effective central coordination and planning was not helped by some fairly surreal behaviour by senior figures in London. Wolseley, of course, was in direct personal confrontation with the unsmiling and supercilious regime of Lansdowne, a Cabinet superior he damned as a 'cock sparrow of a Jewish type'.[3] What Lansdowne in turn thought of his military subordinate is not so candidly recorded, although as Wolseley was rumoured to have had a lowly social pedigree, he is unlikely to have been outdone in bigotry. It was the singular achievement of these squabbling imperial warlords to hamper the development and application of strategic thinking from the centre.

The cause of that difficulty was simple: deliberate procrastination or spiteful deception. Lansdowne's response to the competing mid-1899 claims from Wolseley for 50,000 troops to defeat the Boers and

Hicks-Beach's tight-fisted insistence on maintaining a 'Gladstonian' Treasury was thus to be ostentatiously busy with other matters, and then to select August as a handy time to go off on holiday to his ample Irish estates. Having little but contempt for the bureaucratic authority exercised by despised War Office 'clerks', Wolseley's riposte was to economize on his urgent minutes to Lansdowne about the South African military situation, leaving out the increasingly detailed field information at his disposal from some accurate and sobering intelligence assessments. If these critical calculations did eventually reach Lansdowne, it was through the novel channel of Chamberlain and the Colonial Office. The effective outcome of these astonishing exchanges was that the Commander-in-Chief's prescribed 'preparation of schemes of offensive and defensive operations' failed to be enacted 'in any systematic fashion'.[4] All one had from the imperial core was Cabinet approval of a fairly loose plan of a direct expeditionary force advance to Bloemfontein through the Orange Free State, the weaker and more exposed of the Boer states. In the periphery, its only contribution was the local defence strategy for Natal and its strategic coal supplies, planned by the now deposed General Butler. The British had no clearly prepared or structured offensive beyond a vague grasp that their forces would have to be deployed forward for a conquest of the Boer republics. 'We would advance until there were no longer any Boers in sight, and then pass through all such openings' was the sarcastic recollection of one West Yorkshire Regiment officer.[5]

As already noted in an earlier chapter, what first bit a chunk out of a nominal British 'interior strategy' was White's defensive predicament in Natal. The idea of lancing Steyn's republic with a western offensive which would at the same time cauterize Natal was discarded; it was too late to assist White to repel an invasion by easing pressure in the east. Arriving in Cape Town on 31 October, Buller had just over a week in which to fix upon a strategy and get a move on. His original proposal had been devised on the basis of intelligence estimates and War Office thinking during 1896 and 1897. These had envisaged a 'main line' of advance running west of the Drakensberg, based on the Cape Colony and steering well clear of any potentially dangerous entanglements in the tricky mountainous terrain up the Natal route to the Transvaal. Buller knew enough about South Africa to appreciate which ground would be easiest to traverse. That was to be found by ensuring that the hub of an offensive rolled along the rail line through Bloemfontein to Johannesburg and Pretoria; the open plains of the highveld would provide a good road for marching

British forces and their large flow of supplies. But, for the Army Corps, central strategy was now superseded by a decision to salvage Natal. Much of November was spent preparing for the Buller offensive, pushing troops into position, attending to transport and provisioning needs for various fronts, recruiting Africans to service army field requirements, and awaiting the arrival of further reinforcements, not merely from Britain but also from Canada, Australia, and New Zealand.

The most pressing problem confronting the British had obviously been a shortage of troops in the operational theatre; with an Army Corps numbering 47,000 and rising this difficulty was being eased. Asserting a bluff mastery over the developing situation, Buller divided his assembled forces. With 20,000 soldiers, Lieutenant-General Lord Methuen was to retrieve things to the west, carrying an assault along the western railway to relieve Kimberley, and thereafter opening a straight line of advance into the Orange Free State, crushing the enemy's northern districts. Lieutenant-General Sir William Gatacre and French were to stage a counter-offensive in the Cape Colony, putting an end to the Orange Free State invasion by descending on commandos in the midlands, around Colesberg, Stormberg, and Naauwpoort, and by clearing the upper interior route to East London.

Buller took upon himself the crucial responsibility for getting the Natal menace out of the way, committing to this more than half of his Army Corps. Given that there was probably little room for second thoughts by November, there was no obvious flaw in Buller's strategical thinking, or nothing 'intrinsically misguided', to quote a modern military historian.[6] For all that, there is something wayward and brittle about Natal and Buller which captures the early aura of calling and destiny around the advancing imperial enterprise. White's commanders, Lieutenant-General Sir Francis Clery and Major-General Neville Lyttelton, were unsentimental about an unlucky superior whose authority seemed to have been reduced to a plaintive heliograph from Ladysmith. With others, they implored Buller as South African Commander-in-Chief to move swiftly to turn the Boers out of Natal and win the war from there.

From London, an appalled Wolseley denounced White and his 'little army' for an 'ignorance of strategy' which had proved disastrous for 'all the scheme of this war'; put into retreat more by his own feeble tactics than by the Boers, his consequent precariousness had made it obligatory 'that we have to relieve him'.[7] As for Buller, he was rather fond of Natal, familiar and fortunate campaigning country for a brave soldier who had won the Victoria Cross for rescuing British wounded in the 1879 Anglo-Zulu War. South Africa's 'garden' colony was in some ways a familiar cultural continuity, as inviting, bucolic, and replenishing as Buller's own Devon estate. Self-indulgent, and reputedly fond of a daily pint of champagne, the 60-year-old general resembled the empire at its most stertorian: ponderous and 'blimp-like' in appearance, he possessed 'great girth, multiple chins, flushed complexion and walrus moustache'. Attentive to the welfare of his troops, he was held in high regard by the rank and file, and is said to have inspired 'devotion'.[8]

Buller fended off strong political opposition from Milner, who wanted him to make the Cape his first order of business and not undertake a 1000-mile coastal voyage to Durban. He had a firm sense of the kind of mark which needed to be made in the context of the South African crisis. Although he had previously rarely commanded more than a couple of thousand men against virtually unarmed peasants, his considerable experience of war against colonial enemies had convinced him that a strategy of conquest directed at taking towns or capitals was often insufficient to bring hostilities to a successful conclusion. Ultimately, that could only be attained by severe methods of attrition, to eliminate or subjugate every belligerent in the field. With the major Boer forces infesting Natal, the republican war effort could be fixed and destroyed there. The British had been handed an unmissable opportunity.

One factor in all of this was that Natal was in no imminent danger of sliding any further under the republican thumb. Once in the colony, Buller himself did not exactly behave as if this were the case either, taking time in Durban and Pietermaritzburg and only ambling up to forward positions in Frere after 11 days. Joubert's commandos, meanwhile, had done little more than work their way around Ladysmith; after much strategic hesitation and delay, the Boers had ventured the barest advance southwards of the siege sector. Merely 3000 men had ridden on, with no more forthcoming. Natal's military outlook was simultaneously urgent and relatively assured.

Elsewhere, with Kimberley in his sights, on 23 November Paul Methuen commenced his advance from Orange River Station near the western border of the Orange Free State. In the glory of his first independent command, he notified Kekewich that his 1st Division field force of 8000 infantry would arrive to lift the siege within a week, bar any check at Modder River. In readiness after thorough reconnaissance, the Boers had begun to disperse their disposable troop strength in small contingents at a number of raised positions with good observation and wide fields of fire to stall the British advance. North of the Orange River near Belmont, Commandant Jacobus Prinsloo and 2000 Orange Free State commandos topped a hill position, under orders to hold off Methuen's force until Cronjé could slip down reinforcements from Mafeking. Closing up, and knowing that they were the stronger, the British decided to take the Boer position in order to remove any flanking threat to their line of communications.

In a way, Methuen prepared well. His attacking troops made their way forward under cover of darkness, their officers covering shiny buttons and sword hilts, or discarding swords, and stripping the shine off rifle butts to make themselves less conspicuous to beady eyed Boer marksmen.[9] There had already been ample indications in Natal of the threat to exposed officers in battle. A greater intermingling of appearance between officers and men was one obvious way of countering a disproportionate loss and its likely effect upon morale and effective line command.

Unfortunately for Methuen, dodgy scouting and sketchy mapping meant that the the coming of dawn caught his force at an alarming distance from the enemy position with virtually no screening. One soldier recalled a heart-stopping moment, clawing forward through a strangely 'full stillness'[10], and expecting the Boers to open up with every passing second. This came in the form of concentrated crossfire, its costs borne mainly by the Grenadier Guards. Nevertheless, overall losses were reduced by Methuen sensibly having thinned out and not massed his advancing troops; moving across the veld in open formation deflected some of the deadly force of concentrated, repelling rifle-fire, and tenacious republican resistance could not prevent the British from getting on to the slopes of their defended kopje and swarming on until it became clear that the outnumbered commandos could not sustain their defence. Before their losses mounted further the Boers slipped away from their fighting lines and fled northwards. For the British, a frontal infantry attack had done the trick in the small Battle of Belmont, but at a disagreeable cost. The losses suffered by the republicans were only a third of those sustained by Methuen, and all that Belmont represented was a delay overcome. Having pushed Boer outposts further up the railway corridor, the British then resumed their move against enemy strongpoints.

In the Boer camp, command was having to confront a price for the experience of killing and dying. Aware that Methuen's march had only been temporarily hindered, the ordinary burghers grew increasingly disenchanted with Prinsloo's command and tactics, a large number finding this sufficient cause to leg it home to check on their crops and the welfare of their families. The arrival of de la Rey with advance reinforcements and provisions despatched by Cronjé did something to raise morale and enforce more cohesion, but the sapping influence of the burghers' personal and private concerns continued to erode levels of service commitment and combat performance. With so many commandos having trickled away, all Cronjé's contingent did was to raise Prinsloo's strength to around 2000, its original size at Belmont.

On 25 November four of Methuen's infantry regiments pounced again. At Graspan, de la Rey had positioned his force along the summit of an arc of kopjes, thickly fortified with earthworks and with swift and smartly secured evacuation outlets. This position was fairly easily located and targeted by Methuen's observers. Preceded by heavy artillery bombardment of republican frontal entrenchments, which drove the enemy firing-line back from the summit, the British infantry stormed in. After a bitterly fought engagement the Boers again yielded to superior odds and fled on horseback, harried by British shelling, and dragging most of their dead and wounded along with rifles scooped up from abandoned corpses.[11] Once more Methuen prevailed; but again, it had been a costly and bloody effort, with the British casualty rate of 300 more than double that of the Boers. As victories, Belmont and Graspan were minor affairs, however fiercely fought. And by tactically abandoning their posts to regroup, the Boers were still able to elude being brought under British control.

More fighting, in greater earnest, lay almost immediately ahead. If his advance was not going quite like clockwork, Methuen was still certain of reaching Kimberley almost as scheduled, his objective now only some 25 miles away. In his calculations the last remaining defensive point of any consequence left to the Boers was Magersfontein, 12 miles southwest of the town. By then it was anticipated that the republicans would be too spent to put up any further stiff resistance. But something unforeseen happened next. With the British line of advance taking them inexorably to the Modder River, de la Rey saw a chance to exploit position and fixed upon shrewd tactics to do so.

Discarding the traditional basing of defence upon rocky kopjes because they were a vulnerable temptation to artillery attack and provided good covered space for advancing troops at their lower base, de la Rey exploited other natural defences in the terrain. He entrenched 3000 commandos along the banks of the Modder. Here, rather than use the river as a barrier ahead of his trench defences, de la Rey resolved on fronting it with well-prepared and well-concealed trench lines and a dispersed cluster of well-prepared battery positions. A dense line of vegetation aided concealment and provided cover, while the ground behind the defenders sloped down sharply to the river line, hampering enemy observation and granting strong defensive protection from British fire.

Conversely, the ground southwards between the Modder and Methuen's advancing troops was both very exposed and rising neatly, ideal for delivering the quarry to de la Rey's guns. For that, the Boers had actually watered the ground ahead of their trench line, setting down rows of marker stones in measured distances to aid the accurate adjustment of rifle sights in immediate preparation for firing; at short range, and across a flat trajectory, this camouflaged and level sweep

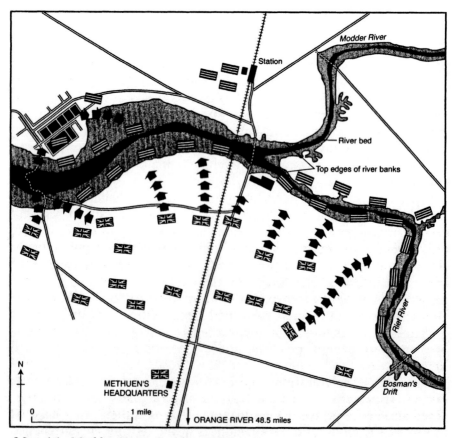

Map 4.1 *Modder River, October 1899*

of field marked a diversion from the customary republican battle tactic of firing downhill from a crest.[12] De la Rey, who was no self-sacrificing romantic, recognized that Modder River provided two crucial factors vital to sustaining the fighting efficiency of his troops. One was the strength of concealment and the known advantage of inevitable surprise as assurance of an impregnable position; the other was the knowledge that the choice of terrain made it difficult for commandos to break and run precipitately if their defences were to come unstuck. As any retreat or escape would involve fording the river, the Boers would first need to inflict sufficient casualties to make the British waver or to cause disarray, for a necessary breathing space in which to accomplish a withdrawal through the rear barrier.

Methuen set off at dawn on 28 November for the Modder, a man on the make who considerately scheduled a late breakfast for his force alongside the railway stop on the other side of the river. He had been advised by advance scouts of Boers milling around ahead, but took little notice of reported sightings, believing that the enemy were all falling back towards Magersfontein. Counting on nothing more than a rough-and-tumble skirmish with retreating Boers, Methuen ruled out the possibility that their command might have made any tactical innovations to utilize the Modder River as a defensive line. Given previous British experience, this was probably a fairly reasonable judgement. It also meant that Methuen set out in ignorance of the precise whereabouts and intentions of his hidden enemy.

The Modder River ambush, for that is what it was, pinned down the exposed British with raking volleys for the whole of 28 November, forcing virtually an entire broad front to go to ground and stay there while attempting to return fire at an unseen enemy whose smokeless powder helped to keep things that way. With little by way of defensive fire control, conditions for the attackers were horrendous, in an unrelenting engagement which cost the British dearly in blood. With voracious ants and searing temperatures adding to their misery, desperate soldiers, exhausted by heat and lengthy marching, and maddened by thirst, were cut down as they fumbled for water carts. While part of Methuen's force eventually managed to stage an assault which broke through a section of the Boer lines and crossed the river to turn on their enemy from the rear, they were beaten back in pitched battle. Here, the Boers were not to be panicked into flight, despite losses which included the death of de la Rey's own son. The Boer commander's objective had been to delay and strike a blow against Methuen's advance, and in this Modder River had been satisfactory. A 10,000-strong British force lost 500 men, with Methuen himself wounded. While de la Rey wanted to build on his strong show of force by running in further reinforcements from Cronjé, he now came up against the limits of the republican model of command by mandate. A Council of War vote directed an orderly retreat towards Magersfontein for a major stand in order to retain the Kimberley position. Methuen looked to the morning of 29 November for a renewed assault, only to find that the enemy had abandoned its position during the night. The Boers can hardly be said to have been beaten in battle, and they remained uncaught.

As Methuen's shaken army now wound its way on towards Kimberley, the travails of Buller's generals elsewhere were just about to begin. In the Cape midlands or central front, French's mounted force was brought up to seal off the Colesberg area against further Boer probing. This was to be the beginning of over three months of duelling, virtually without pause, with neither side showing any inclination to give serious battle. Numerous expeditions were sent out from field bases, but the republicans continued to overstay, leaving the British to increasing frustration and fatigue. While French was in no danger of falling, the same could not be said of Gatacre, who was now about to make a calamitous move.

In the third week of November, several days after he had established his headquarters in East London, Orange Free State commandos occupied Stormberg junction. A man of some political intelligence, Gatacre judged that the upholding of imperial face in such vulnerable districts was a vital requirement if estranged Cape Boers were to be kept in line. Pressure had to be applied, and quickly. But here, time and distance were to be the beginning of his troubles. His own force was too distant to block the republican incursion on 22 November, and French's cavalry brigades were almost 100 miles away to the west, combing the countryside around Naauwpoort. Aware that republican command could take immediate advantage of this gap to feed forces into the very heart of the exposed midlands, Gatacre moved. Arranging to have his force of 3000 troops railed to Molteno, the station closest to Stormberg, the British planned for a surprise, concerted attack on the enemy position, held by 2300 commandos under General J. H. Olivier, before the Boers could do another run. To consolidate his strength Gatacre counted on drafting in a further 500 men from an established post in the area.

This scheme required good logistics, and here problems set in immediately. No troop reinforcements were diverted to Gatacre's command because, in some tangle of confusion, his orders were never delivered. Furthermore, the trains failed to run on time, raising much anxiety that the British force might not all arrive in time to take part in the Stormberg operation. While Gatacre eventually had a full complement in Molteno, some of his soldiers, worn out after spending hours in the sun before being corralled into a train for a lumbering journey, only reached Molteno very late at night. As he planned an 8-mile night march to his target so as to launch a dawn assault, mounting delays obliged Gatacre to drive his already tired troops extremely hard.

The envisaged line of attack for the British column had been directly through the known terrain of the pass through which both the rail line and the road fed into Stormberg junction. But a report that Olivier had concentrated defenders in the pass to meet anything head-on quickly caused Gatacre to turn his force in a flanking westerly direction, pushing troops through the Kissieberg heights, a natural bastion of steep kopjes. This involved a considerably longer march over rough and broken countryside which had not been adequately reconnoitred. In a slight lapse over attention to detail, the commanding officer of the Molteno garrison was not advised of Gatacre's abrupt change of direction, thereby making sure that the British medical and supplies column rolled on grandly along the main road towards Stormberg and a hideous muddle.

On the evening of 9 December Gatacre commenced his planned descent, with a night advance by weary and cursing troops who were sorely in need of rest and refreshening. Unused to night operations, they had also badly needed some prior training, but there had been none to give. In another bizarre piece of carelessness, no scouts were dispatched to go ahead, even though there was uncertainty over the exact positioning of Boer forces on the approaches. By now this offensive was inviting grief. Something close to pantomime came next. In the dark, threading their way through a clogged terrain of rocky outcrops and confusing defiles, Gatacre's novice guides became hopelessly lost. Bafflingly, they failed to inform their commander; perhaps they thought that suicidal pretence would allow them to live to guide another day.

When dawn broke, 3000 British troops, exhausted and disorientated from a punishingly hard march on light stomachs, had indeed reached the Stormberg valley. On the map, however, this actually increased their peril, for they plainly did not know where they were. Gatacre certainly had no reliable clue, and seemed to assume that his path was taking him towards the targeted railway pass. His officers and men were sure that they had ended up just ahead of the front range of the identified heights. In fact, they were about to be caught behind them, and at a nasty disadvantage.[13] The more advanced of Boer pickets on the crest of the Kissieberg swung around in disbelief, and sounded the alarm. A bewildered Gatacre turned to face an enemy thought to be in defensive strength, and launched an attack, thrusting frantically to get battle under way at full strength. The British appeared to have no inkling at all of the real weight of republican positions along the Kissieberg; Gatacre's information about enemy numbers was about as reliable as that of their location. This position was in fact relatively lightly held; but it was formidable high ground. Even fresh, naturalized troops would have found an upward assault impossibly hard going given its steepness, pugnacious rock outcrops, and baulking precipices. It was to be neither the first nor the last occasion in this war when the run of lumpy terrain played a crucial role in determining the balance of advantage between opposing forces.

Inevitably, Gatacre's fatigued infantry largely spent themselves on the unremitting roughness of the Kissieberg, trying doggedly to scale its heights. Some managed to secure a precarious position near the summit, squeezing into crevices to prepare for a closing assault. Even this advance was to be destroyed, this time at a stroke by poor fire-control of their own supporting artillery; trying to aim against blinding sun, gunfire ripped away many troops who had found a foothold. The assault was a disaster, and within a short time the British turned tail and began to move down in demoralized retreat. With the operation in considerable disarray, Gatacre now attempted to march his dispirited force back to Molteno, only to run into more trouble. Commandos put the British under flanking fire from the west, thus squeezing their enemy from a second direction. As it was, the republicans did not press their advantage very heavily; their mounted riflemen also had other fish to fry. To Gatacre's relief, this engagement inflicted only 90 casualties, and he resumed his retreat.

If ever there was a South African War general with a knack for forgetfulness, it was William Gatacre. By all accounts, in beating a retreat he seems to have forgotten the plight of 600 of his men, still stranded on the Kissieberg slopes as the triumphant Boers converged. After hours under a blistering sun, they slunk down to surrender. Conceding that its admiration for British arms was beginning to take a few knocks, the *Cape Mercury* suggested that the 'painful' and 'shameful' 'Stormberg disaster' was indicative of a lack of proper attention to 'growing examples of proper Boer strategy'.[14] Britain's local African auxiliaries were a bit more blunt. At Queenstown remount depot a comic dance mocking the débâcle, in which General

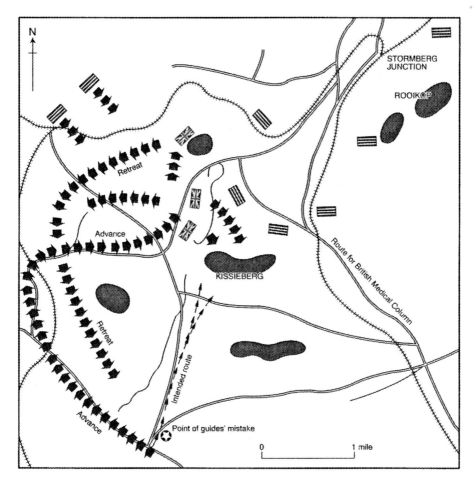

Map 4.2 *Stormberg, December 1899*

'Backacre' (as he was increasingly dubbed by his own men) was played as a cornered beast by a 'whitened-up' mule wagoner, so incensed a Rifle Brigade transport officer that he docked his mule-teers' monthly bonus.[15] Hereafter, Gatacre re-consolidated in the Queenstown area, protecting it until March 1900 without much fear of the enemy trying to take ground from him.

While Gatacre was being pursued to defeat, Methuen was enlarging his force to 13,000, confident that an offensive dominance would enable the British to take Kimberley. But Cronjé, too, was busy finding the commandos to fatten his entrenchments positioned around Magersfontein mountain. All was set for a strike. Methuen suspected that the Boer positions were reasonably strong, but he could not know exactly how strong. In planning his attack, he moved methodically. The British began with a heavy artillery pounding of the Magersfontein hills to spike republican defences, before advancing on 11 December. The standard tactic was Modder River simplicity: a brisk night march sticking straight to the course of the railway with no flanking diversions, followed by a hard dawn strike to overwhelm the enemy position.

But again, as at Modder River, the defending enemy was not stupid. As battles grew larger, they were learning tactically. Instead of bunching their forces on high ground to hold the Magersfontein summits, the Boers had opted to form a long defensive belt along the base. This was another de la Rey plan, stark and effective. Under his watchful direction, the Boers dug a substantial line of deep trenches and rear pits (as medical and supply stations), snaking across some 12 miles in a crescent formation at virtually ground-level. The ambitious length of the trench-line reduced the risk of the Boers being outflanked. In addition, its sculpted narrowness and thick internal earth cushioning provided maximum protection from British shrapnel, and helped to ensure that if a shell did fall in directly, casualties would be minimized.

A further obstacle complemented this. Commandos ran a profusion of barbed wire across the line of approach ahead of their trenches, firmly compacted into the earth, and studded with clanking tins as a trip warning. As a biting barrier against British advance this had been extremely effective at Modder River, where a Highland Light Infantry assault in poor light had been upended by a wire line, with troops in disorder trampling one another in the frantic shove to break clear. Historians have often tended to identify the use of barbed wire with the British, as a grim weapon of encircling and caging a weakening enemy in a later stage of the war; yet its earlier and defensive unpeeling should not be overlooked, not least the robust proficiency with which republican command turned wire stock-farm fencing to repel Highlanders instead of jackals.

Although the Boers had committed a force of 8500 men to Magersfontein by 11 December, an instinctively tentative Cronjé thought that De la Rey's frontal deployment was potential folly, too risky a method for making a stand. But Steyn, on another of his back-slapping tours of the republican front, gave de la Rey an overriding free hand. And luck was to be with him. The British problem was now once more to be lack of foresight, shaky coordination, and rolling confusion. Thinking that he had battered the enemy to pieces through an intense

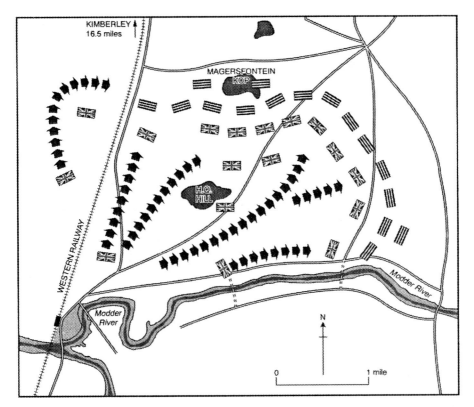

Map 4.3 *Magersfontein, December 1899*

artillery bombardment of the slopes of the main Magersfontein Hill, Methuen tried to storm this position, assigning a dawn assault to the Highland Brigade under the energetic and pushy command of Major-General Andy Wauchope. On this occasion, however, Wauchope was apprehensive ahead of a night march. There had been little basic close reconnaissance, poor weather had grounded a vital observation balloon, and his troops, clinging to guide ropes in the dark, were having to advance across a choppy sector turned to mud by a tumultuous thunderstorm. Bunched up in close formation, Wauchope's 4000 Highlanders negotiated their way to reach a forward position, about 600 yards from Magersfontein Hill, in the early dawn hours of 11 December. The exact whereabouts of the enemy were still not known.

At almost exactly the moment that the British force began to disperse from thick assembly to group fighting formation, it was enveloped by concentrated Boer rifle fire. Dying, wounded, and terrified, Wauchope's column halted in surprise and disarray before losing any meaningful sense of direction. Amidst such stumbling confusion and panic, there was little organized return of fire, nor was there consideration of how to recover or to effect a managed retreat. For the British, the consequences of misjudgement at Magersfontein were atrocious. The majority of Wauchope's kilted force clung to the base of Magersfontein all day, raked by commando fire, scoured by fierce sun, alive with ants and flies, out of cartridges, and short of water. A few small parties ripped off khaki to camouflage their kilts and crawled up to huddle on higher slopes, further imperilling themselves.[16] Estimating that the full Highland contingent had gone to ground at the foot of the heights, Methuen's rear gunners pulverized the upper slopes and summit areas with shrapnel. Doing virtually no damage to the Boer positions, their field-gun barrage shredded their own troops. And their battery support was also wasted for another reason: the sporadic igniting of powder charges well away from the Boer line deceived artillery observers about enemy positions.

During the course of the day there were a few desperate spurts towards de la Rey's trench line, but steady and accurate fire cut down attackers. One storming party did eventually prise open a gap in the republican barrier and charged through in force, with the intention of scaling Magersfontein Hill to threaten the flanks of their entrenched enemy. But as this body of some 120 troops heaved forward, they collided with none other than Cronjé himself and a detached body of commandos, short of their bearings, but alert. This confrontation quickly flared into a vicious battle in which the outnumbered and outgunned British either died or capitulated. Then, a concealed Orange Free State commando wormed out in force around the edge of the Boer entrenchments and closed in to attack the right flank of the immobilized Highlanders. Even the defence provided by remaining prostrate was now being torn away, and any remaining British cohesion was dissolved. Sensing that their line of retreat was coming under threat from a flanking assault, Wauchope's bloodied force broke into panic-stricken flight, their dark kilts a clear target for Boer marksmen, who were soon joined by gunners to press home the rout. Methuen's reluctant ordering of a full retreat amounted to little more than painful recognition of what had already been decided by his men. As it had become clear by the following day that the Boers were not planning to repeat Modder River and abandon their positions after repelling the enemy, the British had no option but to withdraw in the teeth of exceptionally stout defence. Their casualties were considerable, numbering about 1000 against Boer losses of 250. Among the dead was Wauchope himself, no more to be the beneficiary of the hefty dividends of his Scottish family coal mines.

Reined in by his own instincts as well as Buller's command, Methuen then took no further initiatives. Falling back onto the defensive, he trod water until Cronjé evacuated Magersfontein three months later. The ghastliness of Magersfontein was a tragic experience, and among the combatants there seems to have been some grasp of its significance. During a natural lull in the fighting, medical officers and stretcher-bearers were by common consent permitted to move freely and work on those wounded who were marooned on the battlefield. Wounded survivors of the British frontal assault who had been felled very close to the Boer trench line testified that commandos had yelled out promises not to fire upon any walking wounded, provided they discarded all weaponry. Finally, following the completion of Methuen's retreat to Modder River, a lenient armistice arrangement between imperial and republican forces permitted the return of some Highland infantry to retrieve their wounded and to inter their dead, a sombre and hushed assignment in which Boers, vaulting from their trenches, offered the assistance of blankets and shovels. Some observers at the time, and some later historians, have argued from evidence of such humane transactions that the nature of soldierly combat in this war was governed by levelling ethical or chivalrous manly restraints. These were such as to have upheld standards of honourable 'fellow-feeling' between adversaries, or to have expressed the moral spirit of some final nineteenth century 'gentlemen's war'.[17] Although this kind of construction might actually have been no more than illusory or specious romanticism, in the aftermath of Magersfontein there perhaps was something to the elusive vision, if only in the sense of mutual shock that this was a colonial war in which European lives were not being shielded.

As Gatacre and Methuen slumped into the ignominy of decisive defeat in the central west, Britain's eastern campaign went ahead in Natal, with Buller trying to retrieve the situation by personal intervention. Around Ladysmith, little had changed by December; the siege was rumbling on, with neither side displaying any flexibility. Buller encamped at Frere on 5 December, in very low spirits about the way the war was going. In a classic lament to Lansdowne, he conceded initiative to the republicans, declaring that they 'have had the whip hand of us ever since the war began' in obliging the British 'to attack with inferior forces their superior forces in selected positions'.[18] How Buller saw things is perhaps even better reflected in his peculiar perceptions of enemy strength. So grossly over-estimated were these that he insisted that there were a fanciful 120,000 commandos around Ladysmith when the real figure was nearer 8500 men. This was moving beyond illusion into something approaching fantasy.

On the day following Methuen's flight from Magersfontein, Buller left Frere with 18,000 troops and set out towards Ladysmith. His opponent, Louis Botha, commanding a comparatively modest commando force, anticipated that the British would again follow the direct railway-line routing to their objective, and planned to repulse an attack by building weighty trench systems in the huddle of kopjes just north of Colenso, a rising which commanded a naturally wide view. Dimly aware of the strength of this Boer position, Buller had initially decided that he would not be drawn into an encounter, and contrived an advance which would neatly bypass the waiting enemy. If things had been going well for his generals in the Cape, that would possibly have been that. But news of the Magersfontein disaster, coming hard upon the setback at Stormberg, impelled Buller to action through a direct strike against the main Boer position around Colenso. Abandoning his earlier intention to reduce the risk of over-exposure by simply holding the Boers to their Colenso lines and then marching on to Ladysmith along a westerly outflanking route, Buller now chose to force a spoiling battle at a fairly serious geographical disadvantage.

The Tugela River, running through several miles of the direct approaches to Colenso, was backed by immensely solid heights on its north bank which dominated the more navigable southern slopes. There were passable drifts, but as these fords were obvious funnels for any enemy assault, the defence grip was kept tight to spike any offensive. Behind this outer line lay a further strong reserve position, to which republican defenders could withdraw in any event of their frontal chain being snapped. This comprised a forbidding base of mushrooming kopjes and massed rocky outcrops, a sheltered backland into which commandos could fall back, dig in, and sit tight. In Buller's command there was certainly some appreciation of the terrain advantages enjoyed by the republicans along their nine-mile front, but not nearly enough to have productive planning consequences.

While Buller's straight advance may have been playing to Boer strengths, in preparing to repel the British Louis Botha also faced a few difficulties. Devastated by reports of the size of enemy British columns, hundreds of Boers lost their stomach for volunteering for a battle which looked likely to be fearsome, and left their lines for home. The experienced commandants knew something of Buller's hard-nosed earlier pursuit of war in South Africa against the Zulu, and his steely reputation made some of them jittery. A third problem was simply assembling adequate numbers of troops to hold the lengthy front required to ensure that defences could not be out-flanked. Posting commandos to hold vital high positions which were not integrated into the defensive line posed morale and discipline problems. Botha's men flatly refused to occupy any detached point which ran the risk of being encircled and toppled, and deployment to the defence of Hlangwane Hill only proceeded after threats and bul-lying, and then on the chilling basis of the drawing of lots, a method insisted upon by growling commandos.[19]

Dispensing with any attempt at secrecy in the timing of attack, on 13 December the British launched an intensive bombardment of the Boer position with an assortment of heavy field and naval guns, blast-ing enemy entrenchments and earthwork entanglements with lyddite shell. Having taken on the challenge of running at the enemy at its hardest points, Buller counted on his artillery easing a British break-through by dismembering republican defences and rolling away occu-pying commandos, by crushing or demoralizing them through intense shock. Although two days of this ensured that the defenders did not get off scot-free, the weight and depth of republican placings pro-vided ample protection against both explosive and shrapnel. If the bombardment was all but useless as an aid to the British, it proved a help to Boer preparation by clearly signalling enemy intentions of launching a major assault.

The British plan of attack was spectacularly inept, and would prove to be very costly. Buller's striking force would push forward at a slow pace over dangerously exposed ground in full daylight, attempting to fix on an enemy whose defensive density was not properly known and whose advanced positions had still to be definitely located. The main attack committed two brigades to a parallel offensive, one to mount a frontal strike against the Boers' Colenso stronghold and the other to force its way around to peck at the right rump of the republican position. This was designed to lift the British forces across the Tugela River, in order to join up and establish a commanding position. Buller easily had the troops for this, and more. At the same time, a mounted brigade was unrolled to take the upper reaches of the Hlangwane position, with the cushion of two additional brigades retained in reserve. Conscious of the power at their disposal, many of the officers of Buller's army were bristling to get at the Boers before they could resort to running away; it was all as if Colenso were some grouse moor. Such sporting bloodlust, however, was misplaced.

Right at the start, the Colenso battle brought a grim repetition of the Magersfontein disaster. Colonel C. J. Long, in command of the

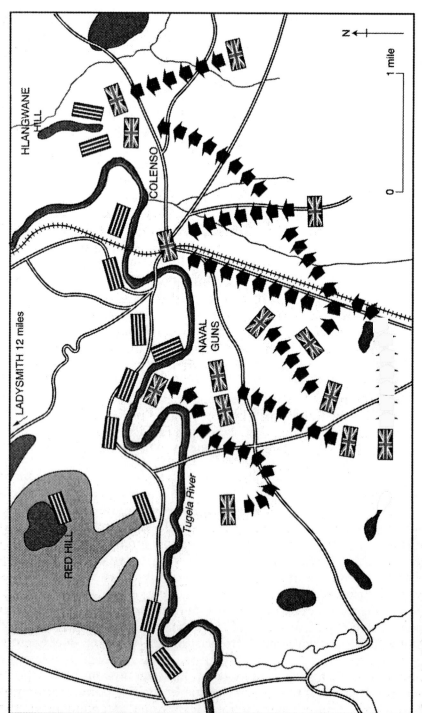

Map 4.4 *Colenso, December 1899*

artillery brigade division, had been assigned to protect the central advance with what was expected to be the customary method of shelling the enemy front from the rear of his advancing infantry. But the impetuous Long was no stick-in-the-mud traditionalist. Together with several of his more experienced officers, he had worked out an approach which had already been applied successfully elsewhere in Africa. This was to dash his guns right up to a startled peasant enemy, take up a parade-ground position and firing drill, and then blow down their assembled ranks with a steady discharge of explosive and shrapnel. Long had no authorization to experiment with this tactic at Colenso, and had not advised Buller of his intention to try an inde-pendent initiative in close-quarter gunnery.[20] Still, as this had been devastating against the Sudanese in 1898, there was no serious ques-tion against trying the tactic to break agricultural warriors here.

However, Colenso was not about to be Omdurman. On the morn-ing of 15 December, Long deliberately ran his batteries well ahead of the infantry brigade which he had been ordered to accompany on its march. After one or two perfunctory stoppages, supposedly to permit the trudging infantry to catch up, he shrugged off repeated requests to slow down and raced well ahead, quickening in pace as enemy pos-itions were spotted ahead. Long soon ended up half a mile ahead of his infantry and roughly the same distance from the bank of the Tugela. Selecting a nicely flat and open piece of land upon which to bring his guns into action, he despatched a scouting officer to survey the forward ground to make sure that it was secure and free of snipers or threatening outworks. As the position received the nod, Long galloped to the front of his batteries to direct firing operations. Magersfontein had shown that reliable reconnaissance was hard to come by in largely unknown terrain; but, fatally, Long made no allowance for prudence as a consequence.

As the British guns rolled forward, Long's exposed brigade ran into a dense wall of rifle fire and shrapnel from thickly concealed repub-lican positions 1200 yards ahead across the Tugela. Rapidly finding their range, the entrenched riflemen toppled most of the artillery officers from their horses, including Long. Their stricken gunners, unable to establish the bearings of a thoroughly hidden enemy, fired erratically and to no avail. With hundreds dead and many more wounded, the survivors withdrew to safer covered ground, abandon-ing their artillery and other equipment. Some suicidal sorties were attempted to try to retrieve the guns, but without gain. After several hours, concluding that the battle was lost, Buller called off any fur-ther attempts at rescuing his artillery, discarding the guns. These were smartly hauled off by the Boers, who crossed the Tugela and descended like vultures to grab the tempting spoils.[21]

This was not the only one-sided confrontation. The other main assaulting brigade, under Major-General Arthur Hart, made progress sufficiently slowly as to allow the republicans to plot its advance and button any charge. As Hart's troops cautiously pushed towards a ford in the Tugela, angling through a sharp curve in the river, they were suddenly mown down by heavy fire from three sides. With Hart's brigade trapped in close formation, the ambush was bloody, with the British dead and wounded mounting to over 400 within little more than 30 minutes. Halting and then breaking into scattered and barely coordinated groups, fragments of Hart's force stubbornly formed and re-formed to try to maintain their fight. It was courageous, but futile.

As Buller's reserve brigades began to be led out towards the offensive line, the realization seemed to dawn that he was walking into defeat. Stopping new troop deployment and recalling ammunition and supplies being fed to gun batteries on the bank of the Tugela, he gave up the engagement. He also had finally to relinquish the guns judged essential to blasting away the Boers around Ladysmith. Any continuation of the offensive to relieve the town appeared lost. For the British, Colenso had miscarried horrendously, with Buller's army losing some 1130 men to republican losses of 40 commandos. The *Cape Argus* was not the only paper to call it 'another Majuba' or 'a second Majuba'.[22] Faced with calamity, Buller's responses amounted to something like a declaration of bankruptcy. To a bemused Lansdowne he confessed to being 'frightened' by the 'utter collapse' of his troops, neglecting to detail the damaging route of attack he had inflicted upon them.[23] And on 16 December there was a sensational heliograph missive to the hapless White, in which Buller suggested that if Ladysmith proved unable to hold out for a further month, the garrison should expend as much of its ammunition as possible and seek 'best terms' with the enemy. This was putting it pretty low. The British Cabinet was dismayed by this blushing display of candour by heliograph. Putting it pretty high, a grumpy Lansdowne fired off a warning that the loss of White's force would be regarded as 'a national disaster of the greatest magnitude'.[24] A gloomy Buller returned to the campaign, hoping for no further follies.

Stormberg, Magersfontein, and Colenso were a high-water mark of conventional republican success in the field, in which the advancing British had been fairly easily held at bay or roundly beaten in surprise counter-attack. These 'Black Week' reversals or disasters, as they become unpopularly known in Britain, also sucked down the empire's

South African Commander-in-Chief. Militarist and patriotic sentiment was outraged by the continuation of the South African sieges
and by the humiliation of battlefield reversals inflicted on a powerful
British army by a tiny pastoralist militia. Liberals sprang to the
defence of honest but ill-used British soldiers, attacking the government for taking risks with the Boers while neglecting adequate military preparedness.[25] Stung, the War Office moved adroitly to replace
a now inglorious Buller. Natal had finished him, and his lame-duck
sacking was unavoidable. Critical historical assessments of his South
African leadership are legion, although Pakenham has made a case
for a more fair credit rating.[26] Perhaps the truth about Buller lies
somewhere between his being second-rate, and the fact that it was his
misfortune to be placed in command at a stage when no one could
really have succeeded against the Boers.

His shamelessly intriguing successor, appointed just two days after
Colenso, was Field Marshal Lord Frederick Sleigh Roberts, who had
already been badgering for some time to be given the British army's
South African command.[27] With the spartan Horatio Herbert Lord
Kitchener as Chief of Staff, Roberts had much to do, and he was
soon receiving the men to do it. In the days immediately following
Black Week the full Field Force of 47,000 troops reached South
Africa, and before the end of 1899 further divisions of 20,000 regu-
lars and 20,000 volunteers had been mobilized and put to sea. Their
new command, Roberts and Kitchener, reached Cape Town on 10
January 1900. Now, if any confirmation were still needed, it could be
nothing but war to the finish.

Equally, in this temporary lull the republicans were not doing very
much to try to settle that outcome. The failures of Black Week
had prised things open, almost inviting a capitalizing counterstroke
from some bold and resolute Boer generalship. Exposed to a broader
offensive, the Cape Colony virtually asked for deeper penetration to
throttle the strategic junction of De Aar, thereby severing Methuen's
supply lines. On the eastern front, almost half of Natal remained
under the enemy thumb, with the British confined or paralysed by
rampant Orange Free State commandos who, in their most southerly
groupings, had pegged out a substantial swathe of land running down
to within 120 miles of the Indian Ocean. With the British rocked back
on their heels, one purposeful strategy at this stage might have been
to launch a counter-offensive against Gatacre and Methuen's forces,
who were dispiritedly binding their wounds and counting their corpses.
Yet the Boers failed to press their advantage. Aside from a few minor
scraps in the Cape, there was barely any further contestation or

serious fighting. Admittedly, republican command could not always assume that all of their men would have the constitution for another test. But a key factor in their restraint was the calibre of older and reticent Boer generalship which was chronically inclined to be dilatory rather than dynamic, even when the going was good.

However galling to the imperial psyche and however injurious to the well-being of more vulnerable sections of the civilian besieged, therefore, republican siege warfare ground on in its pedestrian way. In Natal, younger Boer generals increased pressure upon Joubert to move more decisively against Ladysmith, particularly now that the Buller–White débâcle had added the advantage of good timing to an already strong position. He finally ordered a heavy strike on 2 January, aimed at snatching the commanding heights of Platrand ridge from which further fire could be directed at the town. The Boers failed in their objective, but only after a lengthy, raging battle in which the hard-pressed British held on at a cost of over 400 casualties, more than twice the losses of their enemy. Meanwhile, to the west around Colesberg, General French also came to a decision at New Year. Fixed on the need to prevent the republican tide in the Cape midlands from lapping further into the colony, a 2000-strong British force pressed forward against Commandant Hendrik Schoeman's strong point, held at Colesberg by 4000 commandos. French's initial charge was damaging, but a renewed night attack on 5 January to further turn the Boers was unexpectedly heavily repulsed. While French had contained the enemy, reassured by Buller that his was the 'right policy. Worry them',[28] British losses were once more disproportionately heavy.

To the east, Buller himself had not yet played out his hand. Roberts allowed him continuing command of the Natal army, either through thoughtful tact or some perverse calculation that a sidelined rival might as well be given more rope. So Buller's campaign position was duly strengthened, with his forces profiting from the rising flow of reinforcements to South Africa; by early January he had 30,000 troops at his disposal. For all this, Roberts had no intention of permitting him to go completely about his own business. While on the way to South Africa he repeatedly cabled his Natal commander to remain on the defensive and mark time. Any operations under subsidiary command would have to be under Roberts' overall direction. But a peeved Buller declined to dance to this tune. Colenso had got him the boot, but this setback did not mean that his dented reputation was beyond all repair; there was still the chance of a renewed offensive to unseat the Boers around Ladysmith.

And sure enough, on 10 January, the day of Roberts' and Kitchener's arrival, Buller headed out from his Chievely camp to have a second stab at Ladysmith. This time he reverted to his original approach, which had been just to hold the republicans at Colenso while his forces pushed around to bear down on Ladysmith from the west. The operation involved propelling the main British forces some 18 miles upstream to Trichardt's Drift, the chosen avenue of penetration across the Tugela, and then to close in by cutting between the hills of Spion Kop and Twin Peaks. Buller left the implementation of this advance to Lieutenant-General Sir Charles Warren. As accurate estimates confirmed that there were few Boers menacing Warren's chosen passage when the British set out, all he apparently needed was the confidence to keep pushing through. But Buller's army was to have a bad time before it bumped into its first commando. The rivers were in flood, the roads were waterlogged or so washed away as to force repeated diversions, and the British were themselves so overburdened by supplies and indulgent baggage (on the grounds of 'why lug along one mess table when two would suffice') that a journey of 21 miles took the best part of a week. As Buller's force panted onwards, the republicans limbered up in preparation, pondered danger points, and issued brisk instructions to reposition their front, leaving a few light lines behind outworks to keep up the deception of established positions. The dozy British reconnaissance failed to ascertain the feverish moves which had been taken by the Boers to reinforce the steep heights running to Twin Peaks, nor the fact that the western limits of the republican position had in fact been pushed several miles beyond where it was thought they ended. From various crests, the doings of Buller's columns lay under sharp and continuous surveillance while the British hopes of working their way round without bringing down anything upon them were about to be horribly undone.

On 20 January and again the following day, having found a secure foothold on the bank of the Tugela, Warren's assault column tried to rush the enemy encampment on Twin Peaks. These attacks were beaten back with intimidating effect. Combined with Boer pressure elsewhere, the setback soon disabused the British of any idea of easily outflanking their enemy. An apoplectic Buller urged a further sortie against the Twin Peaks position, but Warren only foresaw a third reversal against steep ground and hardened defences. With withdrawal not the most ideal option at this probing stage, Warren then proposed taking Spion Kop, an assault to which Buller consented. Swelling all of 550 yards above the level of the Tugela, Spion Kop was seen as a commanding fire-point for volleys with which to enfilade enemy trenches tucked into surrounding lower kopjes, thereby breaking the Boer lines.

In settling on Spion Kop as a way in against the republicans, Warren made a sorry misjudgement. For far from trapping the defenders, it would prove to be a hole for their attackers. Spion Kop was inherently unsafe ground, forming a salient reaching into the enemy position, its exposed flanks and impermeable topping making it so indefensible that the Boers had themselves only committed a very light holding force there. That slight picket defence, and the fact that this time surprise was achieved by the British, eased their opening intervention. On 23 January, a rampant night assault with further cover provided by thick mist saw the Boer sentries gutted by the bayonets of Lieutenant-Colonel Alec Thorneycroft's infantry, and other commandos put to flight by the British charge. Backed by a stout artillery bombardment to deter anyone from contemplating a return to the fight, Thorneycroft's troops deposited themselves on the summit and awaited light in which to begin exploiting their occupied hilltop stronghold.

But as the sun rose and the mist dipped, chilling realization set in. For a start, the British were once again not where they thought they were. Instead of squarely occupying the summit, they had based themselves on a hazardous front ridge, an extremely shallow depression below which the ground fell away sharply to a wide plateau. Second, all the close approaches to the British position were situated in classic 'dead' terrain, sterilized by its angle against downwards defending fire. This was ready-made for darting commandos to wriggle their way to within close striking distance of the lip of ground which held their crouching enemy. Thirdly, Spion Kop lay wholly exposed to Boer fire from Twin Peaks and other adjacent heights. Lastly, defensive burrowing for entrenchment foundered on the immensely hard hill rock, against which the desperately flailing picks and shovels of Warren's men could make only the barest excavation. Their risky positioning was also not much helped by their makeshift commander, who seemed to have calculated little beyond successfully delivering his force to its assigned location. Warren had neglected to improvise proper defensive support, failed to lay out navigable paths for withdrawal, and would not countenance surrender. The inevitable impression was one of no great concern for preserving the lives of his men.

The republican picket which fell back from Spion Kop gave Joubert and Botha plenty of time in which to react to an assault which would clearly end by pinning the enemy to a fixed point. Early in the

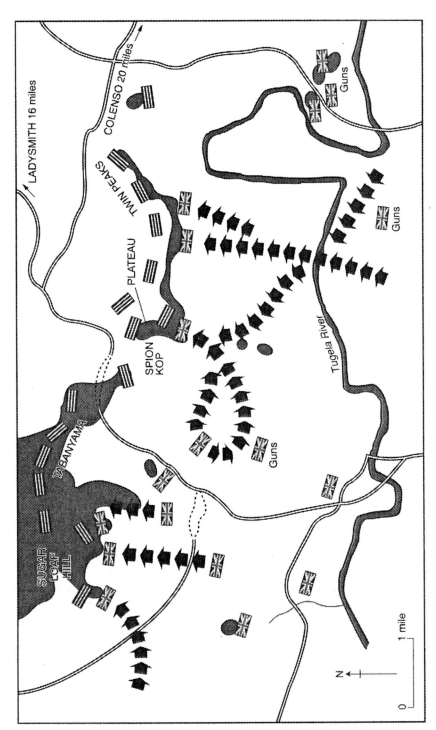

Map 4.5 *Spion Kop, January 1900*

morning of 24 January they proceeded on horseback to review their positions, distributed an encouraging wire from Kruger to the officers, and told commandos to their face of the dangerous confrontation which now loomed. Urging their men to oust the British from Spion Kop at all costs, Boer commanders threatened the usual stick (flogging) for any slacking, cowardice, or attempt to dodge orders. The final and bloody phase of the Spion Kop action now began.

Once the early-morning light was sufficiently clear for the republicans to roll their guns forward and fix their range, devastating artillery and rifle cross-fire from the adjoining heights blanketed the British position from three sides. The Spion Kop location virtually funnelled fire into a huddled mass of unprotected troops. Warren stopped gloating over what had seemed to be the easy capture of the hill and, dismayed by the unexpected savaging of his position, he now looked for a way out. Reinforcements under Major-General Talbot Coke were scrambled up to fortify the ridge, under the accurate noses of Boer guns which tore through the advancing force. Coming at a run across open country, they had no covering bombardment, Warren holding off for fear of striking his own troops. 'It was utter madness,' recalled one infantryman, 'to have placed ourselves in that spot.'[29]

Meanwhile, in the rear, Buller's zest was not yet blunted. Heartened by reports of Thorneycroft's night assault achievement, he ordered Warren to hand him command of Spion Kop, which looked increasingly like a pit which was swallowing those who had dug it. Inexplicably, Warren neglected to advise Talbot Coke, whose nimble force was feeling the weight of casualties, of this new command arrangement. Well into the evening of 24 January, with his eyes still fixed on the Spion Kop plateau, Talbot Coke slipped down its slope for a briefing with Buller to try to establish exactly what was going on. Then came a truly astonishing turn of events. As Talbot Coke's reinforcing troops more or less ground to a halt, a troubled Thorneycroft decided quite independently that his brief hour was over; breaking off, he ordered a rapid evacuation of his over-exposed position. This bizarre lapse in British coordination has been part of virtually every account of the battle of Spion Kop. It bears retelling perhaps only as a textbook illustration of the poorly controlled line of command which beset imperial operations in the earlier stages of this war.

While the British fell back, every advantage did not flow to the Boers. For, as the enemy withdrawal was developing commando fire also began to die away, as the men crammed around the flanks of Spion Kop and on Twin Peaks evacuated their ground, gradually overcome by an infantry counter-attack in a belated forward diversionary action. It was altogether an odd moment of battlefield symmetry: the Boer commandos who could walk in to carry the shattered Spion Kop ridge now abandoned their own positions to the King's Royal Rifle Corps. In effect, the two sides almost cancelled each other out, although in the end the republicans prevailed in the bloody Spion Kop engagement.

Strategically, ground lost or taken in this battle was of trivial significance; it did nothing much to alter the balance of power in the Natal theatre. Those writers who have judged it a 'futile day', or a 'useless waste of life',[30] are clearly right. The action saw great efforts made by both sides and a heaving confrontation of shattering intensity. Casualties from the relentless heavy shelling were terrible, with the weight of losses pressing heavily upon the British, who lost over 1100 troops killed, wounded, or taken prisoner. With most of Buller's army not even released into battle lines, this was a telling cost. Blind to the weakening condition of their men, neither Buller nor Warren fed reinforcements towards the perimeter of the engagement as a diversionary measure to dilute the sting of Spion Kop. While the Boer casualties mounted comparatively slowly, they too had topped 300 by the end of the day. In glinting heat, across hard and jagged terrain, with little cover and less water, the costly tactical pattern of fighting consisted of virtually endless republican bombardment, each side keeping the enemy lines under almost constant attack and counter-attack through frontal assaults, Boer flanking attempts to carry British defences, and opposing formations variously wilting, barely holding firm, or falling back briefly before having their front sufficiently stiffened to surge back to regain position. On and around the British defences just about every piece of ground was frantically and bitterly contested in pitched confrontations. Entrenched or rutted belts of that ground held the stark remains of those who had been in at the kill, most of them British, in a kind of no-man's land: the crawling or expiring wounded, torn corpses already darkened by clumps of ants or flies, and more isolated bodies slumped in rocky extremities which were already being nosed down by dismembering hyenas as night began to draw in.

For the wounded, the only reliable passage away from the battlefield was the Natal Indian Ambulance Corps. Funded and fanned on by the pro-imperial merchant and professional interests around M. K. Gandhi, a company of around 1100 bearers, consisting mostly of sugar-estate indentured labourers together with a sprinkling of artisans and middle-class volunteers, stuck it out perilously near the firing line to stretcher Buller's casualties from Spion Kop. While the locally raised Ambulance Corps was to be used in a number of major eastern front engagements, clearing this arena was by far its bloodiest business of battle.[31]

Perhaps more than any other single photographic image from this stage of the conflict, it was the grisly sight of hundreds of dead infantrymen stacked up in their own trenches, some visibly mutilated, which underlined the reality of an imperial offensive which was now taking an ominously bad turn. That said, Botha and Joubert had troubles of their own in the Tugela sector. In the republican lines the horrific conditions around Spion Kop had begun to tell heavily on morale. So, too, did the exhausting burden of launching attacks on the cornered British, being beaten back repeatedly, and having to build up a wave to stage a thrust all over again. This may have produced a few more yards' progress each time before attackers were repelled, but that was that; a deciding breakthrough remained elusive. One part of the republican problem was their lack of numbers to sustain an offensive spirit. Fatigued and drooping commandos, close to breaking-point, had few reserves to hand to provide line relief. Again, a familiar index of collapsing resolve was defiant desertion, with increasing numbers of Boers ignoring the pleas and threats of their commanders to stay to continue fighting. As the day ground on, disenchanted and demoralized burghers flitted away homewards, sometimes taking only their rifles and ammunition, while leaving behind almost all their personal belongings right down to tobacco and bibles.[32] A number of observers have credited the moral exertions of Louis Botha with having saved the Boer forces in the Tugela basin from complete rout. Botha's persuasive zeal notwithstanding, it seems apparent that by nightfall the hard centre of the defence line was crumbling away inexorably. In truth, here, too, it was just about all up. As it was, curiously little advantage came of it for Buller.

If there was an oddity about Spion Kop, it was that neither side grasped quite how badly its adversary was doing. Close to the end of their tether, the British concluded that before orderly movement around their tenuously held position became impossible they should break off and retreat in advance of any authorization from Warren. Feeling the odds, they seemingly had no inkling of how much Botha's lines were buckling, leading the enemy to quit the battlefield as well. Far from exploiting any moment of advantage for fresh onslaughts, faltering, combat-fatigued men relaxed their grip. When Warren heard that commandos had given up their Spion Kop fight altogether, he was most intent on pressing a renewed assault. But Buller had come to accept that his battered troops had already borne enough. In ordering a comprehensive withdrawal across the Tugela, he gave up; and there was no republican stomach for any pursuit. In the very early hours of 25 January, sniffing Boer scouts found Spion Kop empty; an incredibly driven Botha then performed one further prodigy of endurance, scratching together a band of commandos to dart up to the summit to claim their showy reward. The republicans had won, although with so many fighters having fled speedily and far afield, relatively few were there to recognize this.[33] It was victory in a battle which, in a sense, almost ran down of itself.

Not greatly perturbed by the outcome of Spion Kop, Buller returned to the focal point of his strategy, an offensive large enough to deal with Ladysmith. A blackened Warren could be blamed for the late-January failure. As the siege situation worsened, with mounting hunger, dysentery, and general misery, Buller prepared another offensive to relieve White, who was now wrangling with the War Office over a surrender of the town. Like some other early British planning in South Africa, this consisted of charging at the enemy at secure holding-points, where the likely depth and line formation of the republicans had not been adequately probed. While Buller had plenty of anxieties, unfortunately too few of these seemed to be technical.

Resolving to simplify and hasten the line of advance, he arrowed in to carry the Boer defences on the Vaalkranz and Doornkop hills. Closing on either side of a direct route through to Ladysmith, once it was overrun the British could look forward to an unimpeded push through to White. With many dissembling commandos having fallen back to republican territory, and with Botha himself having left the fighting zone, it seemed that success would at last smile on Buller. With only very minor forces holding the hills, it was assumed that a really heavy attack would do the trick.

On 5 February Buller forged ahead with an army of 20,000 men, some of its officers convinced that, with such weight, Boer nerve would now break completely. At first, matters did indeed seem to go well, as a force under Major-General Lyttelton cut through to the dominating Vaalkranz headland, beating down fiercely held Boer defensive lines. Lyttelton's brigade then looked to having its initial successful push consolidated by a converging assault which would close up Doornkop; the entire advance was based on a fairly method-ical unrolling of diversionary troop movements and feint attacks to try to bluff the defenders as to where the British really aimed to make gains with a superior force.

But Buller's opponents were not bamboozled. Unexpectedly heavy and concentrated fire struck the British head-on, severing their planned coordination between the attacking infantry and cavalry. Buller then stopped. Wheeling away from his Doornkop target, he was inclined to break off the action. Now, instead of having his position improved, Lyttelton found it significantly more precarious. Ahead of him the republicans, anticipating further blows, moved rapidly to switch resources into the depleted defences commanded by a distinctly nervous General Ben Viljoen. Drawing back Botha from Pretoria, and strengthening their delaying capacity to over 2000 men, by sunset the Boers had thwarted further British actions to capture Vaalkranz. With neither side having anything to spare with which to clinch an advantage, Lyttelton urged an uncertain Buller to stop hanging about and to reopen the original strike against Doornkop. Although this seemed to stir him, Buller did not like it; neither could he conceive of any other way of going forward. So he hesitated, committed reinforcements to Lyttelton but then watered them down, consulted with Roberts, who was alternately reproachful and wearily resigned, and tinkered with offensive preparations. Well into the following day, he had still not plunged in.

By then the Boers had decided not to await any further attack. Towards dusk they concentrated their commandos, ensured that the wind continued to rip towards the enemy, and fired the grass and scrub as screening to cover a coordinated angling assault which struck hard enough to set back the British. Late on 7 February a wobbly Buller decided at last to withdraw, having lost over 400 killed, wounded, or missing. Four days later the entire Natal force slumped back to its Chievely starting-base, having sustained a further 2000 casualties in all in this effort to demolish the republican defences.

The failed confrontation at Vaalkranz and Doornkop marked the end of the opening British drive in one important sense: it was to be the last set-piece action in the old Black Week style. Even Redvers Buller seemed finally to realize that something was going badly wrong, and that the successful resumption of a British advance required other ways of retaining the initiative and finally snuffing out the republican challenge. The key to that leap forward, to which we now turn, had little to do with consuming sieges or formidable battles, and rather more with logistics and improved mobility, adherence to more shrewd techniques and tactics, and elaborately prepared movements of encirclement. A considerable change was impending.

Chapter 4 Notes

1. *Ons Land*, 26 Oct. 1899; *Het Zuid-Oosten*, 30 Oct. 1899; *Natal Witness*, 8 Nov. 1899.
2. Michael Glover, *Warfare from Waterloo to Mons* (London, 1980), p. 208.

3. Quoted in Thomas G. Fergusson, 'The development of a modern intelligence organization: British military intelligence, 1870–1914', Ph.D. diss. (Duke University, 1981), p. 334.
4. J. M. Grierson, *Scarlet into Khaki: The British Army on the Eve of the Boer War* (London, 1899).
5. *Rifle Brigade Chronicle* (1900), p. 86.
6. Howard Bailes, 'Military aspects of the war', in *The South African War: The Anglo-Boer War 1899–1902*, ed. Peter Warwick (London, 1980), p. 76.
7. Thomas Pakenham, *The Boer War* (London, 1979), p. 161; Byron Farwell, *Eminent Victorian Soldiers* (Harmondsworth, 1986), p. 166.
8. John Keegan and Andrew Wheatcroft, *Who's Who in Military History from 1453 to the Present Day* (London, 1996 edn), p. 43; R. J. J. Hills, *The Royal Dragoons* (London, 1972), p. 68.
9. Michael Barthrop, *The Northamptonshire Regiment* (London, 1974), pp. 54–5.
10. *Household Brigade Magazine*, 51/3 (1902), p. 115.
11. A. J. Barker, *The West Yorkshire Regiment* (London, 1974), p. 43.
12. H. Wood, *The King's Royal Rifle Corps* (London, 1967), pp. 79–80.
13. Norman F. Dixon, *On the Psychology of Military Incompetence* (London, 1979), p. 59.
14. *Cape Mercury*, 23 Dec. 1899.
15. *Rifle Brigade Chronicle* (1901), p. 185.
16. L. B. Oatts, *The Highland Light Infantry* (London, 1969), p. 67.
17. J. M. Brereton, *The British Soldier: A Social History* (London, 1986), p. 103.
18. Wood, *Rifle Corps*, p. 69.
19. H. J. C. Pieterse, *My Tweede Vryheidstryd* (Kaapstad, 1945).
20. Robert Scales, 'Artillery in small wars: the evolution of British artillery doctrine, 1860–1914', Ph.D. diss. (Duke University, 1976), p. 211.
21. *St George's Gazette*, 19/203 (1900), p. 29.
22. *Cape Argus*, 24 Dec. 1899.
23. Quoted in Bailes, 'Military aspects', p. 84.
24. Quoted in Pakenham, *Boer War*, p. 244.
25. W. S. Hamer, *The British Army: Civil–Military Relations, 1855–1905* (Oxford, 1970), p. 177.
26. Pakenham, *Boer War*, pp. 457–8.
27. R. J. Q. Adams, 'Field-Marshal Lord Roberts: army and empire', in *Edwardian Conservatism: Five Studies in Adaptation* (New York, 1988), pp. 53–4.
28. *Official British History of the War in South Africa, 1899–1902*, eds Maj.-Gen. Sir Frederick Maurice and M. H. Grant (London, 1906), vol. 1, p. 282.
29. *Light Bob Gazette*, 2/9 (1901), p. 25.
30. George Blaxland, *The Middlesex Regiment* (London, 1977), p. 67; Alan Barker, *Battle Honours of the British and Commonwealth Armies* (London, 1986), p. 94.
31. Peter Warwick, *Black People and the South African War, 1899–1902* (Cambridge, 1983), p. 133.
32. *Oxfordshire Light Infantry Chronicle* (1900), p. 91.
33. *The War Memoirs of Commandant Ludwig Krause 1899–1900*, ed. Jerold Taitz (Cape Town, 1996), pp. 58–9.

5

The Second British Offensive

On 17 February Buller embarked on another stab at Ladysmith, now into its fourth month of sustained siege and increasingly anxious for his liberating army. After the early sour story of three consecutive setbacks, his luck finally began to take a turn for the better. Again the familiar crawling progress of his heavily burdened army (its commander never one to stint on troops' provisions), further impeded by ground grown tidal through severe rains, gave the republicans ample opportunity to make a stand on their threatened Colenso front. It looked as if the old story might well be repeated. The Boers cantered in reinforcements to strengthen their key hilly positions, but could only bring up 5000 commandos, as their generals were now facing serious distractions to the west which were bottling up men. This time, instead of drawing the enemy into a single concentrated battle the British sweep towards Ladysmith took the incremental form of well-rehearsed assaults against a crop of defensive kopjes to the east of Colenso. For this Buller decided to direct the whole of his army, now swollen to 25,000 troops, against his opponents' positions. Crucially, in carrying their renewed attack the British began to do more. In approach, troops constructed defensive field positions as a forward screen, and tighter signals coordination between moving infantry and artillery meant that the bombardments of Boer defences could be lifted at the moment that troops stormed out of trench lines. For all this, it was still a hard, dangerous, and taxing passage against ambushing sharp-shooters. In the face of heavy fire Buller's troops broke through, overrunning a succession of hills and triggering republican flight from a further hill base. With these defensive strong-points put out of action, the Tugela line was finally broken and Buller had secured an opening to Ladysmith, although not without further loss. Aware that the republicans had no defence in any depth, the British banked on having to dispose of little else other than some brittle rearguard resistance. Exhausted, hurt, and depressed by the great strength of the enemy, by now the Boer defensive effort was shot. As their front began to flake away into mass flight, a hard-pressed republican command bickered over the conduct of affairs in Natal. A grimacing Louis Botha, realistic in his perception of the odds against him, was resigned to the unstoppability of a spreading commando stampede, and argued for abandoning Ladysmith before all remaining order went. Kruger, however, was all for staying in the game, believing that the despatch of the increasingly vintage charisma of Piet Joubert to the Tugela would somehow persuade the burghers to get on with the manly task of fighting.[1]

At the same time the remaining republican core was not completely at a loss over what to do about the continuing British advance. Having acquired considerable bridging proficiency in the sodden Natal countryside, Buller's force hardened its breach of the Boer defences by throwing a pontoon across the Tugela to shift men and equipment into and through the opposite valley. As the British slowly pushed the head of their column beyond the far shoreline, the Boers struck back. Pressed into a cluster of flanking hills, they caught the British on the move, subjecting their enemy to solid fire. Having lined up his army, Buller nevertheless continued to tip his troops across the river, cram-ming them on the narrow bank where they simply backed up behind their disabled advance column. In four days of hard fighting the British struggled to hack away the defences on the upper reaches which were checking their thrust, while the Boers maintained a desperate assault to try to close off the advance. The remaining kopje positions then fell into Buller's hands, but not before his force had sustained 1400 casualties. On 25 February fighting died away, Buller and Botha having consented to a ceasefire for their men to turn from the business of killing to bind up their wounded and inter their dead. During this interlude the British withdrew across the Tugela, prompt-ing some commandos to hope against hope that they might yet have prevailed. But their position was lost.

Buller was only drawing back to re-form in order to attack afresh, and this came on 27 February, the Majuba anniversary date. Battered by an immense weight of shell, and shrouded by thick clouds of dust and spinning stone splinters, the panicky defenders took off in complete disarray as the assaulting infantry closed up behind lunging bayonets. Botha had no hope of holding a firm rearguard behind which commandos could fall back along an orderly riding escape route. It was just as well that Buller stayed his hand and did not press pursuit.

After the best part of a fortnight's heavy fighting over the Ladysmith position, the British were building up momentum and conserving an offensive surplus, while the Boers were on their knees. Piet Joubert, now a sick and ailing man, merely drifted, while around him the erosion of morale intensified with awareness of serious reversal on the western front. Never one to keep out of the way, Kruger again urged that the Boer forces stand on the defensive against Buller. Cronjé heard him out respectfully, but had sense enough to discount presidential pleas. In no state to deter fresh onslaughts, he issued the tired command to abandon the Ladysmith siege lines altogether. Few, if any, of those holding these lines were much put out by this, swiftly rolling up tents and loading wagons to wind their way back to the homesteads of the republican countryside. It was stark confirmation of the blunder in barrenly sticking it out around Ladysmith; having failed to break in and entrench conquest from a superior position, the Boers now melted away

On 28 February a British mounted brigade pushed through an open door to relieve the town at last. Buller sealed this two days later with a more grandiose, stage-managed show in which he and White turned out for a solicitous pumping of hands. Hitherto he had not exactly been a friend of the press, empowering Natal Military Intelligence to censor news telegrams and intercept letter dispatches conveyed by African runners; he did not want any correspondents' reports on the sliding Ladysmith morale, its diminishing supplies, and the atrocious state of its hospital camp to be disclosed to the Boers, fearing that news of the real state of affairs could have encouraged an attack. Having generally infiltrated the runner circuits, the Boers probably knew all this anyway.[2]

Re-imposing control over Ladysmith had cost the British Natal army around 5500 casualties, something which took the gloss off Buller's memorably hearty special order of 3 March, in which the offensive became an enthralling enterprise, a further 'glorious page' to replenish 'the History of the British Empire'. Even within contemporary imperial opinion there were a good many observers who suggested that it was nothing of the kind, and well General Buller knew it. Not that this mattered in any way to the dislodged republicans, who by early March were in full and disorganized retreat.

The only attempt to curb this came from their own despairing commanders, who issued hollow threats to shoot their horses, confiscate their stores, or torch their wagons. Among some younger and more resolute officers, there was still a lingering if forlorn hope of keeping a bit of something going in the Natal theatre. Falling back at a trot up a familiar route, the commandos pilfered their Elandslaagte provisioning base of anything portable and incinerated the rest in a rip-roaring bonfire. Leaving a fiery scar, they were out of Natal, although not out of the war.

By this time Roberts was well into extending his controlling share of the imperial advance. He foresaw that the obvious physical problem of South Africa was its size and the exposure of its vast veld. For all the extensive table calculations and strategy briefings, he had an equally simple solution that the only way to choke the enemy was to penetrate through to strategic points to carry that veldt and deny it to the Boers. Part of Roberts' solution lay in numbers. With major imperial reinforcements continuing to stream in, by early 1900 he had amassed a force of more than 180,000 soldiers, an army whose size now already exceeded the total combined white population of the republics. Another part of the solution lay in the manner of advance. Roberts concluded that a push all the way up the railway routes in order to keep close supply lines would bring on the Boers on unwelcome terms: it would give the enemy the latitude of knowing when and where best to strike, and where to base or shift defensive strongpoints. Having massed his forces, he therefore decided to assemble just north of Orange River Station, and then to run hard east and west, pocketing strategic gains in a lunge right into the marrow of the Boer states.

The opening stroke was intended to carry the British across more than 120 miles of open countryside, in a westerly move up the rail line to Kimberley, and then to unleash forces in an eastwards push away from the railway to a central consolidating point just south of Bloemfontein. There, astride the railway and menacing the Orange Free State capital, Roberts envisaged that so critical a national situation for the Boers would force them to catch up, which would mean summoning commandos away from the Mafeking, Kimberley, and Ladysmith sieges as well as the Cape midlands in order to hold imperilled republican territory. No longer extended, the war would be rolled back into the Boer states, and there its outcome would be decided by British imposition: brought to battle, the increasingly disorderly Boer armies could be destroyed. The great thing was first bringing Bloemfontein to capitulate, and then carrying Pretoria; the

British could then snuff out any remaining defiance by cutting off final points of entry. That meant taking command of the eastwards branch line to Durban, and also attending to control of the inland coastal link from Mozambique.

Imperial offensive preparations were made on the customary elaborate scale, its details chronicled in quite stupefying detail by several previous histories of the war. In fact, the makings of an effective Roberts field force may be fairly easily grasped by way of summary. For the British, the running of the war now became both more composed and more exact in intention. Thus Roberts made a basic contribution to the education of his troops through the wide dissemination of instructional 'Guidance' notes on 'South African Warfare', stressing the survival imperatives of improved shooting, rapid movement, proper systems of concealment, and a freer hand to take independent, individual initiative against their opponent. Colonel Percy Girouard, who as Director of Railways had been moving on from Sudanese labour to the recruitment and control of Ciskeian and Transkeian workers in South Africa, was entrusted with rail schedules and timetables to see that things were shifted in good time. With barely 14,000 mounted men available in October 1899, the British also desperately needed more horsemen to throw against an enemy comprised of natural mounted riflemen who were well able to control things from the saddle. Under the robust and bristling French a new cavalry division was formed and, to beef up deficient reconnaissance capacity and make British mobility tell, the complement of mounted infantry was greatly increased. Every battalion had to provide a mounted company, and these were augmented by local colonial mounted-rifle contingents. These irregular settler units, such as Rimington's Scouts or 'Tigers' (so dubbed because of the strips of wildcat fur worn on their hats), mostly enlisted riders who knew the countryside well, could speak Dutch, and had some interpreting facility in African languages.[3] Some of those enlisted had further qualities: the resentments of marginal men or drifters with a taste for violence, or antisocial misfits with scores to pay off and an eagerness to take on any dirty work.

This mounted infantry expansion was accompanied by enhanced efforts to make the British forces less conspicuous targets; grey horses were dyed to provide a camouflaging zebra effect to make them more difficult to pick up at a distance, cavalrymen's buttons were dulled by brown leather, and mess tins and lance butts were painted over to stop them from flashing in the sun. In addition to having to train urbanized infantrymen as riders, some of whom thought that horses were fed on beef or mutton, animals had to be obtained. Commandeering or the costly purchase of mounts from Cape colonist farmers or beady eyed African peasants produced something, but not nearly enough; in any case, local ponies met light Boer requirements, but tended mostly to buckle under the weighty paraphernalia of a fully equipped cavalryman or infantryman.[4] By early 1900 Roberts had already brought in more than 12,000 horses from Argentina, Australia, and Britain itself, with hundreds of thousands more to come. The keeping of forage and other supply systems going would soon overwhelm a poorly staffed and massively overburdened Remount Department; by the end of the war, 66 per cent of all the horses used had been ridden to death, turning South Africa into a kind of imperial knacker's yard.

Roberts took two other steps to try to increase field force efficiencies and nail down an expanded and more predictable communications environment. Colonel George Henderson, the Director of Military Intelligence, began to coordinate the compiling of a comprehensively detailed map of Roberts' planned theatre of operations, hoping thereby to reduce that persistently worrying margin of territorial self-deception. Secondly, he and Kitchener reorganized and unified the existing dispersed regimental transport and supply system into a general transport train, splicing together column ox-wagon and mulecart companies into a makeshift single-service department, staffed by mostly inexperienced transport officers who found themselves floundering. With moving from Cape Town to Pretoria being roughly the equivalent of shifting from Vienna to St Petersburg, demands on British supply, from raising transport and procuring forage to rolling through food and stores, was already a daunting enterprise. The wonderful plan for technical cohesion managed to make matters worse, as trickling consolidated convoys became stuck through error and misfortune. Unintelligent meddling in this sector did Roberts no credit, and after groaning under it for an alarmingly long time the army was finally driven to restore a version of its own traditional, decentralized, and dedicated transport system.[5] Roberts liked to be in charge, but by no means everything was run competently.

Away from the dogmatic reform of logistics, some other early signs were more encouraging. In selecting their renewed avenues of advance under Roberts the army sought to guard against further defeat in the field by preserving the advantage of surprise. Up to now the republicans had had plenty of warning all too often. But Roberts hit on a clever ruse. By the beginning of February he had concentrated roughly 60,000 soldiers in an assault column in the forward ground between the Modder and Orange rivers. Tailing south, they reinforced French's force outside Colesberg, and their itchy presence induced Cronjé, entrenched behind Magersfontein, to assume a direct British move from there towards Kimberley. To cultivate this perception, military intelligence turned from assiduous mapping of the sectors ahead to the shrewd peddling of rumour and semi-confirmation, some of this carefully crafted misinformation dribbled by well-paid African hucksters of British intelligence officers. Taking the bait, Cronje drew in around 8000 soldiers to repel an anticipated frontal attack.

On 11 February the British came, but they cut eastwards in a wide circling movement from their Orange–Modder base, with the intention of outflanking Cronjé's defensive position and then readying themselves in strength to fall on the republican headquarters. Confronting this approach, the Boers could have punctured the British supply lines at De Aar and Naauwpoort, but this vital opportunity was not taken. The Cavalry Division under French was pulled up from Colesberg and given orders quickly to grab the fords across the Modder and Riet rivers as a corridor of infantry advance, and thereafter to wheel around the republican position at Magersfontein for a run at Kimberley. Astutely leaving behind their tents as a further glimmering of deception, the British set out in darkness, with Cronjé only some hours later dispatching General Christiaan de Wet to keep pace with French's manoeuvre. The uncertainty created by intermittent British changes of direction began to wear on enemy nerves as the frustrated Boers waited for a sign of clear resolution. When and where would their enemy try to strike a blow?

In a toiling drive through fierce heat from 11 to 15 February, French kept his nerve but lost a good many horses, over 500 dying or broken through lack of water, adequate forage and exhaustion from pulling a train of heavy guns. As the British force advanced to within several miles of Cronjé's main camp, the republicans, still unsure of their enemy's intention, loaded their defence of the southern approaches, throwing a shallow crescent-shaped front south of the Modder river around Klip Drift. But while French had planned well, the Boers were too out of touch with the threatening enclosure of their position. The fords were seized, and the Kimberley advance then opened in a thundering rush. Early on 15 February 6000 of French's cavalrymen moved in a frightening charge across the open, flat, undefended countryside between Klip Drift and Kimberley. Turning briefly to face the British swoop, over 800 Boer riflemen broke and fled after a few discharges at random, knowing that to stand against such odds would bring not merely swift defeat but the near-certainty of death or mutilation by being cut down. Through guile and size, French grabbed the opening he wanted, thereafter wasting no time in pushing his fatigued troops in a closing line of advance around and above Kimberley. In the face of this commanding encroachment, backed by the replenishing weight of a large army now moving northwards, the republican siege position began to break up.

As French moved in to crack Kimberley, Roberts' following infantry columns were not without something to do. Part of this army was drawn off to take Jacobsdal, where Cronjé had very recently abandoned his headquarters, and to obliterate what was left of a resisting Boer presence in the area. But elsewhere not quite everything was bending the British way. Towards the very rear of Roberts' advance his inviting transport column of some 200 stockpiled wagons provided a turn for de Wet to make trouble. Leading around 1000 horsemen, he attacked the supply train, cleverly worsening the commotion by firing into the oxen to make them stampede, and in due course seeing to some of their African and Coloured drivers with the usual leniency. Roberts, worried about exposing his lengthening communications line between the Riet and the Modder to possible attack from Cronjé, decided against any doubling back to recapture lost transport and stores, leaving his sweating men to pay the price with remaining half rations or less.

The Boer forces around Kimberley were now more than ever in the wrong place. With their numbers already falling off, they were too weak to make a stand and were also unable to strike any reinforcing connection with Cronjé's distracted force at Magersfontein, which was being squeezed hard by a Methuen onslaught. There were a few half-hearted attempts at staging a fighting retreat, but these dissolved on realization of the strength of the British cavalry bearing down on the thin republican lines. Flattening themselves as best they could, the commandos crawled off in a general abandonment of their position and headed for home. In some rough semblance of coordination, Cronjé retreated east while General Ignatius Ferreira ran off his Orange Free State force in a northerly direction, saving the burghers from having their heart completely torn out. Meanwhile Rhodes, never one to let an opportunity slip, muscled forward to welcome French as one John the Baptist to another, bold men of empire who had done the right thing by taking up Kimberley's need.

After this, brushing aside urgings from some subordinate officers to regroup for a counter-attack, a dispirited Cronjé decided to drop out of the central sector and pull back towards Bloemfontein. Snatching the cover of darkness, the Boers vacated their Magersfontein defences. Some 5000 commandos, some with their familial cushioning of women and children, 500 wagons, and thousands of reserve horses, found an exit gap in the British lines through which to ship themselves towards an Orange Free State refuge. Heavily encumbered, Cronjé's force made exceedingly slow progress, and this gave French an opportunity for a further turn of the screw. Counting on the strength of British combat motivation, he risked a smaller force of 1200 troops to head off Cronjé and his lumbering wagon convoy. Aware that they were being pursued in turn by over 1500 fresh commandos under Ferreira, who was committed to carrying a distracting fight to them, the British met the retreating enemy force at a drift on the Modder near Paardeberg on 17 February. Keeping at a distance, French shelled the Boers, splintering wagons and pitting the ground. Cronjé became immobilized.

On the alert for Ferreira and another looming republican advance in the shape of de Wet and his 1500 commandos, French's worries were eased on 18 February by the arrival of Kitchener's ample infantry to add to British strength. Having pounded his flushed troops, covering over 30 miles in a day, a headstrong Kitchener moved immediately to an all-out assault on the republican laager, evidently relishing the latitude of command granted him by Roberts. Eager to wipe out the Boers and achieve quick victory, however, he made no great effort to think through the offensive coordination of his 15,000 troops. Most of his subordinate officers appear to have been left in the dark, while any who may have perceived coming confusion stifled their doubts before an aloof and intimidatingly hard-faced commander.[6]

Sure enough, the British ran into resolute resistance. A series of heavy attacks broke down against a repelling line of fire from commandos dug strongly into concealed defensive positions around the river bed, and Kitchener's assault waves subsided into fragmented formations. Advancing or stopping in haphazard fashion, some units were plucked forward by impetuous younger officers, who wanted to see them eat fire. They did. When, late in the day, the British eventually moved to combine a moving line of attack, this was upended by a diversionary assault from de Wet, whose twisting horsemen rode up close without being detected and then stormed in to capture a commanding British hill position which would later become known as 'Kitchener's kopje'.

This audacious incursion, and the arrival of Ferreira's force and some other light reinforcements from Bloemfontein, did something to calm the Boers by slightly easing the pressure. By nightfall of 18 February Kitchener had slackened his relentless and bloody offensive, withdrawing men and rolling back guns to pick off an approaching attack from Ferreira and Bloemfontein burghers, and to retake the controlling position carried by de Wet. Lifted by some brand of cold courage, the entrenched commandos against whom Kitchener had launched his piling assault had not given up their position on the Modder. They could do little more than hold on, but they could still make the enemy pay. By the time Kitchener finally decided to call off the fighting and dying, almost 1300 British troops were dead or wounded, while the defending Boers had suffered 300 casualties.

But the outcome at Paardeberg was not to be decided by this particular piece of brutal cost–benefit balancing. Cronjé's ravaged position, split between commandos dug in on one bank of the river and a bunched wagon laager on the landward side, was desperate. A break-in by more strong reinforcements might have opened a fighting way out, but nothing was forthcoming. De Wet and several of Cronjé's own subordinate commanders pleaded with him to strip down to minimal essentials and implement a running evacuation before his encampment became entirely surrounded. The general's adversities were growing all the more cruel as the odds climbed. A good many of his men lacked serviceable horses or, indeed, any escape mount, while the ditching of trundling wagon transport put at risk the lives the of accompanying Boer women and child camp-followers. It was a condition of pure pathos.

Paardeberg illustrated that the departure of Cronjé's commandos for the offensive front did not necessarily mean leaving behind the agitating older and married women or the children. One or two women in the Natal Boer lines had already been killed or wounded; again, for some of those destined for this battle zone, there was no gendered (or generational) division of safety. Sucked directly into the arena of armed struggle, the resistance and welfare of wives and children became a frantic part of the struggle for existence.

What was Cronjé to do? Clinging to a faint hope that Bloemfontein would surely find something to spare to help to tide over his crumbling position, he decided, wrongly, to stay put and soldier on. Elsewhere, nerves cracked at the thought of trying to make a fighting stand, with numerous recoiling and hysterical commandos having concluded that the game was already up. To assume any universal mentality has obvious historical risks, but even a passing familiarity

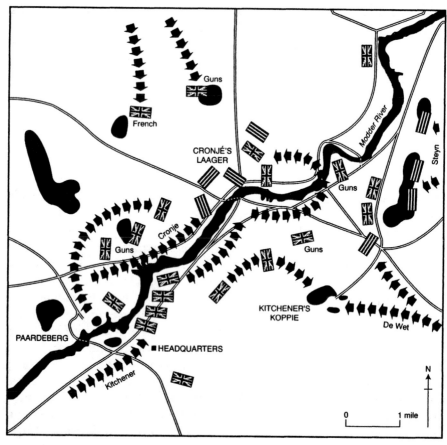

Map 5.1 *Paardeberg, February 1900*

with this war suffices to confirm the pervasiveness of an inherited
Boer combat culture in which commandos would sooner shirk duty
and duck away from a grossly unequal pitched battle than stand and
test the prospect of wanton destruction. Not always being prepared
to risk their lives at an officer's command did not simply mean
'unmanly' cowardice. It meant maintaining an ethos that taking up
battle was an elective business, and also reflected a Boer way of war
built up from earlier tactical experience against large forces of Zulu
foot warriors, when commandos were tough in defending strong
positions, but were always ready to ride away when it looked as
if they might be overrun.[7] Although increasingly unable to run at
Paardeberg, men sensed that a call for acts of courage had little to do
with providing for survival and escape.

Determined to confirm this, Roberts hastened up, arriving on the morning of 19 February to take direct personal command of the action. His opening hand confirmed the republicans in all their fears of a ferocious encounter. Roberts' response to an envoy sent out to propose an armistice in order to attend to the dead and wounded was brusquely dismissive; surrender alone would halt the battle. Cronjé rejected this ultimatum and hardened his intention to fight it out rather than submit. While his opponent was confident, he was not as fully confident as he expected to be in the light of sudden British setbacks near Colesberg and Arundel, which unlocked an opening towards his creaky and exposed supply lines. As he now needed to resolve matters at Paardeberg without any further delay, the pressure became relentless as he turned his entire force on Cronjé's enclave.

The only opposing tug came from some brief diversionary skirmishing. After Ferreira had been fatally wounded in a shooting accident, his commandos were roped in by the agile de Wet, who for some days harried the British with rifle charges, inflicting losses. Forcing the enemy to commit a superior force of both cavalry and infantry to run against his elusive commando, he succeeded in easing away to Poplar Grove, a spot much further along the road to Bloemfontein. Meanwhile, Roberts kept his grip and subjected his enemy to a constant and concentrated bludgeoning. On 21 February, the fourth day of battle, he slackened, formally recognizing the endangered presence of women and children in the Boer position. Bowing to some remote instinct of humanity, Roberts made Cronjé an offer of safe conduct, promising to see them through the British firing line and away from Paardeberg so that they would not be harmed. Now Cronjé imitated Roberts: the offer was spurned, and a fight to the finish reaffirmed. If the women and children with Cronjé's force did not leave their sinking ship, it was only because they refused to leave, or because the bridge refused to release them. For the moral sense of both sides, this must have been a sobering moment. It was one which passed.

Justly known for efficiency rather than squeamishness, Roberts then returned to battle, keeping up an endless artillery bombardment with lyddite shell with the intention of creating the pieces for his infantry to be sent in to pick up. For an enemy hemmed into an enclosed area, the power of the British bombardment, backed by a generous shell supply, must have been a nightmare, as were the rapidly deteriorating conditions of survival. Flayed by heat, without sanitation, and assailed by the reek of decomposing animal carcasses which increasingly polluted the waters of the Modder, the trapped

Boers faced the prospect of succumbing to illness, disease, starvation, or sheer exhaustion. The lives of some shivering commandos bearing festering injuries from earlier engagements were preserved with stubborn dedication by their nursing kin, or by fellow burghers and agterryers with traditional healing skills. Meanwhile in the republics, the agonies of Paardeberg provoked national dismay and a clamour for the dispatch of all available troops.[8]

Little came of this. De Wet, never timid, was still in a kind of secondary relieving position, or thought that he was. He believed that the pressure of a sharp diversionary strike could loosen the British grip sufficiently to enable Cronjé to find ground across which to try to break free. But this required bringing Cronjé into prearranged planning and timing, which did not go well, for poor weather persistently frustrated de Wet's heliograph transmissions to the Paardeberg force. It was not only the British who found the war a struggle against adverse terrain and climate. On 24 February de Wet finally managed to slip one of his best available men through the enemy lines to bring Cronjé into the picture: pack up and await the signalled break.

Again, the elements intruded. The swampy Modder rose rapidly under sudden heavy rain, necessitating a bridging effort before any move could get under way. A frantic start was made, but on 26 February the British hauled up additional howitzer batteries and the Boers' last leg, open to destruction, was taken from them. The next day Roberts launched an attack in full fighting strength, aggressively advancing his men to within 50 yards or so of the enemy entrenchments. He was as eager as any British officer to get Cronjé by now, being determined to turn the taste of Majuba into ash. At the end of their tether, and with nowhere to bolt, the defending Boers refused to hold out any longer and surrendered under their commander in a spontaneous ripple of white flags. A reluctant and dejected Cronjé fell into line, formalizing surrender on 27 February, just a day before Ladysmith would be retaken by his enemy.

Owing to the depth and thickness of their entrenchments, the commandos in Cronjé's laager had mostly escaped the worse of Roberts's bombardment, losing 150 casualties. But the overall republican loss was heavy. The Boers sustained over 4000 casualties and had close to 4000 fighting combatants taken captive. British losses were not light either, accounting for 1300 men. They also lost any possibility of grabbing Boer armaments, shrewdly tossed into the Modder river by Cronjé's force.

The collapse at Paardeberg, with the surrender of virtually 10 per cent of the small Boer army, was a quite devastating blow to the republican war effort. In some respects it even looked as if it might bring the conflict to a sudden conclusion. Engulfed by a sombre crisis of defeat, home-front morale in both republics plummeted. Many fighting burghers out in the field simply saddled up of their own accord, and raced homewards to widespread female anxiety and even animosity for abandoning their duty to defend republican territory from invasion. In occupied southern pockets, shaken commanders had more pressing demands than that of earnestly debating what to do in war councils. Their greatest difficulty lay in keeping their troops still. But Boer retreat was now in full flood. If not in disorganized panic, but with impressive speed, Koos de la Rey and Hendrik Schoeman galloped most of their men back to Bloemfontein, effectively abandoning the central front. The western front became a similar story. With the exception of the holding of the siege line at Mafeking, the barrier of advance in the west more or less collapsed. Some republican 'progressives' who had had misgivings about the whole armed enterprise now had their qualms confirmed by crushing defeat in the field. Following the turnaround from the Tugela and the Modder, it all seemed to have become 'everlastingly retreat, retreat', in the words of Smuts, 'wearying, dispiriting retreat'.[9]

Predictably, such pessimism bred recrimination. At its most extreme, disenchantment with Cronjé saw him being blamed for the whole Boer offensive having come to nothing. Within republican command he was roundly censured for his obstinacy in disregarding repeated warnings in the field from de Wet and de la Rey, as well as other informed senior officers, of the risk of being caught at the Modder in a trap of his own pedestrian making. But there was no need to engineer his dismissal from the sinecure of an ageing generalship; this was attended to by the British, who conveyed him to Cape Town with other prisoners from Paardeberg. Accompanied by his wife and his Tswana attendants, Cronjé was then shipped off to live out the war in island exile on St Helena, behind an Atlantic curtain of historical amnesia. For the republicans, while Cronjé's failure was undoubtedly far greater than that of others, his real sin was to have promised more, yet lost all gain.

At the same time his removal, and the fact that Joubert was fast dying, provided an unanswerable argument for restocking high command with a younger military leadership which would be more able and enterprising, and also less likely to throw things away by fighting the wrong battles. Louis Botha was made Commandant-General of the Transvaal, while Christiaan de Wet rose to Orange Free State Commandant-General. Increased authority also flowed to Koos de la

Rey, while Jan Smuts was given the chance of showing more of himself at the operational level. In a sense these figures were quintessential male partisans, nationalist military entrepreneurs who would bring to high command a greater stringency and capacity to prepare for and face the next round of war.[10] De la Rey and de Wet in particular had a consuming warrior itch, and were cunning commanders, swift and relentless in the field. In the throes of a critical struggle simply to hold the republican position together and to prevent their war from falling apart, the next step for this new generation of Boer generalship was the tall order of trying to come back in force, yet with dejected troops and desertions galore. Some of these were men aching for some rest and respite, or just ready to quit. Others comprised those opting for a determined run homewards to save their personal holdings rather than the republican cause.

Meanwhile, Roberts' great advancing army wound on with every hope and intelligence indication that the Orange Free State capital would fall into its grasp quickly. Unlike most African or Asian peasant adversaries, the Boers were European colonial opponents with a defined capital as their centre. Although Buller was sceptical of a capital strategy, believing enemy territory too big and its key rural communities too fragmented to be intimidated into surrender in this way, Roberts assumed that the conventional toppling of their capitals would finally finish off the Boers.

Given the lack of attachment or indifference felt by parochial rural Boer commandos towards the national point of an 'Afrikaner' state capital, Bloemfontein was not a town that too many felt would be worth fighting for. But for commanders like de Wet something was at stake. Determined to disrupt the British advance, he mustered 6000 commandos and entrenched them at a fancied Poplar Grove along the route to Roberts' objective, in an extended 22-mile line along twisty ground on both sides of the Modder. Here they awaited the British, hoping that disciplined and accurate fire would still halt an advancing force which hugely outnumbered them.

On 7 March Roberts moved to the attack, committing a large enough number of men for a long encirclement of de Wet's line of resistance in order to squeeze the Boers into rapid defeat by cutting their flanks. Instead, however, the gathering confrontation turned into a fiasco. Kruger had arrived that very morning for consultation with de Wet, and the closing impetus of the British advance caught the Boer camp on the hop. With French's cavalry circling towards the bonus of an exposed political target, the republicans rapidly drew up their transport and pulled back towards Bloemfontein. With his way open, Roberts and his bulky force of 40,000 men surged on towards the capital, moving at will, with some units on the fringes looting provisions here, gutting livestock and incinerating property there.[11] Already beginning to lay waste by March 1900 by burning the homes and crops of burghers on commando service, leaving farm inhabitants without shelter or sustenance, the British moved to secure control of the administrative centre of the Orange Free State.

And all the while their enemy combatants continued to reel back in growing numbers, with those who caved in shaking off threats of increasingly brutal sanctions from Boer command, including bluster from Kruger that police reserves would be used to hound men back, if need be shooting any fleeing deserters. Equally, while there was a ragged, bitter, and disconsolate giving way of republican formations, the Boers still had reliable troops, including ideologically tenacious foreign irregulars in the Orange Free State whose republican attachment was especially relished by Steyn and his immediate circle. Although in no state of strength or preparedness to fight off British regulars, Steyn and de Wet bustled about in an attempt to improvise the last-ditch defences of Bloemfontein and continuing to flag defiance. Formal Kimberley–Bloemfontein confrontation between the two armies was now close to being over. Outside the capital, however, de la Rey still had claws. Although only able to cluster a small force of 1500 commandos, he tensed in wait near Driefontein or Abraham's Kraal, tracking enemy movement to lure them on. All that was left was to force some sort of spoiling encounter. In due course de la Rey collided with French and his force of 10,000 cavalrymen, obstructing their advance for a full day before being forced into withdrawal, as every horizon became closed by British horsemen.

Bloemfontein fell on 13 March 1900. Steyn's belief in running things to the wire with some improbable national blood sacrifice came to nothing, superseded by the more prosaic spectacle of a handover managed gently by the town's leading white landowning and commercial élite. The Attorney John Fraser, a former speaker of the Volksraad, and B. O. Kellner, the mayor of Bloemfontein, embodied an Afrikaner–Scottish and Afrikaner–German leading urban interest which liked to make speeches. Provided his position was flattered, Roberts liked to hear them. Driven by remorseless self-promotion, he was an experienced manipulator of a kept imperialist war press, and he ensured that, in the taking of the town, the sunny side of affairs was fully covered.[12]

With Steyn having slunk off northwards on 12 March on one of the

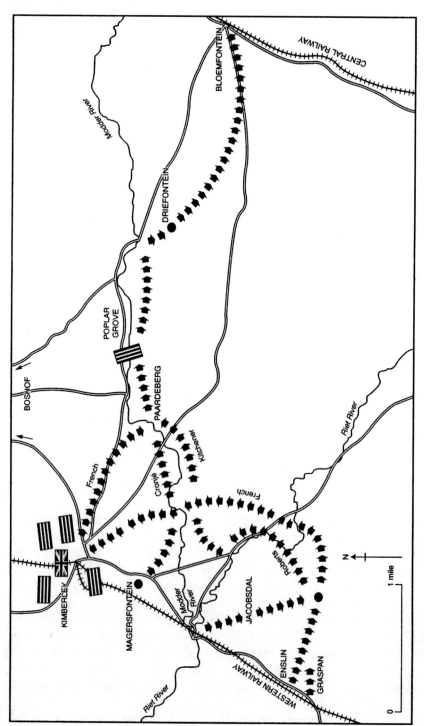

Map 5.2 *British Advance on Bloemfontein, March 1900*

last trains to roll out before the British cut the line, Roberts and his spouse found an open door to the presidential residence. Another such door was Bloemfontein's mostly wealthy and welcoming British Uitlander citizenry, the men with a good grip on the decanter and the women a dab hand at running up silk Union Jacks. The capital's Sotho labourers also bore an inviting expression, with some demonstrating their gratitude by ransacking the Orange Free State artillery corps barracks and looting other Boer property.

For the British the seizure of Bloemfontein was not the grand controlling objective; but it would do as a base from which to strike the really determining blow at Pretoria. Still, the military occupation itself was not without its troubles. Although an important theatre for republican nationalist politics, the Orange Free State capital was a little town, with just over 4000 white and black inhabitants. Its realistic garrisoning capacity stopped somewhat short of the 50,000 soldiers now marched in by Roberts. The trying conditions in and around the capital proved debilitating for already tired, indifferently nourished, and chronically neglected troops. More than just stretching sick parades, the concentration of the British camp in Bloemfontein stretched sanitation facilities and hygiene maintenance to fatal limits. A severe outbreak of enteric fever, or typhoid, quickly turned a packed capital into a swelling military hospital, the hunt for beds and accommodation leading to the widespread commandeering of buildings and usable trappings, including schools, clubhouses and the parliament house itself. By early April almost 1000 troops had died in what was to become merely the first of a series of flaring typhoid outbreaks.[13]

Another factor which retarded the rapid renewal of Roberts' active campaigning was seriously depleted supply levels on occupation. A necessary prior step was the bringing in of replenishing columns, which rolled up some of their fresh provisions while on the hoof through the surrounding countryside. Boer farms which had been losing African labourers and tenants to auxiliary service with the British army now began to lose foodstuffs too. While resting and resupplying his tired army, Roberts moved to clarify the tough new political position for the subject Boers. In March, the British published a local proclamation which specified that men within a surrounding 10-mile jurisdiction of the capital had to surrender or else face the outright expropriation of their property. While the effectiveness of such intimidatory regulations was obviously highly variable, the British were signifying an early sovereignty with sharp teeth. More broadly, the Boers had to be made to feel the loss of their own statehood; in due course, Roberts extended an amnesty to every Orange Free State burgher (with the exception of their leadership) on condition of a return home, the relinquishing of arms, and the taking of an oath of allegiance.

The circumstances in which the republican leadership laboured were dire. Not only had the short war ended up in the doldrums, but the prospects of fighting a longer encounter had been dreadfully damaged. Displaying just how short it was in its understanding of the intricate business of wheeling and dealing between international powers, the Boer command gamely tried to unlock European patronage and protection through official high strategy. Given that the imperialist will to prosecute the war looked rather unlikely to falter, what might make Britain hesitate? Conceivably, the restraining factor of European assistance for the Boers.

In pursuit of an anti-British imperialist aid alliance, three envoys, cap in hand, were dispatched to several overseas capitals. Two members of this mission, A. D. W. Wolmarans and C. H. Wessels, were drawn from the prominent 'Hollander clique' of the Kruger faction, with the third, Abraham Fischer, dispatched by Steyn. But, while they found the Netherlands government a beaming countenance and its Hague and Amsterdam populations a nest of singing Boer birds, the Dutch state had no desire to act provocatively. For Queen Wilhelmina's restraining ministers, it was the Kaiser's voice alone which might draw together some collective anti-British initiative on behalf of the republics. But Germany in turn looked to the United States for support, fully aware of the potential leverage which America was acquiring through the increasing flow of its financial credits to London after the outbreak of war. There was no need to read the *Economist* for Berlin to know about British borrowings not only of American capital, but of American gold as well. Yet there was always something more to the Anglo-American connection: in this case it lay principally in a reciprocity between British and American war aims in their respective colonial worlds. In contrast to other European states, Britain had adopted an indulgent attitude towards the United States in its pursuit of war against the Spanish in Cuba and the Philippines in the later 1890s. In turn, Washington shrugged off political pressure from organized Irish-American and German-American groupings at least to disavow Britain's South African war policy. Unable to bring other governments to consider any assistance, the republicans' emissaries of March 1900 had to content themselves with trawling in public funding for the Boer cause, of which there was a good deal forthcoming through lotteries and other subscription drives by prominent Dutch pro-Boer societies such as the beavering Haagsche pro-Boer Vereeniging.

Meanwhile, as Roberts prepared for the next stage of the British advance and the Transvaal began to nerve itself for a coming onslaught, there were growing suggestions that the Boers did not have to stand helpless in the face of such odds, for they had another card to play: republican control of the wealth and strategic power of the Rand. Always a lingering undercurrent in Boer thinking after the outbreak of war, talk of how to exploit it grew louder after the completed capture of Steyn's capital. In March, Transvaal papers with a close ear to the Kruger government carried insinuations and increasingly outright argument that not only should the gold mines be destroyed, but that any Uitlander property which could not be requisitioned or confiscated should also be demolished. Indeed, both within the ruling executive and among ordinary Volksraad representatives, there was hard discussion and debate over the radical option of wrecking the mines ahead of a British invasion. Some of its advocates did not mind much about consequence or measured purpose; it was a simply a fine chance to whip Britain. Others were made eager by an incoherent Boer anti-capitalism, with the gold industry reviled not so much because it was capitalist as because it was alien, or foreign. A number of influential radical republicans, including F. W. Reitz, favoured blowing up the mines as a delicious retribution upon the Randlords, whose capitalist greed was still considered largely responsible for having brought on the war.[14]

On the other hand, some, including Kruger and Joubert, took a little more effort to think out the strategic issue of what to do about the golden calf. Killing it in a rush of blood was imprudent: it would not do for the reputation of the Transvaal for it to be stung by European accusations of state recklessness with property and market rights. Besides, the republican war-chest dilemma was that they needed gold production to continue rather than to end. It came back to finding the balance necessary to energize a war of recovery, by squeezing the owners of the mining industry – the Rand's jumpy mine-owners were vulnerable to sharp impositions or to being intimidated by the threat of wholesale confiscation or dynamiting of their properties. For a little while the gold industry seemed to offer some illusory prospect of a way out. By threatening the future of Rand production, the Transvaal could remind German, French, and Belgian financiers that their customary returns could not come cost-free. One suggested possibility was that by taking the mines hostage, the republic might even compel foreign states to take a share in its cause, if only to ensure that, in their desperation, the Boers did not jeopardize key world financial assets. Another, even smarter variation was to have done with idle threats and simply to seize the mines from their British owners. By then selling them off to non-British foreign interests, the Boers could redistribute some of the burden of their war effort to a new breed of Rand financiers and speculators, who would have a tidy and obligatory stake in propping up continuing Transvaal independence.

Rumours of preparations to have the mines dynamited soon saw the likes of Sammy Marks scuttling off to prevail upon Kruger and his Executive Council, Joubert, and even commanders in the field like de la Rey and Botha, not to sanction the wanton destruction of mine property. The call was to stand firm against the apocalyptic visions of an overheated Reitz, who felt that if his state was to be conquered by the demonic English, it ought to be left wholly ruined, 'like Sodom and Gomorrah'.[15]

Sensing that the basic economic future of the Transvaal was what mattered, most class guardians of the Boer republican order were firmly against any war strategy of domestic state depredation of this kind. In its social nature Boer society was probably incapable of such absolute action in any event. A powerful constraint was surely the formal ideological field of Boer colonial society; by the 1890s, one of the more settled determinants of its character was the national hedging of property and the protectionism of individualist capital resources. Joubert and other well-connected members of a parasitic Boer élite with a zest for mining and land share speculation were rather unlikely to lead some communitarian national assault upon crucial property, whatever its ownership and whatever their cause. These were men with a healthy appreciation of production and profit.

While de la Rey, Botha, and other Boer commanders agreed on preserving the mines, they had no desire to leave the military situation in the hands of Roberts and an uncontested march to imperial victory. Brushing aside entreaties from some influential Transvaal citizens to consider laying down their arms now that things looked lost, at a key War Council on 20 March it was decided to continue the struggle. A fairly energetic affair, it was shaped by an appreciation that the nature of the war was already changing rapidly, that fixed head-on contests were over, and that as the hunt was on for the British, so their Boer prey had to become even less cumbersome in the field.

For a start, de Wet urged the general abandonment of burdening wagon laagers which stunted speed, stifled flexibility, and offered too obvious a target for enemy guns.[16] Abolishing wheeled columns for pack horses also meant tightening male combat solidarities by removing the guardianship entanglement caused by the continuing presence in some commandos of a number of older women and children. What were needed were better selected and domestically unencumbered troops, younger fighters who would take on the harsh rigours of campaigning in open veldt and bush, and who would be far more accustomed to travelling light. Smuts, in proposing that *landdrosts* form systematic recruitment committees to scour local districts and dragoon every available able-bodied man into service, had in mind such newer men, a sort of pastoral Boer Samurai with Protestant perseverance. With a true sense of what it meant to be a responsible and selfless patriotic combatant, they were urgently needed to repair a campaigning position in which 'the great majority thought more of their farms, their families and their private affairs, than of the fate of the Republics'. Their forces could have no reasonable hope of making headway while 'a spirit of civil self-interest as distinguished from military self-sacrifice'[17] continued to contaminate the Boer rank and file.

These worries certainly counted, underpinned by the burgher response to Roberts' proclamations, in which some 12,000 to 14,000 commandos were to down arms and surrender between March and July 1900. But they did not halt local moves to try to improve the Boer position in late March, any more than did the death of Piet Joubert around the same time. While the republicans were in no state to beat back Roberts, they could still make him bleed. To do this, de Wet conceived a renewed two-pronged offensive which would draw his forces into the wide spaces north of Bloemfontein to bring on the British, and then to strike at them from the southeast.

This was all conducted with some considerable efficiency. On 30 March Christiaan de Wet in alliance with his brother Piet, and General Andries Cronjé, turned the British into quarry, with de Wet's creeping scouts invigilating the movement of a British force from Thaba Nchu to Bloemfontein from distant patrolling margins. Able to anticipate the precise march route of the British column, the commando leadership made its plans. At Koornspruit at dawn on 30 March 400 Kroonstad and Bloemfontein commandos, armed with Krupp field guns and other artillery pieces, took their mounted adversary completely by surprise. The British commander, Major-General Robert Broadwood, had neglected to run forward any scouts to scent out what might lie ahead. While his troops held on and wriggled free of the ambush, they suffered severe casualties, with 150 soldiers killed or wounded and 480 captured; in equipment losses they were relieved of ammunition carts and provisioning wagons, several hundred rifles, hundreds of horses and pack animals, and a batch of Royal Horse Artillery guns. One of the first acts of de Wet's concealed riflemen was to fell gun-battery horses, to impede their deployment and eventually force the retreating British to leave them behind. In their withdrawal eastwards the Boers were jubilant, having taken negligible losses of 5 dead and 11 wounded.

Their spirits lifted by a satisfactorily one-sided clash, de Wet's forces derived an immediate tactical opportunity. The very next day, 31 March, the commandos mounted a direct assault in the same area, this time against a small pocket of British infantry holding the pumping station and waterworks at Sannaspos. Situated on lower, undulating terrain to the east of Bloemfontein, a section of approaching ground could not be tracked by its lookout point and heliograph warning station. This provided a sneaky corridor along which de Wet's force, riding at night and quietly holed up during the day, squirmed forward. Again, the British were caught napping at dawn, and de Wet attained his objective of seizing the waterworks in order to cut off fresh supply to the town. This worsened the typhoid epidemic which was eating at Roberts' army with close on 2000 deaths before the end of April. A regular counter-offensive had begun, even if based more on military blows than on any gaining of ground or effective extension of power. Early in April de Wet detached 800 men from his snaking column of 1500 commandos and struck at the British for a third time, at Reddersburg, about 30 miles south of Bloemfontein.

Their foe, under the blighted command of Gatacre, had been assigned the task of bringing the southern districts of the Orange Free State firmly under the British heel. Staging a rapid approach and preparatory bombardment with quick-firing Krupp guns to press his advantage of timing and dominant position, de Wet then completely enclosed the enemy, and squeezed hard until the British accepted that they were beaten. Handing over their arms, they passed into captivity and confinement behind barbed wire on some republican farm. British casualties exceeded 590 killed, wounded, or taken prisoner, while republican losses were once more slight. For the simplest surprise, a considerable reward had been reaped.

Although the republican forces were still haemorrhaging burghers from their combat musters, for the moment de Wet's heartening strikes ruled out any further thought of breaking off. Commando strength was now also being augmented by a steady trickle of burghers who, having been permitted to return to their farms upon submitting to an oath of non-belligerence, now slipped back to join the fighting ranks. It seems doubtful that all of them had meant to honour their submissive undertakings: where the British were passing, or had established a clear and undisputed hold, farmers had to act in a compliant way to try to restrain the invading enemy from a retributive sacking of their property. Furthermore, the present round saw the Orange Free State Boers being joined by batches of migrating Cape rebels from northern and northwestern districts, and by European volunteers such as the Irish Brigade, the Russian scouts attached to de Wet's commando, and the Kroonstad foreign corps under the pushy ex-French Legionnaire George-Henri de Villebois de Mareuil, who had been promoted to a general on the sidelines after the fall of Bloemfontein. While foreign volunteers were few, their bunched, clannish loyalties and fierce ideological adherence to the republican cause provided purpose and motivation; their position as mostly single, urban men also meant that combat readiness was unlikely to be hampered by the occasional need to skip engagements to trot off to some cattle auction.

With the freedom to continue on the hoof and to stay on the attack, early in April de Wet launched a fourth sally, this time advancing 6000 commandos to put under threat the settlement of Wepener, where he was opposed by a force of around 2000 colonial loyalists, mostly unsentimental Cape Boers who were taking to the Crown for five shillings per day. With a sulphurously hostile determination that the enemy would pay, the republicans tried to crack British defences with repeated assaults, compelling their foe to maintain a frantic vigil against ferocious raiding. De Wet seemed to relish lengthening the line of a new front, boldly laying siege to the well-entrenched Wepener garrison for over two weeks, and with troops to spare to post as a forward approach guard to cover his position at some distance from the action.

The British lines held. They were aided by having Basutoland directly at their rear, where the Resident Commissioner, Sir Godfrey Lagden, authorized a Sotho frontier guard of 3000 men to deter de Wet from attempting any flanking movement across formally neutral terrain, and from which Sotho collaborators tried to feed livestock and ammunition to the colonial force and to transfer wounded and sick soldiers over the border under darkness to be given medical aid. The stealthy movements and disregard of danger showed by the incoming Sotho awed members of the Wepener garrison, one of whom recorded his gratitude that they were not standing by the republicans, given their infiltrationist skill and night silence, barely talking in whispers and lighting no incriminating fires around the Caledon river rearguard.[18]

After more than a fortnight a strong reinforcing column under Ian Hamilton arrived from Bloemfontein to relieve the standoff. Roberts' intention and expectation had been to maroon de Wet with a thick encircling movement and then to push him back against the garrison defence, forcing his enemy to choose between slaughter or capitulation. But the Boers kept themselves fully apprised of Hamilton's manoeuvres through the wily exertions of de Wet's élite scouting corps, and they engineered a proper rearguard barrier behind which to fall back. Abandoning the Wepener position, they careered off before the approaching British could bring them to fight.

After a longer than anticipated pause in Bloemfontein, on 3 May Roberts' Bloemfontein army of 45,000 troops got under way in several columns, on its 300-mile march to clinch the war at Pretoria. To his east, Buller was crawling northwards through Natal, on a direct route to the Transvaal through Laing's Nek. The British could be delayed, but not blocked, as western and eastern offensive strategies converged. The sense of that closing advantage could not have been expressed with greater confidence than in the contagious spread of the popular processional song, 'We are Marching to Pretoria', a jaunty imperial hymn to the rising dominion of the English in South Africa. Hopelessly outnumbered, the Boers could do little more than attempt to check the impetus of the enemy advance by deflecting their passage through the tricky river system. So demolition squads blew the bridge across the Vet river, and shortly afterwards also dynamited the Sand River bridge. This produced some twists to the line of advance, but did not stall the British, who merely sidestepped.

In a change of base, Botha angled away from Natal to the western front to carry the fight to Roberts' enormous invasion columns in the Sand river area. Here, in an effort to disjoint the connecting concentration of the British army, he pulled off a diversionary encounter with its cavalry spearhead under French. But, despite keeping French under fire for virtually a full day, Botha could not avoid having to pull back to avoid being outflanked. With the opposition shaken off the British advance closed up again, and on 10 May threw its line across the Sand river without meeting any further spoiling opposition.

By now, political command in the Orange Free State was in tatters.

None the less, Steyn and his associates continued trying desperately to keep their ruling inheritance together, even if only a minority of their subject burghers showed very much intention of helping. Ousted from Bloemfontein, the leadership had moved its capital to Kroonstad, just over 130 miles north of the fallen town. There, Orange Free State and Transvaal war deputations had deliberated over what organizational combination and strategy might yet save them from rapid defeat. On 12 May the republicans had to find another seat as Roberts rolled up Kroonstad. Heilbron then became the new capital, those sitting there knowing fully that it would probably be exchanged for Lindley before very long: as assuredly it was, and then only briefly, as the incursion of Hamilton's brigades on 8 May put Steyn and his government to flight even further north.

With Kroonstad tucked away, Roberts tied up his force for well over a week, despite prodding from some subordinate commanders who wanted to stay on the trail. It was not a question of lacking the will to move. Extended campaigning over South Africa's distances was aggravating already acute problems of transport and supply. While the republicans had not succeeded in hitting the railway hard enough to break it up and deny the British its vital use, there was scattered damage behind and ahead, making it difficult to bring up regular troop supplies. The exultant Fenians of the republics' Irish Brigade had commenced vigorous, ably coordinated sabotage action on the communications route between Bloemfontein and the Vaal river, blowing up crossings and culverts, and twisting rails. Efficient repair and river bridging were undertaken by a rugged, nomadic army of African railway labourers under Girouard, the favoured Kitchener standby from the Sudan, with his handy background in engineering and colonial labour recruitment.

Until the network was adequately restored for the ferrying of supplies the advance slowed down, for troops who gathered in spots not fed by the railway ended up grievously short of rations through the gratuitous folly and miscalculation of Roberts' and Kitchener's transport mess. Physical strain and dietary deficiencies obviously took costly toll of efficiency and morale, a situation added to by continuing problems with ravaging typhoid and the neglect of sanitation by the field medical services. As more than one historian has pointed out, typhoid and the associated medical crisis experienced by the British army in the Orange Free State during May produced a casualty rate worse than that sustained in all the fighting of Black Week.[19] This time it was plainly Roberts' administrative bungling, a rigmarole quite unsuited to meeting the urgings of his force.

Meanwhile, far to the west, the problem of Mafeking was not being neglected. Lieutenant-Colonel Herbert Plumer, the commander of the closest based British force, an irregular regiment of white Rhodesian mounted infantry, had already made several shallow attempts to force the siege, but with fewer than 700 colonial volunteers and no effective guns had managed to get no nearer than about five miles from Mafeking before being beaten off by the Boers. Even after Cronje had lumbered southwards to respond to the Methuen move on Kimberley, a depleted siege force of 1500 commandos under General Jan Snyman still had the superior strength to trip up any run by Plumer. With a decomposing Mafeking defence line unable to hold out for very much longer, Roberts despatched a 2000-strong flying relief column from Kimberley under Colonel Bryan Mahon. As Mahon's agile force, its brisk movement closely tracked by the Boers, hurried in for a converging attack with a Plumer contingent expanded to over 1100 colonial irregulars and braced by Royal Horse Artillery, Canadian guns, and Australian infantry, the republicans slipped in a last desperate raid.

The defence was sustained, largely by Baralong residents who bore up in ferocious fighting and then helped to harry the attacking force of around 300 Boers into surrender. Mafeking's largely African dead and wounded totalled 20, with Snyman's losses much higher, 'at 60 battle casualties and over 100 commandos taken prisoner. Having staved off the last fight reserves of the besiegers, the raising of the siege just four days later on 16 May came with far less fuss, in Mafeking if not in London.

Pressing up from the south, Mahon combined with Plumer's column approaching from a northerly direction. The advancing of their guns and opening of a light bombardment were sufficient for the Boers to heed the warning. They quickly gave up their position altogether, and fled. At the end of the siege, Baden-Powell as press censor insistently barred the *Mafeking Mail* from running any account of the critical role played by Africans in repelling the final 12 May republican assault on the town, and brusquely disarmed the angrily protesting Baralong. It was not until after the garrison commander's departure from Mafeking that their crucial participation made it into the published record.

For the British, all was now set for their forces to go through and conquer the Transvaal by taking its capital. Going on from Mafeking to smaller things, Baden-Powell and his Bechuanaland corps returned to his secret July 1899 orders to threaten the Transvaal's northern borders, or even to raid it at the outbreak of war, as a spoiling diversion to tie up a large portion of Boer forces. Their strategic position was now, of course, vastly different. With his force ranged alongside Plumer's colonial regiment, there was preparation for a different kind of penetration, an invasion from the west which would strike deep into a republic held by a weakened and rapidly disintegrating army. In another part of this subsidiary pincer, the Rhodesian Field Force under General Frederick Carrington planned a way in to the Transvaal from the north. In major concerted movements, Buller's Natal army was inching up eastwards to hammer down the southeastern Transvaal and unclog the second key railway artery from the coast to Pretoria, while French's probing cavalry headed the growing concentration of British forces under Roberts, now marching up at a brisk pace from the south. Awaiting them was no military power, but the wasting asset of a Boer soldier-citizenry. The Transvaal's war looked all but over.

By mid-1900 British Liberal intellectuals were already pondering a possible peace, while a wider public sense of the end of the war was reflected in pamphlets, essays, and even a number of books which circulated amongst the more educated British middle classes. A memorable example was *A Retrospect on the South African War*, conceived in 1900 and published early in 1901. It was the misfortune of its sanguine author, Sir Edward May, to start rather ahead of time and to finish rather behind it, too.

Still, the Transvaal itself was not short of inclinations to surrender. In mid-May a small deputation of influential political notables and businessmen, all cosy associates of Kruger, opened peacemaking overtures to the president on the basis that the republican cause was unmistakably lost. Evidently thinking that a peace without victors or vanquished might somehow still be retrieved, their idea was to salvage an honourable alternative to the ignominy of unconditional surrender. Announcing its action to be 'under protest', the republic should lay down its arms and then unilaterally declare the war to have ended. This would cheat Britain of the fruits of complete victory at the last minute, and also impose a moral restraint upon any continuing imperial belligerence. As a diplomatic device, it was fairly odd and remains a puzzle. It was, at any rate, an indication of the desperate state of Kruger's mind that he even toyed with the proposal as a possible means of checking further loss of life and destruction of property. After a brief airing, it was killed by Steyn. He was now far more committed to the republican struggle than the Transvaal leader and was, if anything, all for fighting on to hold off the trauma of defeat at all costs. For southern republican territory, too much had already been sacrificed in smoke to give up the struggle.[20]

But there was little to stop the enemy's immediate onward movement. By the last week of May, the imperial army was breasting the Vaal river on a line of march which would take it through Johannesburg and on to Pretoria. Near its crossing, a small force easily put to flight a puny Boer rearguard trying to cling to strategic command of the important Vereeniging colliery fields. Roberts needed to take the Vereeniging mines in one piece, to lighten his coaling headaches as the rail trucking line grew ever longer. In running, the Boers did not neglect defiant delaying actions, firing the railway station and detonating the railway bridge but sparing the vital coal mines from damage. It seems that no preparatory boring had been authorized for the works to be blown in and denied to the British.

Ahead of them, at the end of May, there was the sticky business of those other mines to be got over once again. With Roberts pressing right into the Transvaal, the republicans could no longer retain the gold workings to fund their war effort, and there was no reason to protect the mines. If anything, leaving them intact to be worked under British administration meant that their bullion extraction would instead go to finance the British campaign. The clarion call was rekindled of strategy-minded radicals such as the energetic republican judge, Antonie Kock, the former state attorney, Ewald Esselen, and Reitz: had not the time come to bring down the house of those culpable of bringing on the war, the mineowners, just as the Boer republican nation was being laid low by British imperialism? Although the special commandant of the Witwatersrand, F. E. T. Krause, remained watchful in defence of mining property, with Roberts' remorseless drive displacing burghers and pushing resentful and embittered Boers and pro-Boer Uitlanders back towards the Rand and its touch-paper, anxieties over the well-being of the mines once again grew.

By this stage, the fear was not so much that the republican government would order the destruction of the mines, for it had already halted some impetuous drilling of dynamiting holes in shafts in April, permitting European investors to sleep more easily. The likely threat came more from retreating Boer and foreign commandos who were falling back through Johannesburg, and from fighting burghers based in the city. These were being ordered by Krause at the end of May to head out for Pretoria to buttress a commando army in the north which would continue a lengthening struggle for 'land, liberty and independence'. Already causing maximum damage in retreat, these sinewy bands of men included no shortage of foxy saboteurs and incendiarists, and foreign anti-imperialists not at all averse to an anarcho-syndicalist line on how to bring down the capitalists' war. John Blake, commander of the First Irish Brigade, recorded how he had pleaded with a Council of War on the Vaal to permit him to dynamite some mines, but in vain. He met an infuriating wall of opposition, as 'they did not believe in the destruction of property'. At a Meyerton War Council, Arthur Lynch, another Irish Brigade firebrand, found some support from the pugnacious Boer commander, Tobias Smuts, who wanted to get rid of what he believed was a wicked system, 'the greed of this gold that had induced the war'.[21]

On 29 May, there actually was an abortive attempt to destroy the Robinson mine, winked at by Kock and Reitz, which only fizzled out at the very last minute. Botha and Krause then succeeded in scotching any further last-ditch moves on the mines, the former not wanting to disown the romantic masculinity of a 'fight as men' by perpetrating 'spiteful things', the latter intent on checking any imported revolutionary radicalism from 'foreign elements, such as Socialists and the like'.[22] As conservatives, they would still not break strategic property for the sake of the cause.

Botha, meanwhile, still with 6000 commandos to put into action, tinkered with attempting a blocking defence of the heart of Johannesburg, but the intimidating strength of his encroaching adversary sensibly persuaded him against anything adventurous. In any case, Boer command knew that they had lost it, or at least that there would be nothing to gain from fighting another unequal battle of this kind. Once across the Vaal, and with only about 40 miles to go, Roberts' army was already assuming tactical angling positions to carry all before it. French and Hamilton's columns were to push round to the west, closing the communications mouth provided by the main Rand road from Johannesburg to satellite towns like Germiston and Krugersdorp; the main force would set off in an easterly direction up the railway line to outflank the target from the opposite approach. The attackers ran into the dregs of republican resistance dug into a hill at Doornkop, appropriately not far from the stricken symbolism of the blackened heads of the Krugersdorp mines.

The line to try to inflict delay and diversion consisted of several hundred Johannesburg commandos under Ben Viljoen and a Lichtenburg commando led by de la Rey. Supremely confident that by this stage no fight could be fair, Hamilton chanced his luck by turning his infantry brigades on the Boers in an extended frontal charge without directing covering fire or bringing up artillery support. In widely separated waves, small parties of troops advanced in dispersed order up the hill in staggered stages, until Hamilton's Gordon Highlanders could close in to rip out the Boers with a raw bayonet charge. The defenders were routed, and Doornkop taken, but not without some cost to the British through well-sighted lines of enemy fire. Hamilton's infantry casualties exceeded 100, a loss which could have been avoided by a diversionary advance around Doornkop through a gap to its west. The heart of it all was that British general-ship was probably mesmerized by a Doornkop war cry, for it was here that a squirming Jameson had been forced to concede that everything was up.

What followed was a confused period, with a scatter of skirmishes and sniping exchanges between British and Boers in and around the Elandsfontein railway junction just to the east of Johannesburg. The prospect of a dangerous new phase of hostilities, that of chaotic and nightmarish urban street fighting, now threatened to superimpose itself upon what had been an essentially agrarian contest. But after some banging away, bands of defending commandos gave up their fir-ing lines behind covering mine heaps and brick walls, and dropped away to join the growing northwards retreat. The moment had come, but Roberts did not drive on his divisions to chase down and destroy the withdrawing Boer army. Instead, he opted for a delaying armis-tice, so that the handover could be tidied up.

On 30 May, the Commander-in-Chief's bicycling representatives settled on a peaceful handover of the whole Johannesburg district, an agreement which pleased the Krause administration which wanted to protect the city and its mines, and was also jittery about the effects of continued fighting on the African labouring population; in the end, it was wiser for the British and the Boers on the Rand to make their peace so that black workers would keep their place. Boer officials then struck a good-behaviour bargain, in which the republicans would hold off any burning or plundering in return for being allowed a day for the evacuation of the bittereinder rump of the republican army, which promptly retreated towards Pretoria with its arms, including heavy artillery, other war supplies, loot, and commandeered gold. On these terms the British took Johannesburg peaceably on 31 May. There was agreement on non-belligerence from burghers or pro-Boers, while Roberts issued a paper assurance that women and children would not be harmed by his troops, and permitted anyone with resistance left in them to leave without interference to resume the military fight elsewhere.

There were a few kicks at Krause's doings with Roberts. Invoking de la Rey as a trusty general who would have no wish to see Johannesburg relinquished without a decent struggle, there were thin cries for armed resistance; there were also rumours of daring malcontents plotting to raze the city around Roberts, and some outbreaks of frenzied looting by blacks and poorer whites, while stiff-necked Boers, Transvaal Irish volunteers, and Roberts' Australian scouts fought a few final running scraps at close quarters. Thereafter, the British had to turn to governing the city through a new Rand administration, finally realizing the claim to political power of the Uitlander élite. The rigorous new occupation regime was ready to enforce the disciplinary needs of a British Johannesburg, one of which was the deportation of various foreign 'undesirables'.[23] Another was to set right a popular misconception among its African labourers that they could continue to tear up their oppressive passes, as the arrival of Roberts had brought a liberalizing imperial freedom. This was not a cause for which Roberts was campaigning.

The conduct of hostilities at Johannesburg may well be seen as another of the more obvious might-have-beens of the war. The armistice dangled and struck by the British was certainly a little strange in military terms, for while it wound down the fighting it did nothing to prevent the Boers from reassembling to renew it later in another place and on other terms. For Louis Botha's army, the last straw had not broken their back. One cosy explanation is that Roberts held off through some velvet-glove tactical strategy of trying to bring the war to a 'speedy and humane conclusion'. What mattered was the saving of the gold mines and the screwing down of the Boer capitals, and along the way setting shrewdly discriminating terms of conquest for ordinary Boers, lenient for some, stern for others. With the enemy demolished and the war virtually over, it seemed 'sensible and humane'[24] not to squander any more British lives by attempting a final successful showdown. Much is speculative here, and probably something can be made of this. By now, Roberts obviously judged the war to be virtually at an end, and it would have been sensible to avoid more costs in a campaign already won. Also, storming the city could have jeopardized the mines, an indication that this was a war not entirely without some sense.

At the same time, there may have been other, more cogent reasons for Roberts playing the accommodating old charmer. Having experienced something of its deadly intensity in Kabul in 1880, the British commander wanted to avoid a big tussle for Johannesburg based on indisciplined street fighting, indecisive by its nature and an environment ripe for frustrated troops to vent their rage gratuitously or to commit atrocities against inhabitants. Another factor was the acute hunger and thirst of British troops, who could be run short no longer. When they reached Germiston on 30 May, Roberts' strained soldiers had barely a day's provisions left. An obvious and serious worry was British forces being penned into an exhaustive battle over Johannesburg, waiting who knew how long for the Boers to come across to parley, and inevitably running out of stores because supply lines could not easily be maintained across an unpredictable urban grid. Still, spitting on the enemy rather than urging on the fight in May 1900 has been judged 'probably the most serious strategic mistake'[25] of Roberts' South African career, both by some of his contemporaries and in hindsight. In the view of Buller's Chief of Staff, he had 'annexed a country without conquering it'.[26] The implications of this form the next and final phase of the South African conflict.

Chapter 5 Notes

1. J. H. Breytenbach, *Die Geskiedenis van die Tweede Vryheidsoorlog in Suid Afrika, 1899–1902*, vol. 1 (Pretoria, 1969), p. 466.
2. Jacqueline Beaumont, 'The British press and censorship during the South African War, 1899–1902', Rethinking the SA War Conference paper, UNISA, 1998.
3. Emanoel Lee, *To the Bitter End: A Photographic History of the Boer War 1899–1902* (Harmondsworth, 1985), pp. 61–2.
4. R. J. Moore-Colyer, 'Horse supply and the British cavalry: a review, 1066–1900', *Journal of the Society of Army Historical Research*, 70/284 (1992), pp. 259–60; S. R. Badsey, 'Fire and sword: the British army and the *arme blanche* controversy, 1871–1921', Ph.D. diss. (University of Cambridge, 1981), p. 135.
5. G. Crew, *The Royal Army Service Corps* (London, 1970), pp. 90–3.
6. Byron Farwell, *Eminent Victorian Soldiers* (Harmondsworth, 1986), p. 335.
7. Badsey, 'Fire and sword', pp. 78–9; Michael Glover, *Warfare from Waterloo to Mons* (London, 1980), p. 207.
8. *Het Zuid-Oosten*, 22 Feb. 1900.
9. *Jan Smuts: Memoirs of the Boer War*, eds Gail Nattrass and S. B. Spies (Johannesburg, 1994), p. 39.
10. R. W. Schikkerling, *Commando Courageous* (Johannesburg, 1964), p. 66; Pretorius, 'Afrikaner nationalism and the burgher on commando', Rethinking the SA War Conference paper, UNISA, 1998.
11. *Cape Daily Telegraph*, 7 May 1900; *Green Howards Gazette*, 89/8 (1900), p. 63.
12. S. F. Malan, 'Die Britse Besetting van Bloemfontein, 13 Maart 1900', *Historia*, 1/1 (1975), pp. 41–2.
13. Lt.-Col. J. H. Plumridge, *Hospital Ships and Ambulance Trains* (London, 1975), pp. 90–1.
14. *African Review*, 23/387 (1900), pp. 96–8.
15. Diana Cammack, *The Rand at War, 1899–1902: The Witwatersrand and the Anglo-Boer War* (London, 1990), p. 102.
16. R. L. V. ffrench-Blake, *The 17th/21st Lancers* (London, 1968), p. 97.

17. *Smuts: Memoirs*, p. 45.
18. *Oakleaf*, 1/8 (1900), p. 26.
19. Thomas Pakenham, *The Boer War* (London, 1979), pp. 381–3; Lee, *Bitter End*, pp. 109–13.
20. *Lloyds Weekly Newspaper*, 21 May 1900.
21. Arthur Lynch, *My Life Story* (London, 1924), p. 194.
22. Cammack, *Rand at War*, p. 107.
23. *Cape Times*, 12 Aug. 1900.
24. Pakenham, *Boer War*, p. 428.
25. Ibid., p. 428;
26. D. H. Doolittle, *A Soldier's Hero: General Sir Archibald Hunter* (Rhode Island, 1991), p. 229.

6

A Protracted and Pervasive War

With Johannesburg in Britain's pocket, and measures in place to weed out its Boer agitators and those suspect Europeans identified by Milner as 'disagreeable foreign riff-raff', Roberts now moved on to conclude his relentless offensive. This involved fixing Pretoria, which lay about 300 miles away. The final and most destructive phase of the war now began. Continuing the flanking tactic of closing and enveloping republican defence lines, which by now amounted to punching through gossamer, on 4 June the British reached the hills overlooking Pretoria. 'That holy of holies of the Republic in South Africa,' observed a flushed Smuts, 'was generally expected to mark a decisive stage ... to the British commanders the expected final Boer stand at Pretoria and its capture' would deliver 'the *coup de grâce* to the Republics'. This was certainly how Lansdowne, Milner, and Roberts and his generals saw things. For once, colonial opponents had a fixed 'European' capital which they seemed to prize, making its capture a clinching strategic gain. 'To the republican rank and file,' continued Smuts, the conception of Pretoria was that of 'the great Armageddon where the Boer forces, concentrated from all points of the compass in defence ... would deliver that final united blow from which perhaps the British forces might be sent reeling back to the coast. Perhaps – and perhaps not.' Despite the weakened condition of forces retreating from Johannesburg and continuing desertions, in Smuts' view the fact that thousands of men still 'stuck to their commandos'[1] was animated by an expectation that the war's decisive action would be fought at Pretoria, a place which contained all the republican currency reserves and reserve ammunition stores. It also had surplus food in the hands of wealthier classes, having drawn heavily from surrounding farms and organized stockpiles. Within the city, petitions, meetings, and the press called upon commandos to show some manly staying power in the face of a conquering enemy, and to stand and fight for their homes and women and children.

Scrabbling desperately to find troops after the defection of 20,000 burghers who had been struggling to halt the British drive north-wards, Boer command was able to muster some 7000 men to meet the British attack. Pretoria also had fortifications. These included several formidable gun bastions, thickly proofed against artillery and with integrated electric power, and a German Siemens field telephone system, a pioneering use of modern communications in war.[2] This may have been something to get the pigeons fluttering, except that operational demands on the Boer artillery corps had kept these forts short of heavy Creusot cannon and gunners. With the British advance too rapid for timely rearmament, Pretoria's forts could barely put up any blocking fire. But this had already ceased to matter.

At the beginning of June, several Boer commanders, including Ben Viljoen and Louis Botha, proposed to Kruger that the war be brought to an end at Pretoria. Their case was that the Boer armies had dis-integrated, and what fighting remnants had been left behind were spent. Already on the brink of extinction, to continue the war would be to invite only death or captivity. Given the crushing weight of defeats and losses since the start of Roberts' raging campaign, the Boers lacked the means even for tit-for-tat warfare. Paralysis was too great to even contemplate a counter-effort. Finally, with destruction already advanced, if the war went on devastation could only spread until it consumed the whole of republican territory.

The Transvaal President was, by all accounts, dismayed by so defeatist an assessment; in particular, Botha's argument that several thousand men could not hope to contest Roberts' seizure of Pretoria looked unanswerable. Among the senior military leadership it was only de la Rey who strongly dissented, hissing that if the Transvaal was meekly surrendered, he would run his best troops westwards to regroup and resume hostilities from there. Ahead of a major War Council on 2 June to consider what to do about the Pretoria position, Kruger conferred with Steyn, still on his toes in the far northeast of the Orange Free State. After this exchange of cables, no Transvaaler of substance would ever again risk Orange Free State susceptibilities in favour of Transvaal needs. Steyn's answer to the capitulation pro-posal was blunt, releasing some pent-up resentments. The Transvaal had harried his republic into war solidarity, even though Britain had not been endangering Bloemfontein's independence; furthermore, Orange Free State authorities had even gone on to induce neighbouring colonial rebels to risk all. Now that their republic had lost its independence and was being flattened in parts, its ally was prepared to conclude a 'selfish and disgraceful' peace the moment warfare lapped over its borders.[3] Kruger's concern for peacemaking in order to prevent continuing devastation seemed to Steyn a poor joke at his expense; too much was already carcasses and cinders for the Boers not to do the honourable thing and fight on. If it ended as defeat for the Transvaal, so be it; even if the Orange Free State was left on its own, it would remain in combat, prepared to go to the wire.

With this terse position digested by the War Council, the chance of peace was lost. If Pretoria *was* defeat, few now seemed willing to admit it. Curiously, remarkably little needed to be done at this political level to repudiate any separate Anglo-Transvaal peace. Talk of ending resistance was condemned as traitorous by increasingly self-sacrificing, younger nationalist hotheads; the government was denounced for desertion in packing its bags; and there were calls for all of Pretoria to be turned into an armed enclave, regulated by a military regime under a Commandant-General. So that this spot would not necessarily become a final stand, the War Council planned a staged defence and fighting retreat; but the ground was poor.

Those disgruntled commandos who were not already surrendering to the advancing British or sidling off to their homes in surrounding districts were limping into Pretoria to get drunk and feast on the proceeds of widespread looting. As conditions grew increasingly chaotic, the appetites of some republican soldiers made them more to be feared and restrained than trusted with fighting responsibility. Contact between retreating soldiers and urban civilians was not particularly helpful to national morale. Nor was the show put up by a *rust en orde* (peace and tranquility committee), disparaged by pro-war leadership as men scared of war, and most especially of artillery bombardment. Quickly dubbed an *oorgee* (surrender) committee of fair-weather patriots, their attempts to grasp at peace was 'an exhibition of treachery and double-dealing, sickening to behold'.[4]

As the British closed in, Kruger's executive council sensibly put aside thoughts of serious resistance, relieved the increasingly inert Commandant, Lukas Meyer, of the impossible task of defending his capital, and withdrew before the President himself ended up being nabbed by Roberts. Together with senior members of the Transvaal government, Kruger rattled away by train to Machadodorp on the

Delagoa Bay line, with the sanctuary of Portuguese East Africa ahead. Until he was forced finally to flee the country in September 1900, this rolling stock served as a puffing capital, spewing out desperate telegrams to more stationary capitals like Paris and Berlin. The government left behind a little window-dressing in the shape of Vice-President Schalk Burger, Smuts, Botha, and de la Rey.

Theirs was an urgent time. Money and gold to the value of around half a million pounds was prised from the republic's National Bank and its Mint, and a special war fund of £25,000 was also hunted down by Smuts; the South African Republic's paltry reserve wealth was then transported eastwards on a police train in the direction of Mozambique. Having two kinds of capital on the same line was perhaps one of the more novel moments in the history of the railway and colonialism in Africa. As fighting commandos evacuated their lines and rode east towards the Magaliesberg, Roberts did not even have to mop up. On 5 June, with his usual exceptional sensitivity to press needs, he put up a great triumphal show of marching into Pretoria to run up the flag. The publicity was immense. Ever ready to give Buller the benefit of any doubt, several Boer observers, Smuts included, wondered whether his advance through the Drakensberg had been deliberately slowed down politically to ensure that Roberts had the chance of first bite at the Transvaal. Even by his usual standard, Buller's pace looked suspiciously arthritic.

The idea of a free republican state order had become a fiction; now a secondary imperial political formation, a recently proclaimed Orange River Colony, would soon be joined by a new Transvaal Colony to solve the South African problem. While the government and its generals had not stayed in Pretoria to surrender, thousands of their broken burghers were doing just that. *Hensoppers*, or 'hands-uppers' were flocking to accept Roberts' neutrality-oath proclamation extended from the Orange Free State. In the eyes of more speculative British commanders, any continuing Boer hostilities had to be a hollow bluff, for between March and June their military power had been wasting away. Before the end of June almost 8000 Transvaal commandos had voluntarily surrendered their arms; to this could be added around 6000 Orange Free State surrender losses from March to July. As Albert Grundlingh has pointed out, this was a dismal yardstick of quite how bad things were. A combined wastage of 14,000 men represented over a quarter of all those liable for military service in both states, amounting to around 40 per cent of the level of initial mobilization.[5]

On 5 June 1900 Roberts had almost every advantage with which to conclude the war, most of all a huge superiority in fighting numbers and equipment. His advance against a virtually unprotected Pretoria had been exceptionally easy. The remaining Natal commandos on the Drakensberg stayed clear, having nothing to spare from their thin lines of defence thrown up to try to block Buller's advance. The commandos from the western border were falling back towards Pretoria, but too slowly and too few in number to be a disruption. Directly ahead, what Botha and de la Rey had left as a command would have fallen apart at the prospect of any more hideous battles. Meanwhile, Roberts had done his calculations, and these included what to do about any possible Boer retreat. He was not too perturbed. Sent off fast in a northerly direction from Krugersdorp, French's stroke was to cut through the Magaliesberg and to turn east to seal off any gap behind the republican lines; that would give Roberts the option of a rear assault on Pretoria, and choke off what he guessed would be the probable line of any Boer retreat northwards.

For one usually so well-informed, it was a seriously wrong guess. The logical line of retreat was east: that was where the republic's government and reserves were going, and if supply and communication were to continue filtering in it could only be through Delagoa Bay. To the north lay strategically barren terrain, lightly populated with settlers, notoriously unhealthy, and poorly provided for foraging. To go fully into such unprotected country was to be too easily plucked. Although he had a large enough force to deal with Pretoria and to catch out the Boers in any attempt at an eastern movement, Roberts failed badly in dispatching French to close the wrong back door. His opponents spotted this blunder and for once were able to rejoice at the air they were being given; had French covered the right, seaward flank rather than the left the Boers would probably have been well and truly caught. This, as Smuts recognized, 'might have dealt a massive blow to further resistance by the Transvaal'.

The reorganizing Boers soon showed that if down, they were not yet out. On 7 June de Wet staged a lightning raid on railway garrison posts north of Kroonstad, inflicting 700 British casualties, cutting communications to the south, wrecking supplies, dynamiting a bridge, and destroying several miles of line. He was a dab hand at the railways, blasting track or even heating rails on bonfires until they were hot enough to twist, making it difficult for the British to quickly straighten bent rail through hammering. In such destructive proficiency, the Boer leader was a carbon copy of Sherman on the march in the last phase of the American Civil War. Moving rapidly, de Wet's Orange Free State force continued to strike out, blowing up more bridges, bottling up tunnels, and laying risky but skilful traps in which to strike glancing blows at the enemy; this involved allowing British parties to pass along routes unmolested, to build up an illusion of safety before suddenly ambushing an isolated convoy when its guard was down.

The effect of this audacious and sophisticated work was to draw on Kitchener with 12,000 mounted men; but by then the damage had been done. By fits and starts, the Boers were getting something going, with their governments settling on a new defensive plan in which their armies would separate. By now, of course, Orange Free State forces were down to 8000 commandos at the most. Still, with the great rump of the British army across the Vaal, Christiaan de Wet's own small unit of experienced and accomplished veterans could be unhitched to position themselves behind the enemy and make continuing trouble with guerrilla warfare. De Wet was showing what could be done with small infiltrationist forces, using surprise to deliver some nasty knocks.

This action was followed by a collision on 11 and 12 June in a serried clump of hills east of Pretoria, which became the battle of Donkershoek or Diamond Hill. Using an imaginative assortment of emissaries, Roberts devoted almost a week to trying persistently to persuade Botha to come out from behind his mountain screen of the Magaliesberg and to accept surrender; if continued, the war could not possibly last more than a further fortnight, and what could be gained by stubbornly prolonging its bloodshed and agony? When the penny finally dropped, Roberts, confident that Botha's force was not a serious threat, sent out his army on 10 June to apply stronger persuasion. Although the British frontal forces had by now been depleted, 16,000 troops were considered more than adequate for this purpose. But Botha and his commanders had managed to assemble 5000 desperate yet determined commandos from various districts, few of them untried, to plug the tops of a triangular hill position.

Realizing the holding strength of the Boers in the front apex, Roberts sidestepped and ran his attack at the enemy's flanks, menacing their usual prized line of retreat. He finally succeeded in collapsing Botha's defences on the left, but the right flank was reinforced, stabilized in a cut of ground which provided a natural firing trench, and proved rather more resilient; a recoiling Roberts lost 180 men, while Boer casualties were a negligible dozen. Having frustrated the British advance, Botha abandoned his Diamond Hill wing, leaving Roberts an empty capture. The flying Boers then withdrew their guns and transport further east, towards Kruger's headquarters at

Machododorp. This was to be one of the last real battlefield actions of the war.

While Buller was at last approaching the northern Natal borders, Botha was pulling back east, and de la Rey was occupying the deep western Transvaal, Roberts had continuously had at least one eye on the wriggling Steyn. To break continuing Orange Free State resistance in its northeastern corner, the British now applied pressure to drive the republicans further and further east. This forced Steyn into a series of retreats, with the Boers having to transport their administration from Heilbron to Frankfort, and then to Bethlehem, to stay a jump ahead of their enemy. Inevitably Bethlehem proved another narrow squeak, and in July Steyn and his commanders sped southwards. Here they had increasingly little latitude for manoeuvre; a combination of Lieutenant-General Sir Archibald Hunter driving down from the north, and Lieutenant-General Sir Leslie Rundle stalking from the east, gave the Boers no recourse other than to retreat into a wedge of land hemmed in by hills known as the Brandwater Basin. This virtually locked in Steyn, de Wet, Marthinus Prinsloo, the Chief Commandant of the Orange Free State, and their muster of around 9000 troops. With the nearing Hunter able to concentrate 16,000 men under his command, the trapped republicans faced encirclement.

But before the British could seal every exit the Boers divided and attempted a breakout through a handful of navigable mountain outlets. A large column led by de Wet and accompanied by Steyn filed through successfully on 15 July and got clear away. Part of Prinsloo's command was assigned to hold open the passes until two further groups squeezed out, and then to form a retreating rearguard for any remaining dribs and drabs. But the cover scheme came unstuck as the British poured into the Basin, turning the Boers back. Completely boxed in, the exhausted, fearful, and demoralized commandos lost all sense of order and discipline, with Prinsloo himself locked in bitter leadership squabbles with subordinates who were trying to edge him out. It was proving virtually impossible to keep men together for any kind of defensive alignment.

The Boers thus sued for an armistice in which to try to negotiate some resolution of their predicament by conferring with Steyn's headquarters. This thoroughly bemused Hunter, who anticipated that what the Boers wanted was a slackening of pressure in order to race away. As the assured winner, he refused, demanding unconditional surrender. Rather than prolong the inevitable, Prinsloo submitted, surrendering 4500 troops (or half the Orange Free State forces), along with 6000 horses, 4000 sheep, and baggage containing everything from surplus weapons to family heirlooms. Burghers without blankets asked for permission to dispatch African servants to collect them from their farms.[6] Psychologically, this was another Paardeberg. Prinsloo and his officers instantly earned themselves the withering contempt of crusading patriots from the more impetuous, and more rabidly nationalist, younger Boer officer caste. Christiaan de Wet and Jan Smuts created a contagious republican myth of guilt or a treasonous stab in the back of 'the nation' to account for Brandwater Basin. A supine Prinsloo became Cronje's phantom, his image not helped by the mellow manner of his captors. Rather than being shipped out to a remote Ceylonese prison camp with the rest of his men, Prinsloo was obliged to live out a miserable captivity in the soothing hell of Simonstown.

Aside from the frustration of pursuing Steyn, de Wet, and the rest of the Orange Free State army in the north, Roberts had still to attend to business in the southeastern Transvaal. Here, his obvious strategic objective was the cutting of the eastern railway link to Portuguese East Africa, to block the inland passage of Boer supplies from Delagoa Bay and to try to reel in Kruger from his railway-base exile. The plan was for Roberts to drive east, while Buller's northern advance from Natal would become the right flank of the offensive line to carry the war towards Portuguese territory. By early August 9000 of Buller's heavily encumbered soldiers at last swung away from the Natal railway passage just north of Laing's Nek and pressed up northeast to coordinate with Roberts. With the odds against them absolutely overwhelming, any remaining pockets of republican resistance were progressively closed, and the British advanced upon Komatipoort effectively to sever the Boers from any remaining communications link with the outside.

As his enemy was striking east, de la Rey saddled up west of Pretoria to show that its position was not as yet secure. He had around 7000 loyal commandos with which to gamble. Moving fast, and aided by good scouting, this skirmishing force crashed into British posts within a 100-mile radius west of the town, capturing some and destroying others, and brazenly taking the railhead site of Klerksdorp to the southwest of Johannesburg. On 5 August, de la Rey even laid cheeky siege to a British garrison of 500 at Brakfontein, near Rustenberg, 100 miles west of Pretoria. The Boers were rushed by Rhodesian Field Force reinforcements, but held them at bay.

The Boer forces which were continuing to hang on were by now split roughly into three fighting groups which, despite intermittent lapses in their command system, maintained reasonably unbroken lines of consultation and report. With de la Rey mounting a campaign in the western Transvaal, Botha concentrated his forces in the east, leaving de Wet to move out and cause aggravation in the Orange Free State. By now fighting virtually as soldiers on the run, the Boers attacked trains, cut telegraph wires, fired stores, bombarded outlying British military posts, and even fleetingly occupied small towns. They could not secure their trivial victories in these weeks, but neither could the British settle the contest definitively, for their occupying hold on areas such as the Transvaal's western districts was slight. As more than one historian has remarked, however, the idea that British commanders were already fighting a guerrilla war seemed as yet to be in few minds.[7]

On this sustaining basis the fighting began to fan out. In August de Wet and his hardened Brandwater Basin veterans broke away north into the Transvaal to swell de la Rey's western concentration. Confident, clear-headed, and aggressive, he wasted no time in throwing his forces against the British in battering raids from a number of directions, trying to baffle his opponent through pressure across a wide front which criss-crossed the Vaal. One of these strikes was sufficiently fierce to break the security of Potchefstroom on the rail line from Klerksdorp to Johannesburg, briefly forcing its evacuation. For all this, concentrating their attack on supply and communications lines quickly simplified matters for the British; with his thicker lining of disposable reserves, Roberts soon moved to reinforce key garrison posts on the railway south of Pretoria.

His other move was a major effort to chase down and rub out de Wet and his mobile raiders. As a starting-point the hills west of Pretoria were not good hunting ground, and the Boers were able to manoeuvre and slip their way past their attackers back to their operational base south of the Vaal. To end an embarrassing southern crisis, Methuen and other commanders were handed 30,000 troops to flush the republicans out of their lair in the northwestern Orange Free State. For six edgy and exhausting weeks Roberts kept up a determined pursuit, utilizing his enormous numerical superiority and the speed of his fastest-moving cavalry to outflank snaking Boer lines of retreat. Harried hard, de Wet's commandos were compelled to stay on the hoof throughout this chase, covering over 500 miles of wild and jagged terrain. Although the British had the numbers, the large distances over which troops were having to perform and the exceptionally rough terrain undoubtedly sapped energies and diluted striking power. Already building up popular prestige as some republican military wizard, de Wet's ability to slip the British net only increased his stock. 'Too much and too quick on his heels to make it possible for us to finish this',[8] was the grudging compliment of one British officer.

His army encountered less trouble elsewhere. Sent to clear the countryside between the Natal and Delagoa Bay rail lines, Buller's force, which outnumbered its opponents by twenty to one, advanced on Botha's flank and broke through, swatting aside minor resistance in its path with crushing ease. Augmented by men released from the unproductive charge after de Wet, Buller's troops finally had a frontal encounter with Botha later in August, the Boer general having decided to stop giving ground. In the last major republican defensive siting, Botha lined up and entrenched about 5000 commandos and disciplined Transvaal police *Zarps* along a lengthy 40-mile front (to try to block any flanking penetration) near Lydenburg as a spoiling action. With a comfortable command of 20,000 soldiers, Buller launched a heavy assault against the defenders on 21 August. Performing prodigies of endurance, Botha's force held up for an astonishing five days, but his front was too thin and rickety to maintain a coherent firing line against attackers; perilously wide gaps between Boer trench positions merely widened, enabling the British to dart through and fire upon them with slanting volleys. Staggering back as their adversaries charged in to close quarters, the commandos turned and fled in general panic.

East of Pretoria the door was now permanently open. Roberts rapidly occupied Lydenburg, Barberton, and Carolina, and soon moved up on Nelspruit, where Kruger and Steyn were both running out of what remaining steam they had. In the eastern Transvaal, Boer forces still committed to the fight were also running out of secure base camps and natural shelter from which to run surprise, evasive attacks to slow the British. Before remaining exit points were blocked, worn and dishevelled commando formations broke their camps and fled in various stages of disorder. Some of the most war-weary sought out the advancing British to surrender, including a number who took along a short spoon with which to sup. Turncoat ex-combatants slid into new roles as imperial army guides, transport conductors, and veterinary assistants.[9] Others simply migrated away from the whole war business, resuming a civilian identity and collecting their families, servants, and livestock to trek to the safety of surrounding territories like Rhodesia, Mozambique, or Basutoland. They were mostly received with permissive tolerance, and some tribute-bearing burghers even sought to put themselves under the patronage of Tswana or BaSotho chiefs as protection against any possible cross-border Boer re-commandeering of renegade men. Yet others fell back in a straight retreat to the Komatipoort border position, staking something on a stand backed by a Portuguese safety cushion. Not everybody dodged. Botha's most committed commandos, 'very hard' and 'most stubborn', also dropped away, but only to regroup and 'wait and see' behind the mountain barriers of the northern Transvaal.

Now in real jeopardy, the republican presidents could procrastinate no longer. In response to urgings from Steyn and others, Kruger travelled to Delagoa Bay on 11 September to board a cruiser provided by the sympathetic Dutch monarchy to convey him into neutral European exile and a welcome from anti-British continental factions. It was a curiously immigrant fate for an essentially anti-immigrant politician. Leaving behind Burger to discharge residual state obligations, he was never to see South Africa again, dying in Switzerland in 1904. It is hard to resist the conclusion that the quality which the ageing and frail Transvaal president lacked most was luck. An increasingly marginal figure, some within the rising new progressive military élite were not sorry to see his back, believing that with him would go the soft-blooded inner-circle culture of toadyism and greedy living which had so damaged the Boer war effort through lacklustre leadership, mistakes, and indiscipline. Flushed of the likes of Kruger, Cronjé, and Prinsloo, martial blood would only course all the stronger.[10]

For Steyn, flight was also the logical course, but he opted to stay and take his chances. His state had made immense sacrifices, and he was not about personally to give up the patriotic cause. So, with an escort of 300 first-rate commandos, his party loaded up the republican gold and currency reserves and departed northwards on a planned route which would swing him around and back into his annexed and increasingly ravaged state.

By now Roberts no longer saw the need for any further big blows. After a faltering start, under his command the British had regained the initiative, and in just under a year had defeated the enemy forces and destroyed the general fighting will to resist. Or so it seemed. On 13 September he issued a triumphalist proclamation announcing Kruger's flight and conveying the assurance that the war was effectively over. By the end of that month Roberts' drive towards Komatipoort was completed and the Mozambique communications line was gone. As the British approached the Boers wrecked their wagons and destroyed surplus stores and artillery to deny their use to the enemy. Botha then halved what was left of his force to increase the burden of pursuit, leaving the like-minded Ben Viljoen to command the other section. Many of their men had by now lost all heart; with each onward step taken by Roberts' soldiers, Boer morale in the eastern Transvaal continued to fold. A British intelligence officer concluded that many dispirited enemy combatants were welcoming the arrival of troops, because 'they know our growing presence means the end of this calamitous war'.[11]

They had also encountered few stories of gratuitous British mistreatment of captured Boer soldiers. Saddled with almost 3000 unwarlike commandos and foreign volunteers who were desperate for a way out of continuing hostilities, Botha decently pushed them off towards Komatipoort and a choice between being interned by the Portuguese colonial administration or being taken prisoner by the British. Irish and other foreign nationals were combed out and repatriated to Europe and America, to a chorus of republican growls from Dublin, Paris, and Boston. In the last week of October 1900 Roberts proclaimed the annexation of the South African Republic. He had no second thoughts on winding down the war, assuring London that troop withdrawals could commence shortly, as all that was still required were a few policing sweeps to round up rebellious stragglers. Also in October the Natal army was disbanded. Buller returned to Britain and some considerable popular acclaim as the common soldier's general, the ostentatious South African embodiment of Victorian military achievement. But the critical knives were out in the War Office, and he would soon be weathering a few awkward questions about his managing of the Natal campaign. On 28 November, with the war publicly declared as good as over, Roberts appointed the cerebral and unlikeable Kitchener his successor in command and left for Britain as yet another imperial army totem, rarely to be out of full dress.

While the falling Boers were plainly losing force in the concluding months of Roberts' command, some problems were not only persisting but growing in this transitional period. Estimating that de Wet had at most 3000 fighting burghers to hand in the Orange Free State, Roberts almost ended up under-prepared. In its tense and battered northeastern region, the attrition already being waged against farmsteads and other rural resources and the harrying of both women and men had an ambiguous impact. For some, the rising sacrificial costs of the conflict obviously simply intensified their war-weariness. But others were put in a bind. For the burghers the choice was either falling back to rural immiseration and an uncertain hold on the means of life, or throwing in one's lot with resumed commando activity. This meant more than joining improvised movements to hit back at the enemy: in banding together as a fighting group there would be enemy stores to plunder, or foodstuffs to be carried off from cowering African peasants.

Zealots such as Smuts, de Wet, and Wynand Malan were inclined to see in this a renewed patriotic commitment to the republican cause despite mounting adversity, but in the absence of much reflection of immediate experience from unlettered or lesser-educated burghers, we cannot be certain of the depth of such convictions. What can be ventured is the idea that worsening conditions in parts of the countryside probably aided the task of some of de Wet's propagandizing veterans, who were dispersed into farming districts to prod disconsolate men into returning to fighting duties. In these circumstances, what was beginning to show, as it was virtually bound to, was that it was easier getting beaten men back to arms than those holed up in calmer districts which had escaped the more harrowing experiences of the Roberts firebug. The farm-stripping and burning already well in hand under Roberts was by no means aiding the British conquest objective. Far from it; some affected burghers were sticking to commandos because they no longer had homesteads and a fixed family to which to go.[12]

The republican commandants were already becoming aware of this unpleasant irony by mid-1900. So were the more far-sighted British officers, who noted that 'excessive' destructiveness would only end up benefitting the enemy cause by keeping combatants in the field. 'The Burgher out on Commando is bound always to his farm,' wrote one; 'by burning it and sending his family packing, we are only making him a roving desperado, consumed with hatred.' Captain Francis Fletcher-Vane was one of a good many who concluded at the war's end 'that if farms had not been burnt the war would have been sooner over'.[13] It can be and indeed has been argued that Roberts made one of the great mistakes of the war by getting scorched-earth measures under way so early in his campaign across republican soil. Not only was its terror disproportionate for an enemy which was already buckling; instead of bringing on an end to the war, it was far more likely to prolong its duration. If we grant this, as a strategic error it would make Buller's bungling in Natal look like small beer.

By October 1900 there were between 8000 and 9000 burghers back in the field. The British had not anticipated having to keep vigil against an opposition force of this size, and certainly not one out to create havoc. Sure enough, Orange Free State commandos tried to start up a minor counter-offensive designed to hinder British movements, interrupt the flow of supplies, and sever telegraph communications. Abandoning their own use of wires, the Boers split into small sabotaging parties which moved about energetically at night to disable telegraph loops, forcing much greater use of the heliograph upon the British. While the bright, clear air of the South African interior permitted mirror signals to be sent across impressive distances of up to 100 miles, they had the disadvantage of being easily monitored and read by the enemy.

De Wet also closed in more boldly. On 20 October his force attacked an enemy column on the banks of the rail line at Frederikstad, holding the British to a fierce pitched encounter for all of five days before reinforcements arrived from Krugersdorp to shove the commandos into withdrawal. For Roberts the day was saved, but only just. Believing that he had come close to routing the British, de Wet blamed his men for not occupying the entire frontal position. For their part, some of his more wary commandos felt· that at Frederikstad he was taking unnecessary chances with their lives. As always, there was a limit to what their leaders were celebrating as a renewed and more ardent sacrificial spirit.

Later in October the Boers began to take small towns by surprise in a string of attacks on their British camps, perhaps most notably in a daring assault in bad light on the enemy encampment in the Jacobsdal market-place, a spot which had been a former Orange Free State field headquarters. They remained denting incursions rather than a strategy to accumulate solid gains; by now, the spread and constantly improving mobility of the British meant that reinforcements could mostly be run in at quick notice. Still, for de Wet, de la Rey, and Botha not everything was lost from a strategic point of view. These generals still clung to the hope that by prolonging hostilities they might sap Britain sufficiently to bring about an end to the war by negotiation, not by their having to succumb to a clear-cut imperial victory.

At the end of October Steyn, Botha, de la Rey, and Smuts held a prolonged planning session at a hideaway west of Pretoria. This took stock of republican possibilities and problems, as the emerging picture now looked clear enough. Britain's hope had receded of detaching one or other republic so as to have a greater chance of finishing off its ally: the fight could therefore be continued as a fully pan-republican guerrilla struggle. As their fortunes had contracted in tandem, so commandos north and south of the Vaal were growing more willing to mix things up and to defer to each other's officer authority. Boer field forces were not as yet down to the halt and the lame, and in irregular operations combat casualties would be relatively light and sustainable. The ranks of good riflemen had been denuded, but the remaining rump was skilled, committed, and could move fast.

The problem was the harshness of the burnings and sackings. While it was not breaking the Boers, and paradoxically was helping to keep the burghers in the war, its cost to civilians was awful and growing heavier by the day; in the northeastern Orange Free State and eastern and western Transvaal women and children were being lumped in as virtual contraband of war. Rural destruction was not only razing the means of livelihood for the resisting commandos but was also threatening the elimination of their remaining campaigning grounds. For evasive riding and counter-riding, mounted Boers needed avenues of retreat to replenishing bases and protective enclosures like the lost Brandwater basin.[14] They could not fall back to stubble. In this at least, something of what Roberts was doing was effective.

The only way of easing pressure would be a strategic initiative to distract the British. Here Botha and Steyn were not without foresight, however short they were on means. The Boers hit on a fresh campaigning solution, almost a grand design; it was to carry the war on a guerrilla basis back into British territory. In Natal and the Cape it would be politically tricky to teach the more refractory rural settler population the hardships and terrors of war through farm incendiarism and other devastation of private property. And if good routes of advance were properly worked out, and surprise was sustained, then a breakthrough was possible, disrupting British second-line colonial garrisons, as they would not know where to move until it was too late to prevent their opponents from lashing down new positions. This was to be preceded by a strategic return to the old bewitchment of the Rand and its gold supplies.

Drawing up Steyn and de Wet behind a combined Transvaal-Orange Free State strike and pushing others who were more timid, Smuts laid out a far-fetched move to settle accounts through agility and intrigue. Early in 1901 the enemy in Johannesburg would be bearded in a diversionary action to draw them away, while a republican force of some 12,000 to 15,000 would be held back in preparedness to strike in a straight line through the Witwatersrand. After seeing 'all mines and mining property blown up and completely destroyed', in the ensuing confusion Botha would immediately nip down into Natal, and de Wet and de la Rey would thrust a wide wedge into the Cape.

For one thing, Smuts had decided that as the gold mines were now a British political possession, economic sabotage would be a defensible expedient. For another, there was a morale need for a big gesture of reprisal. Although 'an extreme measure', the blow inflicted by mine-wrecking would 'not be one-tenth of what the policy of farm-burning and women-driving was inflicting on the Boer people'. That accomplished, the ruining of the gold industry and a new offensive breakthrough could 'have had a very different influence on the future of the war'.[15]

Perhaps, but it was not to be. After the western Transvaal talks Steyn slipped off to catch up with de Wet's commandos, and was in their midst during one of his flying visits on the morning of 6 November. Lounging on a farm northwest of Kroonstad, the Boers were unexpectedly caught in broad daylight with their guard down, either snoozing or plainly idling. As the British closed in, the startled Boers scampered in leaderless flight, ignoring de Wet's frantic efforts to *sjambok* or whip them into making a stand. In addition to over 150 men the Boers lost artillery, wagons, and stampeding horses. While Steyn wasted no time in getting away, a small Boer rearguard took a grip and held off their attackers until de Wet was able to compose his commandos and range them against the British in a flanking counterattack. This seesaw took another dip with the arrival of British reinforcements in much superior strength. After a short-lived but ugly exchange involving snipers, the desperate use of women and children as improvised cover, firing of mutilating dum-dum or fragmenting bullets, and some brusque post-battle reprisals, the Boers were forced to give up. Astonishingly, however, de Wet squirmed away to fight another day. This abrupt retreat, and the simultaneous quick turning of de la Rey and Smuts, threw out any serious prospects of still carrying through a coordinated joint strategy. The ends of any republican advance were loose: what remained was to make it difficult for the British to knot them.

The last month of Roberts' command turned out to be particularly bumpy. Fresh pockets of Boer resistance flared up in the northeastern Orange Free State, with convoys captured and plundered, supply-train stoppages in which drivers were targeted by proficient Boer marksmen (less effort than blocking the line), and the blasting of various communications points. There were numerous such episodes of tormenting resistance, although few worthy of much individual record. By mid-November de Wet, not one to hover about, determined a penetrating route south to start lining up things for a republican invasion of the Cape Colony. Alert to this, Roberts quickly sent a column charging in pursuit in what would become known in war folklore as the second of the great De Wet Hunts. Moving rapidly to the attack when an opportunity was offered, the Boers struck at Dewetsdorp (de Wet's own home town) on 23 November, duelling fiercely with its British garrison for three days until they forced an enemy surrender. Personally exulted by this blow, de Wet rode on defiantly.

Although eventually headed off by their more numerous and better provisioned pursuers, his commandos kept a wide margin of ground across which to wheel. So, even if obliged to turn around and run back to less risky northern positions, they tied up the British long enough to give Generals J. B. M. Hertzog and Piet Kritzinger enough slack to take around 2000 commandos across the Orange river and into the northern Cape on 17 December. Exactly one week earlier Roberts had been finally seen off by Milner, who made a big effort to be agreeable to his departing Commander-in-Chief, despite his inner feeling that there was something 'almost repulsive' about the fawning over 'Bobs' (Roberts) when they were inescapably still 'in the middle of war'.[16]

By now the Boers were striving to demonstrate this in other areas which had been made into their boltholes. Their drowsiness broken in part by cheering news of de Wet's fleet-footed accomplishments, the forces in the northeastern Transvaal and on the high plateau south of the lost Delagoa Bay rail corridor began to raise their fighting temper. Louis Botha and Ben Viljoen had now raised numbers under their respective commands as well as a greater will to move. Hungry for the credit of some striking victory, the Transvaal leadership consolidated their commandos for a coordinated offensive manoeuvre in the west through which to try to regain some forward initiative.

Early in December de la Rey and Smuts sniffed out a heavily provisioned but lightly guarded British convoy outside Rustenberg. Led on by their advance scouts, they swooped, killing, wounding, or capturing 120 British soldiers, flogging or executing over 20 African drivers, torching 115 wagons, and making off with the remainder, which contained much that, as guerrillas, they needed – medical supplies, clothing, and boots. The fact that they tossed aside the Bollinger, *Grand Cru*, and port can only have confirmed some British officers' prejudices about the Boers' debatable grasp on civilization. Thereafter, the Transvaal forces looked for bigger fish, and hooked it in Nooitgedacht gorge in the Magaliesberg on 13 December.

Making an exceptionally bad choice for a camp site, Major-General Richard Clements discounted danger in placing his men at the foot of steep cliff faces, neglected basic intelligence, skimped on pickets for his crucial outer line, and paid the price. Smuts and de la

Rey extended the striking power of General Christiaan Beyers and General Jacobus Kemp, so that when the Boers attacked they outnumbered the British by more than two to one. Sustaining negligible losses through their tight command of the imposing terrain running downwards from kopje firing positions, the Boers inflicted almost 640 casualties amounting to half the strength of Clements' force, ran off hundreds of their draught animals, seized over 120 mule carts and ox wagons, and fired other transport and combustible equipment. If this could be kept up in the Magaliesberg, mused one hardened and hopeful veteran, the enemy could become so depleted of supplies and impaired in fighting capacity that it might be forced to give up the countryside and retract to holding only the towns.[17] In the end there would be nothing left to requisition and the British would have to bargain for peace. This was so optimistic that it could only have come from reading one republican war bulletin too many.

What Nooitgedacht did reveal was a mixture of Boer confusion and timidity on the battlefield. Despite outnumbering, outmanoeuvring, and pinning down a force which had little effective cover, and also knowing that any enemy reinforcements were certain to be late in coming, the Boers did not press home their advantage to squash Clements. Without trenches the British troops would have been slaughtered or forced to capitulate by the republicans' continuing their accurate artillery bombardment. As it was, however, the Boer generals held off, allowing the surviving enemy troops to retreat to Pretoria.

In one respect they could do little else. Given the choice between foraging through the British camp or straightening up to finish off the fight, the tired and hungry burghers followed their stomachs. With the basic job done there was no need for them to chance their lives in continued hostilities, however much Beyers or Kemp might admonish them with a customary fatherly whipping. Furthermore, the British prisoners were now a drag, not a gain, as there was little food to sustain them and no handy holding places to which they could be consigned. There also remained divisive differences in command objectives within republican leadership, a clash of styles between a clinical and disciplined Smuts who wanted to stay on the attack in any and every way possible, and a coarser and lower-minded Beyers, who rather enjoyed the deflections offered to his force by plundering opportunities. The real problem was the old one of fluctuating militia resistance to a common elementary discipline and forthright conflict in command structure, both likely to affect efficiency in field conditions.

While the new year did not bring any unified republican direction of the war, at local levels it continued to flicker. Early in 1901 Botha and Viljoen linked up their columns and sought out a new operational base in the east, near Machadodorp.

Here, on 7 January, they chanced their hand in a daring timed assault on seven thinly screened enemy garrisons along the Delagoa Bay line with the intention of running the British off these points, thereby bisecting their control of the eastern corridor zone. The thinking behind a stalking attack to open up a disruptive gap was enterprising, but this time the terrain and weather worked against the Boers; heavy night fog and twisted ground sent the commandos fumbling rather than stealing forward in attack. Surprise was quickly lost, and the aroused British held firm. Meanwhile, knots of mounted commandos elsewhere continued to bring on running fights on ground where they felt tactically most at home, and where they judged that lighter, detached enemy forces could be beaten. While these forays produced little more than glancing scraps, they still drew blood. A costly shock attack in the far northeastern corner of the Orange Free State brought down a British company, with close-range rifle volleys killing over 150 men. These were sharp blows, but were in the nature of playing a hand. What the Boers required for 1901 was someone to conjure up a renewed offensive initiative, with a sense of purposeful direction and a realistic end in view. The alternative was to resume contemplation of a grinding and inexorable defeat.

An attempt of sorts came from the Orange Free State leadership pulled along by de Wet. This was a return to the aborted October 1900 scheme of a wide, deep offensive to relieve the pressure of attrition being waged against the social bases of republican society. In a four-pronged advance to cram combatants into the Cape, on 27 January de Wet began to track south to cross the Orange into British territory to find and hitch up the commandos and colonial rebels already there and to impose some positioning discipline and direction over roaming bands. Second, Judge Barry Hertzog was also dispatched from the Orange Free State in a westerly direction across the trackless landscape of the northwestern Cape to the Namaqualand coast, to open up Lambert's Bay for a shipment of European munitions and volunteer infantry. Wholly illusory, this was probably the closest Boer society ever came to some island cargo cult of European maritime liberation.

But then this was not always a war about sense. Raising additional recruits from the large number of Cape republican loyalists believed to be willing to take up arms, de Wet would rendezvous with Hertzog and then march southwest in earnest to threaten Cape Town. In a third entry, the hard-riding and hard-talking General Piet Kritzinger was given a force of about 1000 commandos and set loose in the handy, settler-farm-supplied interior lands of the Cape midlands, to accumulate rebel hands, harry white and black British loyalists, and cause a commotion to encourage generalized local resistance to British control.[18]

Then there was whatever Louis Botha was contemplating against Natal. His brief called for him to clip down with around 1000 horsemen from the eastern border of the Transvaal and to plot a fast invasion route into Natal. His eyes were on the British encampment at Dundee and then a plan at a stab at the railway at Glencoe, to deprive the Transvaal occupation force of its principal trunk route for supplies. And although Kitchener set the hard-headed French and his large eastern Transvaal mounted force of 21,000 men after Botha, it would not be enough to chase down his commandos. There was another burning need, which was to ensure that the harried enemy could not loop back and dissolve into territory which provided the necessities of life, as well as scatterings of spies, farmhouse snipers, and arms caches. Not famous for being 'soft when it came to the enemy',[19] French intensified Roberts' scorched-earth strategy behind Botha, scouring areas clean, indiscriminately destroying crops, livestock, and wagons, and firing farmhouses. A punitive scouring to chill the spines of those in the field, it included the drama of a single artful blow: the dynamiting of Louis Botha's own house. French was no milksop. Having served in the Sudan with Kitchener and Buller, he well knew what it took to fight tribesmen.

Ahead of the Transvaal Boers, the key entry points into British Natal were too well-guarded or patrolled to be broken, and now enjoyed effective intelligence and communications systems. Break-ins by the familiar routes were solidly blocked, and while intermittent raiding scooped up British arms and ammunition, it did not bring in good horses with feed or replenish vanishing food stocks. There were sufficient troops not to become over-extended in standing on the defence, and the effect by September 1901 of blocking Botha's attempts at a passage was to drive his force in on the southeastern border of Zululand. To continue would be to press deeper into new danger, as the British approved of 10,000 to 12,000 bristling warriors turning out mostly with assegais, and some firearms, to chase away any invaders of their territory. After a couple of expensive reverses against British positions in the vicinity in late September, Botha's heart appeared to be in it no longer, and his beaten commandos broke off and sprinted back to the Transvaal.[20] At least 15,000 British bloodhounds followed to ensure no slackening of pace.

Elsewhere, the fluttering wings of combined Boer operations had also been having to cope with heavy odds. During the course of February, Hertzog and Kritzinger's forces were slimmed down and pushed in a westerly direction back towards the Orange Free State by flying columns of British troops. While on a forward campaign the Boers were, in effect, having to act defensively. Their being stuck in a larger column made it easier for the British to fix their location and place them in a tight spot; dissolving into small commando units enabled them to survive parasitically, but it dissipated their striking capacity against the enemy, unless it was falling upon obstructive African and Coloured labourers and smallholders in sporadic raiding and atrocity.

But de Wet could still not be run to ground where the British could get at him. With de Wet over the Orange and into the Cape by the second week of February, Kitchener put in thousands of troops to blanket the Karoo region, using the Colesberg locality as a logistical base. He also proceeded to peg out a thick coil of mounted columns in a line running south from Kroonstad in the Orange Free State to Naauwpoort in the Cape. Using the trusted bush method of picking good troops who could travel light and handle the challenge of troublesome terrain and extended distances, 15 British columns were set off in a third De Wet Hunt. Although his planned northward retreat was cut off for a time by a flooding of the Orange, which forced his commandos to turn around, de Wet did not lose his edge when on the run. Abandoning his remaining guns and any other cumbersome equipment, for six gloating weeks he outran his pursuers, eluding every trap, until finally he was able to make his way back, to be swallowed up again by the folds of the Orange Free State highveld.

Many of the British officers involved in this pursuit found the experience of being persistently misled by an inferior force especially galling; while the threat of de Wet had been removed from the Cape, it was blood that they wanted. A 'humiliating state of affairs', wrote a Namaqualand Field Force intelligence officer, 'the cheeky Boers have again been able to move away ... it is all as vexing as a mysterious robbery'.[21] That de Wet prevailed was no mystery. On the British side, it was down to signalling difficulties between branching columns, some uncertain mapping, and key shortcomings in staff training for tactical field intelligence, with the Boers easily intercepting some sensitive communications passed across in the clear but without encipherment. On the Boer side, it was down to better horses and horsemanship, retention of the best mounts for long-range scouting, cunning knowledge of the stepping stones around the southern Orange Free State and northern Cape, an intelligence grasp resting upon a pro-republican civilian population, and the ability of hardened Boer command to sever the attachment of their men to those cumbersome ox wagons which dragged along such vital worldly essentials as stoves and mattresses. Matters had grown more trim since the first 1900 de Wet chase.[22] Then, with over 50,000 troops bearing down on them, 2000 commandos had still clung to a baggage train of 460 wagons. Orange Free State forces were encumbered partly because the anxious commandos were loathe to sacrifice transport and draught animals to the enemy, who were routinely confiscating such possessions as military resources. Now, whatever the fears about him, de Wet would not contemplate being balked by his own laager; a guerrilla war could not be fought with domestic comforts which slowed movement.

Within this continuing Boer prosecution of the war there was evolving – as Kitchener, for one, rightly saw – a widening conviction among surrendered burghers that there was no point in looking to the battlefield for salvation. It had become futile for commandos still in the field to continue the struggle on the basis of some or other mirage of foreign diplomatic intervention, European aid, or an imperial loss of will. As defeat could not be avoided, it was felt that arms should be laid down voluntarily to end the war and provide for the making of a negotiated soldierly peace, in which the Boers might be allowed to surrender with honour. For this, an initiative was needed before the two sides were driven even further apart, and the country ruined.

Those burghers whose war was over debated what to do. Towards the end of 1900 a couple of urban middle class ex-commandos employed their riches and political pull to get out of the Transvaal and travel to London, where their knocking landed them an audience with Chamberlain. The Colonial Secretary was quite taken with the idea of dispatching 'peace emissaries' to the republican fighting forces to present the case for sense, and authorized Milner and Kitchener to explore the possibilities.[23]

Kitchener, who had been closely monitoring the rough state of Boer morale through personal contact with surrendered Transvaal combatants and interceptions of strategic information by his improved Field Intelligence Department, saw this as a timely initiative. Given the nod, several burgher peace committees were set up in the Transvaal, an activity which then lapped over into the Orange Free State. Their representatives stressed the odds against their countrymen and -women, stressed that no one could be blamed for defeat, and urged the commandos to create peace by disarmament; by demonstrating their pacific intentions, they 'would be assured of better treatment in future'. In the opening months of 1901 a serious attempt at the conversion of fighters was made by the emerging peace interest, aided and abetted by British high command. Communication was not easy given the increasingly scattered and localized distribution of commandos; almost 30,000 handbills and leaflets were sent fluttering into the countryside, and a small body of reliable apostates was saddled up to make contact with individual commandos to 'add reason' or 'bring sane views' to the nightly campfire politics of Boer laagers. The Boer peace movement also tried to make use of potential conciliationist elements which lay beyond the republics. In a memorable contribution to a fighting family bloodline, General Piet de Wet, brother of Christiaan de Wet, led a delegation to the Cape to foster the peace cause among prisoners of war held being held in Cape Town and to try to gain the moral support of the Boer clergymen and influential Afrikaner Bond personalities.[24]

But he and the others had a thin time. The majority of prisoners spurned people regarded as renegades; except for a handful who risked breaking ranks, the male group solidarities of camp life ensured that the captives stayed disdainful. At the same time, prominent Cape Boers professed themselves reluctant to become embroiled in the growing divisions which had become warring sections of republican society. There were merely sympathetic tears for the de Wet peace deputation, some of them of the crocodile kind. Out in the field, the peace burghers experienced rough treatment from commandos who, not surprisingly, viewed them as deserters and traitors. A number were taken captive, fined, or had their property destroyed, while a few unfortunates were flogged and even executed by firing-squad.

Perhaps the most striking of these false peace starts by massaging an enemy surrender was that arranged by Kitchener himself. He had no desire for fighting on if parleying with Boer generals would resolve matters on his terms. Accordingly, feelers were put out for a Transvaal conference with Louis Botha at Middelburg along the Delagoa Bay line. Botha consented to crossing the enemy lines under safe escort, and entered the town for peace talks on 28 February 1901. At this stage Kitchener's political outlook was not especially vindictive. Provided that the Boer leadership accepted that imperial annexation of the republics was final and not to be haggled over, the proposed peace terms would not be without sops. This could include war-damage compensation in the form of a levy upon the gold mines, and an assurance to the Boer political élite that they would have command of their own interests and would not be bossed about by Rand capitalists. They would get to keep an essential share after all. Furthermore, there could be a general amnesty, not merely for republican combatants but for Cape and Natal colonial rebels too. Lastly, an improved legal position for the African majority would not be pushed down the Boers' throats in any peace settlement; Kitchener was in fact rather taken by the big stick of republican 'native laws' in Boer society, and wanted to see them embedded, not diluted by any sentimental metropolitan liberalism over black civil rights.[25]

Never inclined to be lenient, Milner was at best lukewarm about talks with the Boer generals, and he and Kitchener squabbled over this and that point of the concessionary peace terms. In London, Chamberlain and the Cabinet raised difficulties over a rebel amnesty and the absence of any regard for the statutory rights of Africans in any peace agreement. But Milner was interested only in getting things scuppered, such as pruning down Kitchener's ideas on reparation for damage to the rural economy to compensation to farmers for any wartime horse losses. The armistice negotiations were as good as wasted. In the event Botha shrank from the final British 10-point peace plan, advising Kitchener that it would be difficult to persuade his fellow generals to call off warfare on the basis of such stern terms.

Kitchener's chance to make peace through talking with the enemy drained away, leaving him exasperated. He was being given no political latitude by Milner and the British government's unwavering adherence to an unconditional surrender, and Botha could not act alone; those around him were not enthusiastic peacemakers. His objective remained that of ending the war, and quickly, but its resolution would continue to lie in the balance between what was militarily capable and politically practicable. Middelburg demonstrated the dilemma of getting one factor to tilt the other. Had the British already cornered Christiaan de Wet and the obdurate Steyn, Kitchener might have strengthened Botha's restraining hand in persuading other commanders to come in on the Middelburg deliberations.

In an aftermath of renewed pessimism, peace talks of this kind (or, indeed, of any other) were ever more fiercely opposed by groups of Orange Free State officers. This applied most especially to the key figure of de Wet; he was growing increasingly suspicious of Botha, whose apparently cosy correspondence with Kitchener was looking to him as ominously bad faith. The burgher peace movement, too, signally failed in its purpose during this phase of the war, although one scholarly authority has suggested that its propaganda effects on rank-and-file combatants should be seen as a factor behind the distinct increase in the number of surrendering burghers in February and March 1901.[26] That notwithstanding, the difficulty for Boer peace collaborators is that they could not act as neutral mediators between belligerents. Most damaging was their standing: as men who had limply surrendered their arms, and thereby their traditional claim upon republican manhood and citizenship, they had no credit in the eyes of their ex-commanders. In operating under British direction, they were Kitchener's partisan ally against themselves; in a sense, the reviled burgher peace emissaries were sawing off the very branch upon which they had decided to sit.

On the other hand, the emergence of collaborationist peace energies clearly reflected the untidy factional fissures which the war had by now opened within the body walls of Boer society. One tear was the obviously strained attitude between the surrendered burghers and uncompromising patriots, who were set on continuing the independence fight, come what may. Another divorce was that between those of a more moderate nationalist stripe, who had concluded that it was hopeless to continue a ruinous war which was consuming their states, and radical 'rejectionists', including women who had been pushed about or driven off by British soldiers, who supported a struggle to the end.

As a doctrine, actual pacifism never took hold. It is a truism that religious feeling among Boer troops was extremely widespread, but the stiff certainties of a united Calvinist Protestantism probably smothered any humanist or 'secularizing' dissent from the notion of fighting a just English War. Religious faith 'kept the courage and the moral sense of the burghers up to the mark', for this was a sacrificial patriotic war for the nation's survival.[27] Perhaps more interesting than this was the way in which the war crisis unlocked less conventional expressions of primitive religious faith – a mixture of superstitions, prophecies, or millenarianism amongst Boers on the fighting front. The most weird and scintillating embodiment of this by 1901 was undoubtedly the increasingly influential republican visionary or prophet, *Siener* (Seer) Niklaas van Rensburg. Although regarded coolly by educated, more 'European' commanders like the sophisticated Reitz and the worldly Ernst Marais, Siener van Rensburg was able to lodge himself under the credulous wing of de la Rey in the western Transvaal. Under this patronage his richly elaborate prophecies and ranting predictions were listened to avidly by ordinary burghers and the more rustic of commanders, such as de la Rey.

Visions infused with homespun rural symbolism served as a kind of supernatural subsidy to continuing commando exertions; they included warning predictions of precise British attacks on laagers, psychic confirmation of the outcome of impending Anglo-Boer clashes (such as that between de la Rey and Methuen late in the war), and various other occult observances of danger. Both de la Rey and Steyn swore that their survival in a number of close-run encounters was due to van Rensburg's timely premonitions of a sudden closing enemy advance. A good scoring rate boosted his reputation among bittereinders. It is by no means easy to take a full measure of the command of the supernatural over the minds of fighting burghers; at the same time, there can be little doubt of the workings of superstitious practices over some men in the field.[28]

While such republican prophets concentrated on psychic tactical intelligence, the Boers fought on the basis that, if surprise could be achieved, a thinly held British line could always be penetrated, and forward forces and convoys could still be up-ended if caught napping. To increase their ability to ride faster and more freely, the commandos jettisoned most of their remaining field artillery during the latter half of 1901, turning all to small battles and little engagements. A fair part of this consisted of increased attacks on enemy convoys which, with the approach of winter, were bringing in urgently needed food, clothing, and other supplies. These amounted to a mixed bag, with attackers sometimes being beaten off by British fire power. Then there were impetuous dawn assaults on troop concentrations, with riflemen riding down hard to open a fight before wheeling away to avoid being gunned down by superior numbers and fire. There were also a great many night attacks on British camps in the eastern and western Transvaal, with the Boers sometimes preparing hidden positions in advance to provide Maxim and Vickers guns with good flat trajectories of fire. And there were opportunities to move when the enemy strayed too near which were too tempting to ignore.

At this the Boers tried to make up for want of numbers by employing innovative attack techniques. Thus, at the end of May 1901, de la Rey chanced upon a mounted British column camped near Vlakfontein in the Magaliesberg. General Kemp brought his force of 1500 riflemen to bear, advancing in a flanking movement along a rising incline to within 600 yards of the enemy, turning pickets and dispatching their outlying African scouts. Cutting into a favourable wind, the commandos embroidered the veldt with gunpowder to fire up a thick protective smokescreen; it also bemused the British about the size of the enemy force. Firing from the saddle in a storming attack, the republicans inflicted 180 casualties before breaking off after losing 41 of their own men. Yet the outcome of such positive strikes simply posed the problem: stealing a march on the enemy was something, but nothing like enough. The Boers faced a strategic blockage; the enemy could still be damaged, but not repulsed. Kemp's force was cunning and courageous, but was repeatedly trying to do too much with too few men. Time could always be gained, but for what? After the Vlakfontein battle, the British columns shook themselves off and resumed what they had been doing, burrowing away for hidden caches of weapons on farmland.

Remaining obstinate war theatres, the heartland of the Boer territories became a generally confusing maze of attacks and retreats from place to place, governed for the republicans by pure chance and opportunity rather than any commanding strategic aim. With few if any periods of inactivity, it was a tense and exhausting time. In June 1901 de Wet and Steyn had another narrow squeak near Reitz in the Orange Free State when their convoy was trapped by a British drive. A month later, in Reitz itself, Steyn was nearly swept up again when a stealthy encircling British attack netted Kitchener almost the entire Orange Free State government and its war cabinet. Although the President was able to use up another life to run another day, it was a serious psychological loss.

In September and October matters took a slightly different turn. Getting wind of the extent to which British strength in the western Transvaal was being depleted by the need to run troops down to deal with Botha's second Natal invasion, de la Rey and his force of 3000 bittereinders went for a column commanded by Kekewich in the Zeerust area. The ferocity of this onslaught panicked some of Kekewich's soldiers, set horses and mules off in a dozen directions, and inflicted a heavy loss of 200 men. To retrieve the situation Kekewich and Methuen combined their forces to nab de la Rey while he was still loping around Zeerust. Instead, the biters were bitten as the Boers struck again, the weight of casualties and supply losses being borne by the British rearguard.

Just as conventional campaigning included the early destruction of the Orange Free State countryside to bring home to civilians the frightful hardships and terror of war, so the guerrilla confrontation threw up one or two last battles in the old style as hostilities bled on to their conclusion. Towards the end of December 1901, at Tweefontein, east of Bethlehem in the Orange Free State, de Wet seized a chance to turn his 700–800 commandos on a scratch force of drowsing British units. Commandos reconnoitred the enemy camp on a kopje for several days, selecting a prudent approach and preparing well. A slope judged too steep to assail had been left unguarded by the enemy. It was a fatal slip, for a groping de la Rey had picked out a gulley through which his troops could get on to the summit undetected. In the dark, early on Christmas Day, the Boers, many in stockings or with feet bound in rags or smeared in dung to muffle the noise of their upward file, overran the sleeping encampment. What followed was carnage. Using dum-dum bullets at close range, the commando rifle volleys inflicted gruesome casualties, with British losses eventually topping 300 men in addition to 500 horses and scores of laden wagons. The disaster caused Kitchener to roll his eyes. But he remained optimistic, confident that the tide could not be turned by what he perceived to be desperate thrashing. As if to confirm this, at the end of February 1902 driving columns under General Henry Rawlinson neatly enveloped a complete commando on its last legs and falling over to surrender; this handed the British almost 800 prisoners, 25,000 cattle and 2000 horses.

Still, several months later de la Rey was still polishing the art of surprise and behaving like a general who could not possibly return with anything less than victory. In March 1902, in the last major engagement of the war on republican soil, he turned and sank his teeth into his British pursuers, forces under Methuen which were attempting to ground him in the unsparing vastness of the countryside between the Mafeking railway spur and the Magaliesberg. This was ground which de la Rey and his men knew intimately, and upon which they had been able to lay their hands, as British command had been concentrating mostly on a rounding up of Botha and de Wet. After weeks of sharp and evasive moves to hold the British at bay, de la Rey sallied out in a surprise attack on three columns at Tweebosch near Lichtenburg.

His appetite whetted by an action a short while earlier, when his force had cracked open a convoy and removed 380 troops for a loss of 50 of his own men, de la Rey swooped on Methuen himself. A combination of Boer heroics and tactical concentration on the enemy's weakest points, raw British troops and injurious lapses in coordination landed Methuen in disaster and humiliation. Wounded, he fell into de la Rey's hands himself, while his force sustained almost 200 casualties for a republican loss of 35 men. Having done more than his fair share towards the destruction of crops and livestock and the torching of homesteads, Methuen could not have exactly anticipated kid gloves from his captor. But de la Rey was an old-fashioned and chivalrous Christian warrior; in any event, a humbled British general was probably not much with which to barter.[29] Methuen was treated courteously, taken to Klerksdorp for a wound to be treated, and convalesced on roast chicken cooked by Koos de la Rey's wife, Nonnie. In view of his mortifying position, this presumably must have felt more like choking than feeding him. He was then generously released, fully clothed, escaping the fate of other captured troops, who were often run off stark naked after being stripped to ease a critical commando clothing shortage.

The severity of the Boer supply problem was producing another surreal occurrence, remarked upon by a number of British soldiers who would normally have expected it in music hall or pantomime rather than while on armed pursuit. This was the appearance of some of de la Rey and Botha commandos in the distinctive bonnet and black dress apparel of rural Boer women, the only serviceable clothing available to the most ragged men, now short even of adaptable grain sacks or captured British army garments. Here was a social phenomenon probably ripe for more inventive kinds of postmodern historical interpretation; it could be seen as feminized commandos representing some apologetic rite of inversion, or Boer men disguising the weakness of their sex in not fighting hard enough to preserve republican nationhood, or skirts supplanting beards as signifiers of the Boer cause. Carrying on the war for that cause was certainly becoming an ever tougher proposition. From November 1901, adolescent youths or *penkoppe* were being commandeered from the age of 14. Ahead of them, Britain's solidity, steady pushes, improved logistics, and army management were bringing on a victory through round-about pressure rather than a decisive stroke.

Chapter 6 Notes

1. *Jan Smuts: Memoirs of the Boer War*, eds Gail Nattrass and S. B. Spies (Johannesburg, 1994), pp. 39–41.
2. M. E. Jooste, 'De Boeren hadden Radio-Beheer voor hul Kanonnen', *Historia*, 28/1 (1983), pp. 108–10.
3. *Smuts: Memoirs*, pp. 43–4; J. H. Breytenbach, *Die Geskiedenis van die Tweede Vryheidsoorlog in Suid Afrika, 1899–1902*, vol. 5, pp. 298–9.
4. *Smuts: Memoirs*, p. 41; *The War Memoirs of Commandant Ludwig Krause 1899–1900*, ed. Jerold Taitz (Cape Town, 1996), p. 81.
5. Albert Grundlingh, 'Collaborators in Boer society', in *The South African War: The Anglo-Boer War 1899–1902*, ed. Peter Warwick (London, 1980), pp. 258–9.
6. R. L. Wallace, *The Australians at the Boer War* (Canberra, 1976), pp. 213–14.
7. Howard Bailes, 'Military aspects of the war', in *South African War*, p. 95; Frank Myatt, *The British Infantry, 1660–1945* (Poole, 1983), p. 157.
8. *Globe and Laurel*, 59/8 (1900), p. 119.
9. *Navy and Army Gazette*, 5 Nov. 1900.

10. Pretorius, 'Burgher on commando', Rethinking the South African War conference paper, UNISA, 1998.
11. *Cape Mercury*, 19 Oct. 1901.
12. *Naval and Military Record*, 16 Nov. 1900.
13. Capt. F. P. Fletcher-Vane, *The War One Year After* (Cape Town, 1903), pp. 5–8.
14. Leopold Scholtz, 'Die Strategiese Oogmerke van Genl. C.R. de Wet tydens die Eerste Dryfjag, Juli-Augustus 1900', *Historia*, 22/1 (1977), p. 14.
15. *Smuts: Memoirs*, p. 132.
16. Quoted in Thomas Pakenham, *The Boer War* (London, 1979), p. 485.
17. *Suffolk Gazette*, 131 (1900), p. 44.
18. P. W. Vorster, 'Generaal J. B. M. Hertzog as Kampvegter vir die Kaapse Rebelle, 1902–1903', *Historia*, 39/2 (1990), p. 116.
19. Philip Bateman, *Generals of the Anglo-Boer War* (Cape Town, 1977), p. 14.
20. Dermot Michael Moore, *General Louis Botha's Second Expedition to Natal* (Cape Town, 1979), pp. 96–101.
21. *Oakleaf*, 8/7 (1900), p. 39.
22. 'Die Eerste Dryfjag op Generaal C. R. de Wet', *Historia*, 17/3 (1972), pp. 201–2.
23. *Cape Daily Telegraph*, 8 Jan. 1901.
24. Grundlingh, 'Collaborators', p. 263.
25. Pakenham, *Boer War*, pp. 489–91.
26. Grundlingh, 'Collaborators', p. 264.
27. Dietlof van Warmelo, *On Commando* (Johannesburg, 1977), p. 112.
28. Albert Grundlingh, 'Probing the prophet: the psychology and politics of the Siener van Rensburg phenomenon', *South African Historical Journal*, 34 (1996), pp. 226, 231–2; Adriaan Snyman, *Siener van Rensburg: Boodskapper van God* (Mosselbaai, 1995), pp. 49–66.
29. D. Scholtz, 'Die Slag van Tweebosch, 7 Maart 1902', *Historia*, 24/2 (1979), pp. 53–5.

7

Squeezing Through
to Peace

As the whole axis of the enterprise swung to guerrilla struggle, Kitchener had one or two blinding flashes of extremism. Frustrated and embittered that things had not gone his reasonable way in the Middelburg talks, back in June 1901 he had caused a stir by proposing that the whole population of irreconcilable Boers should be swept up and deported to somewhere like Madagascar or, preferably, Fiji, where they could be left to decompose. 'A little bluff'[1] to finish things off was one facile suggestion. Through July and August, for once he and Milner saw eye to eye over a much milder fantasy: that of the banishment from South Africa of the republican leadership. The government was quite taken by this stiff threat, and early in August endorsed the issuing of an aggressive proclamation, warning Boer officers and anyone in command of 'armed bands' that they would face permanent banishment if they failed to surrender by mid-September. This fitted well with Milner's iron purpose, that of surrender being unconditional. Again, this political stroke did not exactly carry the veldt; very few commandos were scared into giving in.

But Kitchener's prime job was the forcible defeat of the enemy, and in this respect the military promise was more potent than political threat. Under his stern and sweeping command the army advanced gradually and highly methodically. Core staff work became more exacting and systematic; the size and scope of the Field Intelligence Department was vastly increased, so that by 1902 it had almost 140 officers, over 2300 civilian subordinates, several thousand African and Coloured scouts and spies, and a number of Boer *hensoppers* winkled from their farms to work as spies; overall coordination of command was also improved.[2] As this fell into place, around it Kitchener assembled part of his striking force of some 220,000 troops into bustling flying columns. The objective was to establish an almost continuous north–south front, bisecting the interior of the country from the Transvaal down to the southwestern Cape Colony. By robbing the enemy of ground and closing off exits, the British moved to squeeze the commando rural war into an ever more bounded space.

By 1901 Kitchener had also grasped the necessity of throwing an impregnable bridgehead right under the noses of his mobile enemy and beginning to use it as a field base artery of communications, supply, and intelligence. It required the rapid and efficient construction of thousands of small forts or blockhouses as a fixed grid across which British columns could conduct sweeping drives against the commandos. At first built sturdily of thick stone, cost and speed requirements soon obliged Kitchener to base his protective lines upon galvanized, corrugated iron and timber blockhouses. Less squat than stone structures, these lighter bastions could be easily raised on top of thick cushions of earth and stone, providing commanding elevation over the veldt and well-protected firing positions. Proofing blockhouses against assault also became increasingly easy as Boer fighting formations diminished in size and, crucially, in firepower as the hurrying commandos gradually discarded their remaining artillery.

Their mere jutting presence was an important stamp of imperial military authority. Looped together with barbed wire, and thickly compacted at vulnerable spots, the cheap blockhouse noose employed a dense system of outlying alarms and traps in defence, and rigged up telegraph, telephone, carrier-pigeon and other signal connections to maintain communication over lengthening field fortification lines. A stark and simple scheme, it was a great feat of military engineering, providing Kitchener's army with a mechanical backbone further increased in strength by the enrolment of loyal colonist guards and many thousands of armed African and Coloured 'watchers', 'guards', 'scouts', and 'police' to augment garrison strength along blockhouse lines. The British were strung out, but systematically; and gaps for the enemy were few and steadily decreasing as the telegraph wire controls spooling out behind their columns, and power and light provision from Royal Engineers' sappers, tautened surveillance capacity.

Thus thickened, Kitchener deployed close to one hundred columns across large belts of mapped and defined territory. Mostly brigade-sized, these became tactical areas of independent responsibility in which commanders were given their head and a fat purse to engage local black field hands and herders for scouting, snooping, and other kinds of useful service. Large columns of between 1200 and 2000 soldiers and accompanying black auxiliaries then undertook a series of drives or sweeps into the countryside between fortified British lines, to box in and pick off their prey; as an operation to scour areas clean, by early 1902 Kitchener's flying columns had come to resemble vultures swooping on the bones of the Boer armies.

The course of these gnawing operations in which the British overhauled and then increasingly ran down more flagging opponents involved numerous expeditions of varying effectiveness; some were huge combined operations, such as French's 1901 sweep between the Natal and Delagoa Bay rail lines, which nabbed some 273,000 head of stock, 'a devastating blow to the Boer economy',[3] and a converging drive between the Modder and the Vaal some months later, to squeeze commandos against the westerly blockhouse line between Jacobsdal and Bloemfontein. It is not easy to plot a meaningful narrative pattern to these rolling actions. In general, they killed or wounded small numbers of commandos, but took thousands more captive, and carried off wagons, weapons, horses, cattle, grain, and forage supplies. Of course, the outcome of individual drives was often mixed; British hunters could not always set good snares or bridge the intelligence gap between them and their quarry. Cumulatively, however, this relentless tidal method made a crucial contribution to settling the outcome of hostilities, as a gradual cordoning of the countryside with anti-guerrilla blockhouses and wire now limited the range and effectiveness of commando raiding parties.

In addition, Kitchener's exacting methods of enclosure began to break the will of some of the most bittereinder parts of his enemy, such as Meyer's 800–strong commando, which simply ran out of ground and crumpled into submission in February 1902. Unremitting scouring movements struck out further and faster, formed continuous barriers made up of a mesh of soldiers, blockhouses, wire, and even prowling train-mounted searchlights, and further tightened the screw by laying in large numbers of armed African mounted scouts. Of course, it took time for this pattern to harden, and there were also regions, like the western Transvaal, where tricky terrain, troublesome water shortages, and communication obstacles made it difficult to unfurl the blockhouse net. But by constricting available territory and penning in the enemy Kitchener gradually countered the Boers' evasive warfare. It was not so much that de Wet's veterans in the northeastern Orange Free State and those of de la Rey in the western Transvaal kept slipping away as that the guerrilla war became less elastic and more habituated to the synchronization of Kitchener's territorial adjustments. Commando movements then became increasingly regulated by the rhythms of great British sweeps, with the compulsions of repeated flight leaving many burghers exhausted, demoralized, and on the brink of paralysis. A further territorial factor tipped the balance against the commandos, denying them possible flanking country in which to regain breath. Friction and menacing hostilities left them checked in the southeast by wilful Swazi and Zulu, and by Pedi groups to the northeast; to the west they were hemmed in by hostile Tswana. Any movement in these directions was risky.

Kitchener also forced the pace in turning imprisonment into isolation, withdrawing most prisoners of war altogether from the scene of hostilities. It was cheaper, made them less conspicuous, knocked the morale of those still under arms, and would perhaps teach the Boers just how large the empire was. Following Roberts' dispatch to Ceylon of Cronjé's troops after Paardeberg, prisoners of war were removed to camps in Ceylon, India, Bermuda, and St Helena. A couple of these economies were revived by a novel new import industry: the good fortune of keeping prisoners of war, over 5000 in the case of Bermuda, which consequently increased its population by more than a quarter.[4] These camps were rough and ready affairs with inadequate services, and stressful tropical conditions led to a considerable number of deaths. Given the remoteness of their locations, Boer captives, some of them young boys, were left mostly to tend to themselves, their pursed lips opened by religious assembly, sports, music, carving, and other rural cultural practices carried to a distant frontier of incarceration. While nutrition levels were uneven, there was at least a tobacco and chocolate subsidy from Dutch and Belgian sympathizers. And while, for most, this was a crushing kind of war tourism on the imperial fringe, a few found enough to begin life anew, staying on in Ceylon after 1902 as imperial service veterinary officers or returning from Asia as advocates of Oriental philosophy and religion.

The fighting fortunes of the commandos were also jeopardized by increasing Boer collaboration with the British. If Kitchener did not create this, he did more than any other imperial commander to mould it into a fairly effective auxiliary asset. Since mid-1900 some hensopper burghers under oath had been tilting from neutrality towards providing assistance in the field for casual payment or reward, and towards the end of the war their numbers were increasing significantly, reaching almost 4000 by April 1902 and close to 5500 when hostilities ceased. With no more than around 17,000 bittereinders still out at the end, the reviled spectacle of Boer traitors had become a real worry to fighting republicans. Most of these were in no doubt about the position: as British annexations had not ended the war and continued to be contested, Crown authority remained illegitimate. The states which burghers had been charged to defend continued to live, and it was to these and these only that Boer populations could owe any political allegiance. For surrendered neutrals to keep their peace and their place was one thing; the act of becoming a British 'joiner' (as it was contemptuously termed) was quite another. Technically, such treachery amounted to treason, and anyone captured ran the risk of being summarily executed; and the quandary of a hard-pressed Boer society deepened as a flank of its anti-imperial war began to mutate into a bitter head-on civil war.

Kitchener grasped both the military advantage and the political value of making the most of this. The patchy and largely informal system of irregular scouting and guiding with untried local burgher corps and Farmers' Guards which had been in train since late 1900 was greatly extended, put on a more organized basis, and made subject to a more unified direction. Variously, thin strings of Burgher Police and Farmers' Guard 'joiners' in the Orange Free State were run through a 'protected area' around the capital as a protective blanket for surrendered men who were trying to resume farming, and as a force to help in nailing down British authority. This deployment was evidence of intelligent thinking: propertied members would have a stake in trying to defend their localized interests against commando incursion. Yet the execution of this strategy was never entirely easy; there was a lack of defensive depth to cover all key points, a particular difficulty when the enemy tactic was to raid as it pleased wherever possible, and then to wait.

Further strengthening came from burgher guiding and scouting which, along with black expertise, came to form part of the intelligence operational capability of every British column by early 1902. Across the Orange Free State, and especially in the Transvaal during later 1901 and 1902, renegade burghers sharpened the strike of column commanders. Reconnaissance estimates of enemy movement and disposition became more accurate, confusion over place and terrain diminished, and spying and other clandestine operations (such as sneaking reliable 'joiner' agents into commandos) picked up in effectiveness. So, too, did the predictive side of the tactical intelligence field; many ex-commandos had a good nose for where their former bands were likely to lie up in laager, thereby assisting British night assaults on resting Boers. 'Big coarse fellows,' wrote one Intelligence Officer, 'but in slyness and quiet they would surprise my sister's cat.'[5] The boost this provided has to be seen against guerrilla war conditions which, right to the end, provided the Boers with an explicit intelligence advantage. Aside from splinters into British colonial territory, the annexed republics remained the rib-cage of irregular fighting, and occupation forces found it virtually impossible to saddle up without the closest commando being alerted.

In all of this, Kitchener's calculations were never without a shrewd political core. In 1901, and again in 1902, he was thinking hard about enemy divisions, concluding that if there were 'already two parties amongst them ready to fly at each other's throat', then the way forward was to nudge this along. Thus, 'if the Boers could be induced to hate each other more than they hate the British', the outcome would be obvious, he assured the Secretary of State for War. It would be to cultivate and deliver 'a party among the Boers themselves depending entirely on British continuity of rule out here'.[6] He had no intention of neglecting calls from a number of more conspicuous hensoppers, like Piet de Wet, that more should be done to enable lapsed commandos to aid the British, so that sense and compromise could win the day. Responding to such urgencies, and his tactical perception that the use of armed Boer collaborators would ease the pressure of competing needs on his columns, in the closing months of 1901 Kitchener sanctioned a scheme to amalgamate the burgher corps. Some of them were ill-armed and performing little more than clearing livestock from the countryside in return for scraps of loot; they were now to be combined with less mediocre units, properly attested, and placed under uniform conditions of service and standard British army disciplinary codes. Commencing in October 1901, local corps and scout bodies in the Boer territories were pulled into the (Transvaal) National Scouts and the Orange River Colony Volunteers. Their very names established their valued membership of Kitchener's professional army establishment, yet with a certain ironic imperial detachment; these were the kind of volunteers for parading in Kroonstad, not Canterbury.

Enlarging their complement of enlisted men required recruiting, and Kitchener got this under way with impressive dispatch, becoming personally involved in campaigning, which largely took the form of plucking surrendered burghers from concentration camps. In addresses his message was stark: the guerrilla war was hopeless, and would only bring on more bloodshed and ruining of the country. By responding to imperial need, 'joiners' would both improve their own mean circumstances and assist in bringing needlessly prolonged hostilities to a close. Although Scout and Volunteer pickings were not huge, the availability of good wages, regular rations, clothing, and equipment, along with intimations of land or farm rewards, put over 1800 men under British arms by the end of the war. Mindful of hostilities and potential retaliation from bittereinders towards their families, some of whom received perks for loyalty, the British tried to provide an insulation for them through separate camp and house accommodation in Pretoria and elsewhere.

National Scouts continued to be the skirmishing outriders of mobile British columns, their various units never combining as an independent Boer-British fighting force against their countrymen and women. But they were more damaging in another way, for through armed collaboration the festering divisions within Boer society were fused with the British army. There may be an argument that Kitchener's burgher corps was misconceived, and that it made matters more awkward for the British by contributing further to the bitterness of resisting commandos, hardening their determination to hold out. But it is more likely to have been otherwise, demoralizing in spirit and deflating of morale. Leading figures like Louis Botha, Lukas Meyer, and Schalk Burger were all keenly sensitive to the depressing tactical and moral climate engendered by the Scouts' formation. 'Faithless', 'unfaithful', or 'failed' people were now aiding the British to get the better of the patriots in the most wounding way imaginable: teaching the enemy the Boer way of 'how to wage war', how to muffle hooves and equipment to trek silently through the night, or where there were mountain channels through which to squeeze unobserved. While commandos were counting their losses, their opponents were so growing in strength through the infusion of traitorous blood that the dread time might come when fighting partisans behind the republican cause could be outnumbered by 'their own people' who had turned on it.[7] If by no means a principal factor in bringing about Boer defeat, the plague of collaboration was there in the final losing equation between actual hardship and loss of faith.

The leading historian of 'joiners' and their treason as a social phenomenon has provided cogent argument that it can mostly be understood as a symptom of the deep agrarian inequalities of Boer society.[8] At the start the war provided a social cement, but once things began to go badly, not only did it flake off, but economic and social divisions worsened. Undeniably, ordinary burghers would have had a range of motives influencing their actions, whether to stay on the run as a die-hard or to turn in as a 'handsupper' or 'joiner'. Rank-and-file bittereinders included poor landless burghers as well as 'socially sunken' individuals whose possessions had been eaten by the scourge of the war: displaced, and with no anticipation of ever being able to rebuild a known material existence, there was nothing left but the fight, and pride in not yielding. Equally, not every 'joiner' was a bywoner; Piet de Wet, a leader of the Orange River Colony Volunteers, was not short of an acre. Even so, in the closing phase of the war, the broad profile confirms a conspicuous class differentiation in the social base of National Scouts and bittereinders.

Overwhelmingly propertyless and underprivileged 'joiners' were drawn from that discontented stratum which had long resented having to bear the costs of unpaid commando duties, and were now not always charmed by having to look after the assets of the wealthier while they themselves had none. In some cases coerced into armed service by landlords, they had never been that much of a sacrificial repository for national cause. The post-1900 bittereinders, and especially their leadership, were mostly individuals of a different type, a new, younger Afrikaner landed, urban, and semi-urban professional grouping, the 'well-to-do'. By 1902, unable to be rejuvenated by anything telling in the way of increased fighting numbers, they were sustained precisely because they had contracted to tried, able, and trusted burghers, had nurtured more stringent commando discipline, and saw themselves as the moral kernel of their cause, with 'a magnificent sense of righteousness'.[9] The war had cost all of them money, and some their relatives, and the sense of being a distinctive war generation came to mark them. Like General Ben Bouwer, they had outlived the scoundrels like Kruger and Cronjé, and had become that fabled Afrikaner samurai, a 'select', prowling, warrior 'company' who would endure 'to the end without hope of reward'; for what hung over them was 'the threat of banishment from their country'.[10] Theirs was a confinement more bitter than that of Britain's camps, from which some surrendered burghers were now liberating themselves as Kitchener's National Scouts.

Once these camps moved beyond being conventional male prisoner-of-war camps, they were to have immense consequences for the prospects of continuing republican resistance. Right from the outset of his command, Roberts had had no doubt as to where and how to crush the resistance of his agrarian enemy. A scorched-earth policy had been implemented from March 1900 as a punitive measure for continuing resistance to British occupation and, undoubtedly, to bring home the hard hand of war. 'The problem of the Boers lies not only in their armies,' wrote a Sussex Regiment lieutenant, 'they are in the main a rather hostile people, who have also to be subdued in order for our present business to be brought to an end.'[11] He was by no means alone in this early realization.

Neither Boer government had the administrative, transport, and food-supply capacity to evacuate families from districts which were being overrun by the enemy, and farm inhabitants had to face the harsh consequences of a hostile army moving through their territory, doing more than stripping homesteads of food supplies and animals. Families faced complete displacement as crops were burnt and houses fired or dynamited. The official targets for demolition were properties occupied by the families of burghers who were away on commando duty, fighting on against British columns or raiding communication and supply lines, grievously worsening a long-range transport problem already aggravated by Roberts' and Kitchener's ingenious restructuring. But the destruction grew increasingly indiscriminate. In some instances, incendiarism razed property contaminated by the absence of male heads who were continuing acts of war, but both proportionately and in total number the destruction bore most heavily on non-combatant homesteads which had no direct link to operational commandos in particular districts. A few officers in Roberts' army grasped the risk posed by setting too much ablaze, worrying that 'gross burning and gutting' was 'needlessly spiteful' and could only increase 'the offence and hatred felt by these people'.[12] Roberts, however, was firm about rigour across all fields of battle. In the closing months of his command, he again insisted that 'unless the people generally are made to suffer for the misdeeds of those in arms against us, the war will never end'.

During that command, nothing systematic was done to deal with the problem of evicted families made destitute as a consequence of burning and culling. While a few senior officers had families assembled and dispatched to British-controlled towns, for the most part women and children were left to drift through the countryside, having to fend for themselves by foraging and taking what shelter they could get, sometimes being lifted into commando laagers, sometimes even straying into the odd African homestead, which received them decently. Some Africans were themselves having stock confiscated by the British as a means of trying to stop Boer fighters from commandeering food- and supply-convoy resources to keep them in the field.

In the midst of general neglect of those uprooted by the British advance, there were one or two displays of improvisational virtuosity during the course of 1900. In May Major-General Edward Brabant had proposed establishing protected camps for surrendered burghers, many of whom had families drifting in their wake. A few months later, some army officers north of Pretoria suggested that the only thing to do was somehow to round up the civilians and then send them lurching towards the areas most infested by commandos; that would give their mobile enemy an unwanted anchor which they would then be obliged to drag along. Roberts obligingly provided a sample test from July, when he evicted around 2500 women and children from Johannesburg and Pretoria and railed them to the Boer forces as they were retreating along the Delagoa Bay line. This was followed by a decree that all families of active commandos residing in occupied districts were liable to be dispatched to be accommodated by the enemy, without exception; this was sweeping in intent, and applied both to the pauperized and to the better-off spouses of any government officials and office-bearers.

For Roberts, the Boers were the architects of their own deportations. Instead of behaving as neutrals, the families aided commando strength in the field by dripping intelligence; and Roberts was also short of food supplies because of repeated republican strikes against the Cape and Natal rail supply lines. Not surprisingly, Louis Botha and others in the Transvaal leadership saw this as a deliberately cruel act of retribution, forcing the severe costs of the continuing republican struggle 'upon our wives and children' in order to intimidate those commandos who were keeping up the fight. In the event, two curious twists followed those expulsions which did proceed. First, families who had been bundled off to be accommodated by the combatants simply slid back into British hands as the commandos retreated. Second, the impact of driving women out to commandos seems to have been ambiguous. At one level, it hit at morale: this can be seen in popular attitudes, as distressed fighters realized just how uprooted they were, with even their families 'run away' or 'chased from this place to that'.[13] But equally, the entry into fighting laagers of embittered women moving defiantly under republican colours may have encouraged and shamed some crumpled burghers into straightening up.

By September 1900, the month in which camps for surrendered burghers were established at Bloemfontein and Pretoria, it had become obvious that the problem of displaced non-combatants could not be solved by depositing them with enemy forces; encumbered by furniture, grain, and even stoves, they were being left behind by commandos who were already having difficulty in providing for themselves. As scorched-earth and population-clearance policy became more systematic under Kitchener, affecting not only Boer resources but also small African peasant settlements and crop and livestock holdings in the republics, something had to be done about the chaos in the countryside. Towards the end of December, Kitchener instituted a policy of what was termed 'refugee-camp' provision for the whole of South Africa; by then there were already over 40 camps, a number holding larger populations than most middling republican towns.

Usually bonded to the railway supply spine, and close to the administrative pulse of military administration in small towns, these concentration camps absorbed thousands of inmates, and came to house not only surrendered burghers and their families, but also thousands of non-combatants who had been swept from farms by burnings and the great mounted drives set off by Kitchener; these comprised women and children as well as old men. Along with them came large numbers of dislocated refugee Africans, for whom the military authorities established separate camps. The size of the incarcerated population grew during the course of 1901, as Kitchener tightened the screw, ordering the removal of all people from designated hostile districts which were persistently housing commandos. In the Commons, the British government position was that the camp system solution had been imposed on it: with unprotected women and children being left at risk on the veldt, the only humane thing to do was for the British army to extend aid by accommodating and feeding them as best it could. There was, no doubt, an obvious reality to this: unavoidable burnings and confiscations were leaving families on the loose in the most dire straits. Through its camp provision the army was therefore seeing to Boer women and children who had been deserted by callous male breadwinners, selfishly putting war above the crying needs of love and family. Outside the protective confines of bell-tents lay a nature black in tooth and claw, as *The Times* advised in June 1901, for to return women to the open veldt would be 'to send them to starve and to expose them to outrages from the natives which would set all South Africa in a flame'.[14] As Paula Krebs has argued, the combination of a sentimental humanitarian protectionism and anxiety over what unbridled Africans might do 'brought together two central ideologies of Victorian Britain – that of the weakness of woman and that of the sexual savagery of the black man towards the white woman'.[15]

British anti-war activism from the middle of 1901 through to the end of the war focused squarely on the incarceration of Boer women and children, and demanded a great deal of defensive humanitarian rhetoric about the function of the camps from government spokesmen and the pro-war press. The great underlying thing, of course, is that they were serving a military purpose based upon a paradox: families, and women in particular, were not classified as combatants, yet were in effect being made prisoners of war through confinement to camps. At one level, Kitchener's camp system had to expand because of tactical need. 'Every farm,' he told Brodrick in December 1900, 'is an intelligence agency and a supply depot so that it is almost impossible to surround or catch' the enemy. Again in March 1901, he stressed that the position of 'women left in farms' was proving intolerable, 'as they give complete intelligence to the Boers of all our movements and feed the commandos in their neighbourhood'.[16] To exist in inflamed parts of the countryside was a potential act of deception, a subversion of effective military operations which required that the enemy neither see nor hear. The show could only go on if there were enclaves of controlled 'undesirable' populations, thereby denying information and sustenance to republican commandos.

At another level one thing stands out. In the eyes of Kitchener and Milner (and, for that matter, Roberts) internment was a strategy to pressurize the enemy into giving up the fight. The camps were to serve as hostage sites; only by laying down their arms would burghers ever again be reconnected with their families. For Kitchener, fear of perpetual separation and loss could 'work on the feelings of the men to get back to their farms'. And through camp confinement the contagious influence of those more bittereinder women who were 'keeping up the war' could also be nipped. Here was the only 'solution' for women 'more bitter than the men'; the only way to 'bring them to their senses' was to 'remove the worst class'.[17] Kitchener was again a ruthlessly exact organizer of what needed to be done for a satisfactory outcome. It was not enough to unleash force and firepower against burghers on remaining commandos. Their surrounding families had to be scared into orderly behaviour, and kept away from feeding the fight.

So brisk a summary can hardly convey the significance of the traumatic camp experience, reflected in letters from some of over 116,000 inmates who fought a submerged battle to keep body and soul together in what had become an audit of life and death. 'As far as one can see, the veldt looks quite beautiful,' wrote Gezina Pretorius from her Bloemfontein camp in November 1901, yet 'terrible numbers of people are dying around us'.[18] Nor can we provide a full picture of the 1901–2 camps controversy and humanitarian scandal in Britain over the imperial army's conduct and prosecution of the war. The 1901 first-hand account of the severity of conditions by the Liberal humanitarian Emily Hobhouse is still credited by many as being largely responsible for awakening sections of the British public to the plight of interned Boer civilians, prodding on Henry Campbell-Bannerman's famous denunciatory Commons speech on British 'methods of barbarism' and other Liberal anti-war critiques. Many of the most pungent (and overheated) came from Lloyd George who, early in 1901, warned that 'brutal policies' might be exploited as a worrying pretext by European powers to justify their intervention on the side of the Boers. This had happened before in 'America's colonial revolution' and could do so again. If that were to come to pass, Britain would 'have to pay the penalty, not merely of the shame of transactions in these colonies, but the more substantial penalty of facing the world in arms against us'. Salisbury remained shameless, instructing a humanitarian that, as war was a terrible thing, the Boers 'should have thought of its horrible significance when they invaded the Queen's dominions'.[19]

The Liberal moral revulsion over the Boer camp system and Britain's perceived perversion of the rules of civilized warfare forms the most single-minded political issue of the war, and of the establishment of black concentration camps, with their internment of thousands of Africans, creating no contemporary fuss. For present purposes, however, the key question is rather different: not that of how horrendous the camps were, but rather, of whether they were effective in bringing on Boer surrender. It cannot be doubted that forced resettlement of both Boers and Africans became a crucial link in the Kitchener chain of attrition, part of the massive loop of blockhouses and their interconnecting patchwork of barbed-wire squares through which flying columns conducted big sweeps to scour the countryside clean of any hostile or impeding presence. Against an enemy conducting an undulating struggle based on rising, lying low, and rising, the veldt had to be rendered sterile. Scorched earth was more than evacuating farm populations and handing them over for resettlement; its ultimate objective was the removal of all civilians, crops, and livestock from the republican countryside. In the end the Boer commandos would experience what the Spanish resettlement strategy had produced in the recent Cuban War of Independence: exhausted, demoralized and skinny rebels would surrender, leaving their opponents the easy task of rounding up any stragglers who might still be resisting.

Just as there is a strong argument that the early commencement of wholesale farm burnings lengthened rather than shortened the war, so there is a view that the pressures imposed by the concentration-camp policy did not of themselves bring determined bittereinders to quit. Within the camps themselves, female opinion seems to have been divided. Some collaborated with camp authorities or struck up friendships with soldiers in the hope of earning favour or perks to ease their deprivation; others sometimes communicated their desire for the war to be ended to burghers in the field, 'berating us,' as a Transvaal commando noted in February 1902, 'for forcing them to keep on living in the midst of misery and the dying.'[20] But many did not waver in their continuing adherence to the republican struggle, remaining a constant source of disaffection to the British and an emotive subsidy to Boers still out in the field. By 1902 many had lost more than their lands and burned homes; with kinfolk incarcerated, there remained precious little to be saved through a voluntary, compromising surrender.

Still, as the purest encapsulation of Britain's war of attrition, there can be no doubt that the camp policy was a weighty contributory factor to the ending of republican resistance. For the camps added something to the destruction of shelter, supplies, and subsistence bases in devastated parts of Boer territory: they added fearfully high death rates, which peaked towards the end of 1901, reaching a mortality rate of 344 per 1000 by October. Metropolitan and local anti-war critics of British 'death camps' accused army administrators of near-genocidal maltreatment of inmates, including mass poisoning to wipe out the Boer population. For their part, British propagandists blamed the Boers for running up their own death lists due to their ignorance of modern sanitation, and for clinging to their own 'primitive' therapeutic practices, such as the use of 'Dutch medicines'.[21] The basic fact is that the British army was unable to maintain a hygienic environment for its own troops in South Africa, who were far more likely to succumb to a faecal–oral disease borne by water, dust, or flies than to a Mauser bullet. The poorly prepared and insanitary camps run by officers seconded as general superintendents were an invitation to catastrophe – and it came, in the shape of winnowing epidemics of measles, dysentery, pneumonia, and whooping cough, which bore particularly heavily on children and cut down black as well as white inmates. The devastating impact of this high civilian mortality on the morale of republican leadership cannot be overestimated; it seemed to be threatening the very reproductive future of the Boer people. Smuts, for instance, was to estimate that by the end of hostilities over 10 per cent of the Boer inhabitants of the republics had died in camps. Here was a most compelling restraint against holding out for a continuation of the war. So, in addition to civilian suffering, was a rising social fear among men that the upright, Calvinist character of what General Hertzog called 'our female sex' was being eroded by 'immorality' or 'destructive moral influences', increasingly unable to keep good order 'under the influence of a godless enemy'.[22]

By now there was also a further damaging factor, one with a worrying chemistry all of its own. Since the start of war black people in various operational zones (and even outside them) had been aiding the British to defeat the Boers through irregular armed service, scouting, spying and intelligence, supplying crop, livestock, and other goods, and in providing remount, transport riding, and other labour for logistical services. This was a tide which was always running the British way, and was rising beyond politically tolerable levels. As commandos in areas like the southeastern Transvaal topped up their provisions in the only way now available, through the pillaging of Zulu homesteads, so resistance intensified and began to grow increasingly more violent. In forced conditions of almost constant pursuit, night riding, and the rapid creaming off of peasants' supplies, burghers had increasingly to manoeuvre through lands occupied by Africans, whom they routinely harassed and who then either informed on them to chasing British forces or turned on them themselves, infuriated by the disruption and losses caused by the commandos. One shock example of the latter, and a chilling indication of how things were breaking up, was a Zulu surprise night attack in April 1902 upon a small commando encampment at Holkrantz, near Vryheid, in retribution for periodic Boer confiscation and labour conscription; 56 burghers were speared to death, with the vengeful impi itself losing about 100 warriors, dead or wounded. Matters were no easier elsewhere, for either there was no longer room in areas such as the far northern Transvaal, or what there was had become too hostile to run into. Thus, as Louis Botha ruefully concluded at the end, 'in only one portion of the country, namely Zoutpansberg, is there still food, but how do we obtain our provisions there? It must be taken, and thereby we create more enemies...if the enemy were to pour into that district the kaffirs will join against us.'[23] The Boers could only sustain their guerrilla strategy through wide dispersal, drawing off the British and forcing them to campaign over the largest area possible; this could not be done in an infected countryside or in areas like the western Transvaal, where armed Kgatla had grown teeth sufficiently sharp to deter any commando attempts to get them to budge.

Roaming south into the northern and northwestern Cape Colony was beginning to produce some encounters with armed Coloured inhabitants which were also less one-sided than in previous incursions. In the northwest commandos met with little else but good intentions from local Boer farming communities, but they were greatly outnumbered by a brown-skinned majority determined to fight what they saw as an enslaving republican rule. British colonial authority could not but rest upon the enlisting and arming of 'coloured corps', like the Namaqualand Scouts, Bushmanland Borderers, and Northern Border Scouts. Skilled horsemen and accomplished hunters like their enemy, between them they landed some commandos in a tough spot during 1901 and into the early months of 1902, handing defeat to an Edwin Conroy commando in a cross-fire ambush, a pounding engagement which has now been retrieved for the historical record as the battle of Naroegas.[24]

As if to add to a sense of impending doom, back in Boer territory communities of rural African tenants were taking up the habit of armed threat or violence in disturbingly large numbers as they commenced occupying Boer land across many areas, particularly in the Transvaal, spurning customary master-and-servant or landlord-and-tenant relations. The Boers naturally resisted moves to contest their authority and ownership of land, but as hostilities wore on many began to lose all ability to act and even faith in their strength. So extensive was this decomposition, and so intense the Boer–African belligerence to which it gave rise, that one historian has characterized it as the eruption of a peasant war or a 'rebellion from below'.[25] Without exaggerating its influence as a driving force behind Boer defeat, it has become quite clear that black anti-republican resistance and collaboration with the imperial occupation moved the Boers along towards surrender. 'An unbearable condition of affairs in many districts of both Republics' was what the Boer peace delegates eventually saw. Several British intelligence officers saw it no less clearly, if somewhat more approvingly, recording the 'discomfiture' and 'jumpiness'[26] of the enemy and its crisis of black resistance as the Transvaal buckled, hit from the outside and gnawed away from the inside.

Ultimately, what was left for the republicans was the Cape Colony. An unwelcome place, regulated by martial law and punctuated by rebel imprisonment and military court executions, there was not much here, what with French using his standing court-martial machinery against captured rebels 'with the utmost vigour', and compelling the 'disloyal Dutch' to observe the public execution of rebels in Middelburg and Dordrecht. Milner worried over the long-term political damage such military harshness would cause, 'but who in practice was to decide which actions were necessary and which excessive'?[27]

Hertzog and de Wet had had a stab themselves at carrying war deep into the Cape between the end of 1900 and early 1901, of course, but had effectively ended up being worn down by their own offensives without creating any meaningful breach. Smuts had another try in August 1901, despite his own pained perception that victory over Britain was no longer possible and that the only option for the Boers would be to try for a negotiated end to hostilities. If sufficient colonial recruits could be raised, and that crucial but maddeningly elusive general Cape rebellion be got under way, the republicans might survive on strengthened terms after all. Barely slackening, Smuts nipped through British lines across the Orange Free State, got through the southeastern Cape, and settled into a westerly prowling movement along the lengthy Atlantic seaboard. It was another impressive Boer dash by no more than a handful of selected commandos, distracting the British and forcing the diversion of large numbers of troops to take on Smuts' force of just over 300 burghers; although ill-equipped, some men answered its driving call, increasing numbers to around 3000 commandos. Then the old story was repeated; the invading expedition covered too much too thinly. And although Cape Boers were 'better-conditioned'[28] than their scorched-earth northern counterparts, far fewer than anticipated took up arms to strengthen Smuts; they knew what they stood to lose.

Smuts' appeal to Transvaal forces to reinforce his Cape position said all there was to say about a colonial rebellion, as did his May 1902 assessment of the military position there. With no more than about 3300 men in the fight, crippled by remount and forage shortages, and panting for relieving reinforcements, he was at a loss. With no harvest to be reaped, he concluded that if the war was to be kept going, its southerly direction would have to be reversed. A 'continuance of the war', said Smuts, 'will depend more on the Republics than upon the Cape Colony'. That, in a way, clarified matters on the spot, stripping away illusions. As a member of Smuts' party, Deneys Reitz met with Botha and a group of 300 representatives from every surviving commando in the eastern Transvaal. What most brought home to him that 'the Boer cause was spent' was the sight of 'starving, ragged men, clad in skins or sacking, their bodies covered with

sores, from lack of salt or food'. However steely their faith, their pitiful physical state meant that they could not fight for much longer. If
these 'haggard, emaciated men were the pick of the Transvaal Commandos', concluded Reitz, 'then the war must be irretrievably lost'.[29]
In truth, despite few if any reserves, Smuts' forces and other republican units in the westernmost Cape were still in a position to keep up
operations, trying to adapt to the changing social and political ecolo-
gies of various districts (more hostile British colonists here, more
open-handed Boer settlers there), and remaining an unvanquished
nuisance. But it could never be more than one little thing at a time,
and when that amounted to no more than sacking Coloured mission
stations or executing suspected British spies and other collaborators,
it was not much of an initiative to hold. In any event, scrappy southern fighting bands were well outside the influence of the disciplinary
screen erected over northern bittereinder commandos in the closing
stages of the war. Efficiency was much impaired by familiar militia
friction over such matters as captaincy, geographical and political
connections, and personality squabbles. Right to the end, commandos were electing or deposing officers for reasons which often had
little to do with their soldiering abilities.[30]

By now the leadership on both sides wished to end a wasting war
and to conclude peace. There was no popular gain in the war for
Britain, and for Milner the ruin of the overrun republics had gone far
enough: very much more would jeopardize any prospects for
reconstruction and the installation of a new and more amenable
civilian administration. In January 1902, convinced that the republicans were all in and that unconditional surrender was imminent, he
foresaw 'settlement with a free hand', declaring that the 'advantage of
a war ending as it is ending is enormous'.[31] Kitchener had gone a lot
further than Roberts towards a conclusive military defeat of the
enemy, and already had his eye on the plum of an Indian army
command. But first he wanted to see a sustainable Anglo-Boer
settlement.

With the Middelburg talks having come to nothing, the war had
already ground on well into the next year, until in April the republican
governments came together at Klerksdorp in the Transvaal and
resolved to re-open negotiations with Kitchener. Typified by the
figures of Marthinus Steyn and Schalk Burger having stayed out
in the field within fighting ranks, these were emphatically war
governments, for whom peace was something to be negotiated by
belligerents. Their Klerksdorp proposals stuck to the fundamental
March 1901 principle of a retention of the republics' independence.

Predictably, Steyn was adamant that if Britain 'did not wish the Republics to remain independent, the struggle must continue'. If the moment to yield had to come, he would not be drawn into making peace terms with the enemy, preferring instead to 'submit unconditionally' to the British 'for ever'.[32] Through all the laborious months of his command, this is what had always worried an astute Kitchener. Unconditional surrender, without terms, would not bring in all the Boers; the most hardened opponents could continue their resistance. Even if they could not get far, the British would continue to be dragged along for uncertain gain and at further financial cost, against the background of a public mood which had grown weary of the war.

Provided there was no wrangling over independence rights, the Boer leadership offered to make a compromise peace based on several republican concessions. Going along with a general amnesty, the Boer states would undertake to 'demilitarize' their offensive capacities, extend the vote to Uitlanders, sign a binding treaty of friendship with Britain, and accord English equal rights with Dutch. With the republican forces by now numbering at most between 15,000 and 17,000 combatants, the British had considerably more guns to which to stick in the form of a quarter of a million troops. The government rejected the Klerksdorp terms, and responded essentially by dusting off the proposals which the Boers had repudiated at Middelburg. With a relinquishing of national independence as the starting-point, the assembled commando leaders were in some difficulty, for negotiations could not go forward without the legitimacy of a mandate from those in the field. In due course, with British consent, a conference of 60 Transvaal and Orange Free State representatives, elected as their delegates by commandos, was convened at Vereeniging to discuss British peace terms and decide if they were tolerable for ending the war. One of them was Smuts, plucked up from an inconsequential siege action in the northern Cape and conveyed under British safe conduct to Vereeniging for the more humdrum business of getting through agendas.

With one side as good as defeated, it was inevitable that the Vereeniging negotiations would end in the signing of peace, however impassioned and agonized the discussion and debate between delegates over what to do, however painful the exchanges with British peace representatives, and however sunny commandants tried to sound in their reports on 'splendid' and 'strong' Boer combat morale. What that assertion signified was no more than a dignified impotence. The republican representatives with whom the decision rested had to take realistic stock, and the picture which they painted at Vereeniging was sombre in the extreme. Externally, the Cape and its Afrikaner rebellion was a shrunken sideshow, and the Boers seemed to know better than Lloyd George that the war would not bring anti-British foreign intervention.

Internally, the impetus of Kitchener's ruthless drives and his blockhouse and wire noose showed no sign of slackening; while the scale of armed 'joiner' and other kinds of 'unfaithful' collaboration had also become deeply troubling and a source of immense nationalist bitterness. It was as well that the British did not try to usher in the 'handsupper' and 'joiner' interest at Vereeniging: negotiations would in all likelihood have stalled. While camp conditions had been improved by the British administration following the horrendous losses towards the end of 1901, this was only tainted relief. From December onwards, the British authorities had been refusing to pull any more women and children into camps, landing the worn-out commandos with the daunting job of providing for and protecting dependants in a field with few material resources. Lastly, and far from least in importance, was the fatal Vereeniging realization that republicanism had visibly lost too much ground and too much grip. Forced to abandon large chunks of the Orange River Colony and Transvaal Colony by devastation and scarcity of the essentials of grain, horses, and cattle, many Boers were becoming rusticated ghosts, beset by 'murders and all sorts of cruelties' perpetrated by the 'Kaffir tribes' who had been egged on by the enemy into 'taking part in the war against us'.[33]

Louis Botha was eloquent on this, and, together with Jan Smuts, he was also persuasive on another crucial matter concerning present defeat. This was to convince fellow delegates that while the Boers could not go back militarily, neither could they go forward. For more radical bittereinders, the Boers were not yet sufficiently flattened to have to submit to an unconditional surrender and, as guerrilla resistance, hostilities could be kept going for who knew how long, perhaps a year or even more. As long as the commandos could escape final defeat in the field, a negotiated settlement would always be achievable. This was a strategic notion based on elephantine faith, and we need not delay over it. Smuts had recently spent enough commando time in the Cape to know about going on too long and having little to show for it. He and Botha argued vigorously that the Boers' only chance had already come; if Vereeniging failed and the war sputtered on into 1903 and even beyond, the republicans would be so run down as to lose altogether any sort of treaty bargaining position, which might bring the worst kind of defeat, that of capitulation to imperial ultimatum. This argument carried sufficient delegates to move along negotiations, although not without some sulking from the most zealous and ill-at-ease die-hards. Leaders like Steyn, and commanders like Koos de la Rey and J. B. M. Hertzog, had long been scornful of the wing of the progressive new Afrikaner élite represented by the like of Botha and Smuts; from this quarter there had been too many signs before Vereeniging of dispirited introspection and a willingness to consider callings things off for a peace of conciliation. From some anti-monopoly capitalist spirits, there was brief discussion of trying for a conditional peace through some appeasement, such as handing over Johannesburg and its gold mines to Britain as an imperial enclave, in return for the retention of an agrarian-based independence. They can only have forgotten the truth of Kruger's 1899 judgement of what Milner wanted, or have been hitting the brandy.

The result was a sharp republican division. The Transvaal delegates were overwhelmingly for calling off the war to avoid a national catastrophe. This prospect was obvious to Smuts, who declared that if, 'humanly speaking', there was 'no reasonable chance to retain our independence as Republics, it clearly becomes our duty to stop the struggle in order that we may not perhaps sacrifice our people and our future for a mere idea which cannot be realized'.[34] Orange Free State representatives were, with few exceptions, unwilling to trade that idea through what amounted to a dictated peace. Taking things to a forced unconditional surrender still suited Steyn and his circle well enough, the very eventuality which had always worried Kitchener, for whom 'no terms' implied that the Boers could 'hold themselves absolutely free to begin again when they get a chance and see England in any difficulty'.[35] But it had been an alliance war, and there could be no separate repudiation of any military consequence. Bloemfontein could not be a check upon Pretoria, and the making of a final peace agreement.

Milner and Kitchener had never got on over the strategic consideration of the war aims of defeating the Boers, and were constantly at loggerheads over the terms to be settled with the Boer leaders. The High Commissioner, in fact, disliked having to enter into *any* peace negotiations with colonial forces who had demonstrated so great a threat to a British South Africa. He wanted the Boer leadership left high and dry by defeat, the influence of republican generals destroyed to open the way to Anglicization. If Milner was vindictive and tactless, an aloof and hard-headed Kitchener was scarely a more winning imperial figure. Yet he was an experienced imperial general of no small political judgement, and had a calculating sense of the need for magnanimity. Defeating the Boers required the making of peace so as not to produce a Roberts victory. At war's end, that could only be clinched through a fair measure of conciliation with the Boers, who had to be an accepted, indeed an essential, co-element of a reconstructed white settler order. This is surely what underpinned Kitchener's belief, aired before Vereeniging got under way and more than once reiterated, that the Boer leadership be accorded due honour and generosity, so that they would not go down in history as traitors who had sold out their countries.[36] Although the dominant influence on the British side, Milner did not get all that he wanted, nor did Kitchener get agreement on every fine detail that he wished to see as part of peace terms. But the Commander-in-Chief's influence in the accommodationist direction of those terms is apparent: an open-handed and 'honourable' peace as a basis for treating with the Boer generals.

The detailed political and administrative issues and activities in bringing Vereeniging through are quite exceptionally tedious, and do amount to small beer. Broadly speaking, the war had turned essentially on Boer claims: while severely cut back, they could never be completely excised. Even in Milner's fond vision of a significant British dominance within just a few post-war years, what mattered was that Afrikaner wants be reconciled to this. But the problem of the war had first to be resolved. This was achieved in the signing of peace in Pretoria shortly before midnight on 31 May 1902, ending the negotiations which had commenced at Vereeniging on 15 May. By 54 votes to 6, the republican delegates consented to surrender their independence and recognize the sovereign authority of Edward VII. The British object was accomplished, and to be made good it required a non-retributive aftermath. Many of the now around 20,000 bittereinders still out were said to be 'shattered' by news of the peace treaty, scarcely believing that they had just become British subjects; there were tears, and some declared their loss of faith in God.[37] The British troops were relieved that it was all over at last, but wobbled less at news of peace. That was predictable: they had been fighting a different war.

For their part, the Boers came away with the substance of a negotiated, not a dictated peace. In return for signing away their independence, they secured arrangements for the repatriation of all prisoners of war and the provision of an almost universal general amnesty; the ratification of economic rights, such as the maintenance of property ownership and non-punitive taxation; the provision of economic relief and renewal, through Britain meeting the bill for the republican war debt for anything up to £3m; and reconstruction relief for war victims. The terms also made provision for the eventual introduction of self-government in the two newly annexed colonies, and stipulated that limited franchise rights for blacks would not be pushed down tight Boer throats; that unwelcome consideration would be left for contemplation only after the introduction of responsible government. There would also be a measure of legal protection for the Dutch language.

Coined as 'surrender' by Milner (but not by a more tactful British government), and as a credibly negotiated settlement or treaty by Botha, the Treaty of Vereeniging brought to an end the British Empire's Boer republics. The South African War was over, ended by peace talks which had begun in a place with a name which meant, roughly, 'join' or 'unite'. A drab and ugly spot, it was not a promising town in which to sow the seed of a South African New Jerusalem. Eager to see the harvest, a new Liberal British government commenced the handing back of authority to the Orange River Colony and Transvaal Colony Boers in 1905, granting local self-government some five years after the end of hostilities. Union came in 1910, creating a unified white segregationist state presided over by Louis Botha and Jan Smuts, won over as the empire's Afrikaner colonial collaborators. When self-rule came, those men who came to constitute its governing nucleus were drawn from the generals who had made things so difficult for Britain. Afrikanerdom had not been obliterated, and in this sense Milner had come up short.

Having made up sufficiently with the right kind of realistic and amenable Afrikaners, the Liberal government had now gained 'good British subjects, whom we desire to be loyal', hoping that there would never again be a need to keep against them 'an enormous garrison at an enormous expense'.[38] In turn those subjects, in the shape of Botha and Smuts, sang sweetly, arguing for the reconciliation of 'white people in this land' as 'one solid, united and strong race'.[39] Invoking the American Civil War analogy much favoured by well-disposed British observers, Winston Churchill welcomed the day 'when we can take the Boers by the hand and say as Grant did to the Confederates at Appomattox, "go back and plough your fields"'.[40] They did, but, for many, not without a grudge. Among militant nationalists, 'the long history of conflict had aggravated a strongly anti-British sentiment ... leaving "the reverberations of menace"'. Wounding memory of the war 'could not be so easily wished away by the strategic logic of élites'.[41] Having finished one war, traditionalist republican malcontents would in time be ready for another, a political rather than a military struggle. The creation of the memory which helped to fuel it lay partly in how the opponents came to see the war, and to view each other, once hostilities had got under way. As we approach the end of this consideration of the South African War, we turn now to this question.

Chapter 7 Notes

1. Quoted in S. B. Spies, *Methods of Barbarism? Roberts and Kitchener and Civilians in the Boer Republics, June 1900–May 1902* (Pretoria, 1977), p. 237.
2. Thomas G. Fergusson, *British Military Intelligence 1870–1914: The Development of a Modern Intelligence Organisation* (Frederick, 1984), p. 161.
3. John Keegan and Richard Holmes, *Soldiers: A History of Men in Battle* (London, 1985), p. 243; Charles Townshend, *Britain's Civil Wars: Counterinsurgency in the Twentieth Century* (London, 1986), p. 183.
4. C. A. R. Schulenberg, 'Boerekrygsgevangenes van Bermuda', *Historia*, 23/2 (1978), pp. 83–5.
5. *Globe and Laurel*, 75/8 (1902), p. 74.
6. Quoted in Albert Grundlingh, 'Collaborators in Boer society', in *The South African War: The Anglo-Boer War 1899–1902*, ed. Peter Warwick (London, 1980), p. 268.
7. J. D. Kestell and D. E. van Velden, *The Peace Negotiations* (London, 1912), pp. 94, 179–82, 195–6.
8. Grundlingh, 'Collaborators', esp. pp. 272–5.
9. Keith Macksey, *Technology and War* (London, 1986), p. 46.
10. O. J. O Ferreira, *Memoirs of General Ben Bouwer* (Pretoria, 1980), p. 95.
11. Archives of the Royal Sussex Regiment, du Moulin Papers, RSR Mss.1/101, Journal entry, 15 Dec. 1901.
12. West Yorkshire Regimental Museum, Cayley Journals, entry for 27 Aug. 1900; S. B. Spies, 'Women and the war', in *South African War*, 165.
13. M. A. Gronum, *Die Bittereinders, Junie 1901–Mei 1902* (Kaapstad, 1974).
14. *The Times*, 18 June 1901.
15. Paula Krebs, '"Last of the Gentlemen's Wars": Women in the Boer War Concentration Camp Controversy', *History Workshop Journal*, 33 (1992), p. 45.
16. *Naval and Military Record*, 11 May 1901.
17. Quoted in S. B. Spies, 'Women and the war', p. 168.
18. F. A. van Jaarsveld and F. J. Pretorius, 'Tussen Lewe en Dood: Briewe uit die Bloemfonteinse "Refugee Kamp", 1901–1902', *Historia*, 28/1 (1983), p. 57.
19. Quoted in N. O. Goulart, 'Back bencher against war: a rhetorical analysis of the parliamentary speaking of David Lloyd George during the Boer War', Ph.D. diss. (Indiana University, 1982), p. 230; Malcolm MacColl, *Memoirs and Correspondence* (London, 1914), pp. 230–1.
20. Castle Museum, York, Records of the Friends South African Relief Fund, memo of committee meeting, 12 May 1902.
21. Bruce Fetter and Stowell Kessler, 'Scars from a childhood disease: measles in the concentration camps during the Boer War', *Social Science History*, 20/4 (1996), pp. 596–601; S. B. Spies, 'Women and the war', pp. 169–71; Elizabeth van Heyningen, 'Women and disease: the clash of medical cultures in the concentration camps of the South African War', Rethinking the SA War Conference paper, UNISA, 1998.

22. Kestell and van Velden, *Peace Negotiations* , p. 175.
23. Ibid., p. 85.
24. Martin Legassick, 'The battle of Naroegas: context, historiography, sources and significance', *Kronos: Journal of Cape History*, 21 (1994), pp. 32–60.
25. Jeremy Krikler, *Revolution from Above, Rebellion from Below: The Agrarian Transvaal at the Turn of the Century* (Oxford, 1993).
26. *Household Brigade Magazine*, 49/5 (1902), p. 43; *Oxfordshire Light Infantry Chronicle* (1902), p. 166; Beckett, *Johnnie Gough, V.C.* (London, 1989), p. 82.
27. Charles Townshend, *Britain's Civil Wars: Counterinsurgency in the Twentieth Century* (London, 1986), p. 185.
28. Deneys Reitz, *Commando: A Boer Journal of the Boer War* (London, 1931), p. 314.
29. Reitz, *Commando*, p. 320.
30. Rodney Constantine, 'The guerrilla war in the Cape Colony during the South African War of 1899–1902: a case study of the republican and rebel commando movement', M.A. diss. (University of Cape Town, 1996), p. 23.
31. Bodleian Library, Oxford, Milner Papers, MP 1V/B/221/fols.172–6, Milner to Dawkins, 16 Jan. 1902.
32. *Selections from the Smuts Papers*, vol. 1, eds W. K. Hancock and Jean van der Poel (Cambridge, 1966), pp. 151–2.
33. Kestell and van Velden, *Peace Negotiations*, pp. 185–6.
34. Ibid., pp. 188–9.
35. George Arthur, *The Life of Lord Kitchener* (London, 1920), vol. 2, p. 93.
36. Keith Surridge, 'The politics of war: Lord Kitchener and the settlement of the South African War, 1901–1902', Rethinking the SA War Conference paper, UNISA, 1998.
37. Fransjohan Pretorius, 'Waarom het die "Bittereinders" Gedurende die Anglo-Boereoorlog van 1899–1902 op Kommando Gebly?', *Historia*, 35/1 (1990), p. 72.
38. G. H. L. Le May, *British Supremacy in South Africa 1899–1907* (Oxford, 1965), p. 154.
39. Quoted in Leonard Thompson, *The Unification of South Africa, 1902–1910* (Oxford, 1960), pp. 30–2.
40. Quoted in Le May, *British Supremacy*, p. 112.
41. Anthony W. Marx, *Making Race and Nation: A Comparison of the United States, South Africa, and Brazil* (Cambridge, 1998), p. 90.

8

Anglo-Boer Attitudes
and Beliefs

Numerous historians have characterized the years from roughly 1870 to 1914 as a distinctive new epoch of frenetic nationalist war psychology and war culture. In this period the general attitudes of European society turned to embrace the increasingly belligerent 'realities of modernity', one of its more influential notions being an acceptance of war as both desirable and beneficial, a supreme competitive test of national virility and racial fitness.[1] In Britain, mounting concerns over the empire's place in the wider world led to excessive fears of foreign states and nationalities, not helped by great external national humiliations such as Majuba and Khartoum, which seemed to expose a worrying lack of real imperial power. By the end of the 1890s such circumstances had led to a great flowering of popular patriotism, actively and even violently hostile to anything perceived to be endangering British power. Whether those threatening were large, like Russia or France, or small, like the contentious Irish or the Boers, there was to be no toleration of nonsense.

The classic conception of this brew of nationalist patriotism and intoxicating militarism was the collective pathology of jingoism. As depicted by radical intellectuals like Charles Masterman and Hobson, this was a warped patriotism in which national feeling was transmuted into hatred of another nation, feeding into a primitive impulse to destroy its members. In Daniel Pick's fine summary, Hobson's famous *Psychology of Jingoism* conjured up a cynical imperialist 'world of war, a world contaminated by ... fanatical masses ... a Boer War world which ... unmasks illusions about the "purity" of British national character'. The war in South Africa shattered any liberal imperial notion of a John Bull who favoured a fair fight, instead peeling open 'the darker face of Britain, unmasking hidden and disturbing propensities'. Abandoning reason, the whole of British society had embraced a rapacious xenophobia, crowing over the plight of a weak and minor enemy. For Hobson this was best exemplified by hysterical public celebration of the lifting of the sieges, 'the saturnalia of Ladysmith and Mafeking Days', other ostentatious displays of war enthusiasm despite 'breaches of ... civilized warfare', and strident press calls for the slaying of Boers 'with the same ruthlessness which would be shown to a plague-infected rat'.[2]

The crusading force of this argument rested on the assumed pervasiveness of anti-Boer feeling in British society, partly directed from above by the Conservative and Liberal imperialist war interest, and swelling partly from below through substantial social sectors which eagerly absorbed war propaganda. Incubating hostility towards the enemy was a powerful imperial patriotism, inculcated by music hall and theatre, schools, military pressure groups, churches, paramilitary youth bodies like the Boys' Brigade and the Church Lads' Brigade, rough house jingo mobs who broke up anti-war meetings, and 'yellow' newspapers, periodicals, and books. The more sensational kind of cravings for blood which so disturbed Hobson could be seen in the views of the jingo socialist, Robert Blatchford, who by September 1900 was lamenting the failure of British 'kindness' in South Africa. 'We have killed some of them with kindness, but we have not killed enough ... Dispatch more. Those in St Helena and Ceylon might be rendered down into beef extract. It will be too expensive to send them back to South Africa.'[3] Blatchford was famous for a number of things, but not for heavy irony.

Commencing with the florid picture painted by Hobson and several of his contemporaries, we are used to the notion of mass patriotic enthusiasm for the war, demonstrated by the crowd-based nationalism of 'mafficking' to celebrate British mettle in the face of difficult odds, the disruption of anti-war gatherings, and the roughing up of prominent pro-Boers and attacks on their property. Once hostilities had got under way, and particularly after the dispiriting early British reverses, anti-war or equivocal Liberal, Labour, trade union, and socialist positions split, and minority opposition to the war became ever more marginal and muted; there continued to be such radical voices, but they were few and diminishing. While the issues of the war may have meant precious little, if anything, to working-class people, its rights or wrongs were quite secondary to the need that it be won.

Where popular attitudes might have differed sharply over something like Irish Home Rule, war against a distant colonial enemy bridged social divisions, creating a patriotic cause which could be shared by enthusiastic working and middle classes as well as the aristocracy. Moreover, the war encouraged more than a patriotic consensus; its emotive episodes of steady advances and heroic victories provided dazzle.

In this perspective, the war was also a winning cry at the polls. On the domestic political front, in some municipal contests and most notably in the 1900 'khaki election', it decisively conditioned political behaviour. Here, the strength of feeling was readily apparent in 1900, when an excitable election fought by the government on national loyalty and its running of the war produced a whopping majority, scuppering many pro-Boer Liberal MPs. In this charged atmosphere, working-class men were entreated not to dishonour or betray the memory of 'murdered' or 'treacherously felled' British soldiers by voting the wrong way. Candidates who tried for a more nuanced position, arguing that political criticism of war motives and of the government's conduct of military affairs did not mean lack of admiration for soldiering achievements and pride in victory, found that this cut no ice. The war was a patriotic cause to be supported to the hilt.

The straight proposition that war in South Africa enjoyed an enthusiastic mass following, that there was no anti-imperialist working-class opposition, and that even if workers did not promote anti-Boer jingoism, they acquiesced in it, has not gone without scholarly challenge. In studies which sought to reinterpret popular attitudes, writers such as Henry Pelling, Richard Price, and Ross McKibbin have argued that there was not all that much from which to conclude that the *mentalité* or political culture and beliefs of the working classes were so emphatically for war and empire. After all, what typically mattered in working-class culture was the immediacy of concrete, everyday experience, a consciousness in which ideals of patriotic militarism would have counted relatively little.[4] Given uncertainty as to what the empire actually meant to the mass of British people, attitudes to its wars were not necessarily unambiguous. While some sense of a common Britishness could be said to be widely felt in the working-class population, attitudes to the wider world rarely ever rose beyond indifference or dismissive contempt.

Given that, one could then turn to more specific factors to explain the weakness of popular opposition to the war. At the outset, organized labour leadership had indeed opposed hostilities; but once war became wartime it was difficult to sustain a united stance, and traditional pro-war, working-class Tory organization was able to extend its social reach. Furthermore, extra-parliamentary anti-war organization was weak not because of working-class attitudes, but because of poor, unimaginative leadership and organizational deficiencies. Crucially, too, the Liberals were damagingly divided. The gulf was between those who blamed Britain for forcing war and those who blamed the Boers for starting it with their handsome preparations and ultimatum, those who were instinctively pro-Boer and those who were not, those who sympathized with the republican case but accepted that Britain could not lose, and those who, like David Lloyd George, were 'secretly delighted' by the early spectacle of British noses being bloodied by farmers.[5] It followed that the outcome of the decisive 'khaki' election lay in Liberal weakness and disunity, and a political culture which was more inert than active; 1900 drew a significantly lower poll than in the preceding 1895 election. In any event, there was 'little correlation between imperial appeal and electoral success'.[6]

Nor was the assumption of jingoism on any firmer ground with the rampant occasions of Mafeking or Ladysmith. 'Mafficking' could be seen as flamboyant, self-indulgent crowd celebration, less an expression of aggressive working-class war motivation, and more an airing of relief at British triumph over adversity and joy at the saving of lives; it was also a social opportunity grabbed, as victory in South Africa provided an excuse (and the licence) to run music hall onto the streets for the solidarities of a festive knees-up. While the war undoubtedly provided the urban working classes with their own satisfactions and view of the empire, these were some way off those of *Quarterly Review* or the *Nineteenth Century*. Nor did they amount to simple jingoism. Arguably, the working class *joined* or attached themselves to Mafeking night, and that in the archetypal sense of the jingo crowd as one which deliberately piled into anti-war opponents, workers were in fact not prominent in such vengeful 'mobs'. These tended to be composed heavily of patriotic middle-class and lower-middle-class men and coarsened youths, often no-nonsense Unionist activists.

A further factor was that British army recruitment in the earlier months of the war, in 1899 and 1900, was disproportionately from the volunteering lower-middle and middle classes; working-class enrolment was more sluggish, peaking only in the last few months of the war and not spurred by ideological considerations. The war just confirmed the traditional place of the Regular army as an institution to mop up the unemployed and the unskilled, with its recruitment patterns moving roughly in tandem with the rising level of unemployment in the early 1900s. It was bleak prospects, rather than patriotism, which induced working men to enrol to fight for the empire in South Africa. Whether as volunteering or as pro-war rioting, the fervour of jingo patriotism was squarely a lower-middle-class phenomenon; in fact, it has been suggested that Boer War jingoism was a distinctive expression of status anxieties, as the lower middle class licked the social adhesive of patriotism and militarism to affirm that it was up there with the war of middle-class Unionism and Liberal Imperialism.[7]

Lastly, we know that general domestic interest in the war was not constant but fluctuating, and was to prove transitory. After the intensities of 'Black Week', and the 1900 victories which marked British recovery, the opening flush began to abate. As hostilities dragged on in their increasingly grim and costly way, there was little to give the conflict a fresh imaginative lease. Concentration-camp deaths, executions of republican rebels, and Boer murders of blacks who were consorting with the British were not the sort of thing to lend tone to a war ostensibly in defence of those famous Chamberlain principles of peace, good government, and the indivisible world rights of Englishmen. Moreover, as the conflict dispersed into shifting irregular warfare, it became that much more tricky for correspondents to report flatteringly and entertainingly on events. With matters less volatile and 'newsworthy', the stakes were simply less. As Raymond Sibbald has shown in his recent study of British war correspondents in South Africa, by mid-1900 '*The Times* was just a little bored with South Africa ... In June 1900 the Boxer Rebellion began in China, and this exotic tale of heroism and barbarous people, coupled with the Victorian obsession with the heroism and stoicism of sieges, pushed the Boer War from its position at the forefront of the British public's consciousness'.[8] By July the large British press corps had almost evaporated, its correspondents diverted to China or elsewhere.

Gradually, too, as awareness grew that attrition and misery had replaced real fighting, so middle-class pro-Boers were listened to more politely, and skilled working-men's clubs and institutes became more tolerant of speakers presenting the moral case against an aggressive war and that of the Boer position on Uitlanders and the franchise. Opponents of the war invariably argued that it was not being fought for patriotic British interests; *they* were the real patriots, with the jingos the pawns of conniving, warmongering cosmopolitan financial forces. Some of these more sceptical interpretations of mass war enthusiasm have again been questioned by historians who do not follow things all the way. Thus, stressing the intimate socializing connections between the late-Victorian military and semi-skilled and unskilled segments of the working class, Michael Blanch has argued that the war induced a sizeable 'excess' of working-class army volunteers above the numbers naturally generated by unemployment growth. Moreover, the number of volunteers in the war years (just over 200,000) did not simply reflect the number of would-be soldiers who pushed themselves forward; many working-class men were obviously rejected on medical grounds, and officers from 'respectable' Volunteer and Yeomanry forces had a class bias, favouring any recruits who could demonstrate riding and shooting ability.

That aside, the weight of militarist and patriotic traditions among unskilled and semi-skilled male workers suggested that they would indeed have been keen on going at the 'primitive' Boers. The lure of adventure, and a bluff preparedness for colonial conflict, was a powerful enough draw; against this, the cause of the war was at best secondary or wholly irrelevant. For enthusiastic recruits, some already apprenticed to meanness and brutal confrontation through gang associations in rough industrial city districts, South African army service promised a new, exotic and institutionalized setting for masculine aggression or 'aggro' against 'the Boer – a kwaint littel creetchur'.[9]

In an accompanying and more substantial explanation, other writers have sketched the emergence of a fairly suffocating imperialist patriotism in the last quarter of the nineteenth century. Hugh Cunningham, for example, has suggested that whatever the different meanings of patriotism for the middle and other classes, by the time of the war it was fundamentally about being loyal to the institutions of the country, and resolute in defence of its honour and interests. Through their effective influence, Victorian youth organizations instilled manly (or womanly) imperial virtues, and the mostly working-class Volunteer Force provided part-time service for young males in the task of defending the country. Even the Regular forces, for so long the last resort for social dregs, had been actively promoted ever since the Crimean War as the incarnation of British Christian bravery and heroism, and for decades there had been earnest talk from the Conservative war party about bridging the divide between the nation and the armed forces.

When one adds to this the more diffuse Tory imperialist attitudes channelled through schools, popular literature, music hall, chapels, and churches, the mass of working-class people cannot be seen as having been 'immunized ... in any thoroughgoing way from the virus of right-wing patriotism'.[10] This measure of the mood has been stressed most by John Mackenzie and fellow writers, who have suggested that the scope of the uniquely intense imperial patriotism of this period was sufficient to create and sustain a semblance of national 'unity across class and party lines'. Its basic articles of faith were traditional Conservatism, expansionist militarism in defence of some perpetual Imperial Preference, a devoted royalism, the identification and aggrandizement of archetypal Victorian national heroes, and the ready absorption of the supremacist racial thinking of Social Darwinism.[11]

In some ways we have, perhaps, come virtually full circle. Historical argument has moved from unquestioned British jingoism to interpretation which has been critical of the perceived influence of working-class imperialist patriotism, to a more recent view which almost takes us back to Hobson's Boer War saturnalia. In any rounded picture there is surely no doubt that imperial war patriotism, whether as intellectual doctrine or as mobilizing street rhetoric, was an extremely important element in British culture. The late-Victorian South African War may indeed have been a moment when it was dominant. But a question which looks destined to remain is whether such factors as Darwinist militarism or racial stereotyping of the Boer enemy were as fixed in popular consciousness as has sometimes been claimed. We do not know, for instance, to what extent such conceptions influenced the war attitudes of working-class women. For that matter, while numerous middle-class and aristocratic women declared themselves repelled by the 'racial degeneracy' and 'polluted stock' of the Boers, others were prepared to ration their favours with the enemy, collecting humanitarian relief funds and actively aiding distressed Boer families. There were even those like the West African explorer and social reformer, Mary Kingsley, niece of Charles Kingsley, who nursed Boer prisoners of war. Her belief was only in healing the war, not in winning it. In a cruel irony, she died on the job, of enteric fever, the disease which accounted for over 60 per cent of British army fatalities in South Africa.

Elsewhere, of course, British attitudes towards the Boers were less charitable. The war did not create the common image of a Boer social primitivism, destined for conquest by a more advanced and industrious order; that, as we have seen, was already being propagated by pro-war elements in the 1890s. Rather, it provided circumstances for this disparagement of enemy society to grow in intensity and to acquire new propaganda variations. Take, for example, British reaction to a stock charge levelled by French, German, Russian, and Dutch anti-war critics. This was that Britain was criminally destroying the republics, that the fruit of the labour of generations of sacrificing Boers was being blighted, and that the harsh methods employed by Kitchener, turned from 'The Butcher of Omdurman' to 'The Butcher of the Transvaal', would cause famine and drive the Boers back to the Stone Age. Far from denying the war's destructive impact, the middle-brow *Quarterly Review* acclaimed it as a positive achievement, one which was sweeping away a slothful and stagnant agricultural community.

The only problem was that prominent Continental critics, such as Pierre Leroy-Beaulieu, failed to grasp this. 'If M. Beaulieu were personally acquainted with South Africa,' explained a writer in April 1902, 'he would learn that generations of Boers had lived, or more correctly, squatted on their soil,' and that 'except in the mining districts' there was an 'utter absence of labour on the part of the inhabitants'. Accordingly, even if 'the whole Boer population had been swept away by an epidemic, they would have left no marks of their rule other than the railways ... constructed for them by the Uitlanders', mostly 'men of British birth'. As the objective of the war between a vigorous empire and flaccid colonists was the establishing of 'an industrial civilization as the basis of Africa's regeneration, even those among us who oppose the war may take comfort'. Its outcome would resolve the tension between 'higher and lower types of civilization'.[12]

It was a logical next step to portray the Boers as technologically immature and intellectually stunted or irrational; the average commando was best seen, according to one homely observation, as an Irish peasant: if given a cannon, he would instinctively roll it home for use as a dairy churn. Another familiar view was to ascribe Boer mental and physical torpor to the easy availability of African labour, perpetually on call to meet the 'primitive wants' of growing 'the necessary mealies' and keeping of 'numerous flocks' which was all that constituted Boer existence. Carrying this hypothesis to a novel strategic conclusion, a journalist suggested in 1901 that the way to wrap up the war quickly would be for the British to round up all able-bodied African youths and men in the Boer territories, thereby making settler life immediately insupportable.[13]

Belittling the character and capacity of Boer opponents sometimes involved exaggerating the supposed superior talents and vigour of Africans. Thus in the early weeks of the war in Natal a West Yorkshire Regiment officer concluded that while his commando enemies were showing themselves to be 'marvels of ingenuity and still more of energy', this was assuredly a consequence of their having 'gone native', as 'both qualities come more from the inspired Kaffirs, than from the Boers themselves'. At the end of 1899, *Under the Union Jack* assured readers that reports of the republicans' positioning Africans 'against us' in Natal fighting lines 'loses its seriousness when it is remembered that it is one of their customs' to have several servants to prop up and fuss about every commando, as they lacked real fighting self-reliance.[14] There was also scorn for more passionate, fundamentalist forms of religious practice among some Boer prisoners of war, seen as dabbling in 'witchcraft', an African contamination. It is not surprising that in the eyes of pro-war Australian, New Zealand, and Canadian politicians, this was a war of 'predestination', to quote a member of the New South Wales legislative assembly, in which the lowest stock of European humanity should be displaced by the efficiency of a better type, such as British Dominion colonists.[15]

More extreme British commentators reinforced the impression of a sub-civilized enemy by turning to apish or other animalistic imagery to depict the Boers as sub-human, or certainly as something less than fully human. Popular weeklies like *Pearson's War Pictures* and *Under the Union Jack* often resorted to such contemptuous representation, in which commandos, stripped of humanity, became 'Boer herds' or 'Boer flocks'; civilian camp refugees were 'swarms' or 'droves', dull and ruminant by nature. 'I much disliked their aspect,' wrote Lady Rolleston in 1901, 'their eyes are generally small and dark, and too close together, the nose is short ... the face is nearly always animal ... the glance is shifty, and reminds me irresistibly of a visit to the Zoological Gardens at home.' In like vein, Colonel Hubert Jourdain of the Connaught Rangers recorded that he found Boer captives 'reptilian' in appearance, and 'quite hideous to look on'.[16]

While republican politicians, their European allies, and British Liberal sympathizers were dipping into Christian discourse to condemn the immorality of the camp policy and to convey transcendent female suffering and sacrifice, some metropolitan observers portrayed the removal of Boer refugees and 'undesirables' from the countryside as rather like the rounding up of cattle. Charges of 'methods of barbarism' and denunciations of inhumanity during 1901 and 1902 by anti-war newspapers such as the *Manchester Guardian*, Quakers, and social reformers were brushed aside. Dramatic investigative uncovering of abysmal conditions and high mortality, such as that provided by Emily Hobhouse in her 1902 *Report of a Visit to the Camps of Women and Children in the Cape and Orange River Colonies*, was troubling, but sentimental and biased; for the Boers were to blame for their own high death rates. In this blunt observation the fundamental irrationality, ignorance, and superstitions of republican society were merely cultural symptoms of some clinical disorder: the pre-modern Boers were congenitally unclean or insanitary. The British army was there to fight, not to solve the enemy's sanitation malaise.

In a neat reversal of the conventional Victorian social perception, in the Transvaal and Orange Free State it was country, not urban life which was unhealthy or diseased, and it was rural, not urban fertility which was producing socially irresponsible racial stock. If camp inmates were dying, this was due to 'filth, carelessness, fatalism and a belief in absurd or disgusting remedies'. According to a Dr John Welenski, writing in the *British Medical Journal* in November 1901, the 'fecklessness, ignorance and dirtiness' of Boer women 'was so ingrained' that 'decent habitation is a thing of which they would have about as much conception as they would have of the aestheticism of Mr Oscar Wilde or the philosophy of Mr Herbert Spencer'. The cause of sanitary ignorance was obvious to the likes of John Buchan. While conditions were undeniably 'distressing', this was because 'mentally and bodily underbred' victims represented 'a class of people who have somehow missed civilization' and the foresight and training in proper 'habits' it provided. If anyone merits the last word here, it is Kitchener; in an irritated comment which has often been repeated, he put down soaring Boer child mortality levels in camps to 'the criminal neglect of the mothers', and disclosed that, in his view, the most wilful culprits ought 'to be tried for manslaughter'.[17]

In imputing criminality to the enemy, controversy over the introduction of uncapped or dum-dum bullets, which expanded on impact to mangle flesh, also played a propaganda role in various stages of the conflict. And here atrocity charges came from both sides. The background was provided by the earlier 1899 First European Peace Conference at the Hague, in which 26 states, including Britain, accepted a convention on the conduct of war which banned dum-dums as too brutal or 'inhuman' for use in European theatres. A fundamental premise, as Edward Spiers has underlined, was the late-nineteenth-century endorsement of a distinction between 'civilized' warfare, or regular war between 'civilized' European nations, and 'savage' warfare, or unorthodox colonial war waged by European armies against non-European tribal opponents.[18] The supposedly innate 'fanaticism' and 'animalistic' strength of 'savage' and 'semi-civilized' enemies made the ferocious stopping-power of the dum-dum a technical necessity, something which had already proved bad news for the Zulu in the 1870s and the Sudanese in the 1890s.

Some of the accusations which whirled among British soldiers and in published popular opinion were quite sensational and wholly imaginary. One recurring story was that commandos were putting poison into soft-nosed Mauser cartridges, or were rolling slugs in faeces to spread disease. Other prominent accounts were rooted in actual occurrences, such as the routine unearthing of arms caches in the Orange Free State which allegedly held 'split-nosed cartridges which had been dipped in verdigris'. While there is no doubting the genuine rage of ordinary British soldiers at the capture of stocks of expanding bullets at places like Colenso and Paardeberg, of greater interest is the way in which such practices went on to be cited as confirmation of the debased nature of the enemy. That Kruger could sanction the use of 'immoral' techniques against 'civilized troops' confirmed that he was, in the words of one newspaper', a 'diseased growth from the worse of the criminal classes',[19] which in turn confirmed that the war was about subduing criminal or anti-social activity by the enemy.

The officer corps also voiced paternalistic and protective concerns for the exposure of their men to 'improper' mutilation and suffering. 'Unsporting and intolerable', protested an Imperial Yeomanry captain, who took particular exception to his 'good class' of men being gouged by dum-dums. Things seemed to be moving in the direction of class war. The Boers were culturally and temperamentally unsuited to observing the 'rules' of combat with 'infantry of civilized stock, men who are clerks, telegraphists and engineers'.[20] At times a sense of a common humanity in war could none the less be seen in British outrage at the horrific wounds being inflicted upon their African and Coloured transport drivers and scouts by expanding bullets, with 'pitiful' men left 'hideously mangled' and 'rarely unmaimed'. Some medical officers even urged soldiers to hit back hard on behalf of black victims. A legalistic and liberal view of war by the rules could also be found among some commanding officers, who considered blacks in British army service to be entitled to treatment under 'civilized' war conventions and Cape auxiliaries to be of 'British' status. Thus, when Carolus Duimpies was caught and executed, a British colonel wrote to the Boers, declaring the shooting not only a 'shameful act against one of our men' but the use of 'barbaric explosive bullets' to be 'against all known rules of war'.[21]

In Britain, socialist militarists like Blatchford, and H. M. Hyndman of the Social Democratic Federation, concluded that Boer peasants had forfeited any rights to restraint, with the former's *Clarion* warning that the lives of British troops were being needlessly endangered by a War Office 'sentimentality' which was denying them the tools to do the job. This chorus was joined by the Tory voice of *Quarterly Review*, which declared the notion of racial conventions of war to be 'curious ... discrimination', when all that mattered was 'stopping power. The enemy, whether civilized or savage, must be stopped in his charge'. Hyndman's *Justice*, which incidentally took the novel and romantic view that the only imperial reason for fighting the war should be to return the country to Africans, proclaimed that the ferocity of Boer armaments had destroyed the pro-Boer mystique of republican virtuousness and Christian piety. Rounding on anti-war Radical Liberals, it taunted them with the mock assurance that 'explosive devices ... are simply carried around by brother Boer as engineering curiosities'.[22]

The grip of the dum-dum story may have become one of the war's more tenacious combat atrocity myths, with republicans for their part claiming British savageness in fire at Spion Kop; there was also the legend of British beastliness in the brutal shooting of pregnant Boer women with cartridges sufficiently powerful to kill the unborn. In the context of scorched-earth actions, these nightmare images fitted with feelings of a demonic war of violation and deliberate extermination. Leaving aside wilder implausibilities, the use in combat of doctored ammunition was not a myth. While there was no authorization from either Buller or Roberts, British command equally turned a blind eye to what by 1902 was being termed a stock control problem in the field. For the honest and upright Boers, according to Ludwig Krause, this British 'want of ordinary humanity' had reluctantly contaminated their fighting practices. 'Such ammunition was unknown amongst the Boers', he insisted, 'until they found it on the bodies of the English soldiers.' When, 'in spite of our repeated protests the English persisted ... our men retaliated ... converted ordinary Mauser bullets ... then both sides continued its use.' The expediencies of imperialist warfare had somehow undone the naturally charitable side of Boer armed conduct. What made this regrettable was that, morally, the Boers counted for more.[23]

In their fighting self-image, others went along this path. For younger, college- and university-educated republican officers, making sense of the war involved more than the belief that their cause of national sovereignty was incontestably just. If God-given national rights of self-determination and liberty were to be successfully defended, that cause had to be righteously upheld through a form of decent fighting, in which European Christian virtues would not be abandoned, and in which Boer warfare would not degenerate into brutalized excesses or atrocity. Within varying levels of idealistic war commitment during the first year of hostilities, this was an article of faith among many leaders in the field: the enemy was barbarous and fought dirty, while the Boers were civilized Christians and fought more honourably. The Transvaal and colonial republican press dismissed as fabrication persistent British accusations of 'treachery' in commando use (or misuse) of the white flag to buy time for regrouping or to stage ambushes, a stand backed by liberal pro-Boer publications in Britain, which declared the charge a shabby invention of the 'jingo imagination' to discredit republican adherence to conventions of civilized war.

By contrast, what was morally repugnant was the use of cavalry wielding the *arme blanche* in Africa to terrorize 'natives' who were in fact Christian Europeans. Critics fastened on the savagery with which imperial soldiers used lances and even bayonets against hapless farmers, in particular the ruthlessness of cavalry officers, whose evident relish in the 'sport' of 'pig-sticking', 'skewering', or 'gutting' in close combat featured prominently in early issues of war periodicals like *Black and White Budget* and *Shurey's Illustrated.* What matter of larger significance this had is well-caught by a metaphor of war in South Africa as the hunt, in which the Boers 'would not stand cold steel', with 'native ignorance of the lance' proving 'a pleasing revelation'. On the republican side it is correspondingly well captured by a Cronje commando's reaction of panic and disbelief that a white enemy would be so 'deranged' and 'barbarous' as to inflict 'tribal savagery' upon the 'civilized'.[24]

To H. R. Fox-Bourne, a leading figure in the British Aborigines' Protection Society, the very campaign against the Boers meant nothing other than the wrong kind of war. Writing to the *Morning Leader* just over a year into hostilities, he condemned the 'wanton brutality of an imperialist onslaught on a small, white, civilized and Christian community'. Warfare, he protested, was coming to resemble the routine 'savagery' associated with punitive colonial expeditions against 'black, uncivilized and non-Christian peoples'. Even if fought far away on colonial soil, the European character of Britain's adversaries called for civilized restraint, or the proper observance of some racial etiquette. According to Lionel Curtis this was, after all, a war in which British soldiers would find that whatever their differences with the enemy, none the less 'hospitality to a white man is a religion with these people'.[25]

Writing as recently as the 1970s, the military historian Eversley Belfield suggested that a defining feature of the war was the lack of hatred felt by British soldiers towards their opponents; sentiment was apparently all for mutual respect, a fair fight, and some primordial recognition of 'their adversaries as Brother Boer'.[26] The Boer states were not some barbarous imperial spot, like the northwest frontier of India. How the war should be fought was one issue; its resolution and settlement was another. Observers like Curtis rolled them together. If hostilities were conducted without meanness, this would ensure an accommodating Anglo-Boer peace. Of course, the British government position was that it *was* being mindful of the European niceties of civilized war. If anything, it was drawing back from the inviting expedient of military alliances with black African societies, which would have been a cheaper and less wearing way of 'doing in' the Boers. 'It would have been easy,' wrote Leopold Amery in 1900, 'for the Imperial Government to have let loose Swazis, Basutos and Bechuanas against their old enemies. Attacked on every side and exposed to the terrors of savage warfare at their very doors, the Boers might have been placed in a terribly difficult situation.'[27]

The Times was not alone in this view, for such observation was representative of a strand in military opinion. The primary reason for not contracting black Southern African levies was not a cultural worry about 'cowardice', as in nervousness over the performance of West African Hausa soldiers in Wolseley's war against the hardy Ashanti. It was, in fact, quite the opposite. For Baden-Powell, it was a distasteful exultation in 'slaughter ... to them, as attractive and entertaining as a bull-fight to a Spaniard or a football match to an Englishman.' The moral risk was dodgy instincts, as in 'a winning fight' the non-European 'want of discipline' would 'lead them to commit excesses as would be unbecoming in allies of the British'.[28] One of many graphic expressions of this was carried by the *Cardiff Western Mail* shortly after the outbreak of war, in a full-page sketch of 'The Savage and the Boer', depicting Milner and Chamberlain gamely leashing a Gurkha warrior 'to stop that horror being added to the rest'.

On the other hand, there were plenty of British critics for whom the war did not seem to be so clearly a European business. Conspicuous among these were those who argued in the pro-war press that in South Africa it was difficult to establish where 'barbarism' ended and 'civilization' began. Rarely one to mince his words, Blatchford claimed that 'the Boer method of fighting is not that of reckless, gallant, untrained peasants. No, it is that of the bandit, the redskin, the Afridi and other savage fanatics.' An indignant Kitchener added his own vintage piece, deploring his guerrilla opponents' for not being 'like the Sudanese who stood up to a fair fight. They are always running away on their little ponies.'[29]

So influenced, a section of British Indian opinion fumed that Salisbury's Cabinet was inadvertently prolonging the war effort and disregarding national interest by sticking to the view that 'in fighting Boers and other semi-civilized white races we are not to employ any of our Imperial resources'. One or two commentators made a point of the 'animal' or 'devilish' behaviour in South Africa of Irish, Australian, and other 'more ruffianly' white colonial volunteers, declaring them demonstrably less disciplined than trained Sikhs and Gurkhas, and already to be taking the conduct of the war downhill. In any event, there was no call for being angelic, as a fight with the Boers did not require 'the usages of civilized war'. While in the Commons Arthur Balfour and Edward Grey underlined their high regard for the quality of 'indigenous' Indian troops, the pro-Indian *Quarterly Review* and *Nineteenth Century* urged the War Office to take this to heart and act on it. As 'Her Majesty's troops' the native Indian army should not be allowed to think that it was 'not an integral part of the imperial military system', just as Russia's Cossacks were now part of 'any of its European conflicts'. What counted by 1901 was soldiering effectiveness to deal with a serious British 'national emergency'; what had this to do with 'possession of a dark skin'? The Boers, of course, could be expected to whine and to cause a commotion at the Hague, noted Sir Henry Howorth, just as 'they have complained of our using balloons and Lyddite shells'.[30]

Most ordinary British soldiers had no interest in abstract theorizing about a colour line; the case for Indian deployment rested on persuasive practical knowledge and experience, especially for those in regiments dispatched from Asia. Accordingly, when the going got tough in Natal because of rain or heavy humidity, Indian combat contingents would have been 'altogether ideal'. Lieutenant Edward Warr wished that he had had Sikhs, Gurkhas, or Punjabis alongside him in the Orange Free State in March 1900, who would surely have been 'fantastically good' against de Wet and his frustating tactics. Had the British been assigned even half a Gurkha company in the first place, Gatacre's problems at Stormberg would have been taken care of, after which 'the splendid little heathens in their grass shoes' could have been set after disabling the Transvaal artillery corps.[31] As the war became more protracted, so did irritation grow that another string to the British bow was not being hooked. It made no operational sense to restrict companies of accomplished Bengal and Madras Lancers to menial remount duties which could be performed by local black labour when what the army desperately needed were more mounted troops to increase its range and raise its speed. Not only were these 'splendid natural horsemen', and more than up to the job of 'cutting up the Boers'; they were, moreover, 'just like white men, only their colour is different'. With such soldiers, declared *The Statist* in 1901, Buller would swiftly have made the Orange River Colony his, and the war would 'long ago' have been over.[32]

Those to be dismembered were also not necessarily always viewed as a white or European enemy. It did not require very much contact with commando prisoners or communities of the very poorest whites for soldiers to recognize an odd thing about the Boer republics. On the one hand, they were clearly states based on rigid racial stratification and white supremacy, places where 'the natives really got bossed about'.[33] On the other hand, Boers at the bottom of the social pile seemed sometimes to be inhabiting somewhat blurred racial communities. One lieutenant was puzzled by what he saw as the 'bossing' and 'enslaving' of blacks when some swarthy commandos were themselves as dark as their agterryers. Private Arthur Dye had a distasteful encounter with 'dreadful low-class' prisoners, a jumble of men, 'half-Dutch, half-Native', and other 'dubious half-castes ... black or several shades of it'. In the closing days of the war, a Yorkshire infantryman encountered a group of young Boer children who had spent much of the conflict accompanying Swazi herders who had been given the task, by a widowed master, of looking after them and keeping his cattle safe. Their lengthy African confinement appeared to have left them thoroughly acculturated. 'It would be interesting to know,' he reflected, 'on what basis some of these Boers assemble their fancy notions as to being European overlords.'[34] For men steeped in the more distancing style of British imperialism, such contradictions and other lax encounters with 'going native' proved yet again that while republican Boers lived in the bush, they did not always dress for dinner.

What of those who did? Here, just as anti-war factions in Britain were accused of prolonging the war by criticizing its conduct and providing moral encouragement for the republican cause, so the pro-republican Cape Boer intelligentsia faced acrimony for war reporting seen as subversive of the imperial effort. Of special concern following the fall of Bloemfontein, Johannesburg, and Pretoria was the external role of sympathetic Cape Boer papers such as *Het Zuid-Oosten* and *Ons Land* in peddling accounts of British excesses and atrocities. What was objected to was not simply highly charged exaggerations or distortions; the offence lay in 'flooding' Boer territories with 'Cape Dutch organs' which were now circulating among the 'unlettered' or semi-literate 'philistines', crude rustics unable to make proper judgements. An isolated class of 'poor farmers' with 'Kitchen-Dutch alone', the northern Boers represented a community of 'unreason', having had none of the rational benefits of the Victorian Sunday School movement. Their mood in Natal amply illustrated this. The ransacking of school buildings in Dundee and Colenso and the feeding of commando campfires with 'school furniture and scholars' copybooks' rekindled the enemy as the new Goths and Vandals.[35] With commandos' anti-educational bigotry extending to the despoilation of Coloured mission station property in the Cape, they seemed to be negating the entire British liberal vision of constructing a better and self-improving South Africa.

In their lack of educated 'good sense' and 'comprehension' the Boers were like worrisome Indian villagers, at the mercy of a prejudiced nationalist press which could mischievously exploit a shortage of proper information and sound judgement. In some quarters this line was carried in a further direction. Through renegade Cape political journalists, meetings, pamphlets, and other kinds of anti-British agitation, conspiratorial and manipulative Boer 'scum' were beavering away to seduce 'responsible' or 'true' peasant Boers from a path of sensible accommodation with empire. For those who believed that the First Anglo-Boer War had been started not by the yokel Dutch but by the meddling of shady 'foreign' elements linked to the 'criminal classes of Europe',[36] presumably history seemed to be repeating itself. Moreover, the notion that the Boers were themselves the dupes of a scheming and amoral war element produced a curious mirror image: it was the clear counterpart of those Liberal, Labour, and socialist assertions that the war had been forced upon Britain by the hidden hand of mercenary capitalists.

At the same time it needs to be remembered that lofty contempt for Boer intelligence and capabilities was by no means equally shared by all the British troops. Their first-hand view of the enemy would have rested on countless small observations, empirical perceptions, and imaginative suppositions. Far from simply dismissing the Boers as inferior or dehumanized opponents, the British could also be impressed and even intrigued by Boer fighting capabilities and technical accomplishments. In general there was grudging admiration for the flexibility of Boer tactics, for their frequent ability to engage unseen, for the planning and skill which went into defence-in-depth systems, for their exceptional mobility, for their camouflaging ability and clever use of river lines and fencing stock, and for their effectively timed use of long-range artillery in the opening movements of the war. Beyond this, there were routinely respectful murmurs about their proficiency of horsemanship, skill in markmanship on or off the saddle, seasoned ability to treat wounds with herbal applications, and rumoured capacity for stupendous campaign endurance, lasting for weeks 'almost entirely' on 'biltong', the odd 'Boer biscuit', and even 'prickly pears'.

Among such positive pieces of mythology there were many admiring perceptions of Boer physiological characteristics. These sometimes assumed an apocryphal or folklore quality, such as the strength and physique of republican warriors, and a contagious belief that the enemy was endowed biologically with 'superior powers of sight', with miraculously 'magnifying' eyes and 'mysterious' night vision. The legacy of 'untold centuries' of evolution as 'natural hunters' and 'nomads', this made them especially perilous riflemen, 'manly, spirited and deadly country folk'. Snatches of this sense of an uncanny enemy ability doubtless fed the superstitions of some British soldiers from Dickensian Coketowns, who found the Boer a capable and gifted mounted countryside foe who was not to be lightly subdued.[37] News that commando ranks sometimes contained prophetic visionaries or sieners also created an unsettling sense that the Boer fighters inhabited an impenetrable field of chance and possibility. Tactical intelligence, use of the mask of terrain, and planning by superstition all coexisted mysteriously to sustain them in the field.

There were also signs of an admiring spirit away from the lines. Certainly much Nonconformist or Free Church Liberal and Labour pro-Boer sentiment did not admire the Boer character or back an anti-imperialist republican cause, merely believing that however reactionary or corrupt the Boer states, this did not justify an aggressive and unjust war. But there was a romantic edge to some of this. At its most extreme, it idealized the Boer republics as some pastoral African Eden, inhabited by a humble, family-loving people who were white, Protestant, and peaceable underdogs. It is hard not to wonder what attitudes would have been had the Boers been Roman Catholic. What they had was now being 'criminally' despoiled by a brutal war; while the Transvaal was perhaps a touch imperfect in its running of affairs, the old-fashioned sobriety and rustic virtue of the yeoman Orange Free State could not but command admiration. While Bloemfontein was not quite Banbury, conceded an Oxfordshire correspondent, its surrounding countryside had its own verdant charm.[38] Not surprisingly, he had yet to survey this during January or February.

In an effort to dispel the prevailing unflattering image of the Boer, sympathetic writers sought to domesticate the enemy by turning him into someone with an amiable and recognizable Anglo-Saxon likeness.

Hence they were not to be seen as some homogenous medieval tribe, but as an improving commercial agricultural society, with customary class divisions into wealthy and poor. 'The average Boer is much like the average Englishman of country birth and agricultural surroundings,' noted one observer, some of them gentry proprietors like middling squires, with poorer agriculturalists resembling the Earl of Carnarvon's tenants. This was so much so that 'any group of the better class Boer farmers might be with difficulty distinguished from a matching group of English farmers'. In the same vein, the Boer landed class were said to be 'just the people you are used to in Hertfordshire and Derbyshire, merely talking another tongue'. Given that 'virtually all the agricultural progress of South Africa is due to the Dutch' it should therefore be no surprise to observe 'the extraordinary activity and hardihood of the Boers in war'.[39] The Boers were not lesser men than the British; they were virtually the same. This was probably the highest conceivable wartime compliment, of sorts.

What, then, of the Boers themselves? Here the evidence is naturally much thinner, but probably sufficient to gain a reasonable sense of some basic attitudes. The most pertinent feature of the republican propaganda lexicon is that while not short on political invective and abuse, there was certainly no counterpart to the Social Darwinist racial dogma which shaped much intellectual British perception of the enemy. It was never the case that the British problem lay in their being, in some evolutionary or scientific sense, an inferior race or nation. What it all came down to was the fact that an offensive war against free republics showed up the empire, killing any idea of its liberal Christian decency. For some sympathizers in the Cape middle-class intelligentsia, what the northern Boers were experiencing was that heavy hand so long familiar to nationalist Irish, and indeed to Jamaican rebels in the 1860s.[40] This threat of a British servitude was a particularly powerful instinct among those under arms across the Orange; imbued by the religiosity of Boer republican nationalism, for many who stuck it out the war became a sacred vocation to preserve a God-given free inheritance. As Dietlof van Warmelo suggested in his chronicle, it was their lot to persevere through an affliction of quite biblical proportions, knowing they would be delivered by grace.[41] Locusts, pestilence and famine had become the British War Office, Kitchener its pale horse of death.

Others in the republics wondered just how aware British citizens were of the raw contradictions between the civilizing assumptions of their empire and the incendiary inclinations of their military conquerors. Equally distressing was that the British seemed not at all averse to enlisting blacks to spy, bear arms, provide incriminating court evidence, or in other ways keep tabs on the Boers. This was surely no way for civilized Europeans in Africa to deal with one another.

Boer officers such as Krause and Abraham Malan had a firm military understanding of British convictions. The war became so severe and retributive because 'the English have never been able to forgive the Boer for having been so ready ... more ready than they were'. It was politically unpalatable for Britain to give the Boers 'credit for ordinary foresight and common sense ... genuine wisdom and cunning'. What must have hurt more than anything was the way in which 'the English boasted' that they would flatten the Boers in a fortnight, only to be pulled up by the shocking surprise 'of the Boer ready for them'. Predictably, 'they have never been able to forgive his "insolence" for daring to be so'. And so Boer society was now having to bear the disproportionate cost of anger over such impudence. That accepted, what still remained hard to take was the haughty imperial assumption that the Boers were too backward or so ignorant as to be unable to rumble British purpose. British arrogance, reflected Krause, reminded him of how the colonists must have felt in the American War for Independence. They too had been slandered as marauders, murderers, looters, and liars, whereas, with nauseating hypocrisy, 'the same acts committed by themselves the English characterize as "reconnoitring parties, executions, collecting cattle ... punitive measures, etc."'. This sort of patrician sophistry well suited the 'aristocratic' British approach, which sought to 'justify the war by equally high-sounding names', while in reality it was mainly intended to cloak 'their want of humanity and the non-observance of the civilized rules of warfare'.[42]

A host of stories, signs, rumours, and legends about the vengefulness of British character and the ferocity of British war-making proliferated during the conflict. Some were ephemeral, others more enduring. One legend was that Britain intended to 'debase' the Boers by assaulting the racial purity of white womanhood. Early in 1900, Dutch Reformed Church clergy in the northern Cape Colony advised male congregants to secure the safety of women, as it was believed that rural towns would be garrisoned by Indian sepoys. Such soldiers, inhabitants were warned, would be coming from an Asian army which had already had a taste of violation in the 1857 Mutiny. Another myth was that Africans with British forces would be accorded new social freedom; war tribute or bounty would include permission to 'enslave' or 'carry into their kraals' defenceless Boer women who had lost husbands in the fighting. The frame of mind which conjured up this story also concocted a brilliant tale of retaliation, in which commandos on British territory would shoot colonial English volunteers and donate their women to Africans; something which circulated around Kimberley during the siege, perhaps it was this masculine racial anxiety which kept Kekewich and Rhodes so much on their toes.[43]

As the war dragged on, female beliefs grew that the British were either soft on the racial protection of vulnerable white inhabitants, or were actually nudging at Africans to rise beyond their station. Such concerns were shared by any number of visiting pro-Boer British women activists, such as Hobhouse and Jane Cobden Unwin, who were alarmed at the exposed position of women both in camps and in female-headed rural homesteads, having to confront the increasing 'impertinence' of Africans, including the threat of being manhandled. Panicky communities did not have to be susceptible to lurid stories to be apprehensive about what an advancing British army might bring. Rumours of rape, destructive actions, or personal mistreatment by the 'kharkis' or 'kharkies', whatever their basis, ran well ahead of the British offensive into the Orange Free State, leaving many civilians frantic or even terrified. Near the Vaal river in May 1900 a soldier observed 'a look of perpetual alarm' on face after face, and found a huddle of women on a farm 'scared stiff by our presence'. After directed questioning, an African scout and interpreter attached to his patrol told him why they seemed so petrified. They had heard that after burning their homes, British soldiers were turning on women to commit all manner of brutal violations, including cutting off fingers to steal rings. Vindictive soldiers sometimes took a malicious delight in indulging such atrocity myths, darkly warning women of further horrors to come, like the abduction of babies or confiscation of all food, medicine, and clothing, 'to frighten them, as they seem to expect us all to be proper demons'.[44]

Moving British soldiers had no need to behave as the devil incarnate to be feared and loathed by many women in the countryside, caught in occupation areas between the advancing enemy and their retreating home armies. All that was needed was the army's destructive strength in the implementation of Roberts' Orange Free State scorched-earth policy and its driving intensification under Kitchener. With this came the usual requisitioning, casual food foraging, and plundering which went with long and fraying supply lines and intermittent ration shortages, and ruffianly indiscipline and spitefulness, of which there was a good deal on the edges of patrolling, given the latitude of a draconian occupation policy. Naturally, however, in the midst of the deepening ruthlessness of a conquering war not all British troops splintered precious family heirlooms or wolfed down the holdings of farm pantries. Nor did all officers nod at unauthorized plundering of homesteads, as regimental punishment books reveal;[45] nor did every roving 'farm party' relish the experience of dynamiting or burning properties. Despite intelligence instructions that the only farms targeted for 'doing' were those of men who were 'spies, or snipers or otherwise behaving dangerously', some sappers and infantrymen could still not avoid feeling queasy about the business of evicting or 'turning out' numbers of 'sobbing women and their children', finding this 'a bit sickening' or 'a loathsome task'.[46] In this view, they may not have been typical of imperial soldiers – but then neither were all soldiers in South Africa wholly without some sense of humanity and conscience.

From a detached perspective, men advancing into enemy territory and enforcing the rigours of occupation could hardly be viewed as anything other than barbarians or devils by a civilian population hauled into confrontation well beyond any immediate battle perimeters. Yet, while occupied areas became a front line of dread, by no means all Boer women were cowed or intimidated. According to one Ayrshire Yeomanry officer, scores of the females he encountered were smouldering and hard, prone to giving 'Tommies looks which would have turned milk sour', while another soldier was shocked by encounters with seething defiance and hectoring abuse; obvious insults 'in their outlandish tongue sounded shocking ... whatever it was, anyone could tell it was not the language of refined women'.[47] Kitchener himself had reflected on this. 'Boers,' he sighed, 'were uncivilized African-der savages with only a thin white veneer ... The Boer woman in the refugee camp who slaps her protruding belly at you and shouts, "When all our men are gone these little Kharkis will fight you" is a type of savage produced by generations of wild, lonely life'.[48]

There are many such small illustrations of visceral animosity which, while scattered, point to the secretion of a web of Boer female hatred of an enemy which was invading its domestic spaces. At times this was expressed through snappy provocation and even violence. While tramping around farms, troops were sometimes spat at, or had stones and hot water tossed at them; numerous men seem also to have been suspicious of any voluntary offerings of 'blarstid Dutch skoff', in case it had been poisoned or seasoned with ground glass.[49] In this supportive gender action, the wives of farmers enjoyed some liberty of hostile feeling and incitement; they were, after all, not recognized combatants, and were neither prodded into swearing neutrality oaths nor forced to relinquish any personally owned rifles.

Quite apart from the natural hostilities of the thousands shovelled into camps, the depth of anti-British feeling among many Boer women could probably have compared with the sentiments of the most motivated male commando, 'as most of the women ... stalwart in respect to the liberty of her country.' If anything their venom and resolve may well have exceeded that of more lukewarm burghers. Captain F. P. Fletcher-Vane was one of many who observed how, after the Paardeberg setback, the wilting commandos 'went home and came back fortified by the example of the heroism shown by the women'.[50]

The stubborness and militancy with which Boer women threw themselves into a nationalist war role has long been recognized by Afrikaans writers. Today, as a radical corrective to highly masculinist portrayals of combat roles and motivation, a leading feminist historian has suggested that it was an implacable wall of women which played a decisive political part in sustaining the republican war effort after the conventional collapse of the Orange Free State and the Transvaal.[51] In a highveldt version of the Victorian four-feathers challenge to male cowardice in war, embittered settler women shamed or harried their beaten or yellow men into resuming the fight. As seconds they were a match for their own soldiers, through whose frailty or irresolution the nationalist war effort was not getting things right. This uncompromising anti-British hostility was impressive; and it certainly hugely impressed those American, Russian, French, Dutch, and Irish nationalist observers who documented the way in which the emotional involvement of the Boer nation translated into an uncompromising female conviction about sacrificing for liberty and patriotism. At the same time, even though British warmaking carried things to the line of the homestead, the gap in experience of the enemy between male and female was distinct. Those middle-class female inhabitants of cities like Pretoria who talked of personally avenging their lost husbands, or who were so contemptuous of commando shirkers who were finding it too hot, could have known little of the terrifying shock of a cavalry charge, of the alarmingly effective British tactical adaptations to guerrilla warfare, or of despair at the inability to muster a decent-sized force when massively outnumbered. And, while grudging battlefield appreciation of the discipline and endurance of detested khakis or *rooienekke* (red-necks) saw some Boer soldiers modify their contempt for a detested foe, the singular angle from which militant women encountered the enemy was as the imperial embodiment of suffering and domestic displacement, men who made war on women. Boer attitudes towards the enemy were undoubtedly coded by gender; they were also not one-dimensional, even as times got harder. Given just how hard they became, it is also not surprising that more compliant camp inhabitants and 'lax' poorer bywoner women succumbed to the sapping effects of war, sometimes 'frequenting the company of soldiers' and engaging in prostitution.[52]

As the power which prevailed, it was British opinion which could ultimately err most charitably about its adversary. However illiberal its prosecution of the closing stages of the war, the imperial army was never without one or two more thoughtful lights who did not shed all the liberal assumptions of their London drawing-rooms when crossing the Orange. A good few officers were prepared to forget occasional abuse of the white flag by underhand commandos for the larger picture: country-bred Boers were honourable foes and admirably hard combatants, more effective fighters for being free of the 'degenerative' defects and weaknesses of their own city-bred privates from overpopulated slums. Consequently, they deserved an honourable peace, one in which their innately virile and outdoor future would not be mortgaged to a Johannesburg or 'Jewburgher' capitalist community.[53]

This mix of anti-Semitism and colonial hayseed romanticism was nicely embodied by General Ian Hamilton. As Kitchener's Chief of Staff in the last spasms of fighting, he divulged his war impressions to Winston Churchill. A soldier who had nothing but distaste for indiscriminate farm-burning and other punitive measures, Hamilton judged the Boers as fine and worthy people who deserved generous conciliation, and merited favourable incorporation into the empire at the very earliest opportunity. By and large, British soldiers in the field tended to respect and even to admire them as opponents, concluded Hamilton, adding that the republics' farming yeomanry were often viewed more positively than arrogant imperial politicians like Milner. Politically, it was the High Commissioner and his squalid bunch of 'Jewburg' capitalists who seemed intent on a continuing death roll and a wholly vengeful peace. Doubtless no commando at Elandslaagte in October 1899 would have judged Ian Hamilton charitable or restrained in attack. But, in attitude, his was a certain kind of liberal steel.

The liberal Hamilton was not an entirely lone voice amongst the upper echelons of the British army officer corps. Others drawn from the Anglo-Irish and Anglo-Indian gentry were instinctively anti-urban capitalist and anti-Semitic, and despised the 'mercenary' nature of the Uitlanders. What such individuals found most disagreeable was the idea of fighting purely as the military tool of mammon; the conquest and annexation of the Transvaal looked to be all too much to the benefit of a manipulative plutocracy of Randlords and bought Colonial Office politicians and officials. 'If our motive for going to war with the Dutch is to secure freedom and right, this is hypocritical to a high degree.'[54] This was certainly how some patrician soldiers saw it, and in this regard it made for a pretty contemptible war, in which national interest seemed to have become thoroughly corrupted by the leverings of a shabby sectional interest.

At the same time, the existence of such whimsy and respect for the Boer enemy should not be overstated. For an appalled and war-weary General Henry Rawlinson, by 1901 they had also done their bit for the war's degeneracy by random killings of black civilians, and in the savagery of many reprisals against African and Coloured inhabitants who had been colluding with the British.[55] In such views, these contemplative members of the officer corps were perhaps not altogether unlike their earlier nineteenth-century counterparts in the United States army. There, too, in fighting flinty and enterprising Indian warriors on the Great Plains, reflective professional soldiers came to despise the political context in which they found themselves, one of government expediency and mendacity, the pathological extremes of settler racialism, and the insatiable greed of mining kings and cattle barons.[56] In one curious way, Britain's South African frontier had begun to echo a North America it had long ago lost.

Chapter 8 Notes

1. Glenn R. Wilkinson, '"The Blessings of war": the depiction of military force in Edwardian newspapers', *Journal of Contemporary History*, 33/1 (1998), pp. 98–104.
2. J. A. Hobson, *The Psychology of Jingoism* (London, 1901), pp. 17–19, 31–40; Daniel Pick, *War Machine: The Rationalisation of Slaughter in the Modern Age* (New Haven and London, 1993), pp. 111–13.
3. *Clarion*, 1 Sept. 1900.
4. Richard Price, *An Imperial War and the British Working Class: Working Class Reactions to the Boer War, 1899–1902* (London, 1972), pp. 132–77; Henry Pelling, *Popular Politics and Society in Late-Victorian Britain* (London, 1968), pp. 82–100; Ross McKibbin, *The Ideologies of Class: Social Relations in Britain 1880–1950* (Oxford, 1991), pp. 23–4.
5. John Grigg, 'Lloyd George and the Boer War', in *Edwardian Radicalism 1900–1914*, ed. A. J. A. Morris (London, 1974), p. 13.
6. Price, *Imperial War*, p. 131.
7. Price, 'Society, status and jingoism: the social roots of lower middle class patriotism, 1870–1900', in *The Lower Middle Class in Britain, 1870–1914*, ed. Geoffrey Crossick (London, 1977), pp. 89–112.
8. Raymond Sibbald, *The War Correspondents: The Boer War* (London, 1993), p. 177.

9. M. D. Blanch, 'British society and the war', in *The South African War: The Anglo–Boer War 1899–1902*, ed. Peter Warwick (London, 1980), pp. 225–9; *Ladysmith Lyre*, 5 December 1899.

10. Hugh Cunningham, 'The Language of Patriotism, 1750–1914', *History Workshop Journal*, 12 (1981), p. 27.

11. John Mackenzie, *Propaganda and Empire: The Manipulation of British Public Opinion, 1880–1960* (Manchester, 1984), p. 2.

12. *Quarterly Review*, 195 (1902), p. 523.

13. Ibid., 193 (1901), p. 239.

14. *Under the Union Jack*, 28 Dec. 1899.

15. Barbara R. Penny, 'Australia's reactions to the Boer War: a study in colonial imperialism', *Journal of British Studies*, 7/1 (1967), p. 103.

16. *Black and White Budget*, 31 Mar. 1900; *On Yeoman Service*, C. E. M. Rolleston (London, 1901), p. 58; National Army Museum, 5603/10/7, Col. H. F. N. Jourdain, Boer War Diary 1901–1902, entry for 29 Oct. 1901.

17. John Buchan, *The African Colony: Studies in the Reconstruction* (Edinburgh, 1903), p. 78; *The New Penny Magazine*, 2/132 (1901), p. 161; Spies, 'Women', p. 171.

18. Edward M. Spiers, 'The Use of the Dum-Dum Bullet in Colonial Warfare', *Journal of Imperial and Commonwealth History*, 4/1 (1975), pp. 3–14.

19. *Pearson's War Pictures*, 31 Apr. 1900.

20. *Lloyds Weekly Newspaper*, 25 Mar. 1900.

21. *Oakleaf*, 8/5 (1900), p. 134.

22. *Justice*, 20 July 1901.

23. *The War Memoirs of Commandant Ludwig Krause 1899–1900*, ed. Jerold Taitz (Cape Town, 1996), p. 16.

24. *Black and White Budget*, 4/59 (1900), p. 232.

25. Lionel Curtis, *With Milner in South Africa* (Oxford, 1951 edn), p. 16.

26. Eversley Belfield, *The Boer War* (London, 1975), p. xxiv.

27. *The Times History of the War in South Africa*, vol. 1 (1899–1900), ed. Leo Amery (London, 1900), p. 138.

28. R. S. S. Baden-Powell, *The Downfall of Prempeh: A Diary of Life with the Native Levy in Ashanti, 1895–96* (London, 1898), p. 177.

29. Quoted in Correlli Barnett, *Britain and Her Army, 1509–1970* (London, 1970), pp. 171–2.

30. Sir Henry Howorth, 'Our Indian Troops', *Nineteenth Century*, 47 (1900), p. 37; Shigeru Akita, 'The Second Anglo-Boer War and India', *Journal of Osaka University of Foreign Studies*, 8 (1993), p. 122.

31. *The Ladysmith Lyre*, 27 Nov. 1899.

32. NAM, 7208/8, Paterson Letters, Cpl. J. Paterson to his brother, 17 Apr. 1900; *The Statist*, 27 Apr. 1901, p. 762.

33. *Black and White Budget ('Transvaal Special, No.2')*, Nov. 1900, p. 27.

34. Castle Museum, York, 'The Wharfedale Yeomanry, 1901–2', ms. typescript.

35. H. W. Wilson, *With the Flag to Pretoria* (London, 1901), p. 459.

36. NAM, 7305/82, Craig-Brown Diary, 1900–1901, entry for 21 Feb. 1900; *Black and White Budget*, 2/25 (1900), p. 31.

37. Charles James O'Mahony, *A Peep over the Barleycorn* (Dublin, 1911), pp. 191–3; Archives of the West Yorkshire Regiment, 78/1, Lothian Nicholson Diaries, Lnt. A. H. Lothian Nicholson, entry for 22 Mar. 1900.

38. *Morning Leader*, 22 June 1900.

39. A. M. S. Methuen, *Peace or War in South Africa* (London, 1899), p. 140; Preben Kaarsholm, 'Pro-Boerism and romantic anti-capitalism on the European continent during the South African War', in *Patriotism: The Making and Unmaking of British National Identity*, ed. Raphael Samuel (London, 1989), vol. 1, p. 113.

40. *De Graaff-Reinetter*, 23 Nov. 1900.
41. Dietlof van Warmelo, *On Commando* (Johannesburg, 1977), pp. 115–24.
42. Krause, *Memoirs*, p. 16.
43. *Under the Union Jack*, 1/7 (1899), p. 162.
44. Archives of the West Yorkshire Regiment, 2nd Battn. Journal, ms. typescript.
45. RSR, Mss. 1/116, Battalion punishment books, vol. 3 (1901).
46. RSR, 1/119, Bidder letterbooks, vol. 5, letter encl. 2 Nov. 1901; John Selby, *The Boer War: A Study in Cowardice and Courage* (London, 1969), p. 217.
47. *Bugle*, 19/4 (1900), p. 18.
48. Quoted in S. B. Spies, *Methods of Barbarism? Roberts and Kitchener and Civilians in the Boer Republics, June 1900–May 1902* (Pretoria, 1977), p. 235.
49. Nasson, 'Tommy Atkins in South Africa', in *The South African War: The Anglo-Boer War 1899–1902*, ed. Peter Warwick (London, 1980), p. 133.
50. Captain F. P. Fletcher-Vane, *The War One Year After* (Cape Town, 1903), p. 7.
51. Helen Bradford, 'Gentlemen and Boers: Afrikaner nationalism, gender and colonial warfare in the South African War', Rethinking the SA War Conference paper, UNISA, 1998.
52. *All the World*, Jan. 1902, pp. 113–14; Nasson, 'Tommy Atkins in South Africa', p. 133.
53. Keith Surridge, '"All you soldiers are what we call pro-Boer": the military critique of the South African War, 1899–1902', *History*, 82/268 (1997), , p. 599.
54. John Lee, 'Sir Ian Hamilton after the War: A Liberal General Reflects', in *Facing Armageddon: The First World War Experienced*, eds Hugh Cecil and Peter H. Liddle (London, 1996), pp. 880–1.
55. Thomas Pakenham, *The Boer War* (London, 1979), p. 534.
56. John Keegan, *Warpaths: Travels of a Military Historian in North America* (London, 1996), p. 310.

9

The War a Century On

In demographic depth and human cost, let alone in geographical scale, the South African War may well be topped by the disruptive pre-colonial *Mfecane* wars which raged across a swathe of the Southern African subcontinent in the early decades of the nineteenth century, pulverizing old African worlds and providing the hammer for building new societies from the rubble. Yet, while the climactic *Mfecane* ('the crushing') conflict is remembered principally in invented rural oral tradition, in popular mythologies about Shaka and the Zulu kingdom, and in scholarly debate in South African and African historiography, there can be little question that in modern South African historical consciousness it is the 1899–1902 war which today still counts in national memory, however historically narrow has been the context of that construction.

In any wide view, it counts with fairly good reason. The war has left many of the more enduring residues of early twentieth-century colonial war. Generating hundreds of books, including even Anglo-Boer spy thrillers like the 1907 *The Secret of the Scarlet Letter*, and a further wealth of other forms of literature, the war's varied literary epitaph remains unrivalled locally, and this cultural deposit may make it the modest South African equivalent of an American Civil War, a British Great War, or even a Spanish Civil War. In part, that reflects the extent to which both colonial and imperial observers were drawn to the obvious contrast between the quick, dashing war that was envisaged or imagined, and the rather more lengthy and arduous war which was actually fought. Given the sobering experience of the

Crimean War and the American Civil War, any major contest of modern arms and prepared opposition was almost bound to be a protracted and bitter one. In part, too, the weight of the war is an illustration of the degree to which even – or especially – after 1902 its meaning continued to be fought over between clumps of South African empire loyalists and defeated but unreconciled Afrikaner republicans. As in post-1939 Spain, a war of arms was to continue as a war of words for those for whom the Anglo-Boer War became the massive building-block of a nationalist 'Afrikaner' history, 'a myth of national origin'.[1]

That war of words was certainly of some importance to the balance of white political forces even into the early post-Second World War years, when the survival of cultivated memories of concentration-camp cruelties and brutal conquest in war remained closely connected with the rise and eventual ascendancy of a republican nationalist Afrikanerdom. The emotive expression of a subordinate yet combative nationality, tilting at the political and economic citadels of South Africa's languid English establishment, Afrikaner war commemoration provided a moral legacy of heroic manly struggle and female fortitude and sacrifice. That reflection began in the 1900s, through pilgrimages to grave sites, the disinterring and ritual reburial of the remains of fallen combatants, the later creation of war memorials, such as the 1913 Women's Monument or *Vrouemonument* as a male-inspired shrine to female martyrdom (some organized Afrikaner women had favoured a memorial of more utilitarian social benefit), the 1920s issuing of commemorative medals to veterans or *oudstryders*, and other resurrectionary modes of expression.

The fatal clash between Briton and Boer was not to be just another miserable vestige of the outrages inflicted by imperial conquest. As leading nationalistic war poets like Jan Celliers, Eugene Marais, and Totius asserted after 1902, cathartic memories of blood sacrifice could kindle consciousness of national identity and help to renew dignity and purpose.[2] It is perhaps not stretching things too much to see the war enshrined as the Verdun of Afrikaner society, or even as its equivalent of a Tsarist 1905, a perilously close moment of complete and final national disaster. In this, Afrikaner nationalist writers and historians worked as hard as anyone to keep the war a live and burning issue within the crucial social networks of religion, politics, family, and friendship. In the first instance, in the aftermath of conflict it was obviously necessary to construct a view of the republican struggle which countered the ludicrous and frequently offensive portrayal of warring Boer society peddled by various imperialist writers. In the

most crude of these depictions the Boer was a degraded rural speci-
men, an untidy pre-modern with no proper place in capitalist modernity and a warrior who displayed shifty fighting qualities in fighting a
criminal war against progress.[3] These stereotypes became refash-
ioned: the bearded toad on Lord Roberts' mess table would turn out
to be handsome and dashing Albert Viljoen, a commando Lion easily outwitting plodding British Tommies.

But there was always more to these representations than mere
counter-history. For popular historians such as Gustav Preller, a former war correspondent on the Boer side, accounts of republican
doings all came to serve an overriding purpose – to awaken the
Afrikaner to the truth about their War of Freedom and their
National Mission. As Albert Grundlingh has underlined, the message
was to make the inheritance of war the powerful core of an immanent
Afrikaner 'nationalist spirit', with popular histories reminding readers of the Christian Boer crusade 'against the mighty British Empire,
and the suffering of women and children'. The experience of war 'had
to serve as a constant reminder of the Afrikaners' bitter fight for freedom. Although they had lost...they were exhorted not to sacrifice a
common identity as Afrikaners...History had to be used in such a
way that it enhanced patriotism and national consciousness...Con-
temporary Afrikaners had to complete the historic mission of the
Boer die-hards – they had to continue the fight for Afrikaner independence in the present.'[4]

The splintering impact of the war upon the fabric of Boer society
did not make it easy going for a bookish, middle-class, nationalist
intelligentsia; it took time to stitch together a meaningful sense of war
and an awakened ethnic nationhood. Ideological industry was also
further hampered by the incoherence and fragility of an Afrikaans literary culture. But once the assertion of a standard Afrikaans language became buttressed by official recognition from the 1920s, magic
could be worked with war writings. Much of this alchemy was pursued in popular magazines like *Die Brandwag* (The Sentinel) and *Die
Huisgenoot* (The Home Companion). By soliciting personal war tes-
timony for publication, they plumbed a rich seam of earthy folk memory of hardship and suffering which appealed widely to republican
patriots, particularly rural women, as well as to veterans and their
families. In this genre the war largely ceased to be a disputed and
internally divided struggle against imperial domination; instead, it
became resurrected in print as the unity of the Boer nation at war, a
tribal defence of hearth and home by a small and virtuous Christian
people.

While few Afrikaans books on the war appeared between the 1900s and the end of the 1920s, the ensuing two decades witnessed a surge of popular works, ranging from tendentious histories like Sara Raal, *Met die Boere in die Veld* (With the Boers in the Field) to spirited historical fiction, like Mikro, *Die Ruiter in die Nag* (The Rider in the Night). Populist writings of this kind helped to harden a consolidating collective mentality and memory, by creating an exalted sense of national character as wiry, valiant, and persevering. While harping on war memories of bitterness, anguish, and redemptive Christian fortitude, it was no less necessary to commemorate superhuman republican bravado, exemplified by the gritty epic of bittereinder resistance and the seemingly clairvoyant genius of the younger Boer generalship. In this mostly masculine legacy, 'the courage and determination of the die-hard Boer fighters revealed those character traits supposedly typical of the Afrikaner and deemed worthy to emulate'.[5]

As in the Francoist historiography of post-1936–39, the overlap between popular and scholarly representations of the war which turned history into nationalist propaganda was quite marked. Through the 1940s and for a time even beyond much academic writing presented the war above all as a militant and emotive moral covenant of Afrikaner nationalist mobilization. Such classic studies of the later 1940s as J. H. Breytenbach, *Die Betekenis van die Tweede Vryheidsoorlog* (The Meaning of the Second War of Freedom), portrayed a war made up of godless and meretricious British and the upright guardians of a freeborn Boer people, men of the elect who listened to the Prophets and women who would continue to carry the seed of a republican freedom whose time would come. Integral to the professional promotion of an Afrikaner people's history or *volksgeskiedenis*, this gloss on the war became its historical truth, part of an 'objective-scientific' truthfulness about the past furnished by nationalist historians.[6] An accepted truth was the pervading resonance of a *Vryheidsoorlog* or War of Freedom, first coined in the 1880s, after the defeat of the British at the Battle of Majuba. Retrospectively, the 1880–1 Transvaal War became represented as the *Eerste Vryheidsoorlog*, or First War of Freedom, the epic struggle of a tribe of Israel for justice and independence in the promised land. As a living parable this imagery went on to season the spiritual plateau of the second conflict. The confection of a *Tweede Vryheidsoorlog*, or Second War of Freedom, served to affirm the spiritual plateau occupied by the war in the long upward slog of a republicanist Afrikanerdom.

At the same time it needs to be remembered that this is not all.

More modern Afrikaans scholarly writing on the war, emerging essentially between the end of the 1960s and the later 1980s, has been less crusading in purpose, reflected not least in the use of a more pro-saic *Boereoorlog*, or Boer War, and *Anglo-Boereoorlog*, or Anglo-Boer War, and in a shift towards a less partisan historical assessment. In this the liberal significance of victory or defeat has probably generally mattered less, as has the search for 'meaning' in the war; it was comprehensible as tragedy, a fateful fissure between English and Afrikaner with profoundly regrettable consequences. In some of this there is an echo of those British officers who were concerned that the bitterness of the war would end up completely alienating the two white 'races' when what the country needed was an alliance of their common European kinship.

There were good reasons for exaggerated nationalist reminders of the moral lessons and animosities of the war to weaken appreciably through the post-Second World War decades. In part this was because many Afrikaners found themselves enjoying unprecedented prosperity under National Party rule after 1948. In these circumstances, brooding over the privations and losses of the English War inevitably became a less important element of *volk* propaganda. Whatever the English had done in the past could now be undone through the soufflé of Afrikaner nationalism; there was a lot of such rising to be done. There were also other factors which made the war a declining factor in identity politics. One was the long-awaited satisfaction at the achievement of a national South African Republic and its withdrawal from the British Commonwealth at the beginning of the 1960s: at least in spirit, the old Boer Republics could waltz again. Another was the need to glide English South Africans into a more companionable and inclusive white supremacist nationalism. This also produced a judicious thaw in war sentiment, with a decreasing tendency for staunch Afrikaners to associate English speakers with the sins and brutishness of old imperial conquest.

By the early 1970s memory of the war as an ideological totem had largely migrated to the khaki-shirt, nationalist ultra-right. Remaining combative, its gaze fixed firmly on the past, this mostly lower-middle-class and working-class cluster began to keep incriminating war memories active on the margins, with a festering bitterness about the fate of the Afrikaners in the war forming a crucial part of an anti-English agenda. Naturally enough, the currency of remembrance was one of facing up to the war from the front. It entailed submerging and forgetting the very large number of those who had had enough of male sacrifice in war: men who hid, surrendered, or became turncoats by enlisting in the British army. What mattered was making remembrance of the trauma of the war an inextricable part of the continued demonizing of an old imperial enemy. Crushing defeat and humiliation are obviously wounding memories, but their regular reflective commemoration has long had its nationalistic uses.

Britain's camps, and their atrocious conditions of internment, continued to be a symbol of the atrocity of conquest, as the Boer women and children of August 1901 became the equivalent of the Belgians of August 1914. The violation and capture of the domestic space of the 'home front' continued to help in knitting together a focused will to remember. And, as a focal point of memory, what the resettlement camps of the occupied Boer states continued to bequeath was victimhood and martyrdom. They had also long been a site of historical mythology. Thus, within contemporary South Africa, it is fair to assume that most people still see the use of concentration camps as a uniquely cruel strategy invented by the British and pioneered by a devilish Kitchener to do in the Boers, while Britain's 'methods of barbarism' lit the way to Nazi concentration camps 40 years later. In fact, as a standard tactic to stop a dispersed rural guerrilla war becoming an indefinite war, policies of forced resettlement and internment had earlier been put into service by Spain in the Cuban War and by the republican Mexican army in the 1870s. Detention was how regular armies came to wrap up the challenge of evasive and irregular warfare. No less tangibly, the invocation of memory of the camps has long been the special path of an Afrikaner war trauma; only now is there a dawning wider recognition that living and dying in internment sites was something shared by African refugees too.

In defining the memory of the war it is always the England of the past which asserts itself in the end. The creation of a unified English-Afrikaner Union Defence Force in 1912 saw Boer veterans and others full of righteous indignation about an Anglicization of military methods and the imposition of a common khaki, a fairly insufferable colour given recent history.[7] Another obvious thing is how the crisis has remained related to the position and claims of the British monarchy in South Africa. Take the 1920s tour of the Prince of Wales when, among some Afrikaner representatives, reconciliatory welcome and lingering war resentment rubbed along very uneasily. Or take the 1947 Royal Visit to South Africa which had as its Churchillian sub-text Britain's desire to acknowledge Prime Minister Jan Smuts for having been the War Office's finest Boer general of 1940. Appropriately enough, on a Transvaal leg of their tour the Royal Family was escorted by a folksy commando, complete with serge suits, slouch hats, republican medals, and vintage Mausers, to a garden tea party, where they met a scraping band of 1899–1902 oudstryders. Radical nationalists, now within a year of electoral office, were unimpressed by so ignominious a ceremonial.[8]

Equally noteworthy were the pricks felt during the first visit of the Windsors since the 1940s, the 1995 tour of Elizabeth II in the wake of South Africa's recent Commonwealth re-entry and its transition to majority rule. In some quarters, old war words and images were rapidly revived. An incensed Afrikaner *Boerestaat* (Boer State) Party declared the Queen unwelcome in the 'Boerestaat of Transvaal and the Free State'. From 'a dynasty of conquerors', she was 'the great grand-daughter of a cruel queen' whose invading armies had not only 'destroyed our Boers' freedom', but had also committed 'the infamous holocaust in which a sixth of our people were murdered in concentration camps'.[9] Other Afrikaner responses were less apoplectic, if still chastening. The blustery former African National Congress parliamentarian Carl Niehaus called upon the Queen to observe a more inclusive act of South African war remembrance by commemorating the Boer dead. 'If she is going to lay wreaths at World War II and World War I graves here,' he declared, 'she ought also to lay wreaths on the graves of the tens of thousands of women and children who died in the camps.'[10]

At the heart of that particular attitude lay South Africa's post-1994 political settlement and the project of national integration for the post-apartheid ruling political élite. South Africa's World War experience and that of its modern colonial war were to be pulled closer together through enlarged common commemorative rites, with Afrikaner losses of the South African War becoming more universally acknowledged as the *nation's* war dead. It was in this sense that Elizabeth II was urged to make a redemptive Boer War gesture in the image of a new South African nation, or in the 'imagined community' of that nation. Far from continuing as a divisive historical legacy, the legacy of the war could become part of the fabric of a newly reconciled and healed country, affirming shared understanding between Afrikaner and English as well as between black and white. Indeed, for some more wide-eyed observers of the Royal Visit the presence of the Queen signified both a final transcendence from Anglo-Boer war bitterness and the ratifying of the 'equal footing' of the three symbolic strands of South African society, 'Bantu, Boer and Briton'.[11]

Perhaps nothing exemplifies this gradual recomposition of the war better than the way in which its commando and internment camps past can now be detached from conservative nationalist Afrikaner history, and imbued with new national patriotic meanings; the purpose of a war imagination is to structure consensus. In 1996, on the fortieth anniversary of a famous African women's march against apartheid pass laws, the ANC Women's League urged the wives of some prominent Afrikaner politicians to stretch 'across the divides', and to join in a commemorative walk to 'cement the unity of South African women'. According to the League's President, what sealed such female solidarity was a shared history of imperial and colonial brutality. Just as African women had been victims of merciless racist decrees, so 'we recognize that Afrikaner women suffered and died under the British'.[12] In an even more grandiose gesture, an ANC judge of the Constitutional Court reclaimed idealism and the universal story of freedom as the meaning of the war. Eliding the language of the present with that of the past, he asserted his personal 'pride in the heroic struggle of the Boer fighters in the history of the world and in our history'. Any history of a liberal human-rights culture had to 'take into account the fate of the women and children in the concentration camps. So much of Afrikaans history is part of the struggle for freedom. *Vryheid* (Freedom) has real resonance and meaning.'[13] If there is any irony here, it clearly comes at the historical expense of the black majority.

Assimilation of the history of the war to a broader new South Africanism is a model illustration of how a populist public agenda may seek to recreate or reinvent the place of armed conflict in modern national identity. Thus, according to one government provincial cultural department in 1996, the purpose of any centenary anniversary would not be to commemorate an Anglo-Boer War but to recognize a South African War, or rather a series of South African wars, in which 'virtually all ethnic groups' played a role, thereby forging 'the common historic destiny of all South Africans'.[14] This version of everyone's war around some military maypole has the cosy ring of a shared bonding, even though adversarial responsibility for the war, and for the running of its operations, did not exactly rest with all of South Africa's inhabitants. In such therapeutic reordering and reconstruction the ugly phenomenon of the concentration camps becomes a levelling time for Afrikaner and African war trauma, as a previously exclusivist Boer martyrdom becomes shared suffering across the colour divide.

At the same time, more needs to be said. Within the lower levels of the ruling party itself, the war is not up for grabs as a war of South African 'people' rather than an Anglo-Boer war. In 1996, for instance, Cape Town ANC councillors denounced war centenary initiatives as 'a celebration of a colonial war which produced a new period of oppression and exploitation of our people'. Having 'just got back our dignity', there was no appetite for remembering 'an insular war which has nothing that unites our people'.[15] By 1997 in some places this feeling had gone further. For one government official the protracted misery endured by black people for most of the twentieth century had been the direct product of the war; for him, there could be no question of official public commemoration. For another, as the cause of the war was no more than a British–Boer squabble over African land it was neither appropriate nor politic for a majority rule government to mark the centenary of an episode of colonial expropriation.[16]

Elsewhere the ground so well-watered by radical Afrikaner nationalism in earlier decades also began to bear its own distinctive fruit. Although by the 1980s well past its zenith as a mobilizing cult of war remembrance, the embers of 1902 were stoked by the terminal crisis of apartheid. In a striking 1993 observation the quixotic Afrikaner historian Floors van Jaarsveld concluded that 'Afrikanerdom has suffered two great defeats in its history: the first at the beginning of the twentieth century in the war with Britain, which inflicted a military defeat on it, and the second at the end of the century – a political defeat at the hands of Africa.'[17]

Elements of a bittereinder aesthetic took shape around this view, as British domination became African domination, with the ANC President Nelson Mandela its odious High Commissioner; for its far right, Afrikanerdom once again faced the prospect of complete deracination in a unitary mongrel state. 'Again,' intoned Ferdi Hartzenberg of the Conservative Party, 'dark days have come to our people.'[18] In turn, to his right there was a rekindled yearning for a Transvaal and Orange Free State Boerestaat or *Volkstaat* (People's State) to secure the bloodlines of ethnic self-determination. In one burst of unvarnished Anglophobia, Robert van Tonder of the Boerestaat Party called for 'Boers' to consecrate a pure 'Boerestaat' as a posthumous revenge upon Queen Victoria, who had seen to it that 'our Boer republics were crushed in 1902 and 14 other "peoples" were forced to live with us in one state'. This had amounted to breaking the rules of warfare to foment civil war, but then, as now, civil war could not defeat Afrikaners as, 'after all, it was the Afrikaners who invented it'.[19]

In the 1990s this dissenting Boer War flank engaged on a number of fronts, not just against the old enemy of rampant Englishness but against a dawning age of racial equality and majority rule, and against now-despised National Party leadership for capitulating to racial and cultural cosmopolitanism. At one tragicomic pole there was the seizure of Pretoria's Schanskop fort and military museum, a place in thrall to a virile Boer commando heritage. Under the billowing *Vierkleur* flag of the nineteenth-century Transvaal a knot of armed vigilantes protested against multiracial political negotiations, seeing their sole purpose as selling off the assets of Afrikaner sovereignty. After their arrest and conviction for illegal armed occupation, their leader, Willem Ratte, wrote from gaol to contest his newspaper depiction as right-wing. All that informed his thinking was a First Anglo-Boer War antecedent. In a torrential yet powerful manifesto, Ratte declared:

> Were the Boers of 1880 called right-wingers, for resisting the imperialist British occupation? Then, as now, you had an alien regime lording it in Pretoria over our people, whose gutless president had betrayed and handed over his sovereign state. Then, as now, the new (neo)colonialist administration pretended to be God's gift to the supposedly 'dirty and dumb Dutchmen' and tried its best to smear the pro-independence party as only a few backward 'Don Quixotes tilting at windmills'. Our struggle has nothing to do with right or left...this being incidental, like religion in the Irish–British conflict, but everything to do with nation having an inherent right to be free, to be able to choose its own representatives and leaders democratically. [20]

At another eccentric pole, an October 1992 Kruger Day commemoration saw a sliver of rough-hewn Englishness regain its lustre in right-wing nationalist Afrikaner life. In a cameo of bonding between Afrikaner and English ultra-right interests, indefatigable ex-Rhodesians and English-speaking adherents of the Afrikaans Conservative Party lumbered into the Vaal River to retrieve rocks from a camp memorial reputedly torn down by departing British soldiers in 1903. Under the solemn gaze of a crowd of several thousand, the rock was piled up close to the official Paardekraal camp monument, thereby symbolically atoning for past desecration. As 'the greatest conciliatory gesture by English-speaking countrymen since before the Boer Wars', Conservative Party leader Andries Treurnicht announced that 'the time has certainly come for all English-speaking patriots to let bygones be bygones, and to join hands with the Boer to resist the common enemy of black domination'.[21] This, as it happens, was a fairly droll gesture from a man who had spent a good chunk of his political career railing against English influence in South African life.

In April 1998 there was appreciation of news from Ireland of stiff opposition in Listowel to the raising of a plaque to commemorate Kitchener's birthplace because of his inhumane prosecution of the Anglo-Boer War. One correspondent noted that it would be received 'with great satisfaction by Afrikaners in general, but particularly by descendants of the Boers who fought against Kitchener's barbarism'. Several others invoked the obvious popular analogy, arguing that Kitchener's concentration-camp policy had been the genocidal work of a 'Hitler' in South Africa, or the creation of an unrecognized British Vietnam. J. A. Marais, 'son of a Boer father' exiled and imprisoned on St Helena, and 'a mother who was interned in the Klerksdorp concentration camp', urged on the idea of an Irish-Afrikaner 'war crimes tribunal for Kitchener' in 1899, to mark 'commemoration of the centenary of the outbreak of the Boer War'.[22] It was all caught neatly in 1999 by a call for the British Prime Minister, Tony Blair, to apologize for Britain's 'appalling concentration camp record' in the light of blushing contrition before the Irish for the potato famine and Indians for the Amritsar massacre. Yet readers were advised not to expect too much sentiment, for while there were 'many Irish and Indian voters in the UK...there is no Afrikaner vote'.[23]

Such flickerings, and Fort Schanskop and Paardekraal, must surely be seen as being among the last prickly episodes of an antique Afrikaner past, dredging up for a self-conscious and ailing 'Boer' minority the nostalgias and resentments of a world with declining points of reference. For those still attached to a *volkisch* war memory it might not be too much to say that in the 1990s they were being undone by history. Indeed, there was a quite knowing sense of this. Likening African political demands to those of the Uitlanders who had been so unwelcome a blot upon Kruger's republic, the *Afrikaner-weerstandsbeweging* (Afrikaner Resistance Movement) leader Eugene Terreblanche growled that not to grant Afrikaner 'freedom' in a people's state would be to 'play with fire', as British statesmen had discovered in the 1890s. Sceptics were referred to Thomas Pakenham's *The Boer War*, a work which, in his view, gave the Boers their due and more. Terreblanche commended it as being as admirable as Shakespeare, and therefore 'not part of any English conspiracy'.[24]

Within the AWB the coming of black majority rule represented 'a second invasion' requiring the invoking of a national Boer state defence, and heightening the inclination to bob about on horseback in an assertive display of Boer commando lineage. Because of the danger to Afrikaners from untrustworthy news editors, slippery politicians, and meddling imperialists (now American, not British), the call was for a 'return' of 'the generals', as historically nationalist Afrikaners had looked for salvation to their tough military men and spirited irreconcilables, the de la Reys and de Wets. Just how much things turned on emotive memory of the ashes of 1899–1902 could be glimpsed in puffy Conservative Party talk of an imminent *Derde Vryheidsoorlog* (Third War of Freedom), the use by the AWB and Boerestaat Party of the old Transvaal flag and its anthem, *Ken u die Volk* (Do you know the People), in swiping gunshots at the British Embassy in Pretoria in 1990, and in a bomb attack on Melrose House, where the Boer leadership had signed its pained surrender in May 1902. Back where it all started, rabid ideologues of national purity demanded the reclamation and renewal of the old Boer Republics. This was not something to be created, for historically they had already been in fully legitimate existence, based on a Boer occupation which had 'enjoyed internationally recognized independence until 1902'.[25]

In a further poignant echo from the early 1900s, there was denunciation of reformist National Party leadership as traitors or *verraaiers* for having submitted to the ANC. Politicians to their right went for the government as 'a lot of traitors', guilty of 'treachery' and 'acts of treason against its own people'.[26] The base appeal of the idea of treachery was to a form of atavism, a replay of the war's closing stages and its full-blown hensopper and bittereinder split between folding for peace and rigidly holding out under arms. In other words, here again were the more flabby of Boer generals turning traitor through capitulation or spineless surrender. The principal modern embodiment of this behaviour was, of course, President F. W. de Klerk, who in 1997 tellingly let slip in London that he had bowed to the inevitable need to 'surrender the right to national sovereignty'.[27] In terms of the conventional content and discourse of nationalist Afrikaner history, the very word 'surrender' has long continued to be particularly pregnant in meaning. Equally, this may be the final historical moment when the partisan fires of traditionalist Afrikaner nationalist bitterness and self-righteousness can still be fanned by consciousness of the moral relevance of the war.

As the 1999 centenary dawns, within South African society it is increasingly clear that a shifting historical context will affect the established ways in which the war has been remembered. In what for want of a better term one might call 'popular society' the legacy of war still remains a sectional business. Outside élite cultural and academic missionary circles the Anglo-Boer conflict is not *felt* to be a shared South African history, let alone a shared tragedy. By and large, the impulse of the black majority is to dissociate; for white Afrikaners and English speakers it is to associate, however reticently in many instances. In this, 1999 may not be entirely unlike 1949. Yet following the decline of Afrikaner power there are obvious other differences. In a new society being directed by the liberation aristocracy of African nationalism, busily creating its own national myths, what will happen to the historical Anglo-Boer War?

One likelihood is that it will inevitably come eventually to be seen as a more and more remote episode from a vanished European imperial age. As the Johannesburg *Sunday Independent* put it on the centenary of the 1895 Jameson Raid, that madcap moment of imperialist buccaneering which Churchill later considered to be the real start of the Anglo-Boer conflict, 'with this tumultuous century drawing to a close, hindsight puts the do-or-die battle between Afrikaners and English-speakers into its proper, smaller context. White men were never going to win indefinite control of this African continent.'[28] This certainly contains a truth, given the social basis provided by the war for a unified South Africa and the form of a twentieth-century South African nationalism. Its direction was made abundantly clear by many local veterans of the war, not least Smuts. When in the 1930s he invoked a 'philosophy of non-racial, inclusive South Africanism',[29] it meant closing the book on Anglo-Boer War divisions rather than anything Whiggish in intention towards the rightless black majority. Towards the end of the twentieth century some members of that majority, now in power at last, seem still to be laying the blame for this on the 1899–1902 war. This is probably misconceived. It is true that it put things straight for a unified national colonial state which tied up a white supremacist order; but in one form or another that was on the way in any event.

Almost a century ago Kipling despaired of the Boer War as a bad business, plainly 'No End of a Lesson'. In Britain it was a lesson rued across a wide spectrum of opinion, from professional military staff to fastidious liberals. For South Africa, something of that became embedded in old republican Afrikaner imagery, while the backward gaze of others has gradually become infused by newer experiences or the need to recast the war's legacy by reflecting long-unacknowledged black sacrifice or loss. Already ambiguous in its significance, in some ways the future of the war in popular South African historical memory looks quite uncertain. It is even conceivable that with the disappearance of a distinctive Afrikaner 'political nation' it will come to have little core meaning at all and will live on in the refined cultural climate of heritage. Consider the fate of the old Orange Free State, central to freehold Boer trekker identity since the mid-nineteenth century and the location of some of the war's stiffest republicanism and most destructive fruition. Moving with African nationalist times, the Orange Free State lost its distinctively Dutch 'Orange' stamp in 1994 to become simply the Free State; in 1997 its ANC provincial government decided to swap Afrikaans for English as its sole official language. Less than a century after the war African nationalism has in some ways begun to realize Milner's failed post-1902 Anglicization policy. And as with Orange, so with Vaal. The Transvaal, too, has been dismembered, retitled, and demarcated as new territorial entities with chunky, non-colonial African names like Gauteng and Mpumalanga. Post-Boer and politically odourless, on a history map reading they may appear to have become the provinces from nowhere.

And yet in our time, let alone in the longer run to come, the erosion of the war's political inheritance, sentimentalized or institutionalized, is unlikely to mean the end of an Anglo-Boer imperial war remembrance. This has little to do with the politics of identity, or with war as a legitimizing myth; moreover, in its imaginative temperament the Anglo-Boer War is first and the South African War still quite some way second. At the time of writing, able-bodied devotees of the renowned guerrilla commandant Christiaan de Wet can take guided hikes along his legendary flying escape route in the Western Transvaal. As war tourism this may be the South African version of tripping along the Ho Chi Minh Trail. In the Cape Karoo region, addicts can scramble up to remote rock faces on which resting or hiding Boer commandos scratched poignant personal messages or etched images of fellow burghers. Visitors to a minor 1900 battlefield outside Bloemfontein can get, as it were, a bite of the cherry by firing a restored Boer Martini-Henry rifle at a British infantryman dummy target, or by guessing the standard provisions and equipment carried by a commando. Boer War enthusiasts from Britain and the white Commonwealth, swollen in number by the pull of the war's centenary, tramp the battlefields of Modder River or Paardeberg, ponder at the still-exposed Boer trenchlines at Magersfontein, amble through the Ladysmith siege museum, or chart the whereabouts of some of the 8000 blockhouses erected over large parts of South Africa by British forces.

The remnants of the *soldiering* war clearly remain as powerful an attraction as ever, the sites of decisive battle or marks of guerrilla attrition a source through which to imagine the concrete realities of a European colonial war. From the perspective of the late 1990s it is the significance of political memories of the war which looks set to decline. Something of that ideological mood may remain; it will just touch ever fewer people. Indeed, it is hard to see how it could naturally be otherwise in a country of such limited commonalities. South African's modern war is not, and has never been, an American Civil War in the sense of a 'never-to-be-forgotten moment' in 'the collective consciousness that makes Americans American'.[30] It produced no Stephen Crane to mythologize a tragic war as a national rite of passage to 'manhood'. To conjure up 'We are Marching to Pretoria' is not to summon up the shared image of a universally transforming war of the kind endowed by 'Marching through Georgia' or 'Dixie'. Unlike the Blue and the Grey, Boer and departing British war veterans were slow in scrambling towards camp-fire brotherly reconciliation. Equally, this was not merely a big war in the modern life of an evolving nation state. It was at the same time the most violent expression of the prolonged engagement between South Africa and empire. In this, it is again high time to summon A. J. P. Taylor who, decades ago, concluded memorably that in the long term 'the eclipse of Boer independence was of less importance than the deflation of British imperialism'.[31]

Chapter 9 Notes

1. Isabel Hofmeyr, 'Building a nation from words: Afrikaans language, literature and ethnic identity, 1902–1924', in *The Politics of Race, Class & Nationalism in Twentieth Century South Africa*, eds Shula Marks and Stanley Trapido (London, 1987), p. 109.
2. T. Dunbar Moodie, *The Rise of Afrikanerdom: Power, Apartheid and the Afrikaner Civil Religion* (Los Angeles, 1975), p. 17.
3. Nasson, 'Race and Civilisation in the Anglo-Boer War of 1899–1902', M.A. diss. (University of York, 1977), pp. 44–50.
4. Albert Grundlingh, 'War, wordsmiths and the "Volk": Afrikaans historical writing on the Anglo-Boer war of 1899–1902 and the war in Afrikaner historical consciousness, 1902–1990', in *Mfecane to Boer War*, ed. E. Lehmann and E. Reckwitz (Essen, 1992), p. 52.
5. Ibid., pp. 45–6; also Hofmeyr, 'Popularizing History: The Case of Gustav Preller', in *Regions and Repertoires: Topics in South African Politics and Culture*, ed. Stephen Clingman (Johannesburg, 1991), p. 67.
6. Grundlingh, 'War, wordsmiths', p. 48; 'Politics, principles and problems of a profession: Afrikaner historians and their discipline, c.1920–c.1965', *Perspectives in Education*, 12/1 (1990/91), pp. 6–14.
7. Sandra Scott Swart, 'The rebels of 1914: masculinity, republicanism and the social forces that shaped the Boer rebellion', M.A. diss. (University of Natal, 1997), p. 55.
8. *Cape Argus*, 26 Mar. 1947.
9. *Die Burger*, 21 Mar. 1995.
10. *Cape Times*, 21 Mar. 1995.
11. *Cape Times*, 18 Mar. 1995.
12. *Cape Argus*, 8 Mar. 1995.
13. Judge Albie Sachs, cited in Grundlingh, 'War, wordsmiths', p. 54.
14. *Cape Argus*, 1 Oct. 1996.

15. *Cape Times*, 26 Sept. 1996.
16. *Cape Times*, 8 Dec. 1997
17. *Beeld,* 12 Feb. 1993.
18. *Die Burger*, 17 Dec. 1993; *Rapport*, 20 Dec. 1993.
19. *Beeld*, 18 Jan. 1993; *Aida Parker Newsletter*, 163 (1993), p. 2.
20. *Sunday Independent*, 31 Dec. 1995.
21. *Weekly Mail*, 16–22 Oct. 1992.
22. *Sunday Times*, 5, 19 Apr. 1998; *Rapport*, 12 Apr. 1996.
23. *Sunday Times*, 26 Apr. 1998.
24. *Sunday Independent*, 31 Dec. 1995.
25. Johann van Rooyen, *Hard Right: The New White Power in South Africa* (London, 1995), p. 43; *South African Foundation Review*, (September, 1992), p. 8.
26. *Patriot* , 5 Apr., 7 June 1991; *House of Assembly Debates* , col.106, 6 Feb. 1990.
27. *Cape Times*, 19 Feb. 1997.
28. *Sunday Independent*, 31 Dec. 1995.
29. Quoted in T. R. H. Davenport, *South Africa: A Modern History* (London, 1987), p. 177.
30. Noah Andre Trudeau, *Out of the Storm: The End of the Civil War, April-June 1865* (Baton Rouge, 1995), p. 422.
31. A. J. P. Taylor, *From the Boer War to the Cold War: Essays on Twentieth-Century Europe* (Harmondsworth) p. 38.

10

Concluding Remarks

Having considered some of the ways in which this war has come to be remembered, we are left with a last intriguing question. At the end of it all, what was the South African War? Or, put another way, what did all this conflict add up to? In the first place it ended a long period of peace for the British empire, the only major European war fought between 1815 and 1899 having been the Crimea. For the Victorian army there had been over 40 small colonial wars and 'punitive expeditions' since the Cardwell reforms of the 1860s and 1870s, but none of these had represented a significant threat to the position of the empire. Second, there cannot be much doubt that this was a war which did not succeed, for all that it left recognizable victors and vanquished. For the British, grinding down the Boers was eventually all fairly effectively accomplished, but really there was little actual glory in it. Too much had ended up morally troublesome, or haunted by the military need to produce improved performance in the light of the early campaign failures. Even long-suffering officers became heartily sick of affairs in South Africa, and the lengthening drudgery of soldiering did little to endear the country to the great Tommy Atkins majority. Relatively few took leave of army service for post-war settlement in 'the white man's country' or 'the country of promises', a few semi-skilled ex-soldiers picking up artisan trade in port cities, joining the police service, or marrying settler and also Coloured women with whom they had made wartime relationships.[1]

In sight and sound and smell, much of the rural interior of South Africa lay blighted by a war of waste. 'A serious crisis,' in the words of the influential Standard Bank, the effects of which 'will doubtless be felt for a long time.'[2] In a material sense, imperial repatriation, resettlement, and reconstruction aided Boer territory and the country as a whole to recover from the ravages of the war; but it took an effort to restore stability and put right Boer dominance over blacks which had been eroded by the conflict. The British produced waste not just for the enemy, but also for themselves. South Africa had produced another of those wars, even if it was to be the last, in which a physically ill-prepared and unhealthy British army sustained more fatalities from sickness and disease than from enemy fire. Viewed in this light, cavalry horses did even worse. The British lost 347,000 out of 518,000 horses used in mounted campaigning, through malnutrition, disease, or relentless exertion.[3] The strains of army life, sanitation hazards, and bleak austerity of the provisioning environment made this a war in which to be British was to be largely unfit and unhealthy, whether on two legs or four. Out of the almost 450,000 troops who had been put in the field by the end of the war, death among the British military amounted to 22,000 men; over 13,000 of these, or close to two-thirds, being fatalities from disease and illness. Several dozen were killed by lightning, and over 270 soldiers drowned; unlike the Boers, they knew neither how to swim nor which rivers were least treacherous.

The manner of this loss, coupled to the wartime rejection of virtually one-third of army recruits because of poor physical condition, made the experience of 1899–1902 seem a low point in the physical health of the British nation. It brought into sharp relief a proliferation of the unfit among the urban working-class masses, and an assumed physical deterioration of the 'racial stock' of the British population. Unease in the aftermath of 1902 that this might lay at risk the imperial future unleashed a flood of chastening prognostication about the state of military fitness and preparedness, and the dark outcome for the maintenance of a strong nation and empire if decline were not vigorously tackled. The mounting concern of the Edwardian élite with the relationship between imperial power and racial vitality as something to be improved through national efficiency and advanced eugenics was very much a product of the hard going in South Africa.[4]

On the other hand, the war was a less deflating affair for the empire's settler dominions. White New Zealanders played a tough hand, creating a self-confident national identity in South Africa as fighting 'Kiwis'; while the Cape authorities would not permit the landing of Maori soldiers, they bestowed upon departing settler contingents that famous ritual of posturing masculinity, the *haka* warrior dance as the mark of a distinctive and evolving New Zealand representation. The role of the war in the construction of national identity was no less the case for Canada. As British North American loyalists, Canadian expeditionary force volunteers with their Maple Leaf Canada badges provided a war experience to underline nationalist patriotism and self-reliance. Flummoxed by the nature of Boer warfare, British army leadership had botched things because of their crusty adherence to red tape and tea intervals, an absence of innovation, and a prostrating class order. In the Canadian critique all this was no more than evidence of the imaginative brilliance and courage of their colonist citizen soldiers. Immensely hardier and more independent than socially deprived and stunted British Tommies, superior Nordic troops had made a better go of it in South Africa, and represented an assertive country ready to control its own future. In helping to create the Canadian archetype of the upright Mountie or lumberjack, the experience of war in South Africa could certainly be put to some use in structuring the national imagination.

Not surprisingly, the war also brightened the star of the emergent 1901 Australian Federation. Making the best of a bad job by the British, the Australian mounted 'bushman' soldier, proficient in open country and not enfeebled by slum life in Birmingham or Glasgow, brought Australian military 'mateship' galloping to the rescue of empire, creating a new breed of loyal white Gurkhas for Britain, old stock renewed as the very best of British horsemen. This turned the war, the third largest in which Australia has been involved, into an early defining moment in national history and mythology.[5] Predictably, perhaps, the war's place in the history of the Irish was somewhat more messy. Roberts himself was but one of tens of thousands of loyalist Irish who fought for Britain, while across the republican divide Irish nationalist brigades lined up with the Boers. Here were some unusual and memorable circumstances for Catholic republicans. The Boers were Protestant, yet anti-imperialist soldiers for freedom; they had to face Buller, as had the Fenians in Kerry and Clare in the 1880s. And this time it was the ally, not the enemy, which was Orange.

So much for the British world: what of continental Europe and elsewhere? In stoking anti-British passions the war had its place in historic Anglo-French antagonisms. Yet its testy political impact was ephemeral; it produced perhaps the last round of vintage Anglophobia before French opinion swung around to the view that Britain (and not Russia) would be the weightiest ally in any confrontation with Germany. In turn, Russia found that war in South

Africa set its eye on high strategy. Intense Russian pro-Boer hysteria which, as elsewhere, was more rhetorical than material, was directly linked to tension and rivalry with British imperialism over the prickly issue of Afghanistan. Only in Japan were attitudes nicer. Here there was popular hostility towards a Boer threat to the British empire at the very moment that Tokyo was snuggling up to London on the grounds of a common interest in blocking Russian expansionism into Manchuria. War sympathies lubricated the passage of the 1899–1902 Anglo-Japanese Alliance, which hitched the fortunes of the Japanese East Asian Empire to British imperialism for decades hereafter.[6] While this war was never at any point likely to be anything more than a colonial one, at least imaginatively the shots first fired south of Mafeking echoed round a good part of the world.

If the wheel is to come full circle we need to return to the protagonists and the circumstances of their war. Here, which perspectives seem to stand out most will obviously depend always on your point of view or angle of vision. In many ways the English War or *Engelseoorlog* represented the lowest point of Boer existence as it cleared the decks for imperialism in South Africa. Its real significance lies in what it did to a Boer republican society of no more than 200,000 people, its losses representing a form of historical trauma. The Boer republics had had at most about 70,000 of their burghers for field service, over 7000 of whom died. This was a significant proportion of their male soldiering complement. Nearly 28,000 women and children (and some older men and prisoners of war) perished in white concentration camps.

Yet, despite the terrible mauling of highveldt society, the Boers survived, retaining the basic core of their social cohesion and inscribed cultural traditions, a hankering for political power and independence, and a simmering capacity for limbering up again to achieve it. Less than five decades after the end of the war nationalist Afrikanerdom, through the institutions of the new apartheid state, was regaining not only most of the ground lost, but quite a lot more. In this respect, the fate of the Boers was not that of troublesome indigenous societies in some other colonial wars, in which military defeat at the hands of superior European power meant that they simply crumbled and disintegrated.[7]

Far from it. For nationalist ideologues, aside from the shadows cast by Cronjé's surrender at Paardeberg and the Prinsloo disaster of Brandwater Basin, the Boers had suffered no heavy defeats in the field throughout the war. The British were only able eventually to win through their preponderance in numbers, financial reserves, military resources, and use of inhumane methods of warfare – not through any equalizing or superiority in combat efficiency against brave and steely bittereinder warriors. So the war left a morale-boosting legend of male heroism and patriotic fortitude, tested and not found wanting against despised British Tommies, moral corrosion of the betrayal, or the treachery of fellow fighters who broke the Boer cause. In what was surely a remarkable nationalist accomplishment, the image of the mythic Afrikaner Boer warrior emerged as a kind of transcendent triumph of Christian fighting duty and perseverance.[8] In this sense the outcome of the South African War became the best victory Boer republicanism never had. For the war was lost by the Boers rather than won by the British, and it was lost to some republican softening, rather than to a conquering enemy.

A few further closing perspectives turn us from the fanciful to the more factual. To the extent that we now recognize the supportive military role played by perhaps as many as 14,000 African and Coloured commando auxiliaries, and possibly 120,000 African, Coloured, and Indian men in armed or non-combatant imperial army service, it is quite obvious that this was never a white war. Even if these latest estimates may be rather overstated,[9] there can be no mistaking the importance of the non-European role in servicing both sides, in keeping them in the field, in flexing their fighting power, and in its distinct irregular contribution to the art of war in South Africa: maintenance, transport-riding, scouting, raiding, cattle-rustling, spying, interpreting, dispatch running and riding, and holding this or that patch of imperial ground. Frequently individuals contested patches which they had probably never known before the war. On the British side, some found it a profitable cultivation. Wages for army labouring were relatively good, and high for service requiring expertise or skill: one of ordinary soldiers' persistent grumbles was that of having to perform 'on the cheap', while valued black auxiliaries were being better remunerated. Peasant communities in more protected areas made a killing as Army Service Corps forage, livestock, and remount suppliers. All this left some sort of positive balance sheet.

But to conclude thus is also to underline the point that one cannot go too far in this direction. Even as an unhistorical, counterfactual question, had the Anglo-Boer conflict's centre of gravity become fully a white and black military collision, it obviously would have been a very different kind of colonial war. That it did not become this left it as an episode with some peculiar features. The republican Boers were implacably opposed to any racial equality, be it peacetime or wartime, and grumbled incessantly about British irresponsibility in sucking in armed black collaborators. Towards the war's conclusion, even on a conservative calculation, the number of authorized black combatants in the field may well have exceeded the remaining force of fighting bittereinders. Moreover, a threatening climate of social fear engendered by sporadic independent black attacks began to drive things ominously hard, and became a factor in bringing on Boer surrender.

Yet at the same time the fiery extinction of farm-burning fell upon the land, crops, and livestock of many African peasants as well as those of Boer landowners. The misery and terrible mortality of Boer concentration camps was more than matched by the fate of interned black refugees, working in white camps or resettled in their segregated camps. The known African camp losses of around 14,000 have recently been revised to 16,000, with a provisional estimate suggesting a fatality rate of at least 20,000.[10] Here was a mordantly ironic kind of shared tragedy, if not exactly much appreciated in 1902. Undeniable, too, was the face-to-face social connection between Boer families and their black servants and tenants, and their heavy dependence upon them for food supply, transport riding, and the entrusting of livestock for safe keeping, often a poor wartime risk. In all of this, the war was of a slippery nature.

No less striking was the difference between the fighting of the South African War and that of other Victorian colonial campaigns. Neither side made serious use of indigenous populations in actual combat. Nor, as in imperial action in West Africa, were black lives put at risk or routinely expended as a systematic tactic to economize upon European troops. For both British and Boers, exploiting available human resources and raw materials was one thing, acquiring the political encumbrance of negotiated black allies was another.

Viewed in this kind of light, the grain of the South African War can still be seen for what it really was: a European war fought in Africa over how best to get on with the colonial order, and what its dominant terms of reproduction should be. To be sure, there is a view in which this war can be passed off as an early twentieth-century anti-colonial African struggle against the predatory encroachments of Great Power imperialism, in which the republicans amounted to another tribal order of armed peasantry. This implies that the warring Boers simply replaced the Zulu as the most intractable people of southern Africa, or became the Zulu with horses.

Such a similarity, however, does not run very far. Certainly in retrospect, republican anti-imperialism tripped over the contradictions of the Boers' own colonizing cause. The independence of their existence rested upon the expropriation of African land and the appropriation of African labour and other resources; doubtless the Pedi or the Venda would have been bemused to hear that the Boer war to defend settler tenure was an anti-colonial undertaking. Accordingly, as one scholar has very recently suggested, both Anglo-Boer wars might best be depicted as European wars fought within, and inflected by, a colonial setting. For, just as the War of American Independence can hardly be viewed as an episode in native American resistance to European invasion, so the South African War cannot really be seen as part of the history of African resistance to imperial incursion.[11]

At another crucial level, it is almost a cliché of South African and British imperial history to point out that the war and its outcome did nothing to solve the 'problem' of the position of Africans, Coloureds, and Indians. On the contrary, the expedient manner of its resolution made the handling of this problem more difficult than ever. Things might have been a little different if Whitehall had pressed home in peace the limited political stand on black civil rights which it had taken in war. In the failed March 1901 peace talks, Chamberlain had obliged a dismayed Milner and Kitchener to include a clause about extending the franchise right of the Cape black élite into the new colonies. Of course, this was conceived of as a long and lowly apprenticeship in civilization under the racial dominance of just English and Afrikaner settlers, but it still implied that the end of the war should bring a small stepping-stone rather than a dead end. However hollow the Colonial Secretary's occasional claim that an imperial war aim was African protection, his fleeting opposition to an unredeemedly 'shameful peace'[12] still provides a lost wartime moment.

Had peace come then, had a successor settler order had its white supremacy slightly diluted by imperial decree, who knows about the possible course of later South African history. But it did not happen. In 1902, peacemaking British and peacemaking Boers had fought a big and damaging war, and Whitehall and the Boer generals had no wish to trade any new blows over the trifle of rights for a small middle-class tributary of 'civilized natives'. Their only interest was in cooperation and imperial-colonial reconciliation, which in practice meant a colour-bar concession to the traditionally racist constitution and custom of the defeated Boers. In classic liberal interpretation, the imperial re-enfranchisement and rehabilitation of its defeated enemy was so magnanimous that it meant that Britain won the war but lost the peace; equally, its easy mortgaging of African interests to settler needs and ambitions represented a deplorable lapse in liberal sensibilities or conscience. A more materialist reading accepts none of this.

For the calculated political and strategic extractions of British imperial interests in southern Africa as a whole, and for the inroads of mining capital and finance, the 1910 Union produced by the war was a splendid political achievement.[13] For it provided a unified and rational national dominion which could rip away those barriers to South African capitalist development which had been the cause of such frustration and crisis before the war. In the long run, the probable truth of the matter is that neither the imperial nor the republican cause in South Africa could be termed righteous. This was assuredly not a war for the conventional liberal explanation that its outcome may have had something to do with the fact that one cause was worthy and the other was not.

If not this, what, then, in the end, defined the war? Within a British ambience, an obvious perspective was its location squarely within a period of tangled and growing crises for the later Victorian imperial order, palpable by the 1880s and persisting through to the Great War. Like some wind across the world, however tangentially in some respects, the war fanned Britain's anxieties about its imperial position, economic vitality, the deteriorating effects of poverty and unemployment, and defence capability. While the British succeeded in South Africa, the victory it brought seemed leaden. For both Unionists and Liberals, South Africa was a messy chapter of accidents, an imperial war best forgotten. Nor, in some other ways, did conquest immediately present all that much for the British to bite at: emigrants hardly sprinted in, and investment beyond post-1902 reconstruction requirements was modest.

While the general significance of the war to modern British imperialism is apparent, this is not to say that historians should make it bigger than it was. Not everything about it was necessarily fundamental in its impact. It is, for instance, conventional wisdom to stress the imposing financial and other costs of the conflict, and the alarm this caused. Five months into the conflict, that estimated cost had increased from £10m to £68m, virtually the charge of the Crimean War, turning a colonial affray into something of European size. By April 1901 expenditure had risen to £153m, with the final cost to the British Exchequer reaching £217m. When war ended not a farthing of indemnity was extracted from the Transvaal. Yet financing the war, and coping with large budget deficits, did not become the major cause of any fiscal crisis.[14] War finance became a mundane, if worrying, part of late-Victorian and early Edwardian living. The state was having to cope with continuously rising national expenditure, and what the war years brought were emergency increases in income tax. For spending growth, arguably the truly significant impact of the South African conflict was its stimulus to a more general state expansion for national and imperial imperatives: experience on the veldt had confirmed rising pre-1899 anxieties about the possible consequences of poverty, ill-health, and declining 'race' quality – they could result in military disaster.[15] Internationally, the modest borrowing needed to ease matters for the British capital market in meeting the costs of the war was actually gratifying to someone like Chamberlain. The first substantive British loan floated in the New York market became a monument to Anglo-American goodwill, something to assure the nation that its American friends recognized that its war motives and aims were as 'high' and 'unselfish' as those which had roused Washington in the recent Spanish–American conflict.[16]

It is also revealing that when it came to rethinking imperial defence the war did not catch on in quite the way which might have been expected. True enough, the performance problems illuminated by the Boer War were extremely important in prodding along further reform and reconstruction of the Victorian army. As more than one authority has emphasized, the experience of South African colonial warfare was crucial to the reworking of British tactical doctrine before the Great War: greater cultivation of mounted infantry, dispersed infantry formations, and coordinated artillery fire and infantry movement.[17] There were also other spheres of new attention after 1902, ranging from making soldiers more drab to improve their survival chances, to marksmanship and firepower and to the planning of more effective logistical systems to cope with the strains of greater dispersion in more mobile circumstances. As for army medical services, South Africa had been another Crimea, with many more soldiers dying from preventable disease than from enemy fire. This time, reorganization and reform was on a very much larger scale than the marginal post-Crimean reforms.[18]

For all this, the evolving army reforms of influential figures like St John Brodrick and R. B. Haldane, culminating in the limited formation of General Staff, a home-based British Expeditionary Force, and a non-regular Territorial Force, were aimed not so much at equipping Britain's army to fight the next case of armed colonial nationalism. If anything, it was more the possibility of dealing with a rival expansionist enemy, much more powerful and close to a vital and lucrative sphere of British influence. While South Africa gave a modernizing push to army and naval thinking, that direction initially was to be prepared for quite another kind of European run-in: an imperialist tangle in India with a threatening Russia. In that sense, experience on the veldt seemed not to leave the army gingered up for improved policing of the empire against unrest, but marking time for the day when European continental fighting could become necessary to preserve the balance of power. Even here, it could not be said that the post-South African War reforms were deliberately designed to prepare British forces for a planned war on the European continent; if there was an army for continental purposes, it remained largely a pragmatic thing, ready for a crisis but to react in an improvised way, and then only if the crisis became a real nuisance. For, politically, 'neither the government nor the country was prepared to accept the massive militarisation of society which a continental strategy implied',[19] despite the best urgings of Erskine Childers' *The Riddle of the Sands* and other seaborne-invasion literature that an unready Britain would now have to square up to an aggressive Germany. Still, South African reverses can certainly be seen to have prepared the ground for this preoccupation of the popular imagination.[20]

As the Boers fired the first shot, they should probably have the last word of the story. This was their mostly guerrilla war, and their longest and leanest armed conflict, one which came to rest on scrawny people fed on scrawny pastoralism. A war rich in suffering, exile, and fratricidal strife, it left an occupied population lifted from desolation and reinstated on their land only by the reconstruction intervention of their enemy. Notwithstanding inequalities and divisions, it was also a people's war, with a knotty and independent-minded civilian character – a strength and a weakness when it came to the imposition of tactics and discipline. And people in this war did not mean only that fighting proportion of the male population. As the effects and implications of the conflict became the felt interior crises of Boer households, women could not but play some active part in hostile transactions.

Looking back in speculative vein, perhaps the misfortune of the Boers was not so much that they fought on doggedly in a lost cause, earning international respect but not much more. Nor was it the fact that, like the winning side, they too were prone to errors, incompetence, and bouts of feuding. That, surely, is a feature of virtually every war. Most of all, it was the fatal delay in plumping for a strategy of guerrilla warfare. Fundamentally, they held the keys to this from the beginning: fine mounted marksmanship and good firearms, skilled auxiliary field support, flexible lower-level command, superior mobility to skip potentially damaging confrontation and pick fights when and where it suited, and proficiency at small-scale tactics. Had the republicans launched a guerrilla war when they still had a rising sense of victory in their sights, rather than when they were more or less already dished, the strategic direction of the first phase of the war might very well have been more productive.

If the Boers chose war with their eyes open, they were perhaps not wide enough. The weight of the blow which fell on them changed the way many thought, not just about the nature of Britain, but about the shattering impact of war itself. The crisis of their English War confirmed the extinction of a Gladstonian Liberal imperialism, with its fond notion of a moral empire bound by acceptance of a historicized nationality in settler colonial areas. It also confirmed empire as the strongest conceivable armed test of national will, whatever the price. For a while, then, the Boers had a taste of the earlier fate of their black counterparts in southern Africa. For the Afrikaner bearers of Western Christian civilization, perhaps the cruelty and dinginess of imperial conquest was an unforeseen turn of the screw in the course of a modernizing trekker history built on Sotho, Tswana, Pedi and one or two other land annexations of their own.

What better epitaph for all who brought on the South African War than a sample of Kipling's memorably sardonic ambiguity:

> Me an' my trusty friend 'ave 'ad,
> As you might say, a war,
> But seein what both parties done
> Before 'e owned defeat,
> I ain't more proud of 'avin won
> than I am pleased with Piet.

Alternatively, and looking at things from a more distant direction, Taylor can again have the last word. Writing on 11 October 1949, his rueful anniversary conclusion was that 'fifty years afterwards, it is clear that victory has gone to the worst elements of both sides... the mining houses and the most narrow-minded Boers have joined hands to oppress and exploit the native peoples who are the overwhelming majority... If Milner could see the results of victory, or Campbell-Bannerman the results of Boer self-government, would either have reason to be proud of his handiwork?'[21]

Chapter 10 Notes

1. Nasson, 'Bobbies to Boers: police, people and social control in Cape Town', in *Policing the Empire: Government, Authority and Control, 1830–1940*, eds David M. Anderson and David Killingray (Manchester, 1991), p. 240.
2. *The Confidence of the Whole Country: Standard Bank Reports on Economic Conditions in Southern Africa, 1865–1902*, eds Alan Mabin and Barbara Conradie (Johannesburg, 1987), p. 494.

3. John Keegan, *A History of Warfare* (London, 1993), pp. 187–8, 361.

4. G. R. Searle, *The Quest for National Efficiency* (Oxford, 1971); J. M. Winter, 'Military fitness and civilian health in Britain during the First World War', *Journal of Contemporary History*, 15/2 (1980), pp. 211–14.

5. J. A. Williams, *The Politics of the New Zealand Maori: Protest and Cooperation, 1891–1909* (Seattle, 1969), p. 150; Carman Miller, 'The Unhappy Warriors: Conflict and Nationality among Canadian Troops during the South African War', *Journal of Imperial and Commonwealth History*, 23/1 (1995), pp. 76–104; Donald Denoon, 'The Isolation of Australian History', *Historical Studies* , 22/87 (1986), p. 255; Richard White, *Inventing Australia* (Sydney, 1992), pp. 79–80; K. S. Inglis, *Sacred Places: War Memorials in the Australian Landscape* (Melbourne, 1998), pp. 56–8.

6. R. A. Bradshaw, 'Japan and colonialism in Africa, 1800–1939', Ph.D, diss. (Ohio University, 1992), pp. 156–60.

7. Michael Howard, 'Colonial wars and European wars', in *Imperialism and War: Essays on Colonial Wars in Asia and Africa*, eds J. A. de Moor and H. L. Wesseling (Leiden, 1989), p. 221; V. G. Kiernan, *European Empires from Conquest to Collapse, 1815–1960* (London, 1982), p. 36.

8. J. A. du Pisani and L. W. F, Grundlingh, ' "Volkshelde": Afrikaner nationalist mobilisation and representations of the Boer warrior', Rethinking the SA War Conference paper, UNISA, 1998.

9. Andre Wessels, *Die Militêre Rol van Swart Mense, Bruin Mense en Indiërs tydens die Anglo-Boereoorlog (1899–1902)* (Bloemfontein, 1998), p. 19.

10. Peter Warwick, *Black People and the South African War, 1899–1902* (Cambridge, 1983), p. 145; Stowell Kessler, 'The black and coloured concentration camps of the South African War, 1899–1902: shifting the paradigm from sole martyrdom to mutual suffering', Rethinking the SA War Conference paper, UNISA, 1998.

11. Bruce Vandervort, *Wars of Imperial Conquest in Africa, 1830–1914* (London, 1998), p. ix.

12. Thomas Pakenham, *The Boer War* (London, 1979), p. 491.

13. Compare Richard Shannon, *The Crisis of Imperialism 1865–1915* (London, 1974), p. 337; Bill Freund, *The Making of Contemporary Africa: The Development of African Society since 1800* (Bloomington, Ind., 1984), pp. 173–5.

14. Porter, 'The South African War (1899–1902): a question of significance ?', SA War Conference paper, UNISA, 1998.

15. James E. Cronin, *The Politics of State Expansion: War, State and Society in Twentieth Century Britain* (London, 1991), pp. 28, 31, 51.

16. Peter Marsh, *Joseph Chamberlain: Entrepreneur in Politics* (New Haven and London, 1994), p. 495.

17. Hew Strachan, *European Armies and the Conduct of War* (London, 1983), pp. 86–7; Frank Myatt, *The British Infantry 1660–1945* (Poole, 1983), pp. 160–6; Tim Travers, 'The Hidden Army: Structural Problems in the British Officer Corps, 1900–1918', *Journal of Contemporary History* , 17/2 (1982), p. 524.

18. Anne Summers, *Angels and Citizens: British Women as Military Nurses, 1854–1914* (London, 1988), p. 205.

19. Gerard J. DeGroot, *Blighty: British Society in the Era of the Great War* (London, 1996), p. 24.

20. R. J. Q. Adams and Philip P. Poirier, *The Conscription Controversy in Great Britain, 1900–18* (London, 1987), pp. 4–5.

21. Quoted in Angus Wilson, *The Strange Ride of Rudyard Kipling* (London, 1979), p. 292; A. J. P. Taylor, *Boer War*, p. 38.

Select Bibliography

The list of available sources for the study of the South African War is longer than the nose of the late General Charles de Gaulle: it would take at the very least the proverbial lifetime to plough through everything. To compound the task, modern war historiography is available not merely in English and Afrikaans, but also in Dutch, French, German, Russian, and even Japanese. Any book of this kind relies heavily on the labour of others, and while the short list which follows gives some of the secondary works consulted, it is intended much more as a guide to further published reading in English for students and general readers. It is deliberately biased towards the literature of more recent decades, although there are, of course, many key works of older vintage which can be tracked down through the bibliographies of some of the general works cited below.

General Histories

The best single narrative of the military story is given by Thomas Pakenham in *The Boer War* (London, 1979) and in *The Boer War: Illustrated Edition* (Johannesburg and London, 1993), the chief merit of which are their meticulous documentation of operations and lively style; there is a handy version, 'The Anglo-Boer War, 1899–1902', in *An Illustrated History of South Africa*, eds Trewella Cameron and S. B. Spies (Johannesburg, 1986). An older general account is Rayne Kruger, *Goodbye Dolly Gray* (London, 1959), which is expressive on the republican side of things, and wobbles attractively between realism and epic. Although they may not take matters very far historiographically, other single-author accounts which deserve mention are Byron Farwell, *The Great Boer War* (London, 1977), Denis Judd, *The Boer War* (London, 1977), and Eversley Belfield, *The Boer War*

(London, 1975), which is nothing if not idiosyncratic. Johannes Meintjies, *The Anglo-Boer War 1899–1902* (Cape Town, 1976) and Fransjohan Pretorius, *The Anglo-Boer War 1899–1902* (Cape Town, 1985), are accomplished pictorial histories, the latter by a leading Afrikaans scholar. Emanoel Lee, *To the Bitter End* (Harmondsworth, 1985), is another useful history, built mostly around previously unpublished pictures. In its own class altogether is Ryno Greenwall, *Artists and Illustrators of the Anglo-Boer War* (Cape Town, 1992), which is sumptuous. A manageable attempt at surveying it all on the basis of modern scholarship is *The South African War: The Anglo-Boer War 1899–1902*, ed. Peter Warwick (London, 1980), a set of illustrated essays which still stands up. Tabitha Jackson, *The White Man's War* (London, 1999) sees the war as responsible for South Africa's apartheid, a rounded view which can be too round. Much of the early and also more modern military historiography is crisply surveyed by Ian F. W. Beckett in 'Military historians and the South African War: a review of recent literature', *Soldiers of the Queen*, 54 (1978), and 'The historiography of small wars: early historians and the South African War', *Small Wars and Insurgencies*, 2/2 (1991). Afrikaner historiography is analysed perceptively by Albert Grundlingh, 'War, wordsmiths and the "Volk": Afrikaans historical writing on the Anglo-Boer War of 1899–1902 and the war in Afrikaner nationalist consciousness, 1902–1990', in *Mfecane to Boer War*, ed. E. Lehmann and E. Reckwitz (Essen, 1992). The definitive military reference work is Darrell Hall, *The Hall Handbook of the Anglo-Boer War* (University of Natal Press, 1999).

Anglo-Boer Crisis and the Origins of War

Perhaps the definitive explanation will never be written; a tortuous topic, this has long been the cause of contentious debate over both fine detail and interpretation. A big attempt to bring in the jury is Iain R. Smith, *The Origins of the South African War 1899–1902* (London, 1996), an exhaustive overview which tends perhaps to overstate its case. Older and more recent approaches can be sampled in J. S. Marais, *The Fall of Kruger's Republic* (Oxford, 1961); G. H. L. Le May, *British Supremacy in South Africa, 1899–1907* (Oxford, 1965); Andrew Porter, *The Origins of the South African War: Joseph Chamberlain and the Diplomacy of Imperialism, 1895–99* (Manchester, 1980); 'The South African War (1899–1902): context and motive reconsidered', *Journal of African History*, 31/1 (1990); Donald Denoon, 'Capital and capitalists in the Transvaal in the 1890s and 1900s', *Historical Journal*, 23/1 (1980); Shula Marks, 'Scrambling for South Africa', *Journal of African History*, 23/1 (1982); Shula Marks and Stanley Trapido, 'Lord Milner and the South African State', *History Workshop Journal*, 8 (1979); 'Lord Milner and the South African State reconsidered', in *Imperialism, The State and the Third World*, ed. Michael Twaddle (London, 1992);

and Ian Phimister, 'Unscrambling the scramble for Southern Africa', *South African Historical Journal*, 28 (1993).

The War and Black Society

An imaginative early probe is Donald Denoon's 'Participation in the "Boer War": people's war, people's non-war or non-people's war', in *War and Society in Africa*, ed. Bethwell A. Ogot (London, 1972). For an overarching account of the war's impact upon the whole region, the standard authoritative work remains Peter Warwick, *Black People and the South African War, 1899–1902* (Cambridge, 1983), while Bill Nasson, *Black Participation in the Anglo-Boer War 1899–1902* (Johannesburg, 1999) provides a short illustrated history. More localized experience can be seen in Bill Nasson, *Abraham Esau's War: A Black South African War in the Cape, 1899–1902* (Cambridge, 1991), and Jeremy Krikler, *Revolution from Above, Rebellion from Below: The Agrarian Transvaal at the turn of the Century* (Oxford, 1993). An informative essay on intervention by African chiefs is R. F. Morton, 'Linchwe and the Kgatla Campaign in the South African War, 1899–1902' *Journal of African History*, 26/2 (1985). The classic personal record of educated African experience is *The Boer War Diary of Sol T. Plaaatje, an African at Mafeking*, ed. John L. Comaroff (London, 1973). The lives of black commando auxiliaries can be seen in Pieter Labuschagne, *Ghostriders of the Anglo-Boer War (1899–1902): The Role and Contribution of Agterryers* (Pretoria, 1999). For the political and cultural legacy of the war experience, there is Bill Nasson, 'Abraham Esau's War', in *The Myths We Live By*, eds Raphael Samuel and Paul Thompson (London, 1991); 'The Priest, the Chapel, and the Repentant Landowner: Abraham Esau Revisited', *African Affairs*, 93/387 (1994).

Military Operations

Specific operations, major battles, and particular campaigns have generated a host of specialized books and essay studies, not least the substantial volume of Afrikaans micro-histories on various Boer commandos and their field performance. Standard treatments of particular battles are provided by Oliver Ransford, *The Battle of Spion Kop* (London, 1969), Julian Symons, *Buller's Campaign* (London, 1963), W. Baring Pemberton, *Battles of the Boer War* (London, 1964), and Johannes Meintjes, *Stormberg: A Lost Opportunity* (Cape Town, 1969). These can be supplemented by a new series, Pam McFadden, *The Battle of Talana* and *The Battle of Elandslaagte*; S. B. Bourquin and Gilbert Torlage, *The Battle of Colenso*; Gilbert Torlage, *The Battle of Spioenkop*; Steve Watt, *The Battle of Vaalkrans*; Ken Gillings, *The Battle of Thukela Heights*; and Steve Watt, *The Siege of Ladysmith* (all Johannesburg, 1999). Accounts more off the beaten track are provided by

Graham Dominy, '"Spoiling his paint": a chronicle of Anglo-Boer naval clashes, 1901–1902', *Historia* , 37/1 (1992), Dermot Michael Moore, *General Louis Botha's Second Expedition to Natal, September – October 1901* (Cape Town, 1979); and I. Greeff, 'Two Victoria Crosses near Krugersdorp', *Historia*, 36/2 (1991). For potted portraits of individual commanders, and one or two perceptive evaluations of generalship, there is Philip Bateman, *Generals of the Anglo-Boer War* (Cape Town, 1977). A spectacularly dyspeptic analysis of British command is given by Norman F. Dixon, *On the Psychology of Military Incompetence* (London, 1979), ch. 4. For the war's British strategic management, and military–political tensions, there is John S. Galbraith, 'British war measures in Cape Colony, 1900–1902: a study of miscalculations and mismanagement', *South African Historical Journal*, 15 (1983); a wide compass and sophisticated treatment is provided by Keith Surridge, *Managing the South African War, 1899–1902: Politicians v. Generals* (Woodbridge, 1998). British national politics and military affairs are discussed by W. S. Hamer, *The British Army: Civil–Military Relations, 1885–1905* (Oxford, 1970), ch. 6.

The Sieges

A great favourite of the established literature is exemplified by Kenneth Griffiths, *Thank God We Kept The Flag Flying* (London, 1974) and Brian Gardner's *Mafeking: A Victorian Legend* (London, 1966), and *The Lion's Cage* (London, 1969). Acute contemporary evocation of siege atmosphere is provided by Edward Ross, *Diary of the Siege of Mafeking, October 1899 to May 1900*, ed. Brian Willan (Cape Town, 1980), and *The Boer War Diary of Sol T. Plaatje* (London, 1973).

The International Dimension

From a fairly considerable literature, the following national accounts are especially absorbing: Jean-Guy Pelletier, 'France and the Boer War', *Historia*, 33/1 (1988); Donal P. McCracken, *The Irish Pro-Boers, 1877–1902* (Johannesburg, 1989); Carman Miller, *Painting the Map Red: Canada and the South African War 1899–1902* (Kingston, 1993); Appollon Davidson and Irina Filatova, *The Russians and the Anglo-Boer War* 1899–1902 (Cape Town, 1998); 'The Russian Red Cross in the Anglo-Boer War 1899–1902', *Historia*, 21/3 (1996); E. Kandyba-Foxcroft, *Russia and the Anglo-Boer War 1899–1902* (Roodepoort, 1981); Shigeru Akita, 'The Second Anglo-Boer War and India', *Journal of Osaka University of Foreign Studies*, 8 (1993); R. L. Wallace, *The Australians at the Boer War* (Canberra, 1976); the Breaker Morant saga, inseparable from the Australian connection, is given nice treatment in *Breaker Morant and the Bushveldt Carbineers*, ed. Arthur Davey (Cape Town, 1987).

British and Boer Society

Much of the literature is broadly spread rather than specifically war-related, but the following treatments are of value: Stanley Trapido, 'Landlord and tenant in a colonial economy: the Transvaal 1880–1910', *Journal of Southern African Studies*, 5/1 (1978); Diana Cammack, *The Rand at War 1899–1902: The Witwatersrand and the Anglo-Boer War* (London, 1990); Tim Keegan, 'The restructuring of agrarian class relations in a colonial economy: the Orange River Colony, 1902–1910', *Journal of Southern African Studies* , 5/2 (1979); Richard Price, *An Imperial War and the British Working Class* (London, 1972); 'Society, status and jingoism: the social roots of lower middle class patriotism, 1870–1900', in *The Lower Middle Class in Britain, 1870–1914* , ed. Geoffrey Crossick (London, 1977); Preben Kaarsholm, 'Pro-Boers', in *Patriotism: The Making and Unmaking of British National Identity*, vol. 1, ed. Raphael Samuel (London, 1989); Keith Surridge, ' "All you soldiers are what we call pro-Boer": the military critique of the South African War, 1899–1902', *History*, 82/268 (1997); and David Feldman, 'Nationality and Ethnicity', in *Twentieth-Century Britain*, ed. Paul Johnson (London, 1994).

Personal Testimony

In general it is Boer rather than British soldiering memoirs which stand out, the finest of which are undoubtedly Deneys Reitz, *Commando: A Boer Journal of the Boer War* (London, 1931), and *Jan Smuts: Memoirs of the Boer War*, eds Gail Nattrass and S. B. Spies (Johannesburg, 1994). Other records of note are *The War Memoirs of Commandant Ludwig Krause 1899–1900*, ed. Jerold Taitz (Cape Town, 1996); Dietlof van Warmelo, *On Commando* (Johannesburg, 1977); and Roland William Schikkerling, *Commando Courageous (A Boer's Diary)* (Johannesburg, 1964). An English view of things from within the Boer world can be gained from *Letters from a Boer Parsonage: Letters of Margaret Marquard during the Boer War*, ed. Leo Marquard (Cape Town, 1967), and Fransjohan Pretorius, 'Caught up in the cross-fire: a British citizen in the Orange Free State during the Anglo-Boer War, 1899–1900', *Historia*, 43/1 (1998). A nuanced presentation of the work of war correspondents is given by Raymond Sibbald, *The War Correspondents: The Boer War* (Johannesburg, 1993). For a moving British humanitarian chronicle of camp and refugee conditions, there is Lawrence Richardson, *Selected Correspondence (1902–1903)*, ed. Arthur M. Davey (Cape Town, 1977).

Colonial War

For overall analyses of colonial operations and imperial armies as a context for this war, useful discussion is provided by Hew Strachan, *European*

Armies and the Conduct of War (London, 1983), ch. 6; Bruce Vandervort, *Wars of Imperial Conquest in Africa, 1830–1914* (London, 1998), ch. 5; David Killingray, 'War and society in Africa since 1800', *South African Historical Journal* , 25 (1991); Michael Glover, *Warfare from Waterloo to Mons* (London, 1980), ch. 11; V. G. Kiernan, *European Empires from Conquest to Collapse, 1815–1960* (London, 1982), ch. 6; Keith Jeffery, 'Colonial warfare 1900–39', in *Warfare in the Twentieth Century: Theory and Practice*, eds C. M. McInnes and G. D. Sheffield (London, 1988); Basil Davidson, *The People's Cause: A History of Guerrillas in Africa* (London, 1981), ch. 4; Charles Townshend, *Britain's Civil Wars: Counterinsurgency in the Twentieth Century* (London, 1986), ch. 5; *Imperialism and War: Essays on Colonial Wars in Asia and Africa*, eds J. A. de Moor and H. L. Wesseling (Leiden, 1989). For the South African conflict and its effect upon military doctrine, there is T. H. E. Travers, 'Technology, tactics, and morale: Jean de Bloch, the Boer War, and British military theory, 1900–1914', *Journal of Modern History*, 51/2 (1979); Frank Myatt, *The British Infantry, 1660–1945* (Poole, 1983), ch. 8.

Index

Printed in the United Kingdom
by Lightning Source UK Ltd.
108634UKS00002B/7-8